ITALY

ITALY

A Grand Tour for the Modern Traveller

CHARLES FITZROY

ITALY

A Grand Tour for
the Modern Traveller

Charles FitzRoy

PAPERMAC

To my wife Diana

Copyright © Charles FitzRoy, 1991
Maps on endpapers, drawn by Leslie Marshall,
copyright © Macmillan London Limited 1991

First published 1991 by Macmillan London Limited

First published in paperback 1992 by
PAPERMAC
A division of Pan Macmillan Limited
Cavaye Place, London SW10 9PG
and Basingstoke

Associated companies in Auckland, Delhi, Dublin, Gaborone,
Hamburg, Harare, Hong Kong, Johannesburg, Kuala Lumpur,
Lagos, Manzini, Melbourne, Mexico City, Nairobi, New York,
Singapore and Tokyo

ISBN 0–333–57475–3

A CIP catalogue record for this book is available from
the British Library

Illustrations by Caroline Mauduit

Typeset by Macmillan Production Limited

Printed in Hong Kong

Contents

Acknowledgements   ix
Introduction   xi

PIEDMONT, LOMBARDY AND LIGURIA   1
   Turin   3
   Stupinigi and Le Langhe   5
   Isola Bella   7
   Milan   9
   Mantua   12
   Genoa   15

TUSCANY: FROM LUCCA TO FLORENCE   18
   Lucca   24
   Villa Reale, Marlia   27
   Pisa   29

FLORENCE   34

TUSCANY: FROM FLORENCE TO ROME   64
   San Gimignano   65
   Siena   69
   Some Sienese Paintings   75
   Arezzo   77
   Cortona   81
   Excursions from Siena   84
   From Siena to Rome   87

ROME   92

ENVIRONS OF ROME   134
   Tivoli   136
   Appian Way/Castel Gandolfo/Ariccia/Lake Nemi/Frascati   142
   Ostia Antica   146

NAPLES	148
North of Naples	156
Capodimonte	168
Pompeii	171
Bay of Naples	173
UMBRIA AND THE MARCHE	178
Perugia	183
Assisi	186
Spoleto	189
Hill Towns of Southern Umbria	192
Orvieto	196
Into the Southern Marche	198
Loreto	200
Urbino	201
EMILIA-ROMAGNA	206
Bologna	211
Parma	216
Environs of Parma	220
Ravenna	221
VENICE	226
THE VENETO	256
From Ferrara to Venice	259
Along the Brenta Canal	261
Padua	265
From Venice to Vicenza	270
Vicenza	275
Verona	283
Epilogue	290
Bibliography	293
Index	297

Acknowledgements

When I first undertook to write this book I had no idea of the amount of research involved, and the project would never have been completed without the help and encouragement of many friends and colleagues. I should like to thank Adam Nicolson, with whom I first discussed the idea, Susan Grossman, for her practical advice, Hugh Honour, John Fleming, Francis Haskell, Bruce Boucher and Sara Menguc, for their constructive criticism, and everyone at 15 Savile Row for their patient support throughout the last eighteen months. I am also grateful to Timothy Llewellyn of Sotheby's, to Dr Joanna Martin and to Jane Whitehead for letting me publish from their documents, and to Dr Kim Sloan for her assistance in using Sir Brinsley Ford's archive. I should particularly like to thank Sarah Lutyens for all the trouble she has taken over the editing, Caroline Mauduit for her beautiful illustrations, and Francis Russell and David Ekserdjian for their care in reading the manuscript from start to finish. Lastly, I should like to express my special gratitude to Sir Brinsley Ford, both for reading the manuscript and for allowing me to publish from his fascinating seminal archive.

Introduction

Italy seemed to me to be Nature's Darling, and the Eldest Sister of all other countryes

Richard Lassels

'A Man who has never been to Italy', Dr Johnson said, 'is always conscious of an inferiority . . . The grand object of travelling is to see the shores of the Mediterranean.' Rather less nobly, his biographer James Boswell – who had the time of his life on the Grand Tour – arrived in Turin in 1765 'with mingled feelings of awe and adulterous anticipation'. These were the two sides of Italy that entranced the English imagination from the seventeenth to the nineteenth centuries. Aristocrats, artists and poets flocked to the ruins, galleries and fleshpots of the alluring south.

Italy has changed remarkably little over the centuries. You can still follow in the footsteps of Grand Tourists, staying in the hotel where the writer Tobias Smollett was eaten alive by bugs, admiring the *Venus de' Medici*, which aroused Byron's friend Samuel Rogers to a pitch of excitement, and enjoying the Venetian Carnival, where Boswell and the eccentric millionaire William Beckford ran riot. It is this unchanging aspect of Italy, so redolent of an earlier age of travel and still alive today – though increasingly hard to find – that this book attempts to uncover.

The idea of the Grand Tour, with Italy as its ultimate goal, originated in the sixteenth century when the influence of the Italian Renaissance, spreading across Europe, brought inquisitive foreigners over the Alps. They modelled themselves on Baldassare Castiglione's *The Courtier* (1528) and came to Italy to complete their education, studying medicine, science and music, and learning how to dance and ride. The treasuries of Florence and Loreto and the arsenals of Venice and Genoa fascinated them as much as any works of art.

At this date there was no set route to an Englishman's travels in Italy but they tended to concentrate on Venice, the first state to which England sent an embassy after the Reformation, and Tuscany, both relatively free from the influence of Spain. The Venetian Republic's university at Padua, one of the most learned in Europe, attracted a great number of foreign students. Galileo taught physics here from 1592 to 1610 and numbered among his pupils Gustavus Adolphus, the future king of Sweden.

Early accounts of what was to become the Grand Tour read like voyages of discovery, full of a sense of wonder. The eccentric Thomas Coryate, who walked to Venice in 1608 and crossed the Alps on foot because he could not afford a sedan chair, thought the city 'The Queen of Christendome' and wrote a rapturous account of his experiences there. His descriptions of Venetian women walking about the streets in *zoccoli*, a bizarre form of shoe mounted on a platform 45 cm high, and his encounters with courtesans read like a fairy tale. But as a Protestant he was in considerable danger: much of Italy, including Genoa, Milan, Naples and indirectly the Papal States, was controlled by Spain, with whom England was at war through most of the Elizabethan era. From 1593 to 1595 Coryate's contemporary Fynes Moryson was forced to don numerous disguises to escape the clutches of the dreaded Inquisition.

Recusants escaping from the religious troubles at home were, of course, more popular with the Catholic authorities. The English government kept a watchful eye on them in case their religious convictions led them to commit treason, and in the early seventeenth century ambassadors such as Sir Henry Wotton in Venice took careful note of the Englishmen lodged in the city. The Government was so worried by the subversive dangers of Catholicism that Rome was excluded from the travel licences issued to Englishmen travelling to Italy until well into the seventeenth century.

After 1630, as northern Italy became involved in the Thirty Years' War and as religious persecution declined in the Papal States, Protestants felt encouraged to venture further south. Earlier travellers such as Coryate and Moryson had visited ancient sites whenever possible and quoted extensively from classical authors, but the difficulty of seeing Rome meant that they had little first-hand experience of the great buildings of antiquity. It was only when a whole generation of travellers experienced the wealth of ruins in and around Rome and Naples that antiquity became the prime inspiration for what came to be known as the Grand Tour.

The two most interesting accounts written by Englishmen visiting Italy in the mid-seventeenth century are by John Evelyn and Richard

Lassels. Evelyn, as befits a future founder member of the Royal Society, looks forward to the eighteenth-century 'Age of Reason' in his scientific curiosity and his study of social manners and customs. Unlike so many later tourists, he was interested in contemporary art, particularly Baroque architecture. Lassels, a Roman Catholic priest, made five journeys to Italy between 1637 and 1663, acting as a tutor to various noblemen, explaining the sites to them and keeping them under control. His *Voyage to Italy* (1670) is the most informed guide of the seventeenth century, and the first to mention the Grand Tour by name. Lassels's Catholicism and his belief in relics and miracles offended many travellers but his learning was much admired, and the various routes he took and his choice of sites to visit, particularly classical ones, were to influence generations of Grand Tourists.

Lassels's main route is the one that I have followed in this book, running down the west side of Italy from the French border to Naples, crossing over the Apennines between Rome and the Adriatic sea, and following the coast up to Venice. The majority of Grand Tourists entered Italy in the early autumn, either crossing over the Mont Cenis pass or arriving by sea at Genoa. After a brief look at Turin and Milan and a quick tour of Florence, they raced down the Via Cassia to Rome, where most of them spent the winter before making an excursion to Naples in the early spring. Once Holy Week was over, they hurried from Rome across to the Adriatic coast and followed it up to Venice for the feast of the Ascension, with a detour to see the main towns of Emilia. Before recrossing the Alps, most stopped to visit the towns of the Veneto. The whole tour would last about nine months and included the most important cities in Italy.

The eighteenth-century obsession with antiquity, epitomised by Joseph Addison's influential *Remarks on Several Parts of Italy* (1705) which concentrates exclusively on classical art, led to a large proportion of the tour being spent in Rome and Naples. Many tourists treated northern Italy, even Florence, as no more than a stopping-point en route to Rome.

Once they had seen the antiquities, there was time enough to relax. The thought of Carnival in Naples and Venice, with limitless prospects of gambling and seducing beautiful, willing women, distracted many from the boredom of sightseeing. The radical John Wilkes boasted of his mistress Signora Corradini who 'possessed the divine gift of lewdness, but nature had not given her strength adequate to the force of her desires'. Boswell recorded how the Mediterranean climate 'inflamed my hot desires, and now it keeps my blood so warm that I have all day long such spirits as a man has after having taken a cheerful glass'.

This was not exactly what most parents had in mind when they sent their sons off on the Grand Tour to complete their education and, partly in order to ward off temptation, most Grand Tourists were accompanied by an older tutor, known as a bear-leader. Horace Walpole, son of the Prime Minister Sir Robert Walpole, was one of the first to be accompanied by a contemporary, the poet Thomas Gray, straight after leaving Eton in 1739. Walpole's account of his travels is laced with descriptions of the balls he attended and the people he encountered: he was soon pitched headlong into a passionate affair with the beautiful Elisabetta Griffoni.

Walpole, like so many Grand Tourists, was quite overwhelmed by the mayhem of Carnival. Caution was thrown to the winds as everyone indulged themselves at the masked balls and processions. Excitement reached fever pitch in Rome, where horse races were held every evening in the Corso; in Naples, where Sir Thomas Gascoigne attended a ball at Caserta in drag to the vast amusement of Ferdinand IV and Maria Carolina; and in Venice, where courtesans stood in their doorways 'with their breasts open and their faces all bedaubed with paint'. Carnival has recently been revived in Venice but more as a tourist event and with little of the bacchanalian excitement of the eighteenth-century original.

Young English milords shamelessly exploited their social connections to secure invitations to all the smart parties, rather as modern school-leavers on their year off before going to university descend on distant relatives all over the English-speaking world. Horace Mann and Sir William Hamilton, the British ambassadors in Florence and Naples, were inundated with visitors demanding entertainment.

Apart from meeting people of rank, Grand Tourists' priorities were to travel in comfort and secure good lodgings. They liked to travel at a leisurely pace, leaving the arrangements to a *vetturino*, who would free them, in Tobias Smollett's words, 'from the annoyance of quarrelling with cheating landlords'. They had little desire to venture off the beaten track and, unlike earlier travellers who had borne discomfort and danger stoically, put a high premium on comfort, grumbling ceaselessly about the appalling roads, filthy lodgings and disgusting food. In 1777 the painter James Northcote entered Rome asleep after he had travelled the last stage in a calash (a type of carriage) 'sometimes standing on tiptoe, then with my knees bent, then kneeling on the seat of the carriage, then resting on my hands'.

Inns rarely lived up to expectations. In his account of Italy published in 1789 von Berchtold advised his readers to beware that the lodgers who had preceded them 'were not affected with the itch, venereal or other disease'. The more sanguine Dr Moore, the father of the hero of Corunna, tried to dissuade travellers from 'fretting at Italian beds, fuming against Italian cooks and execrating every poor Italian flea that they meet with on the road'.

Early travellers, following the route set out by Lassels, paid scant attention to the countryside apart from cultivated farmland, seen as a product of civilisation. They were terrified of bandit-infested mountains, described by James Howell (in Italy from 1618 to 1620) as 'uncouth, huge, monstrous – Excrescences of Nature, bearing nothing but craggy stones'. Until the end of the eighteenth century there was no question of enjoying the experience of crossing the Alps, and many preferred to travel with the carriage blinds down, or, like the painter Northcote, with a nightcap instinctively pulled down over their eyes so as not to suffer further by looking at the view. An exception was Thomas Gray, travelling with Walpole in 1739. Walpole was in a state of shock after watching his unfortunate black spaniel Tory being devoured by a wolf, but Gray's mind was on higher matters, musing on the mountains, 'pregnant with religion and poetry'.

Throughout the eighteenth century Britain played an increasingly important role in European politics, and this encouraged the British to assume a disdainful attitude towards the Italians; they regarded the upper classes as effete, conceited, adulterous and idle, and the lower classes as priest-ridden and submissive. As Randle Wilbraham put it: 'The longer I stay out of England, the more John Bullish I become.' The Italians, not surprisingly, thought the British insufferably arrogant.

The British were, however, fascinated by the bewildering variety of government in the Italian peninsula, which was divided into the Papal States, the Republics of Venice and Genoa, the Kingdoms of Naples and Savoy, and the Duchies of Tuscany, Milan, Parma and Modena. They particularly admired the independent states of Lucca and San Marino, although nothing compared favourably with their own constitutional monarchy. They heartily endorsed Jonathan Richardson's claim that 'there is no nation under heaven that we do not excel . . . since the best times of the ancient Greeks and Romans'.

These tourists were, by and large, rich and consequently seized upon by dealers and antiquarians, who exploited their naivety. Thomas Jenkins, the pre-eminent dealer in eighteenth-century Rome, acted as the unofficial British ambassador and was chosen to entertain the Dukes of Gloucester and Cumberland when they visited the Eternal City. He was utterly ruthless in his business dealings and not only provided the head of the Venus which formed the centrepiece of William Weddell's sculpture gallery at Newby Hall but forged the export licence, declaring the purchaser to be the King of England. His rival James Byres sold sculpture to the Duke of Northumberland, gemstones to Catherine the Great, Poussin's *Seven Sacraments* to the Duke of Rutland and the Portland Vase (as it was later known) to Sir William Hamilton.

Although the cult of antiquity reigned supreme and it was essential to return with a piece of classical statuary – or at least a copy – eighteenth-century collectors increasingly developed a taste for paintings. Jonathan Richardson's *An Account of Some of the Statues, Bas-reliefs, Drawings and Pictures in Italy* (1722) was one of the first critical accounts of the various Italian schools of painting, and encouraged visitors to become connoisseurs. Most agreed with Horace Walpole in his condemnation of the Florentine Primitives, that: 'Their Drawing was hard, and their Colouring gawdy and gothic,' in contrast with 'the qualities of a perfect Painter, never met but in Raphael, Guido and Annibale Carracci'. Consequently, they collected paintings of the High Renaissance and the Bolognese school and landscapes by Claude Lorraine, all of them inspired by the art of antiquity. Pompeo Batoni's portraits of elegant aristocrats posing in front of Roman ruins and Canaletto's views of Venice provided visual mementoes of the Grand Tour.

Italy was an excellent place for artists to meet future patrons, a fact exploited by the socially conscious architect Robert Adam on his tour of 1755–7. His fellow architect John Soane described his Grand Tour in 1779 as 'the most fortunate event of my life, for it was the means by which I formed those connections to which I owe all the advantages I have since enjoyed'.

Italy's unquestioned supremacy in architecture, painting, garden design and music influenced generations of foreign visitors. Inigo Jones, who accompanied Lord Arundel to Italy in 1613–14, introduced the Palladian manner into England, a movement which exerted an extraordinary influence on English architecture for the first half of the eighteenth century and North American architecture right up to the American Civil War.

Many of those who remodelled their houses in the new Palladian style wanted to create a landscape worthy of the setting. William Kent, Capability Brown and Humphrey Repton all reacted against formal gardens and were inspired, in part, by the paintings of Claude Lorraine, who spent all his working life painting views of the Roman Campagna.

Few of the arts escaped the pervasive influence of Italy, and it is scarcely surprising that Handel, Gluck and Mozart composed most of their operas in Italian. Italian music was widely praised by the tourists, particularly in Naples, where Scarlatti and Pergolesi were composing at the court, and Venice, where the amateur musician John Bargrave considered the operas he attended 'the most excellent of all its glorious Vanities'. Vivaldi conducted the choir of the Pietà, whose singing rivalled that of the papal choir in the Sistine Chapel. By the nineteenth century La Scala in Milan took over as the premier opera house in Italy, and witnessed the triumphs of Rossini, Donizetti and Verdi.

The neo-classical movement, with its desire for greater archaeological accuracy in the study of antiquity, was inspired by the discoveries made at Herculaneum and Pompeii. A large colony of foreign artists and architects congregated in Rome, and the movement spread rapidly throughout Europe, influencing architecture, furniture, sculpture, painting and ceramics, from Russia to Ireland. The importance of the Grand Tour for northern Europeans is reflected in the reaction of those, like Dr Johnson, who did not go and felt a sense of loss for the rest of their lives.

This golden era of travel came to an end with Napoleon's invasion of Italy in 1796. The French, in the course of their campaigns, seized all the finest works of art in Italy they could lay their hands on, including the most famous antique statues and paintings of the High Renaissance, and took them to Paris. Napoleon saw himself as the Emperor of a latter-day Roman Empire and created his son King of Rome. On being asked what he intended to do with Italy he is reputed to have called for a lemon, cut it in two and squeezed the juice out of each half before throwing them away.

After 1815 Italy was once again inundated with tourists, many of them coming on the new road Napoleon had cut through the Simplon Pass. These travellers viewed Italy through rose-tinted spectacles, avidly reading Byron and Shelley, both of whom had chosen to live here in self-imposed exile. They eulogised the beauty of the landscape and the softness of the light. The Italians themselves appeared in a picturesque glow, and, apart from some bandit-ridden areas of southern Italy, there was little to be afraid of.

By this date the most famous objects were known from reproductions throughout Europe, and travellers derived their greatest pleasure from coming across the familiar. The classic guidebooks, written by Eustace and Mariana Starke, continued to praise the art of antiquity, the High Renaissance and the Bolognese seventeenth century. Lady Morgan, who expressed her radically liberal views in her book of 1819, declared that 'one brilliant landscape of Claude . . . is, morally, worth a whole army of martyrs' and her opinion is typical of her contemporaries' neglect of the Middle Ages and the Quattrocento. As late as 1857, by far the most popular picture at the great Manchester Exhibition of Old Masters was Annibale Carracci's *Three Maries*.

As more people could afford to travel to the Continent, the Grand Tour became increasingly middle class. The spread of the railways ushered in the era of mass tourism, the cultured bear-leader being replaced by the courier whose job was to ensure that people travelled as swiftly and comfortably as possible, a philosophy of travel encapsulated in the antiseptic character of modern air travel and international hotels. The premium on time meant that there was even less tendency to get to know the Italians. Byron's attempt to go native met with widespread disapproval from his fellow countrymen – even his friend Shelley, who had himself left England for good, regarded him as 'quite corrupted by living among these people'.

Instead of buying masterpieces, tourists took home knickknacks, the secular equivalent of the relics that pilgrims had formerly collected. Byron would have liked to take away the lock of Lucrezia Borgia's hair he saw in the Ambrosiana Library in Milan but contented himself with a piece from Juliet's tomb in Verona. The Victorians filled their houses with more humdrum mementoes. Dickens, who spent a year in Italy in 1844–5, described the Meagles' home in *Little Dorrit* as covered in

> model gondolas from Venice; morsels of tessellated pavement from Herculaneum and Pompeii, like petrified mince veal; ashes out of tombs and lava out of Vesuvius; Spanish fans, Spezzian straw hats, Moorish slippers; Tuscan hairpins, Carrara sculpture, Trasteverini scarves, Genoese velvets and filigree, Neapolitan coral, Roman cameos, and rosaries blessed all round by the Pope himself.

The British, regarding their burgeoning empire as the natural heir of ancient Rome, and the Americans, full of their own moral superiority, tended to despise the Italians, particularly during the first half of the nineteenth century when much of Italy was ruled by Austria. Italian society, so much a part of the exotic thrill of the eighteenth century, faded into insignificance. The Anglo-Saxons imported their own culture, shopped in English shops, socialised with their own countrymen, and even hunted a pack of foxhounds in the Campagna. They showed scant interest in learning Italian, Macmillan's *Guide to the Western Mediterranean* (1901) taking a typically robust line: 'Railway and other officials, are not required to speak any language but their own, and their native indolence makes them disinclined to take the trouble of learning any foreign language.'

The cult of the Middle Ages, with its tradition of chivalry, its legends and myths popularised in the novels of Sir Walter Scott and the architecture of the Gothic revival, replaced that of antiquity. Pugin's *Contrasts*, Lord Lindsay's *Sketches of the History of Christian Art* and Mrs Jameson's *Sacred and Legendary Art*, all published in the 1840s, championed medieval art, which was seen as the product of the age of faith, and attacked the paganism of the Renaissance, especially the art of Michelangelo and his followers.

The Victorians took their travelling very seriously and were rarely to be found without a Murray or Baedeker to hand; on his visit to Italy in 1837 Wordsworth grumbled morosely: 'I never was good at sightseeing, yet it must be done.' This earnest desire for truth led them to question the authenticity of the classical statues they had been taught to admire, many of which were discovered to be copies. Discussing the subject matter of *L'Arrotino*, one of the most famous classical statues in the Uffizi, Murray's *Handbook* of 1856 pushed aside all eighteenth-century speculation over whether the man sharpening his knife was a slave overhearing a conspiracy, and advised that: 'These are questions that have little or nothing to do with its consideration as a work of art.' Ruskin, in a typically sweeping statement, brushed aside classical ruins as 'useless and piteous, feebly and fondly garrulous of better days'.

The first edition of Murray's *Handbook* (1842) was very influential in promoting Pre-Raphaelite painters: Sir Francis Palgrave, its editor – of *Golden Treasury* fame – urged his readers to visit neglected sites such as Padua and Assisi, with their wonderful frescoes by Giotto and his contemporaries. He virtually ignored the art of the seventeenth century and attacked the Bolognese school of painting. But the greatest champion of medieval and Early Renaissance art was Ruskin, whose *Mornings in Florence* became compulsory reading for thousands of earnest Victorians and brought them flocking to the city of Dante and Giotto, which now overtook Rome in popularity.

Late nineteenth-century writers, from the art historians Symonds and Pater to Mark Twain, author of *A Tramp Abroad* (1880), encouraged tourists to venture off the beaten track and visit lesser-known Renaissance frescoes in towns such as Orvieto and Cortona. Berenson regarded his search for the paintings of Lorenzo Lotto as a type of pilgrimage. 'In the remotest villages of the Marche,' he rhapsodised, 'there was often nothing to eat but hard bread, onions and anchovies but every morning I awoke to a glamorous adventure, tasted the freshness of a spring or autumn morning in a Bergamesque valley as if it were a deliciously invigorating draught.' Botticelli, whose graceful Madonnas had been disregarded by Grand Tourists, became widely favoured, and his works in the Uffizi now rival the Sistine Chapel and the Leaning Tower of Pisa as the most popular tourist draws in all Italy.

By the end of the nineteenth century a reaction had set in against the earnestness of the Victorians. Henry James and Norman Douglas, among others looking back nostalgically to the past, advocated a more leisurely way of travelling, and wrote atmospheric descriptions of the places that most appealed to them, trying to capture their individual character. Douglas, a true lotus-eater, was the antithesis of the Victorian tourist in the adventurous journeys he undertook into southern Italy and in his sensuous delight in the climate.

In this book I have attempted to combine their approach with that of the eighteenth-century bear-leader, suggesting, highly selectively, the places which seem to represent the abundance of culture in Italy, and to give an introduction to the main elements in its art history. I have traced the development of taste since the Renaissance, from the earliest travellers braving every kind of danger and discomfort, the increasing passion for classical antiquity in the seventeenth century, the golden age of the Grand Tour in the eighteenth century when Italian fashions swept across Europe, the Romanticism of the early nineteenth century, viewing Italy in a golden light, to the Victorians and the beginnings of mass tourism.

In order to remain selective and to prevent the reader becoming too confused, I have omitted certain places and missed out large tracts of history. Wherever possible, I have recommended shops and restaurants characteristic of their region and which were patronised by Grand Tourists. I have paid less attention to the north-west and to the Adriatic coast, much of which have been built up and industrialised. Instead, I have concentrated on cities such as Naples and Bologna, vital parts of the Grand Tour and still fascinating although out of favour with most tourists. In the more popular sites, Florence, Rome and Venice, I have tried to lead the reader to lesser-known churches and restaurants rather than to the overcrowded Uffizi and Vatican. In this way I hope to convey some of the myriad charms of Italy, from the most intellectual painting to the simplest restaurant selling delicious home-made pasta.

The keynote of any trip to Italy is pleasure, both in the works of art and in the richness of the food and the beauty of the sun-drenched landscape. This is what so many of the Victorians missed, even though Ruskin, their seer, admitted that what he enjoyed most in life was not pursuing worthy causes but enjoying beauty for its own sake.

Nowadays it is a lucky person indeed who can afford the time to cover the whole route of the Grand Tour. You are far more likely to fly into one of the main Italian cities and restrict yourself to the surrounding province. But such is the variety of Italian culture, the product of centuries of disunity, that you can spend years visiting different areas without duplicating your experiences.

PIEDMONT,
LOMBARDY
AND LIGURIA

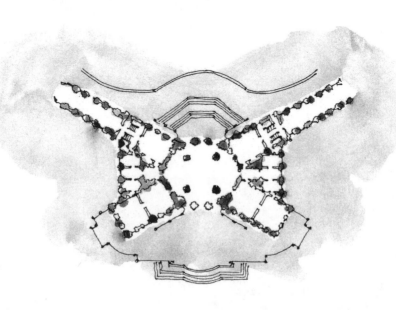

The majestic boundaries of Italy
Mrs Piozzi

The provinces of north-west Italy, possessing some spectacular scenery, and an immensely complex and varied history, introduce the visitor to the bewildering depth of culture which makes Italy such a fascinating and tantalising country to explore. Each provincial capital remains fiercely independent: Turin, the cradle of the Risorgimento; Milan, possessing a wealth of art and (now) the commercial heart of the whole country, and Genoa the Proud, whose beautiful position overlooking the sea entranced generations of travellers. Much of this area has been heavily industrialised and you need perseverance to dig out its treasures.

To reach these cities before the coming of the railways in the mid-nineteenth century, travellers either braved the pirates to sail to Genoa, or, more frequently, followed the Alpine Pass over Mont Cenis, a voyage which filled them with horror. It was the Romantics who first regarded the Alps as 'the majestic boundaries of Italy'. Turner spent his holidays sketching their beauties, Wordsworth hiked through the foothills and Byron, passing through in 1816, on the way to his self-enforced exile in Venice, was delighted by 'avalanches falling every five minutes nearly, as if God was pelting the Devil down from Heaven with snow balls'.

The normal way of crossing Mont Cenis was to be carried by special porters in 'a sort of matted chair without legs, which is carried upon poles in the manner of a bier', as one traveller noted. This peculiar method of transport was obviously very effective; 'the men perfectly fly down with you, stepping from stone to stone with incredible swiftness in places where none but they could go three paces without falling'. Mrs Miller, crossing over in 1770, felt like a witch on a broomstick.

Once he had safely arrived on Italian soil, the intrepid traveller was anxious to press on. The triumphal arch at Susa gave him a foretaste of the wealth of classical art further south, but he had little time for the Romanesque churches of Piedmont and hastened on to Turin. Descriptions of the Grand Tour concentrate almost exclusively on towns, and there was much to see in Lombardy: Monza, whose ancient Duomo houses the Iron Crown of Lombardy, used at the coronation of countless emperors, including Charles V and Napoleon; Pavia, whose Charterhouse is an essential stopping-point for any traveller interested in Renaissance architecture; Cremona, the home of the great violin-makers and the composer Monteverdi; Bergamo, beautifully situated in the foothills of the Alps, and where the great *condottiere* Colleoni is buried, and Mantua, where the Gonzagas created one of the most cultured courts of the entire Renaissance.

The countryside that appealed most to seventeenth and eighteenth-century travellers was the fertile plain of Lombardy, regarded as the garden of Italy, 'all flat and plain, and exceeding rich', as William Bromley noted approvingly in 1691. In the nineteenth century tourists preferred to visit the Lakes, where they could enjoy the beauties of Alpine scenery.

Eighteenth-century travellers complained loudly of the tough journey through the mountains surrounding Genoa. Dr Burney had a particularly rough ride; he recorded: 'However, at length, about eleven at night we arrived at a wretched Inn or pig-stye, half stable, and half Cow-house, with a fire, but no chimney, surrounded by boors and Muleteers, all in appearance cut-throatly personages, with no kind of refreshment but the cold veal, and some stinking eggs.' In the nineteenth century, however, accounts of this journey invariably praise the scenery; Dickens thought it the most beautiful route in all Italy.

Turin

A city of arcades, of pink and yellow stucco
Henry James

EGYPTIAN MUSEUM~GALLERIA SABAUDA

The first major stopping-point beyond the Alps was Turin, where Grand Tourists first took stock of Italian society. Boswell, whose prime interests were great men, willing women and himself, was amazed by the gallantry of the Piedmontese, and whenever he admired a lady, he was told: 'Sir, you can have her. It would not be difficult.' His hopes soared and he confessed: 'The whim seized me of having an intrigue with an Italian countess, and, as I had resolved to stay very little time here, I thought an oldish woman most proper, as I should have an easy attack.' However, it proved more difficult than he had suspected, and after Madame St Gilles had rejected the rampant Scotsman's advances, Boswell had to content himself with a lower class of woman than he would have desired. 'I then went to Billon's, where I had a pretty girl. I was disgusted with low pleasure. Billon talked of women in the most indelicate manner.'

Although you are unlikely to have quite such an exciting time as Boswell – and certainly would not want to describe it as frankly if you did – Turin still surprises most visitors. Its reputation, as a business centre, the home of Fiat and the Red Brigade, gives little indication of its beautiful wide arcaded streets leading into handsome squares. The city centre, laid out on the original Roman grid plan with distant views of the snow-capped Alps, intoxicated William Hazlitt and reminded American visitors, more prosaically, of Philadelphia. Most Grand Tourists, like Edward Gibbon, found it provincial and dull. Those who lingered here had yet to sample the fleshpots of the south, although attendance at court on New Year's Day 'occasions an extraordinary exhibition of bare bosoms', as Peter Beckford noted disapprovingly in 1787.

The best way to explore Turin is to wander through the city centre which lies between Corso Regina Margherita and Corso Vittorio Emanuele, and from Corso Re Umberto to the Po. The cafés of Turin are famous, not only for their excellent coffee but also for their cakes and biscuits; the Caffè Torino in the central Piazza San Carlo serves coffee, which, in local opinion, equals that of anywhere

3

in Europe. Alternatively, you can drink your cappuccino in the Baratti Milano in Piazza Castello in a marvellous *fin de siècle* interior.

The Palazzo dell' Accademia delle Scienze, off the north-east corner of the Piazza San Carlo, houses the masterpieces collected by the House of Savoy. The antiquities in the **Egyptian Museum**, on the ground and first floor, are rated more highly than those in either the British Museum or the Metropolitan Museum of Art and second only to those in Cairo. The science of Egyptology is an extension of the eighteenth-century passion for antiquity, and the finds made by Napoleon's expedition of 1798 made an impact on taste similar to that caused by the discovery of Herculaneum and Pompeii. Particularly impressive are the large-scale statues on the ground floor and the tomb paintings in the last room on the first floor, which vividly recapture the extraordinary life of ancient Egypt.

The **Galleria Sabauda** on the second floor is devoted to the eclectic collection of paintings made by the Princes of the House of Savoy. In the Netherlandish section, a *St Francis* by van Eyck, a *Visitation* by van der Weyden, and a number of scenes of the Passion by Memling are unrivalled in Italy. And for the British tourist, Van Dyck's painting of *The Children of Charles I* is perhaps the finest portrait painted at the court of Charles I. The Italian pictures cannot quite match this superlative quality, although *Tobias and the Three Archangels* by Filippino Lippi (son of Filippo Lippi) is a beautiful work of the late Quattrocento, Lorenzo di Credi's *Madonna and Child* is closely modelled on the work of his master Leonardo da Vinci, and there are some wonderful Veroneses.

The culinary tradition of Piedmont, with its rich sauces, delectable white truffles from Alba and a wide assortment of desserts, is strongly influenced by that of France just across the border. **Del Cambio**, at Piazza Carignano 2, founded in 1757, became the most fashionable restaurant in Turin in the nineteenth century and the favourite of Cavour, who had a regular table looking towards the Chamber of Deputies across the piazza, in case he was urgently needed during a debate. The nineteenth-century ambience makes it a perfect place to sample the best of Piedmontese cuisine and to taste the delightful wines from the Langhe – but it is not cheap and it is essential to book in advance.

Two other restaurants vying with Del Cambio for the honour of claiming Turin's culinary crown are the **Vecchia Lanterna**, at Corso Re Umberto 21, and **Al Gatto Nero**, at Corso Filippo Turati 14. Don't forget to finish your meal with one of the local desserts, such as zabaglione, a Piedmontese invention.

4

Egyptian Museum and **Galleria Sabauda:** Tuesday to Friday 9 a.m.
to 2 p.m. and 2.30 p.m. to 7.30 p.m., Saturday and Sunday 9 a.m.
to 2 p.m., closed Monday

RESTAURANTS

Del Cambio
Piazza Carignano 2, Turin
Telephone: 011 546 690, closed Sunday

Vecchia Lanterna
Corso Re Umberto 21, Turin
Telephone 011 537 047, closed Saturday

Al Gatto Nero
Corso Filippo Turati 14, Turin
Telephone: 011 590 414, closed Sunday

Stupinigi and Le Langhe

The sweete wines of Piedmont
Thomas Coryate

The royal hunting-lodge of Stupinigi, 10 km south-west of Turin on
the SS 23, past the suburb of Mirafiori, where the Fiat works are
housed, is an enormous complex begun by Juvarra in 1730. The
grandiose exterior gives little idea of the intimate rococo decoration
within. Alberoni's painted Sala delle Prospettive, the Chinese wallpaper in Pauline Borghese's apartments and the ceiling of her ante-
room, decorated in mirrors, are all of the highest quality. The walls
are covered in hunting scenes throughout to remind you of the
palace's original purpose, and even in Juvarra's fabulous ballroom
there are stags' heads over the windows and the candles. The ceilings were painted by the finest eighteenth-century masters, the
Venetian Crosato and the French Carle Van Loo, and the walls hung
with some exquisite pastel portraits by Liotard. If you are exhausted
by a tour of the apartments, you can relax in the magnificent park.

Alternatively, you might like to venture into Le Langhe, the home of truffles and Barolo wine. Returning to Turin, take the A6 *autostrada* towards Savona, and turn off at the Marene exit. Following the signs to Cherasco, you suddenly enter an area of rolling, vine-clad hills. If you are here in October, when the white truffles are in season and the vendemmia is in progress, all the roads are jammed with carts overloaded with purple grapes, and every hilltop village, perched beneath a castle, is devoted to the all-important process of making wine.

The village of La Morra, 7 km beyond Cherasco, commands magnificent views towards Barolo. In the Belvedere, at the top of the village, you can try the delicious local wine, which has been widely praised by travellers ever since Julius Caesar stopped here en route for Gaul. These heavy wines need to be drunk in moderation, as Thomas Coryate, one of the first travellers to visit Piedmont, found to his cost. 'I am sorry I can speake so little of so flourishing and so beautifull a Citie,' he wrote of Turin. 'For during the little time that I was in the citie, I found so great a distemperature in my body, by drinking the sweete wines of Piedmont, that caused a grievous inflammation in my face and hands; so that I had but a small desire to walke much abroad in the streetes.'

Barolo itself, the next village south, is more geared up for tourism, but there is an added excitement in drinking the famous wine in situ. An alternative is the village of Grinzane Cavour, 1 km east of the road from Barolo to Alba, where the castle combines facilities for winetasting with a first-class restaurant. If the restaurant is full, or if you are unfortunate enough to encounter a bus load of tourists, try the **Nuovo Ristorante Diana** in the neighbouring village of Diano d' Alba; the service is excellent.

On the way back to Turin, a slight detour 8 km north takes you to Alba, the capital of the region. If you have not yet been tempted to buy some of the local wine, a series of Enotecas offers every conceivable type of Dolcetto, Barbaresco, and the wines of Barolo itself. From Alba, a picturesque back road through the hills, via Canale and Poirino, leads back to Turin.

INFORMATION

Palazzina Mauriziana di Caccia, Royal hunting-lodge, Stupinigi:
    10 a.m. to 11.50 a.m. and 3 p.m. to 5.20 p.m., closed Monday

RESTAURANTS

Trattoria del Castello
Grinzane Cavour
Telephone: 0173 62159, closed Tuesday
Winetasting 10 a.m. to 12 noon and 3 p.m. to 6 p.m., Saturday and Sunday 9 a.m. to 12.30 p.m. and 2 p.m. to 6 p.m.

Nuovo Ristorante Diana
Via Marconi 11/A, Diano d' Alba
Telephone: 0173 69195, closed Tuesday

Isola Bella

A palace in a fairy tale
Président de Brosses

In the nineteenth century, as tourists increasingly admired the beauties of nature, they turned to the Italian Lakes, largely overlooked by earlier visitors. Mark Twain evoked the atmosphere of the houses and gardens surrounding Lake Como: 'They look so snug and so homelike, and at eventide when everything seems to slumber, and the music of the vesper bells comes stealing over the water, one

7

almost believes that nowhere else than on Lake Como can there be found such a paradise of tranquil repose.' The restrained atmosphere of the stately hotels that ring the lakes retains something of that period, and a stay in the Villa d' Este on Lake Como, if you can afford it, captures the flavour of tourism a century ago. If you want to escape from other tourists, Orta, the smallest and the most western of the lakes, remains far and away the most unspoilt.

The mild climate of the lakes and the high rainfall are ideal for the creation of some wonderful gardens. The most spectacular is Isola Bella, near the town of Stresa on Lake Maggiore. Although you are unlikely to find it 'secluded from the rest of the universe', as Gibbon did on his journey to Rome in 1764, it remains an enchanted island, inhabited by white peacocks. The original garden, with its ten terraces, was laid out from 1632 to 1671 by Angelo Crivelli for Count Carlo Borromeo III; it was bare of trees except where they were needed to hide the garden's asymmetrical shape. The crowning feature of the garden is the five-tiered water theatre rising a hundred feet above the lake and decorated with statuary and obelisks. The magnolias, camellias and roses, which give the garden such a luxuriant feeling, were added to the orange and pomegranate trees in the nineteenth century, softening the hard outline of the rocky island.

Even Grand Tourists, immune to the beauty of the Alpine scenery, stopped to marvel at this garden. Bishop Burnet, in 1685, and Président de Brosses, in 1739, were both overwhelmed. De Brosses thought the island resembled 'a palace in a fairy tale . . . it looks as if a portion of the Garden of the Hesperides had been wafted to this enchanted spot'. Byron thought the island and its neighbours fine but too artificial, and was more interested by Napoleon's visit in 1800. He wrote to his friend Thomas Moore in November 1816:

> In one of the Borromean isles (Isola Bella), there is a large laurel – the largest known – on which Buonaparte, staying there just before the battle of Marengo, carved with his knife the word 'Battaglia'. I saw the letters, now half worn out and partly erased.

INFORMATION

Isola Bella: 24 March to 24 October, 9 a.m. to 12 noon and 1.30 p.m. to 5.30 p.m.

Milan

Milan has seemed prosaic and winterish as if it were on the wrong side of the Alps

Henry James

DUOMO~LAST SUPPER~BRERA PINACOTECA~ AMBROSIANA LIBRARY~CASTELLO SFORZESCO~ MUSEO POLDI-PEZZOLI~LA SCALA THEATRE

Milan, strategically sited on the junction of vital trade routes, has always been an important commercial city. It is now the centre of every kind of business from the fashion industry to banking and has its own stock exchange. Earlier travellers regarded it as no more than a stopping-point on the way south; it contained no antiquities of note, and many visitors agreed with Président de Brosses's verdict, that: 'Rome has so many other beautiful things that I have seen since, that they have entirely spoiled Milan for me.' In the late nineteenth century, Henry James echoed this view, finding Milan 'prosaic and winterish as if it were on the wrong side of the Alps'.

However, no one could miss the **Duomo**, so vast and ornate that it took five centuries to complete. Stendhal imagined its flying buttresses 'pyramids of white marble tapering into gothic infinity', and wrote: 'Bathed in the silver radiance of moonlight, Milan Cathedral is a thing of such ravishing beauty that all the world cannot contain its equal.' Shelley was equally impressed by its 'dazzling spires', and read Dante behind the altar.

Leonardo's **Last Supper** (1495–7), in the refectory of Santa Maria delle Grazie, drew many visitors. The fresco, already a ruin within fifty years of its completion, attracted all sorts of stories. In the early nineteenth century Lady Morgan believed that a door had been cut through Christ's legs to enable hot food to be brought more quickly from the kitchen and her contemporary John Chetwode Eustace, a Roman Catholic priest whose *Classical Tour through Italy* was a very popular guide, condemned the French troops for using the refectory as an artillery storeroom and taking pot shots at the heads of the apostles. Artists flocked to study Leonardo's acute psychological insight into the characters of the participants; the artist James Barry, who examined it in detail, was very impressed by 'the wonderful truth and variety of the expressions'.

The museums in Milan contain superlative collections of Old Masters. The **Brera Pinacoteca**, founded by Napoleon in 1809 to house the paintings he had looted from the churches and palaces of Lombardy, has Mantegna's *Dead Christ*, one of the most moving works of the Quattrocento, an altarpiece by Piero della Francesca, several striking early Caravaggios and numerous masterpieces by north Italian artists. However, Grand Tourists passed by these masterpieces in silence in their haste to reach the Bolognese paintings. Stendhal thought Guercino's *Agar* 'a miracle of art created to melt the hardest of hearts, and to soften the most inveterate of misers and the most brazen of sycophants'.

The **Ambrosiana Library**, founded two centuries earlier by Cardinal Federico Borromeo, has an eclectic mixture of Flemish and Italian masters in the picture gallery, including Leonardo's *Portrait of a Musician* and Raphael's full-scale cartoon for his fresco of the *School of Athens* in the Vatican. In the library proper the highlight of the priceless collection of manuscripts and drawings are those by Leonardo, who left Florence to work for the Sforzas in Milan. Byron came here in 1816 and was fascinated by a lock of Lucrezia Borgia's hair and her love letters to Cardinal Bembo. The third of the great museums, the **Castello Sforzesco**, has more superb paintings of the Italian Renaissance.

But perhaps the most exciting collection of Old Masters in Milan, and one that many tourists have scarcely heard of – let alone visited – is the **Museo Poldi-Pezzoli**, at no. 12 Via Manzoni, the collection of Gian Giacomo Poldi–Pezzoli, who left it to the city in 1879. The museum is particularly famous for its paintings of the Quattrocento, including Madonnas by Mantegna and Botticelli, *St Nicholas of Tolentino* by Piero della Francesca and Piero del Pollaiolo's ravishing portrait of a lady of the Bardi family.

Milan was as renowned for its music as for its art. **La Scala Theatre** in Piazza della Scala (begun in 1776) opened in 1778 with *Europa Riconosciuta* by Mozart's rival Salieri. Mozart, who was paraded round Europe with his father in 1772, found the atmosphere very conducive to composing. Their lodgings were surrounded by musicians, as he recorded: 'Above us there is a violinist, below there is another, next to us there is a singing master who gives lessons, in the last room at the front there is an oboeist. What delight it gives us. I feel inspired.'

During the nineteenth century La Scala witnessed the triumphs of Rossini, Bellini, Donizetti and Verdi. Stendhal, a great expert on Italian music, thought it 'the finest opera house in the world . . . Imagination itself can conceive of nothing more grandiose, more magnificent, more impressive or more original than the decor, with its profoundly architectural rhythm.'

But even music and art had to give way to Milanese cuisine, which Stendhal compared favourably with that of Paris. His compatriot Berlioz complained bitterly that the noise coming from the restaurant in the opera house quite drowned the singing of the arias. There is an enormous proliferation of restaurants in Milan, offering every type of cuisine. Capturing something of the Grand Tour atmosphere, the **Brasera Meneghina**, at Via Ciro 10, is on the site of a seventeenth-century tavern, in the ruins of a Roman amphitheatre.

INFORMATION

The Last Supper, the refectory of Santa Maria delle Grazie: 9 a.m. to 1.15 p.m. and 2 p.m. to 6.15 p.m., Sunday and Monday 9 a.m. to 1.15 p.m.

Brera Pinacoteca, Via Brera 28: 9 a.m. to 2 p.m., Sunday 9 a.m. to 1 p.m., closed Monday

Ambrosiana Library, Piazza Pio XI 2: 9.30 a.m. to 5 p.m., closed Saturday

Castello Sforzesco, Piazza Castello: 9.30 a.m. to 12.30 p.m. and 2.30 p.m. to 5.30 p.m., closed Monday

Museo Poldi-Pezzoli, Via Manzoni 12: 9.30 a.m. to 12.30 p.m. and 2.30 p.m. to 6 p.m., Saturday 9.30 a.m. to 12.30 p.m. and 2.30 p.m. to 5.30 p.m., Sunday 9.30 a.m. to 12.30 p.m. and 2.30 p.m. to 6 p.m., April to September 9.30 a.m. to 12.30 p.m., closed Monday

La Scala Theatre, Piazza della Scala: 9 a.m. to 12 noon and 2 p.m. to 6 p.m., closed on Sunday from November to April

RESTAURANT

Brasera Meneghina
Via Ciro 10, Milan
Telephone: 02 808 108, closed Monday

Mantua

A most sweete Paradise
Thomas Coryate

CAMERA DEGLI SPOSI~SANT' ANDREA~
GIULIO ROMANO'S HOUSE~PALAZZO DEL TÉ

Of all the expeditions that can be made into the Lombard plain, the
most rewarding is to the city of Mantua. The Gonzagas, who ruled
the city from 1328 to 1707, were brilliant patrons of the arts, com-
missioning major works by Alberti and Mantegna in the fifteenth
century, Giulio Romano in the sixteenth and Rubens and Monteverdi in the seventeenth century. Considering the wealth of its art
treasures, it is surprising that Mantua did not figure prominently on
the Grand Tour although the peripatetic Thomas Coryate thought it
'a most sweete Paradise' on his visit in 1608. Those who did come
were more interested in Virgil's birthplace and in Giulio Romano's
Palazzo del Té, ignoring Alberti's church of Sant' Andrea and the
Mantegna frescoes in the Camera degli Sposi.

A short morning's walk takes in the main sights in the town
centre, leaving the Palazzo del Té for the afternoon. The Palazzo
Ducale provides a melancholy prelude to Mantegna's unforgettable
decoration of the **Camera degli Sposi**. A combination of the havoc
caused by the Imperial troops who sacked the city in 1530, and the
acquisition of the Gonzaga collections by Charles I, the greatest purchase of its time, have removed everything of merit except a few bat-
tered remains of frescoes by Pisanello.

In the **Camera degli Sposi**, Mantegna's illusionistic frescoes,
painted between 1465 and 1474, give you the feeling of intruding on
the courtly life of the Gonzagas so that you can almost overhear an
intimate conversation between the Marquis Lodovico Gonzaga and
his confidant, while his servants prepare to set off hunting.
Mantegna could not resist indulging his passion for antiquity, and
the landscapes are filled with ideal cities and classical ruins. He
liked to show off his mastery of *trompe l'oeil* and in the centre of the
ceiling an oculus looks straight up into the sky, with sharply fore-
shortened figures gazing down on to the spectator.

Emerging from the Camera, three interconnected squares, the
Piazza Sordello, Piazza del Broletto and Piazza delle Erbe, have a

number of cafés where you can sit outside and enjoy the medieval architecture. At the far end of the Piazza delle Erbe, the charming Romanesque Rotonda di San Lorenzo adjoins the Palazzo della Ragione, with its elegant Torre dell' Orologio.

On the far side of the square stands the basilica of **Sant' Andrea**, designed by Alberti in emulation of classical architecture. The facade combines elements of a triumphal arch and a Roman temple front and the massive coffering of the barrel vault, both in the porch and in the nave, looks directly back to the basilica of Maxentius which had profoundly impressed Alberti on his visit to Rome. Mantegna's tomb and probable self-portrait in bronze stand in the first chapel on the left.

If you would now like to stop for lunch, cross Piazza Mantegna and **Ai Garibaldini**, with a wisteria-covered pergola in a courtyard, is at Via San Longino 7 – just off the square. Alternatively, head back to Piazza Sordello, and the excellent **Aquila Nigra** is in an old stable block at Vicolo Bonacolsi 4, off the left side of the square opposite the Palazzo Ducale.

After lunch, continue from Ai Garibaldini down to the end of the street and follow Via Roma down to Piazza Martiri. Alternatively, if you are coming from the Aquila Nigra, follow directions to Sant' Andrea. Bear right down Via Giovanni Chiassi, an attractive street lined with palaces, and take the fourth left into Via Poma, where **Giulio Romano's House** is at no. 18. Indulging his capricious style to the full, Romano discarded the perfect proportions so beloved of Renaissance architects by squashing the windows into shallow arches and dwarfing them with heavy rustication.

Continue down Via Poma, and turn right into Via Giovanni Acerbi which leads to the **Palazzo del Té**, Romano's masterpiece where the Emperor Charles V was entertained in 1530. This is Mannerist architecture at its most sophisticated, each façade

differing markedly from its neighbours and designed on an asymmetrical axis but done so subtly that it is almost impossible to detect at first glance. The palace became immensely famous as soon as it was completed in 1534. The heavy rustication of the façades appealed greatly to the architect William Kent, who visited the palace in the early eighteenth century with his future patron Thomas Coke, for whom he built Holkham Hall in Norfolk.

The interior, one of the most complete of its type in existence, is covered with frescoes and stuccowork. Each room is devoted to a different theme, the Sala dei Cavalli decorated with the favourite horses of the Gonzagas, the Sala di Psiche with Bacchic scenes of banquets and love-making (whose eroticism greatly appealed to the French neo-classical painter Ingres) and the Camera dei Venti with scenes of hunting and fighting as epitomised by the different signs of the zodiac. Romano was heavily influenced by the antique, notably in the Camera degli Stucchi where a Roman procession winds its way round the walls.

The room that has always attracted most attention is the Sala dei Giganti, which is frescoed with a titanic battle between the gods on the ceiling and the hapless giants round the walls on whom they are raining down rocks, an effect so convincing that the whole room appears to be collapsing about the spectator. This deceit appealed greatly to early Grand Tourists such as Fynes Moryson, who admired Giulio Romano's virtuosity, but by the early nineteenth century the wilful complexity of Mannerism was regarded as distasteful. Dickens condemned 'the unaccountable nightmares with which its interior has been decorated by Giulio Romano . . . so inconceivably ugly and grotesque, that it is marvellous that any man can have imagined such creatures.'

INFORMATION

Palazzo Ducale, Castello di San Giorgio and **Camera degli Sposi:** 9 a.m. to 2 p.m. and 2.30 p.m. to 5 p.m., closed Monday
Palazzo del Té: 9 a.m. to 12.30 p.m. and 2 p.m. to 6 p.m., closed Monday

RESTAURANTS

Ai Garibaldini
Via San Longino 7, Mantua
Telephone: 0376 329 237, closed Wednesday

Aquila Nigra
Vicolo Bonacolsi 4, Mantua
Telephone: 0376 350 651, closed Sunday evening and Monday

Genoa

Their men are as devoid of faith, and their women of shame, as their hills are of wood, and their sea of fishes
Joseph Addison

PALAZZO BIANCO~PALAZZO ROSSO

For those not coming over Mont Cenis, Italy could be reached by sea, arriving at Genoa. Even before John Evelyn caught sight of land in 1643, he 'smelt the peculiar joys of Italy in the perfumes of orange, citron, and jassmine flowers'.

Genoa was known as La Superba because, as Tobias Smollett explained, it 'makes a dazzling appearance when viewed from the sea, rising like an amphitheatre in a circular form'. The Genoese Republic, after decisively defeating Pisa in 1284, became the main maritime rival of Venice, and the great Genoese families such as the

15

Dorias and the Spinolas poured money into the palaces they erected along the Strada Nuova, making it, in Lassels's words, 'the Queen-street of Europe'; Lassels was also amazed at the suburb of San Pietro in Arena: 'We durst not bless ourselves', he wrote, 'lest this enchanted place should have vanished.'

In typical xenophobic fashion, the Genoese were thought unworthy of their city. They had a reputation for pride and meanness, and Thomas Nugent, in his comprehensive account published in 1749, damned them for 'being a treacherous, over-reaching set of people . . . so cunning that it would be impossible for a Jew to get bread amongst them'. Like all ports, Genoa was full of toughs; one visitor recorded: 'They assassinate here as in other parts of this accursed country. I saw a man stabbed in the back in the middle of the day in one of the public markets in Genoa.'

The reputation of the Genoese was not helped by the pathetic sight of slaves rowing in the galleys, which gave the British a chance to castigate the government which inflicted such barbarities on its citizens (British convicts in far-away Australia being conveniently forgotten). Lady Morgan was fascinated by the convicts and wrote a lengthy description of them:

> Their bronzed skins were crimsoned up to their dripping brows; every sinew was starting, every nerve was strained, every vein swelled; their arms were folded on their stooped and panting breasts; they were chained in couples; and on the iron ring, which clasped their worn ankles, was engraved the word 'LIBERTAS'. This was a terrible sight!

The narrow streets of Genoa, flanked by high buildings (particularly those leading down to the harbour) give the city a conspiratorial feel highly appropriate to a centre which played such an important role in the Risorgimento. It was united with Piedmont at the Congress of Vienna in 1815, and Mazzini, Garibaldi, Nino Bixio and their republican followers plotted the unification of Italy here. Byron and Shelley set up their eccentric households here in 1821, and it was in the Gulf of La Spezia nearby that Shelley drowned so tragically in 1822. Byron stayed on until his ill-fated expedition to Greece, keeping up his usual style of living. Lady Blessington saw his bed when she passed through Genoa in 1826, and commented:

> It was the most gaudily vulgar thing I ever saw; the curtains in the worst possible taste and the cornice having his family motto of 'Crede Byron', surmounted by baronial coronets. His

carriage and his liveries were in the same bad taste, having an affectation of finery, but mesquin in the details, and tawdry in the ensemble: and it was evident that he piqued himself on them, by the complacency with which they were referred to.

Genoa was Dickens's favourite Italian city, the people 'good-tempered, obliging, and industrious', although he objected to the myriad flies and the streets emitting 'a peculiar fragrance, like the smell of a very bad cheese kept in very hot blankets'. He came here in 1844 to recover from the disappointing sales of *Martin Chuzzlewit*, and soon found distraction in the arms of Madame de la Rue, which did not amuse Mrs Dickens one bit.

Genoa's handsome Strada Nuova, now known as Via Garibaldi, is still lined with magnificent palaces filled with works of art. The **Palazzo Bianco**, at no. 11, the sixteenth-century Grimaldi palace, has a wonderful collection of paintings including exceptional works by Hugo van der Goes and Gerard David, and a number of paintings by Rubens and Van Dyck, who both worked in Genoa in the early seventeenth century. The sumptuous **Palazzo Rosso**, at no. 18, almost opposite, has a marvellous range of Van Dyck's portraits, showing his gifts as a colourist, and putting even the Dürers and the *Ecco Homo* of Caravaggio in the shade.

Genoese cuisine, as befits a maritime republic, is based on fish. **Rina**, at Mura delle Grazie 3 in the historic centre, is one of the best places in Italy to eat *spaghetti alle vongole*.

INFORMATION

Palazzo Bianco and **Palazzo Rosso**: 9 a.m. to 1 p.m. and 3 p.m. to 6 p.m., Sunday 9 a.m. to 12.45 p.m., closed Monday

RESTAURANT

Rina
Mura delle Grazie 3, Genoa
Telephone 010 207 990, closed Monday

TUSCANY
From Lucca to Florence

You cannot conceive what a divine country this is just now
                                                      John Ruskin

It was not until the Baedeker-touting tourists so lovingly fiction-
alised in Miss Lavish and Miss Honeychurch in E. M. Forster's *A
Room with a View* that the picturesque medieval piazzas and echoing interiors of Gothic cathedrals evoked the awed reactions that
their creators would no doubt have liked.

Seventeenth- and eighteenth-century travellers, with their passion for classical art, dismissed the medieval hilltowns of Tuscany as
primitive and barbarous; only those who chose to stay in one place
for more than a few days, like Boswell in Siena, learnt to appreciate
the peculiar charm of their surroundings. They much preferred
artificial landscape à *la* Capability Brown to the terrors of the
mountains, alive with bandits and other nameless horrors. Tobias
Smollett described his journey from Florence to Rome in 1764:
'Great part of this way lies over steep mountains, or along the side of
precipices, which render travelling in a carriage exceeding tedious,
dreadful and dangerous.' The Grand Tour was essentially an urban
phenomenon, as Thomas Nugent observed: 'Most people of distinction live in the cities, out of which there are very few castles or
noblemen's seats to be seen, especially in comparison with what we
observe in France and England.'

Most eighteenth-century travellers arrived in Tuscany on the
rough overland route through the Apuan Alps, at the risk, as Tobias
Smollett put it, 'of breaking your neck every minute', or braved the
very real danger of pirates to land at the port of Livorno, which they
called Leghorn. The town, founded by Cosimo I in 1571 and the base
for the Tuscan navy, was built by the expatriate Robert Dudley in
the early seventeenth century and declared a free port by Ferdinand
de' Medici in 1618. It therefore became the centre for the dispatch-
ing home of works of art purchased on the Grand Tour, often of
questionable authenticity and certainly without export licences.

From Lucca or Livorno Grand Tourists continued to Pisa, now a shadow of its imperial heyday. Most glanced at the Campo dei Miracoli but restricted their comments to a few feeble jokes on the 'awriness' of the Leaning Tower, which reminded Mrs Piozzi of the leaning tower at Bridgenorth. The Grand Tour is always thought of as a leisurely ramble across Europe, soaking up the atmosphere, but most eighteenth-century accounts complain of the slowness of the journey and the frantic need to press on. From Pisa travellers hastened to Florence, ignoring the Gothic architecture at Pistoia and galloping past the wonderful Filippo Lippi frescoes and the Donatello sculpture in the Duomo at Prato.

From Florence they took the Via Cassia south to Rome, missing out Arezzo and Cortona which lay in the foothills of the Apennines in eastern Tuscany. Even Siena, now universally acclaimed as one of the most beautiful towns in Italy, merited hardly more than an overnight stop. The landscape south of Siena, with its pastoral vistas dotted with cypresses and wild flowers just like a Simone Martini painting, was condemned as desolate, and the effort of climbing up to Radicofani was a source of great irritation; the stupendous views from the town were studiously ignored. From Radicofani a single stop at Viterbo to change horses and grab a quick night's sleep sufficed before the race across the Campagna to Rome.

William Beckford, a romantic by nature, was one of the first to admire the Tuscan countryside for its own sake. He wrote to Alexander Cozens, his Eton drawing-master in 1780:

> You ask me how I pass my time; generally upon the hills, in wild spots where the arbutus flourishes; from whence I may catch a glimpse of the distant sea; my horse tied to a cypress,

and myself cast upon the grass . . . with a tablet and pencil in
my hand, a basket of grapes by my side, and a crooked stick to
shake down the chestnuts.

After the Napoleonic Wars, Byron and Shelley, who followed
Beckford's example by going into voluntary exile, came to live in
Pisa in 1821, and with the descriptive power of their writing inspired
a whole generation to turn away from man-made landscapes and
admire the beauties of nature. Hans Christian Andersen, taking the
same route through the mountains behind La Spezia which had so
upset Smollett, was bewitched. 'Beautiful blue mountains enfolded
the loveliest, most fertile of valleys which seemed to be a crammed
horn of plenty', he eulogised.

Nature was to be enjoyed, though few cared to emulate Shelley
who set an eccentric example by sitting naked in a woodland pool
reading Herodotus before plunging into a torrent for his daily bath.
Love of the natural world provided the inspiration for his 'Ode to a
Skylark', as Mary Shelley recalled: 'It was on a beautiful summer
evening, while wandering along lanes whose myrtle hedges were the
bowers of the fire-flies that we heard the carolling of the skylark
which inspired one of the most beautiful of his poems.'

Nature was not to be tamed so easily, however, and Shelley's stay
in Italy ended in tragedy when he was drowned while sailing across
the Gulf of La Spezia in 1822. Byron wrote to Thomas Moore a memorable account of his funeral on the beach at Lerici:

We have been burning the bodies of Shelley and Williams on
the seashore, to render them fit for removal and regular inter-
ment. You can have no idea what an extraordinary effect such

a funeral pile has on a desolate shore, with mountains in the background and the sea before, and the singular appearance the salt and frankincense gave to the flame. All of Shelley was consumed, except his heart, which would not take the flame, and is now preserved in spirits of wine. [It was buried in the Protestant Cemetery in Rome near the body of John Keats – see page 113.]

Byron, like his contemporaries, was imbued with the cult of the picturesque and fascinated by the peculiar customs and costumes of the inhabitants of each region. Lady Morgan, writing of her journey through Italy from 1819 to 1820, filled her account with descriptions of peasants, those in Tuscany 'generally speaking, brusque and rude, but gay and cheerful – the women resembling Welsh peasants; fresh and chubby, and tight in their dress'.

This love of the picturesque encouraged tourists to visit places off the beaten track and to study the history of the men who built them. Even the ancient Etruscans, about whom very little was known, attracted interest, and George Dennis's *Cities and Cemeteries of Etruria* (1848) provided a very different itinerary from the traditional rushed journey from Siena to Rome.

But the Etruscans could not begin to compete with the bristling towers of San Gimignano, the hallowed fresco cycles in the Campo Santo in Pisa and the Romanesque churches of Lucca, so beloved of Ruskin, all of which became venerated as places of pilgrimage. The history of the medieval city-states of Tuscany, Pisa's rise to power in the twelfth century, Lucca's attempt to conquer Florence under Castruccio Castracani in the 1320s, the battle of Montaperti in 1260 when the Sienese defeated a vastly superior force of Florentines through the intervention of the Madonna (as they imagined), all combined to imbue Tuscany with a glamorous halo. Adam Walker, whose highly critical account was published in 1787, imagined the lifestyle in the walled town of Monterrigioni in 'the days of Knight-Errantry, when Damosels were imprisoned in lofty towers, in wilds, and deserts; among rocks, and precipices'.

The Tuscan Primitives, appreciated by all too few eighteenth-century collectors (such as William Young Ottley, the Earl-Bishop of Derry and the neo-classical sculptor John Flaxman, who greatly admired the Pisani pulpits at Pisa and the paintings of Duccio), became easily the most popular works of art in Italy. Lasinio's prints of the Campo Santo, published in 1828, had an enormous influence on his contemporaries, including the youthful Pre-Raphaelite Brotherhood.

Botticelli and Giotto were the names on every Victorian maiden's lips; even the landscape was seen through the eyes of the Quattrocento. Ruskin described his sensations during the Tuscan spring:

> You cannot conceive what a divine country this is just now, the vines with their young leaves hang as if they were of thin beaten gold – everywhere – the bright green of the young corn sets off the grey purple of the olive hills, and the spring skies have been every one backgrounds of Fra Angelicos. Such softness I never saw before.

Tuscany, regarded as a safe haven for those mistrustful of the noise and dirt of Rome and Naples, became a popular place for convalescents. Following in the train of Montaigne, who took the waters at Bagni di Lucca in 1581, a host of nineteenth-century tourists descended on Bagni di Lucca and Pisa to enjoy their beneficial climate, including Shelley, Byron, Walter Savage Landor and the Brownings.

Such is the wealth of art all over Tuscany that you can still avoid the crowds and enjoy the excitement of 'discovering' a darkened altarpiece in a remote church, or a Renaissance palace in the back streets of a dusty market town, or, when it all becomes too much, simply escaping into the beautiful rolling hills. This is exactly the approach to Italy adopted by Henry James, who wrote of Pistoia, but it could equally well apply to any number of Tuscan towns: 'Pistoia is still medieval. How grass-grown it seemed, how drowsy, how full of idle vistas and melancholy nooks!'

Lucca

The most fly-in-amber town in the world
Hilaire Belloc

78 km from Florence on A 11

DUOMO~SAN FREDIANO~PALAZZO MANSI~SAN MICHELE

'Lucca is a pretty little Commonwealth', wrote the Catholic priest Lassels in 1670 on one of his numerous visits to Italy, 'and yet it sleeps quietly within the bosom of the Great Duke's state.' A century later Mrs Piozzi, full of admiration for its orderly existence, commented: 'A great boarding-school in England is really an infinitely more licentious place.' Hilaire Belloc thought it 'the most fly-in-amber town in the world, with its uncrowded streets, its absurd fortifications, and its contented silent houses'.

As the only city in Tuscany to resist Florentine aggression success-fully, Lucca's sturdy independence appealed to Grand Tourists. Defended by her massive walls, which were completed in 1645 and must have crippled the Lucchese economy, Lucca was besieged only once, by a flood in 1812, which surrounded the walls but failed to breach them. Napoleon's lascivious sister Elisa Baciocchi had been given the duchy as part of the Buonaparte redistribution of Europe. Anxious to retain the affection of her subjects, she was hoisted on to the ramparts in a crane to join the besieged citizens.

Lucca has always been famous for its music. Edward Gibbon greatly enjoyed the opera on his epic tour to Rome in 1764, and in 1780 William Beckford was inspired by the singing of the castrato Pacchierotti, to the wrath of the locals who thought that the jaunts they went on together into the surrounding hills would ruin the unfortunate singer's voice. But the self-centred Beckford paid scant attention, and later persuaded Pacchierotti to come to sing for him at his gigantic Gothic folly at Fonthill in Wiltshire. Lucca's most famous musical son, Puccini, began his career as a choirboy in the church of San Michele, and lived and composed in a villa in nearby Torre del Lago where there is an annual Puccini festival.

Lucca is not awe-inspiring, and you can quite easily see the main sights in a morning, spending the rest of the day walking on top of the walls round the town. The town's chief glories are its Roman-esque churches, which were first carefully studied by Ruskin in the 1840s.

The **Duomo** is, perhaps, the finest of these churches. It was begun in the twelfth century and completed some three hundred years later. The façade has a piecemeal effect, with the top storey missing and its right-hand edge squashed against the base of the campanile. Its appeal lies in its sculptural decoration: a riot of warriors, dragons and lions, interspersed with geometric patterns, covers the columns of the upper arcades. There is more vivid carving in the atrium (porch), particularly scenes from the *Life of St Regolo* by a Lombard master over the right-hand door. It proved too esoteric for the locals, as Ruskin lamented: 'The schoolboys rarely pass the porch without throwing a stone or two at it. The great thing is to knock off a nose.'

The interior of the Duomo was built in the late fourteenth and fifteenth centuries. Lucca's most famous relic stands in the left aisle: a Crucifix, known as the *Volto Santo*, supposedly carved by Nicodemus, which miraculously floated across the Mediterranean from the Holy Land to Lucca. It is housed in a Tempietto by Matteo Civitali, a little-known Lucchese sculptor of the fifteenth century. On 13 September it is taken out of the Duomo and paraded in triumph round the town.

The most beautiful monument in the Duomo is Jacopo della Quercia's tomb of Ilaria del Carretto, dating from 1407–8, in the left transept. The young noblewoman is portrayed lying in perfect repose, her feet resting lightly on her faithful hound. Her stylised figure seems closer to the world of French and Burgundian chivalry than to that of the Tuscan Renaissance, although the putti holding swags round the base of the tomb are one of the first examples of a sculptor using motifs taken from ancient Roman monuments. Ruskin wrote an ecstatic account of Ilaria's tomb, identifying her with his dead love, Rose de la Touche.

Other works of note are the altarpiece by Fra Bartolomeo of the *Madonna with Saints Stephen and John the Baptist* in the chapel next to the tomb, two charming angels sculpted by Matteo Civitali next to the high altar, and a brightly coloured altarpiece attributed to Domenico Ghirlandaio in the Sacristy off the right aisle.

Coming out of the Duomo, cross the Piazza San Martino into Piazza San Giovanni and turn right into Via Cenami, which changes its name to Via Filungo, a handsome street bustling with activity. Halfway up the street you catch sight of the Palazzo Guinigi on the right, famed for the tree growing on top of its tower. Mariana Starke, an eye-witness to Napoleon's invasion of Italy in 1796, and a traveller imbued with the cult of the picturesque, thought it gave Lucca 'the appearance of a fortified wood, with a watch-tower in its centre'. The tower gives a commanding view over the town and the surrounding countryside. Continue up Via Filungo to the Piazza del Mercato which is built on the ground-plan of the ancient Roman amphitheatre. The original format was sensitively reconstructed by Lorenzo Nottolini in 1830, leaving the ground floor uniform and the upper storeys in picturesque disarray.

Just north of the amphitheatre is another fine Romanesque church, **San Frediano**, with a plain façade crowned by a heavily restored Byzantine mosaic of the Last Judgement. Inside, a fascinating twelfth-century font, broken up in the eighteenth century but recently restored, stands on the right side of the nave. The bottom section, by a Lombard sculptor, depicts scenes from the life of Moses, with Pharoah and his army portrayed as crusading knights crossing the Red Sea. Across the nave, the chapel of St Augustine in the left aisle is covered with frescoes by the Bolognese painter Amico Aspertini, painted in the early sixteenth century and depicting scenes from the lives of St Augustine and St Frediano. On the left wall oxen bring the Volto Santo to Lucca, accompanied by all the local worthies and a group of singers with grotesque expressions. Aspertini creates an opulent effect, not only by using rich colours, but also by sticking fragments of gold to the robes and the horses' bridles.

From San Frediano it is a short walk down Via C. Battisti to the entrance to Palazzo Pfanner. From the staircase in the courtyard there is a good view of the formal garden, with classical statues set against the backdrop of plane trees that line the ramparts all around the town.

Continue down Via Battisti and turn left into Via San Giorgio. Via Galli Tassi, the fifth turning on the left, leads to **Palazzo Mansi**. The piano nobile of the palace contains a series of grand rooms decorated in an ornate Baroque style, the most sumptuous of which is the Camera degli Sposi with its exquisite silk hangings. The paintings, with the exception of one excellent portrait by Portormo, are mediocre replacements given to the town by Grand Duke Leopold II in 1847, small compensation for those removed wholesale by the Bourbons.

If you would like to eat some good local food, go back up Via Galli Tassi and turn left into the rather unpromising Via San Tommaso. **Da Giulio**, at no. 29, is a noisy trattoria usually packed with locals. If you would prefer something more sophisticated, take the Via del Toro opposite the entrance to the Palazzo Mansi. The street continues into Via di Poggio, turn right into Via della Cervia, and the **Buca di San Antonio**, at no. 1, an old coaching inn where Grand Tourists put up en route to Florence, still serves the best food in the town.

A few yards east of the Buca stands the Piazza San Michele. From Da Giulio head back to Palazzo Mansi and follow directions to the

Buca restaurant. The Romanesque façade of the church of **San Michele**, like that of the Duomo, is covered in a riot of sculptural decoration. The square was the site of the Roman forum, and is still the market-place, and it was in a room nearby that the triumvirate of Caesar, Pompey and Crassus met in secret in 56 BC to decide how they were going to dismember the Roman Republic.

This incredible breadth of culture, from the intrigue of Republican Rome to the Baroque decoration of the Palazzo Mansi, together with the charm of a sleepy, provincial town, typifies the attraction of Tuscany.

INFORMATION

Palazzo Mansi: 9 a.m. to 7 p.m., Sunday 9 a.m. to 2 p.m., Monday 2 p.m. to 7 p.m.

RESTAURANTS

Da Giulio
Via San Tommaso 29, Lucca
Telephone: 0583 55948, closed Sunday and Monday

Buca di San Antonio
Via della Cervia 1, Lucca
Telephone: 0583 55881, closed Sunday evening and Monday

Villa Reale, Marlia

10 km north-east of Lucca

If you head up the SS 435 for 7 km towards Montecatini Terme, turn left for Marlia and follow signs to the Villa Reale, you will find one of the finest of many beautiful villas in the environs of Lucca. This neo-classical villa was the favourite residence of Elisa Baciocchi, who compelled the reluctant Orsetti family to sell it to her when she was given the Duchy of Lucca in 1806. The informal part of the garden was laid out by her architect Morel from 1811 to 1814. After the fall of Napoleon, the Villa became the property of Maria Luisa, the Duchess of Parma.

Following an anti-clockwise tour of the garden, you cross the sweeping lawn which leads from the Villa to an ornamental lake. To the left is the original fifteenth-century bishop's house, visited by Montaigne in 1581, and a very ornate sixteenth-century grotto of Pan, covered in mosaic tritons and dolphins, and with the usual water jokes for soaking the unwary so typical of Renaissance gardens. Behind the grotto, a formal garden created in the 1930s has unfortunately fallen into disrepair.

Beyond lies the original seventeenth-century garden, perhaps the finest still surviving in Italy, consisting of a series of three outdoor rooms on an axis, divided by identical sets of gate piers. The first, a water garden filled with fragrant lemon trees, has as focal points a nympheum at each end set among the enclosing yew hedges. The second room, with its fountain spraying high into the air, is a circular ante-room to the delightfully intimate theatre beyond, with terracotta figures from the Commedia dell' Arte emerging from the yew hedges and the prompter's box, footlights and orchestra pit all made of box and yew. Elisa Baciocchi's court musician Paganini played here, concealed behind a hedge, while she fainted in ecstasy and was revived by the solicitous attentions of her paramour Bartolomeo Cenami.

If you travel 9 km north of Lucca on the SS 12 to the village of Ponte a Moriano, you might like to stop for lunch at **La Mora**, in an old posting house. The restaurant has been run by the same family since the middle of the last century. It offers regional dishes, including fresh fish caught in the River Serchio, one of the best being fillet of trout with artichokes. The shop opposite the restaurant sells excellent olive oil, for which the Lucchesia is justly famous.

There are plenty of other places to see in the Lucchesia: the Villas Torrigiani, Mansi and Garzoni and the hilltown of Barga are all good places for a picnic and a bottle of Montecarlo white wine, with, instead of your horse tied to a cypress, your hired car cunningly hidden in an olive grove.

INFORMATION

Villa Reale, Marlia: 10 a.m. to 11 a.m. and 4 p.m. to 6 p.m., closed
  Monday

RESTAURANT

La Mora
Via Sesto di Moriano 104, Ponte a Moriano
Ponte a Moriano
Telephone: 0583 57109, closed Wednesday evening and Thursday

Pisa

Celebrated for its profusion of marble, its patrician towers, and its grave magnificence

Joseph Forsyth

100 km from Florence on A 11

PIAZZA DEL DUOMO~CAMPO SANTO~ SANTO STEFANO DEI CAVALIERI

Pisa, 'celebrated for its profusion of marble, its patrician towers, and its grave magnificence', as Joseph Forsyth described it in 1802, was a desolate place during the era of the Grand Tour. Visitors, unsympathetic to the Middle Ages, found it disconcerting, for 'the whole town serves to bring before one's eyes the extravagant superstition of the age of the crusades', as the Marquis of Tavistock commented in 1762. The Campo dei Miracoli seemed out of scale with the emptiness of the rest of the city, its wonderful works of art of little interest apart from some antique sarcophagi in the Campo Santo, nobody knew what caused the Leaning Tower to lean, and all sorts of strange customs survived. Peter Beckford, on his visit in 1787, noted: 'Till lately a very ridiculous custom prevailed on the day of San Martino – The students had the privilege to catch a Jew, weigh him, and demand as many pounds of sugar-plums as he weighed; – you will conclude they picked out the fattest they could find.'

Those who stayed for long did so to escape. One of the reasons that Byron and Shelley came to Pisa in 1820–2 was to avoid English tourists. Later in the nineteenth century it became fashionable to take a cure here and to study the marvels of its medieval art; the Campo dei Miracoli became a place of pilgrimage for the Victorians. Dickens, in 1844, thought the group of buildings on its 'verdant carpet' the most remarkable and beautiful in the world. Recently the airport of Pisa and the quirkiness of the Leaning Tower have made it one of the most crowded places in Italy and it is vital to see the main buildings off peak hours.

The three glistening white buildings in the **Piazza del Duomo**, known as the Campo dei Miracoli, look their best on a crisp winter's morning set against the green expanse of the Campo, mercifully devoid of ice-cream sellers and tourists. Pisa was one of the most cosmopolitan of Italian cities and, during her heyday in the twelfth century, her maritime empire extended to Corsica, Sardinia and the Balearic Isles. The curious black and white stripes of the Duomo and Baptistery, and their blind arcades, show the influence of Sicily and Moorish Spain.

The Duomo, begun in 1064 on the profits of Pisa's wars and completed in the twelfth century on further profits from the Crusades, is one of the most important Romanesque buildings in Italy, and exerted a strong influence on the other great Tuscan cathedrals. Forsyth, perceptively, thought it in 'a style too impure to be Greek [by which he meant classical], yet still remote from the Gothic'. It suffered a disastrous fire in the late sixteenth century, and Giovanni Pisano's magnificent Gothic pulpit of 1302–10, which now stands on the left side of the nave, was taken down and stored in crates, where it remained until early this century. Giovanni carved a number of highly expressive scenes from the New Testament round the exterior of the octagonal pulpit. To increase the dramatic effect, Pisano included various episodes in the same panel, so that completely different scenes, such as the 'Presentation in the Temple' and the 'Flight into Egypt', overlap.

The Baptistery, one of the largest to be erected in Italy in the Middle Ages, was begun in 1152, and work continued sporadically until the fourteenth century, when the dome was completed. The interior contains a fine pulpit of 1260 by Nicola Pisano, Giovanni's father, with six panels depicting scenes from the New Testament. The high relief of the carving and the idealised faces of the figures look back to reliefs on classical sarcophagi, a unique influence at this early date.

The Leaning Tower, which has now become perhaps the most famous symbol of Italy, is, in fact, an extremely elegant campanile, if you can disentangle its picture-postcard associations. Begun in 1173, it had already started to subside by the middle of the thirteenth century. Grand Tourists were fascinated, not only by its peculiar appearance, but also by the experiments that Galileo (1564–1642), a native Pisan, carried out to disprove Aristotle's theory of the acceleration of falling bodies.

If you need a haven from the crowds milling outside the Duomo, head for the **Campo Santo**, the rectangular cemetery on the north side of the square where Pisa notables were buried, named after the sacred earth brought back from the Crusades by Archbishop Lanfranchi. It was badly bombed in 1944, and, in one of the greatest artistic losses of the last war, most of the frescoes, including the series by Benozzo Gozzoli, were ruined. However, the *Triumph of*

Death cycle, dating from 1360–80, has been largely preserved. It appears as a type of moral fable, with a group of richly dressed nobles out riding, suddenly coming across three decomposing corpses in their coffins. Behind this group, the figure of death, armed with a scythe, sweeps down on an unsuspecting party relaxing and playing music. In the centre of the fresco devils and angels fight for the souls of the dead. One can imagine the impact that this dramatic fresco, painted soon after the Black Death in 1348, must have had on contemporaries. Nineteenth-century visitors loved it and Liszt named his *Totentanz* after it.

From the Piazza del Duomo it is a short walk down Via Santa Maria, turning left along Via dei Mille into Piazza Cavalieri named after the Knights of St Stephen, a military order founded by Cosimo I in 1561 as the Tuscan equivalent of the Knights of Malta. John Evelyn began his tour of the city here in 1644, and was impressed by Vasari's Palazzo dei Cavalieri, which was covered in black and white sgraffito.

Vasari also designed the church of **Santo Stefano dei Cavalieri**, whose splendid interior can be visited between 11 a.m. and noon on Sunday mornings. The walls are festooned with trophies taken from the Turks: banners and pennants, lamps from mastheads and wooden carvings from captured galleys. The banners were lovingly restored by Sheila Butler Hancock, a nineteenth-century Irish woman, and provide a compelling image of sixteenth-century naval warfare. Président de Brosses thought they made 'a gallant show', on his visit in 1739, but unkindly wondered whether 'the Turks have not also got some of the flags, which belonged to the Knights, in their mosques'.

On any other day of the week except Sunday the church is shut and you can visit the Botanic Garden, founded in 1543 and probably the oldest in Europe, instead. The entrance is on Via Ghini, a continuation of Via dei Mille, which leads out of the west side of the Piazza Cavalieri.

An interesting walk from the Piazza Cavalieri to the Arno leads down Via San Frediano past the old university, for centuries the most important in Tuscany, and where Galileo lectured on mathematics from 1589 to 1591. The Arno flows in a stately curve through the city, and is the focal point of the major Pisan festival on 17 June, which begins with the Gioco del Ponte, a fight on a bridge between the areas of Pisa on either side of the river, followed by the Festival of Lights, when candles are lit in every palace along the riverbank.

Across the river to your right is the church of Santa Maria della Spina, a Gothic jewel. As late as the beginning of the nineteenth century the Gothic style was still regarded as unpalatable. John Chetwode Eustace described it in detail in 1802, but dismissed it as 'of an appearance whimsical and grotesque rather than beautiful'. Unfortunately it is very rarely open.

Turning left along Lungarno Pacinotti, **Ristorante Sergio** at no. 1 is the best in Pisa, and has delightful views on to the river. Sergio is President of the Tuscan chefs' society, and you would be well advised to settle for one of his delectable set menus; do not miss the pink sorbet of lemon and rose petals. The restaurant is housed in an old inn, where Byron and Shelley came to eat. Byron described the Palazzo Lanfranchi, where he was living, just across the Arno, as 'large enough for a garrison, with dungeons below & cells in the walls, & so full of ghosts, that the learned Fletcher (my valet) has begged leave to change his room, because there were more ghosts there than the other'.

An alternative restaurant is **Al Ristoro dei Vecchi Macelli** (slaughterhouse in Italian) at Via Volturno 49, which you reach by following the north bank of the Lungarno westwards and turning up Via Volturno just beyond Piazza Solferino. Despite its unpromising name, this is an excellent restaurant in a fifteenth-century building, originally a church. For those with a passion for seafood and pasta, this is the place to come.

INFORMATION

Santo Stefano dei Cavalieri: Sunday 11 a.m. to 12 noon
Botanic Garden: Monday to Friday 8 a.m. to 1 p.m. and 2 p.m. to 5.30 p.m. Saturday 8 a.m. to 1 p.m., closed Sunday

RESTAURANTS

Ristorante Sergio
Lungarno Pacinotti 1, Pisa
Telephone: 050 48245, closed Sunday and Monday lunch

Al Ristoro dei Vecchi Macelli
Via Volturno 49, Pisa
Telephone: 050 20424, closed Sunday and Wednesday

FLORENCE

Palazzo Vecchio

Florence is nothing better than a vast museum full of foreign tourists

Stendhal

When you look at the crowds pouring in and out of the Duomo and the convent of San Marco, see the *menu turistico* in every restaurant window, and consider the position of Florence in so much of modern literature, it is almost impossible to imagine that, until the nineteenth century the city was considered no more than an attractive but brief stopover on the gallop to Rome. The extraordinary talent of Florentine artists, from Giotto and Dante to Leonardo and Michelangelo, and the patronage of the Medicis, was little appreciated. As early as 1580, within two decades of Michelangelo's death, Michel de Montaigne was writing: 'I cannot tell why this city should be termed beautiful as it were by privilege. Beautiful it is, but no more so than Bologna, and little more than Ferrara, while it falls far short of Venice.' By 1600 Florence was more famous in England as the scene of a series of bizarre court murders, dramatised by Webster in *The White Devil*, than as the city of Giotto, Donatello and Alberti.

Ignoring the golden age of Medici supremacy, seventeenth-century Grand Tourists pored over the medals, cabinets and weapons of the later Grand Dukes. Brought up on the precepts that were to form the Age of Reason, and horrified by anything that smacked of the dark Middle Ages, they admired the religious tolerance and scientific interests of these Grand Dukes. Hobbes and Milton were just two of the many foreigners who paid their respects to Galileo in his villa at Arcetri.

These travellers and their eighteenth-century successors, weaned on a classical education, were unimpressed by the city's insignificant role in antiquity after its founding by Julius Caesar's veterans in 59 BC. Their favourite guidebook was Joseph Addison's influential *Voyage to Italy* (1705), which concentrated almost exclusively on classical art. As a result they restricted their comments to an appraisal of the antique sculptures in the Medici collections, with a passing mention of Michelangelo and Raphael. In the 1720s Jonathan Richardson was one of the very few to award qualified praise to the Florentine Primitives, calling them 'manly and vigorous, although the style was bad'.

By the later eighteenth century more attention was paid to the fabulous pictures left to the city in perpetuity by the last Medici, the Electress Anna Maria Luisa, on her death in 1743. But no painting earlier than 1500 is included in Zoffany's *Tribuna*, painted in the 1770s, where a group of Grand Tourists are examining the most famous paintings and antique sculptures. The centrepiece of the room is the *Venus de' Medici*, which inspired generations of visitors. Many of them used the excuse of the classical subject-matter to write semi-erotic accounts, marvelling, like Joseph Spence in 1730, over her breasts, 'small, distinct, and delicate to the highest degree'.

Throughout the eighteenth century the Grand Ducal Court was regarded as very dull, and the Florentines were seen as 'niggards and close-fisted', treating balls in the Pitti Palace as a golden opportunity to steal food, to the astonishment of Horace Walpole who gaped at how 'the women fall on with both hands, and stuff their pockets, and every creek and corner about them'. Goethe spent just three hours in Florence on his epic Grand Tour in 1786, and candidly admitted that his only thought was to press on to Rome.

Horace Walpole, on the other hand, had the time of his life on his prolonged visit in 1739–40, describing Florence as 'the loveliest town on earth' and indulging in a passionate liaison with the beautiful Signora Griffoni, to whom he acted as a *cicisbeo* (a male companion to a married woman). Walpole and his friend the poet Thomas Gray stayed with the British envoy, Sir Horace Mann, but managed to avoid dull court functions. The highlight of their stay was the balls they attended during Carnival, where, as the budding architect Robert Adam noted: 'Every mortal was masked, from a Marquis to a shoe-black.' Walpole threw himself into the proceedings:

> I have done nothing but slip out of my domino (a black and white masked costume) into bed, and out of my bed into my domino. The end of the Carnival is frantic, bacchanalian; all the morn one makes parties in masque to the shops and coffee-houses, and all the evening to the operas and balls. Then I have danced, good gods! how I have danced!

For those not privileged enough to stay at 'The King's Arms', as Mann's residence at Casa Manetti near the Ponte Santa Trinita was known, the most popular lodging was Carlo's, owned by Charles Hadfield, opposite the Palazzo Corsini and overlooking the Arno. Social life centred around the Casino (which resembled a London club but with women as members) and the theatre, where much gossip was exchanged over rubbers of whist played during performances. Actresses were particularly prone to scandal, and there was much excitement at Lord Lincoln's affair in 1771 with 'a Strumpet of the Theatre', as the dealer James Byres called her. Mozart dreamt of settling in the city for ever on his second visit in 1773.

The liveliest social circle centred on the Countess of Albany, the wife of Bonnie Prince Charlie who retired here a broken man long after his dramatic attempt to seize the British throne in 1745. The Countess soon tired of his drunkenness and eloped with the dashing poet Alfieri, and their salon attracted leading literary lights such as Byron and the French novelist Stendhal.

The Earl-Bishop of Derry began to take an interest in early Florentine art and history in the 1770s and 1780s, and this increased in the early nineteenth-century, with collectors such as Fox-Strangways and Sanford, and William Roscoe, whose biography of Lorenzo the Magnificent compared Florence to Athens with Lorenzo cast in the role of Pericles. But it was only with the publication in the middle of the century of Ruskin's *Mornings in Florence* and Burckhardt's *Civilisation of the Renaissance in Italy* that the passion for the art and history of Florence and, indeed, for everything Florentine, began. Through these books, eager students learnt how the extraordinary blossoming of the arts at the time of Giotto and Dante was followed by the golden era of Medici rule. Under Cosimo Il Vecchio (1434–64) and his grandson Lorenzo the Magnificent (1469–92), Florence played a key role in European politics, and their patronage of leading artists and humanists established Florence's position as the home of the early Renaissance. The story was hemmed about with enough intrigue, Macchiavellian politics, romance and skulduggery to make the most stalwart Victorian maiden quiver with the drama of it all, and Florence overflowed with diligent sightseers. They soaked in the atmosphere of the Quattrocento, recreating such scenes as the Pazzi Conspiracy of 1478, when Lorenzo's brother Giuliano was murdered in the Duomo, and Lorenzo himself only just escaped with his life; the burning of the fanatical monk Savonarola in the Piazza della Signoria in 1498; and the terrible siege of Florence in 1529–30, when the republican party attempted for the last time to overthrow the House of Medici.

At the same time these Victorians became avid admirers of the art of the Early Renaissance. Clutching their Murray or Baedeker guidebook under their arm, troops of earnest Miss Honeychurches and Miss Lavishes were to be seen peering at darkened frescoes in obscure churches. The church of Santa Croce was a particular favourite, with its monuments to Dante, Galileo, Michelangelo and Machiavelli, and the Trecento frescoes of Giotto and Taddeo Gaddi conjuring up the diversity of the Florentine genius. Ralph Waldo Emerson summed up their fevered enthusiasm: 'I think no man has an idea of painting until he has come hither. Why should painters study in Rome. Here, here!'

The British showed little desire to socialise with Italians but collected in self-contained social circles. The Brownings were at Casa Guidi near the Pitti, and the art historian Herbert Horne, who left his superb collection to the city, was at the Palazzo Gondi in Via de' Benci near Santa Croce. The American community was centred on the house of the gregarious sculptor Hiram Powers, his studio 'a curious, rambling old place, with lofty, spacious rooms succeeding each other, and dark passages leading to remote portions of the structure'.

These Anglo-Americans were anxious not to suffer the indignity of bargaining with Italian shopkeepers. They frequented the area around Piazza di Santa Trinità, cashing a cheque in Maquay and Packenham in Via Legnaioli, browsing in Edward Goodban's print shop at no. 4183, buying groceries from Samuel Lowe in the piazza, and relaxing over a cup of tea at the highly popular Doney's on the far side of the square. Elsewhere in the city, English wine merchants, dentists, doctors and shirtmakers flourished in this expatriate community, keeping Italians at a distance and sending their children to be educated at Dr Broomback's Academy for the Sons of Gentlemen. When there was no escape from entering an Italian shop, they turned to Murray's *Handbook* for some patronising advice: 'Generally speaking', they were instructed, 'the Florentine shopkeepers ask a great deal more from a stranger than they will take: all you have to do is to beat them down with good humour and civility.'

The expatriates took a passionate interest in Italian politics and, inspired with revolutionary fervour and romantic views of the Rights of the Common Man, fervently supported the Risorgimento. Many of them, particularly writers, retired to the wooded hills surrounding Florence, where they could escape from the stifling summer heat in the city. Fiesole, with its beautiful views of the Duomo and the city in the bowl below, became the most fashionable retreat.

A few eccentrics helped to enliven the social scene: Walter Savage Landor, one of the first to collect Florentine Primitives, lived in the Palazzo Medici for years, quarrelling with everyone and even, on occasion, beating up his carpenters. And the novelist Ouida drove around in a silk-lined victoria, proclaimed herself the greatest author of all time and scandalised society with her passion for the Marchese della Stufa.

From 1865 to 1870 Florence was the capital of Italy and, for a brief moment, it seemed as though the city would bestride the world stage once more. The old ghetto was swept away and a facade finally put on the Duomo, but, as the tide of history swept on to Rome, it soon lapsed back to its status as the most popular tourist site in Italy. With its well-furnished apartments, hard-working population and lack of beggars, Florence was the acceptable face of Italy for the well-heeled middle classes, and in contrast with the male-dominated Grand Tour, vast numbers of women, thirsting for culture, descended on the city. The Americans, just as enthusiastic as their British contemporaries, compared the busy, intellectual life of Florence to that of Boston.

At the end of the nineteenth century Henry James was one of those to lead the reaction against the moral earnestness of these tourists, particularly Ruskin. 'I had really been enjoying the good old city of Florence', he wrote in *Italian Hours*, 'but I now learned from Mr Ruskin that this was a scandalous waste of charity. I should have worn a face a yard long.'

As Florence grew in popularity, intellectuals and aesthetes gathered there to study the Renaissance, a tradition enshrined in the scholarship still carried out from Bernard Berenson's villa at I Tatti. Sir Harold Acton, who lives at La Pietra, a villa on the outskirts of Florence, and Sir John Pope-Hennessy, who possesses an unrivalled knowledge of Renaissance sculpture and painting, also represent a continuation of this aesthetic trend.

The modern tourist in Florence is torn between pleasure and duty. Should he queue for hours to see Michelangelo's *David* and the Uffizi, or should he try to enjoy himself even if this means missing some of the most famous monuments in the city? The centre of Florence is too small to offer anywhere wholly off the beaten track, but I have selected two itineraries which include major fresco cycles in lesser-known churches, and a number of sculptures which can be viewed at leisure in their original open-air settings. I make no apology for missing out the Accademia, the Pitti, the Bargello and San Marco. The last time I went to see the Fra Angelicos in San Marco, on a cold morning in March, the floor was so worn out by the weight of tourists that it fell through. Thankfully, the frescoes were undamaged.

I think no man has an idea of the powers of painting until
he has come hither. Why should painters study in Rome?
Here, here

Ralph Waldo Emerson

SANTA MARIA NOVELLA~SAN LORENZO~PALAZZO MEDICI-RICCARDI~BAPTISTERY~DUOMO~MUSEO DELL' OPERA DEL DUOMO~ORSANMICHELE~PIAZZA DELLA SIGNORIA

This walk takes in Santa Maria Novella (one of the most important Gothic churches in Tuscany), the Medici parish of San Lorenzo with Cosimo Il Vecchio's palace and the church of San Lorenzo, the Duomo and the Piazza della Signoria, the ecclesiastical and secular centres of the city.

The Piazza Santa Maria Novella, near the railway station and the venue for political gatherings and open-air concerts, was, until the late nineteenth century, the centre of a district inhabited by a large number of foreigners, including the young John Ruskin, the poets Shelley and Longfellow and the writers William Dean Howells and Henry James. They were able to enjoy the view, now sadly built over, of open countryside stretching away down the Arno valley.

For centuries the two obelisks in the Piazza were used as markers for chariot races held on the eve of 23 June, the feast day of the patron saint of Florence, St John the Baptist. The races emulated those of antiquity, and appealed to classically minded visitors. In 1581 Montaigne enjoyed the sight of the Medici chariot being pipped by the Strozzi's, to the vast delight of the crowd. In 1838 the American James Fenimore Cooper, the American author of *Last of the Mohicans*, was not impressed: 'One may witness the same any fine evening in New York', he wrote, 'between two drunken cartmen who are on their way home.'

The great Dominican church of Santa Maria Novella dominates the square. It was erected in the thirteenth century on the far side of the city from Santa Croce, the church of the rival Franciscan order. The elegant green and white façade, begun by Fra Jacopo Talenti, was largely completed by Alberti from 1456 to 1470, the only Florentine church façade to be completed during the Renaissance. Alberti's ingenious use of volutes to link the nave with the aisles, and the classical pediment surmounting the façade, were widely copied by later Renaissance and Baroque architects.

The Gothic interior, chosen by Boccaccio as the setting for the opening scenes of the *Decameron* (1353) is still filled with masterpieces despite Vasari's whitewashing of most of the frescoes in the sixteenth century. Halfway up the left aisle is Masaccio's sombre fresco of *The Trinity with the Virgin and St John*. The two donors kneel motionless on either side of an impressive Renaissance chapel closely based on Brunelleschi's architecture and showing Masaccio's mastery of perspective. Beneath the deep coffered vault God the Father supports the crucified Christ with the Virgin and St John looking on. The emotion of the participants is very muted, the Virgin's gesture being the only indication that we are participants in the scene.

The Strozzi Chapel in the left transept was frescoed by Nardo di Cione in the mid-fourteenth century with scenes of Heaven and Hell, the latter being one of the most dramatic renderings of the subject in the Middle Ages. The beautiful wooden Crucifix by Brunelleschi in the adjacent Gondi Chapel is the only wooden sculpture by the Florentine architect and was carved to rival Donatello's Crucifix in Santa Croce, which Brunelleschi had criticised for being too crudely realistic, comparing the figure of Christ to a peasant. When Brunelleschi, who had sculpted it in secret, first showed his Crucifix to Donatello he was so surprised that he dropped the basket of eggs he was carrying.

Domenico Ghirlandaio's delightful frescoes of the *Lives of St John the Baptist and the Virgin* in the Tornabuoni Chapel in the chancel give a fascinating insight into Florentine life in the 1480s, and reveal his remarkable abilities as a genre painter and portraitist. The *Birth of the Virgin*, set in a charming interior decorated with friezes in the style of Luca della Robbia, and with a stately procession of maidens come to greet the newborn infant, is perhaps the most beautiful fresco in the cycle. Ghirlandaio was assisted by a number of pupils, including the young Michelangelo. Apart from the isolated figure of John Breval who praised the Ghirlandaios as early as the 1720s, nobody in the eighteenth century commented on the frescoes. Stendhal was one of the first to appreciate the artist's merits. In 1817 he wrote perceptively: 'I confess that I am deeply moved by the steadfast truth to nature which is to be observed in Ghirlandaio and his contemporaries, who flourished too early to be submerged in the strong tide of idealism.' As the science of art history developed, serious figures such as Ruskin and Berenson felt that the Florentine master wasted his talents on genre details. Henry James, on the other hand, felt that it was precisely the charm of the incidental detail which made Ghirlandaio such an enjoyable artist to study.

Filippino Lippi's frescoes of the *Lives of St Philip and St John the Evangelist* in the Strozzi Chapel in the right transept betray the

41

anxiety which overtook Florentine society in the 1490s, with the collapse of Medici rule, the French invasion of Italy under Charles VIII, and Savonarola's terrifying sermons predicting the end of the world. Lippi's frescoes are painted in the bright colours typical of the Quattrocento but the expressions on the faces of the figures betray a deep unease, and in the *Exorcism of the Demon in the Temple of Mars* on the right wall, appear close to hysteria. The beautiful tomb of Filippo Strozzi is by Benedetto da Maiano.

Adjoining the church is the Chiostro Verde (Green Cloister), so called because of the colours of Uccello's frescoes of the Old Testament. The extraordinary depiction of the *Deluge* shows Uccello to have been much more than a painter of tricks of perspective and soldiers on rocking-horses. The scale of the tempest betrays the primeval force of the catastrophe, with death and destruction all around the statuesque figure standing in the foreground; ironically, the frescoes were badly damaged in the disastrous flood of 1966. Uccello was virtually ignored by Grand Tourists, although Sir Joshua Reynolds came here to sketch his frescoes in the 1750s. By the mid-nineteenth century, however, Quattrocento painting was in high fashion, and the Green Cloister was William Morris's favourite place in Florence.

The Spanish Chapel off the cloister, where St Catherine of Siena was summoned in 1374 to justify her outspoken criticism of the papal exile in Avignon, was frescoed by Andrea da Firenze in the 1360s. The complex allegorical scheme depicts the supreme power of the Church, and of the Dominican Order in particular. The *Triumph of the Church* on the right wall includes a view of the Duomo with Pope Urban V seated in front, surrounded by prelates and kings and guarded by ferocious looking black and white dogs, which represent the Dominicans (*domini canes* – dogs of the Lord, as they punningly called themselves). In the landscape to the right, the dogs savage wolves while Dominican saints refute heretics and administer sacraments. The custodian will, if encouraged by a suitable donation, point out the portraits of Dante and Beatrice, Petrarch and Laura, and Boccaccio and Fiammetta, on the right wall. Ruskin reckoned that he needed five weeks to see a quarter of this fresco and called it 'the most noble piece of pictorial philosophy in Italy'. On the ceiling there is a fourteenth-century depiction of Marco Polo in China.

Returning to the Piazza Santa Maria Novella, you might like to look at a pharmacy dating back to the seventeenth century in Via Della Scala, off the south side of the piazza. The pot pourri and assorted lotions and creams in the Officina Profumo-Farmaceutica at Via della Scala 16 are still made to the original formulae. From here, cross over Piazza Santa Maria Novella, head east up Via dei

Banchi and immediately left into Via del Giglio which leads to Piazza degli Aldobrandini at the back of the church of San Lorenzo.

The church is surrounded by a colourful market selling cheap leather bags, gloves, wool sweaters and scarves. This is the heart of the Medici district and the church of San Lorenzo was the family's parish church, where Cosimo Il Vecchio and most of the other principal members of his family are buried. The church, despite its unfinished façade for which Michelangelo, among others, drew up designs, gives the clearest idea of the development of Renaissance architecture in Florence from Brunelleschi to Michelangelo.

The first part of the interior to be built was Brunelleschi's Old Sacristy, at the left-hand end of the nave, constructed from 1421 to 1428 to contain the tomb of Cosimo Il Vecchio's father Giovanni. Brunelleschi designed the room as a cube surmounted by a hemispherical umbrella dome, through which light floods in. He intended the whole chapel to be decorated in muted colours, and objected to Donatello's polychrome reliefs and medallions in the pendentives and lunettes. Lorenzo de' Medici commissioned Verrocchio to design a magnificent porphyry and bronze sarcophagus commemorating Piero de' Medici and his brother Giovanni, which he placed straight in front of the main doors.

The main body of the church is based on the Tuscan Romanesque and on the Early Christian basilicas that Brunelleschi had visited in Rome. The nave and aisles, divided by Corinthian columns, are decorated with white stucco and grey *pietra serena* to give an impression of lightness and harmony very different from the darkness and irregularity of Gothic interiors. Brunelleschi never lived to see his masterpiece completed, but Manetti executed the interior to his designs during the 1450s and 1460s.

The two bronze pulpits in the nave are the last works of Donatello. The harrowing scenes of the Passion are a far cry from the classical serenity of his early sculpture. The principal paintings in the church are Rosso Fiorentino's elegant *Marriage of the Virgin* (1523), in the second chapel on the right inside the main door, and Filippo Lippi's beautiful but badly restored *Annunciation* in the Martelli Chapel at the end of the left aisle.

Next to the chapel is the entrance to the cloister, off which a staircase leads up to Michelangelo's Laurentian Library which houses the Medici collection of books and manuscripts. The vestibule, begun in 1524, is often cited as the first example of Mannerist architecture, a wilful misuse of the classical elements so that the functions of the columns and walls seem to have been reversed. The floor is almost completely filled by a tripartite staircase which flows down from the reading-room, increasing the effect of instability. In contrast the reading-room itself, with its valuable collection of manuscripts, appears an oasis of calm.

Emerging from the church, you may be lucky enough to find that there is no queue behind the apse for Michelangelo's New Sacristy. Pass through the Cappella dei Principi, a sumptuously ornate chapel which served as a mausoleum for the Medici Grand Dukes. Built in 1602 and covered in *pietra dura*, polychrome marble and lapis lazuli, this claustrophobic shrine appealed much more to Grand Tourists than either Brunelleschi's or Michelangelo's Sacristies. It was one of the few places in Florence that Byron noted on his visit in 1817, calling it 'fine frippery in great slabs of various expensive stones, to commemorate fifty rotten and forgotten carcases'.

The New Sacristy is the only one of Michelangelo's sculptural schemes to have neared completion. The chapel was his first architectural commission and was designed to focus on the Medici tombs. Executed between 1520 and 1534, it is modelled on Brunelleschi's Old Sacristy, but filled with a subdued light to provide a sepulchral atmosphere, enhanced by the claustrophobic feel of the blank wall tabernacles. It commemorates Lorenzo the Magnificent, his brother Giuliano and two minor members of the Medici family, Giuliano, Duke of Nemours, and Lorenzo, Duke of Urbino. Michelangelo designed a highly complex allegorical scheme, not all of which was completed. Monumental figures of *Dawn* and *Dusk*, and *Night* and *Day*, symbolising the passing of time, recline on sarcophagi beneath the two Medici dukes. The idealised portraits of the two dukes, whose gaze is directed towards the *Madonna and Child* over the altar, represent the Active and the Contemplative Life.

After escaping from the sepulchral atmosphere, you may like to browse through the market in the square, or have a welcome cappuccino in one of the cafés overlooking it. The **Palazzo Medici-Riccardi**, the original palace of Cosimo Il Vecchio, overlooks the north-east side of the square. To reach the entrance, go down Via de' Gori and turn left into Via Cavour. The palace was built by Cosimo's favourite architect Michelozzo in the 1440s. The heavy and oppressive rustication of the façade was much-copied by later Florentine architects and is in keeping with the tough, masculine image of the city.

Lorenzo Il Magnifico kept many of his greatest treasures here, but the Grand Dukes preferred to live in the grander Palazzo Pitti and sold the palace to the Riccardi in 1659. During the early nineteenth century the palace was inhabited by the eccentric Walter Savage Landor, famed for his uncontrollable temper. On one occasion he was so incensed by a Marquis entering the palace with his hat on that he took him by the scruff of the neck and threw him out, breaking his arm in the process.

The interior, which originally housed Uccello's *Battle of San Romano*, now divided between the Uffizi, the Louvre and the National Gallery, and Donatello's *David* and *Judith*, now in the Bargello and the Palazzo Vecchio respectively, is unfortunately depleted. The only pieces of Quattrocento decoration left are the frescoes in the chapel commissioned by Piero the Gouty from Benozzo Gozzoli in 1459. They depict the *Adoration of the Magi*, a subject which gave an artist a golden opportunity to have fun. Fancy costumes of every conceivable pattern and colour, hawks, camels, even a leopard, portraits of all the local worthies with Gozzoli himself hiding in the crowd, his name written on his cap, all combine to create a decorative masterpiece.

Gozzoli witnessed the Council of Florence in 1439, an attempt to unite the Greek Orthodox and the Roman Catholic churches, and the Magi are traditionally said to represent the Emperor John Paleologus, who led the Greek delegation, Cosimo Il Vecchio and the youthful Lorenzo. The procession is led by Cosimo's son Piero the Gouty.

These frescoes were almost completely ignored by Grand Tourists. Indeed, the eighteenth-century French painter Cochin mentioned everything in the palace except the Gozzoli frescoes. The French magistrate Président Dupaty, who came to Florence in 1785, much preferred the Luca Giordano frescoes of the *Apotheosis of the Medici* in the sumptuous Baroque apartments upstairs. By the late nineteenth century, however, W. D. Howells, in his *Tuscan Cities* (1886), refers to Gozzoli's *Journey of the Magi* as 'perhaps the most simply and satisfyingly lovely little space that ever four walls enclosed'.

Outside the palace, turn right and follow Via de' Martelli down to the Piazza del Duomo, a focal point for visitors to the city. The **Baptistery**, which served as the original cathedral, is believed to stand on the site of a Roman temple of Mars. This confused Renaissance architects, including Brunelleschi, who thought that the present, Romanesque building was ancient Roman and used the green and white colour scheme in his churches. The Baptistery's chief glory is its three sets of gilded bronze doors of which the least important are the south doors by Andrea Pisano with reliefs of the *Life of St John the Baptist*, dating from the 1330s, squashed into awkward quatrefoil shapes.

The north doors were sculpted by Ghiberti between 1403 and 1424 after he had defeated Brunelleschi in the most famous sculptural competition in Florentine history (their panels of the *Sacrifice of Isaac* are preserved in the Bargello). The drama of Brunelleschi's relief, with the angel rushing forward to seize Abraham's knife, provides a striking contrast with the rhythmical grace of Ghiberti's composition. The judges had prevaricated and attempted to split the commission between the two sculptors, but when Brunelleschi refused to co-operate they awarded Ghiberti the whole prize.

These doors continue Pisano's use of the quatrefoil shape but the idealised figures move with more rhythmic grace and are portrayed in greater depth. Immediately after he had finished them, Ghiberti began work on the ten reliefs of the east doors, nicknamed by Michelangelo the *Gates of Paradise*. They are of far greater complexity, with each panel depicting a number of different episodes from an Old Testament story, some of them containing over a hundred figures. Ghiberti's new-found mastery of linear perspective and of composition make these scenes totally coherent and understandable. If the crowds are too unbearable, you can examine four of the original panels at leisure in the Duomo museum.

The interior of the Baptistery is often too crowded to enjoy the wonderful thirteenth- and fourteenth-century mosaics. The most impressive monument is Donatello and Michelozzo's tomb to the Antipope John XXIII.

The **Duomo** dominates the classic view of Florence. It was begun by Arnolfo di Cambio in 1296 and intended to surpass the rival cathedrals of Siena and Pisa. Work continued during the fourteenth century and by 1418 had reached the drum of the dome. After a prolonged debate about the technical difficulties of vaulting the 42-metre span, Brunelleschi provided a solution based on his study of classical building methods in Rome, using two shells to support the enormous stresses caused by the weight of the structure. The dome, the largest to be erected since antiquity, was completed in 1436 and immediately became the symbol of Florentine civic pride. Even Michelangelo admitted that nothing could surpass it. The neo-Gothic façade was erected in the 1880s and unveiled in the presence of Queen Victoria.

The Duomo was the setting for the Pazzi conspiracy of 1478, the most dramatic attempt to overthrow the Medici. Lorenzo de' Medici's brother Giuliano was stabbed to death during Mass and Lorenzo only managed to escape by barricading himself into the Old Sacristy. In the 1490s Savonarola preached many of his most apocalyptic sermons from the pulpit, which so affected the youthful Michelangelo that, until the end of his life, he could still recall the sound of the fanatical monk's voice.

The two main monuments in the interior are the equestrian portraits on the left wall of the nave of two mercenaries: Sir John Hawkwood by Uccello, and Niccolò da Tolentino by Andrea del Castagno. Either because of her proverbial meanness or because she was too nervous of glorifying her *condottieri*, Florence preferred to commemorate them with painted rather than sculptural monuments.

Few visitors have felt much empathy for the barracklike atmosphere of the interior, although the Romantics admired its awe-inspiring size. Berlioz liked to visit it in the late afternoon 'to watch the motes dancing in a splendid ray of the sun as it slanted across the gathering gloom'. Ruskin thought the inside 'a horror, and the outside a Chinese puzzle'.

Grand Tourists made a point of visiting the Duomo on Easter Day. Stephen Whatley, who wrote a virulently anti-Catholic account of his travels, records the service in 1741:

When they (the congregation) come to the hallelujas, at the end of the music, which is very fine, both vocal and instrumental, they all give a hideous shout, then a man sets fire to the combustible pigeon at the altar, which runs along the line to the sepulchre without doors, and blows it up into the air. All this was performed with music, drums, trumpets, ringing of bells, and firing of great guns: meantime the fiery pigeon returns to the altar and the people fall on their faces to worship.

This ceremony is still performed on Easter Sunday, and the successful explosion of the fireworks is taken as an omen for a good harvest.

The **Museo dell' Opera del Duomo**, standing just behind the apse of the Duomo, is a haven of rest compared with the crowds in the Bargello. The most interesting section of the ground floor is devoted to the wooden models made by Giambologna and his contemporaries for a competition for the Duomo façade in 1587.

Halfway up the staircase is the magnificent late *Deposition* by Michelangelo which he carved for his own tomb. According to Vasari, the aged figure of Nicodemus who feebly tries to hold up Christ's sagging body is a self-portrait. As with much of his sculpture, Michelangelo seems to have been unable to complete the group. In a fit of rage in 1554 he smashed the sculpture, but his pupils managed to piece it together. The figure of Christ, his broken right leg unable to support the dead weight of his body as he collapses to the ground, remains one of his most poignant creations.

Upstairs, the Sala delle Cantorie contains the two Cantorie (singing galleries) by Donatello and Luca della Robbia, dating from the 1430s. They were originally placed over the two Sacristies in the Duomo, but removed after a Grand Ducal wedding in the seventeenth century. Della Robbia's work is a model of classical restraint, with pairs of Corinthian pilasters carefully separating each panel of singers and musicians so that even the cheeky children in the left-hand panel who are chasing each other between the trumpeters' legs do not disturb the equilibrium. Donatello, on the other hand, encourages his Bacchanalian children to riot at will in a continuous frieze behind freestanding pairs of columns.

The next room contains a series of hexagonal panels by Andrea Pisano depicting the story of the Creation and the seven liberal arts. The vivid realism of the latter indicates that Giotto may have provided some of the designs. On the far side of the Sala delle Cantorie a series of powerful statues of Prophets, which once stood in niches high up on Giotto's campanile and were designed to be seen from far below, now appear absurdly exaggerated. The most effective are the four by Donatello whose gestures and expressions are kept to a minimum. The room beyond contains four reliefs from Ghiberti's *Gates of Paradise* which, unlike those on the Baptistery doors, may be examined at leisure.

With the exception of the legendary figure of Michelangelo, Grand Tourists paid little attention to any of these Renaissance sculptors. They recognised that, as Joseph Addison put it, 'Florence for modern statues . . . excels even Rome', but only included sixteenth-century sculptors such as Cellini and Giambologna in this category. It was not till the mid-nineteenth century, when the vogue for antique sculpture palled, that the works in the Museo dell' Opera del Duomo and the Bargello began to attract widespread attention.

The shops and stalls around the Piazza del Duomo sell framed reproduction prints, busts and guidebooks. Higher quality antique shops are in the Borgo Ognissanti, San Jacopo, Via della Vigna Nuova and Via della Spada.

The Piazza del Duomo is situated near a wide variety of restaurants. One of the most atmospheric is the **Cantinetta Antinori** set in the fifteenth-century Palazzo Antinori. From the Piazza del Duomo walk past the Baptistery up Via de' Pecori to Piazza Antinori. Palazzo Antinori is on the far side of the square, and there you can sample a wide selection of wine from the famous Antinori vineyards.

An alternative, if you are feeling wealthy, is the **Enoteca Pinchiorri** at Via Ghibellina 87, one of the best restaurants in Italy, with a renowned wine cellar. Take Via del Proconsolo out of the south-east corner of the Piazza del Duomo and Via Ghibellina is the third street on the left. Enoteca Pinchiorri specialises in nouvelle cuisine but includes a number of Tuscan dishes such as *torta manfreda* (pastry filled with chicken livers, eggs and dried meats). Further along Via Ghibellina, **Ristorante Dino**, at no. 51, is an elegant restaurant in a fourteenth-century palace. The menu, set by Dino and his wife Renza, is based on traditional Tuscan dishes: *crostini*, *bistecca alla fiorentina* and *fagioli bianchi*. The *pièce de résistance* is *stracotta del Granduca*, a succulent type of beef served at Medici banquets.

For an afternoon's light culture, you might like to look at the sculptures on the exterior of Orsanmichele and in the Piazza della Signora. From Enoteca Pinchiorri or Dino head west down Via Ghibellina, turn right into Via del Proconsolo and first left into Via Dante Alighieri, which takes you to the Oratory of **Orsanmichele**.

From the Cantinetta Antinori head down Via de' Tornabuoni, past some of Florence's most exclusive designer boutiques and salons, and turn left into Via Strozzi, beside the forbidding mass of the late fifteenth-century Palazzo Strozzi with its heavy rustication and massive wrought ironwork. A biennial antique fair is held here in September and October. Cross over the large and characterless Piazza della Repubblica, built in the late nineteenth century after the destruction of the Mercato Vecchio, and Via del Taviolini, off the south-east corner of the square, leads to Orsanmichele.

In the fourteenth century the oratory was partially converted into a grain store and a trading centre for the various guilds of the city. Each guild was obliged to commission a statue for the Gothic niches on the exterior. Competition was intense and gave wonderful opportunities for the leading sculptors in Florence in the early fifteenth century: Nanni di Banco, Ghiberti and Donatello.

The dominant figure on the south wall is Donatello's formidable *St Mark*, his features wrapped in concentration. On the north wall Donatello's heroic *St George*, his hand resting on his shield, appears the epitome of chivalry. Carved in 1416 for the armourers' guild, the original figure of St George is thought to have held a sword which protruded into the street. The statue has now been replaced by a bronze copy. The predella beneath, carved in 1417 and now also replaced by a copy, is the earliest example of the correct use of perspective in Renaissance art.

Verrocchio's *Christ and St Thomas* on the east wall dates from the middle of the Quattrocento and was designed as a replacement for Donatello's *St Louis*. It is one of the most sophisticated sculptural groups of the Renaissance, with a strong psychological interaction between the two figures centred on the wound in Christ's side.

From Orsanmichele it is a short walk down Via de' Calzaioli, named after leathermakers and still full of shoe shops, to **Piazza della Signoria**, the civic centre of Florence from the Middle Ages onwards. Unfortunately, it is at present a mess since archaeologists have been given permission to dig up the square. After a protracted row, the *comune* finally decided to restore the Piazza to its original state, only to discover that the stones which had been here since 1299 had been sold off by the workmen.

The curious asymmetrical shape of the Piazza derives from the reluctance of the Guelph government to build on land owned by its Ghibelline enemies. The Piazza is dominated by the Palazzo Vecchio, the seat of medieval government; in times of crisis traitors and rebels were hanged from the palace, including the Archbishop of Pisa after the failure of the Pazzi conspiracy in 1478. It was in the Piazza della Signoria that Savonarola organised his bonfire of the vanities in 1497, when priceless masterpieces by Fra Bartolomeo, Botticelli and other artists were consigned to the flames. The Florentines soon tired of this and, in the following year, consigned Savonarola himself to the flames. Cosimo I lived in the Palazzo Vecchio from 1540 to 1565 before moving to the Pitti.

During the pontificate of Leo X in the early sixteenth century, wild beast hunts were held in the Piazza. On the Festa degli Omaggi, held annually to celebrate St John's Day, a procession representing all the territories under Florentine rule passed before the Grand Duke. Montaigne bewailed the ugliness of the virgins in the procession of 1581, but was impressed by the cart carrying a pyramid 'which was as high as the tallest houses, with a man dressed as San Giovanni, bound to a piece of iron'. St John's Day is now celebrated by a football match in the Piazza, the players wearing medieval costume.

You can take in the history of the Piazza over an expensive cappuccino at Rivoire's, Florence's most fashionable café. Michelangelo's colossal *David*, which symbolised the independence of the Florentine Republic, was moved to the Accademia in 1873 and has been replaced by a copy, which stands in its original setting outside the Palazzo Vecchio. On the other side of the doorway is Bandinelli's lifeless group of *Hercules and Cacus*, which was ridiculed by the Florentines when it was unveiled in 1534.

Giambologna's equestrian statue of Cosimo I, based on that of Marcus Aurelius in Rome and the model for countless Baroque monuments of the seventeenth century, stands in the centre of the square. Fynes Moryson, one of many early visitors to admire the statue, was very impressed by its size when he visited Giambologna's studio in 1594 and reckoned 'the belly of the horse being capable of 24 men, whereof foure might lie in the throat'.

Ammannati's *Fountain of Neptune* of 1565–75, by the corner of the Palazzo Vecchio, is an unsatisfactory group. The marble block from which the figure of Neptune was carved had already been mutilated by Bandinelli, the statue is far too large for its surround and the marble does not fit with the bronze figures round the base. The statue is best known for the jibe made at Ammannati's expense: '*Ammannato, Ammannato, che bel marmo hai rovinato*' (Ammannati, Ammannati, what a beautiful marble you have ruined).

The finest sculptures in the square are in the elegant Loggia dei

Lanzi (named after the German halberdiers who stood guard here in the sixteenth century). The statues' violent subject matter reflects the square's bloodthirsty history. Cellini's bronze *Perseus*, a heroic freestanding figure dating from 1545 to 1554, captures his moment of triumph as he holds aloft the severed head of Medusa. The predella (now replaced by a copy) is full of movement as a flying Perseus hurtles himself into the attack. The spiralling composition of Giambologna's *Rape of the Sabine Women* (1579–83), designed to be seen from a variety of viewpoints, prefigures the Baroque. John Evelyn thought it 'most stupendous' and the finest of all the sculpture in the loggia. Directly behind this group, Giambologna's *Hercules and the Centaur*, sculpted from 1594 to 1599, is a brilliant evocation of physical stress as the centaur strains backwards to avoid the impending blow. The loggia has always been a focal point for political rallies, a tradition that still continues today.

INFORMATION

Chiostro Verde, Santa Maria Novella: 8 a.m. to 1 p.m., Saturday and Sunday 9 a.m. to 2 p.m., closed Friday
New Sacristy, San Lorenzo (entrance in Piazza Madonna degli Aldobrandini): 9 a.m. to 2 p.m., Sunday 9 a.m. to 1 p.m., closed Monday
Laurentian Library: 9 a.m. to 5 p.m., closed Sunday
Palazzo Medici-Riccardi, Via Cavour: 9 a.m. to 12.30 p.m. and 3 p.m. to 5 p.m., Sunday 9 a.m. to 12 noon, closed Wednesday
Museo dell' Opera del Duomo: summer 9 a.m. to 8 p.m., winter 9 a.m. to 6 p.m., Sunday 10 a.m. to 1 p.m., closed Monday

RESTAURANTS

Cantinetta Antinori
Piazza Antinori 3, Florence
Telephone: 055 292 234, closed Saturday evening from May to July, and on Thursday evening from October to April

Enoteca Pinchiorri
Via Ghibellina 87, Florence
Telephone: 055 242 777, closed Sunday and Monday lunch

Ristorante Dino
Via Ghibellina 51, Florence
Telephone: 055 241 452, closed Sunday evening and Monday

*I am rather too old to fling chairs and tables out of the
window into the Arno*

Thomas Clarke

SANTA MARIA DEL CARMINE~OGNISSANTI~SANTA TRINITÀ~SANTO SPIRITO~BOBOLI GARDENS~SANTA FELICITÀ~PONTE VECCHIO~UFFIZI

The River Arno, whose beauty has inspired many artists and poets, has proved both a blessing and a curse for Florence. It provided an essential trade route to the coast, but its fickle nature has led to many severe floods and the city has been inundated several times, most recently in 1966 when the water rose up to two metres high in many of the churches, damaging priceless works of art.

The Oltrarno, the area to the south of the Arno, came to prominence when the Medici Grand Dukes moved to the Pitti Palace in the sixteenth century. Many courtiers built large houses in the Via Maggio and other streets around the palace. Today, the Oltrarno still retains a fascinating mixture of fashionable apartments and boutiques alongside working-class shops and restaurants. This mixing of classes intrigued visitors: in 1787 Peter Beckford noted how 'The Noblesse sell wine, and hang out the sign of an empty flask at the Palace window', something that the Antinori, Ricasoli and Capponi families still do, but with slightly more finesse, today. The Oltrarno is also the best place to see craftsmen making and repairing furniture, for which Florence is world famous.

This walk begins at the church of **Santa Maria del Carmine**. The cycle of Masaccio frescoes in the Brancacci Chapel, at the end of the right aisle, revolutionised Quattrocento painting in Florence. Masaccio worked on the frescoes from 1425 until his early death in 1428, after Masolino had begun the cycle, and it was completed half a century later by Filippino Lippi. In the two most powerful scenes on the left-hand wall, the *Tribute Money* and *Expulsion*, Masaccio used his newly acquired knowledge of anatomy and perspective to give his figures a real solidity so that they stand quite naturally in the landscape. The powerful realism of these figures influenced a host of artists including Michelangelo, whose nose was broken by the sculptor Torrigiani on the steps of the chapel. Masaccio's grief-stricken figures of Adam and Eve lead directly to Michelangelo's *Expulsion of Adam and Eve* on the Sistine Chapel ceiling.

In the eighteenth century Lippi's frescoes were considered quite as good as the Masaccios, although the painter Thomas Patch, recognising their merit, made twenty-four engravings of the Masaccios. Horace Walpole was deeply impressed by them. 'I am transported with them', he wrote to Horace Mann, 'I did not remember these works. Oh! if there are more make your Patch give us all.' After a bad fire in the church in 1771, Patch's engravings were used as the basis for restoring the frescoes. By the early nineteenth century Masaccio had begun to be more widely appreciated, and the French painter Ingres described the Brancacci Chapel as 'the ante-room of paradise'.

The frescoes have just undergone a comprehensive restoration which has brought back the richness of Masaccio's colours, and more paintings have been discovered in the process. A window in the original style has been installed at the end of the chapel, dramatically improving the lighting.

Outside the church, cross the Piazza del Carmine, take the first right into Borgo San Frediano, and the first left into Via de' Serragli, which crosses the Arno at Ponte alla Carraia, named after the carts that carried the wool across the river to the centre of the wool industry in the Borgo Ognissanti. Bear left on the north bank along the Borgo Ognissanti, which has some of the best antique shops in Florence, specialising in paintings and furniture, until you reach the thirteenth-century church of **Ognissanti**.

Ghirlandaio's beautiful fresco of the *Last Supper*, which hangs in the refectory, has recently been restored. The serenity of the scene, the fresh colours and the exotic birds and trees in the background make this one of the most appealing examples of a favourite Florentine subject. It stands between Ghirlandaio's *St Jerome* and Botticelli's *St Augustine*, the two saints seated in their studies.

If you would like an early lunch, **Sostanza detto 'Il Troia'** (pigsty in Italian), at Via del Porcellana 25, is one of the best working-men's trattorias. You reach it by turning left out of the church and taking the first left. Try the *calamari inzimino* (squid cooked with greens).

If you would prefer to continue, go down Borgo Ognissanti, cross over Piazza Goldoni, and head up the Via della Vigna Nuova, one of the smartest shopping streets in Florence. Paoli, at no. 26, specialises in straw goods, and Alinari, at no. 46, has one of the best collections of nineteenth-century photographs in the world. Turn right down Via del Purgatorio opposite the façade of Alberti's Palazzo Rucellai, the first Florentine palace to use the classical orders. Take the second right and the first left into Via del Parione, which leads to Piazza Santa Trinita.

The church of **Santa Trinita**, which dates from the end of the fourteenth century, contains some charming frescoes by Ghirlandaio of the *Life of St Francis* in the Sassetti chapel in the right transept. Ghirlandaio's ability as a portraitist and the way in which he places his figures naturally in a readily identifiable architectural setting made him immensely popular with the Florentine bourgeoisie. You can still recognise the Piazza Santa Trinita in the background of the *Miracle of the Spini Child*. The tender devotion of the Virgin and the

naturalism of the shepherds and animals in the *Adoration of the Shepherds* show the influence of Hugo van der Goes' Portinari altarpiece, which arrived in Florence in 1483.

Ghirlandaio, like his contemporaries, was largely neglected by Grand Tourists but became immensely popular with the Victorians, who admired the simple charm of his scenes. This was not enough to satisfy Berenson at the beginning of the twentieth century; he admired Ghirlandaio's abilities as a portraitist but despised him for not rising above the level of genre painting.

The Piazza Santa Trinita leads to the most graceful bridge in the city, the Ponte Santa Trinita, built by Ammannati in 1567 (possibly to a design by Michelangelo) and carefully reconstructed after it was blown up by the Germans in 1944. During the eighteenth century it was the fashionable place to do the *passeggiata*. Horace Walpole spent the rest of his life reminiscing about 'the delicious nights on the Ponte di Trinita at Florence, in a linen nightgown and a straw hat, with *improvisatori*, and music, and the coffee-houses open with ices'.

Sir Horace Mann, Britain's ambassador to the court of the Grand Dukes of Tuscany for more than forty years, lived in Casa Manetti at Via di Santo Spirito 23, off Piazza Frescobaldi on the south side of the bridge. His gossipy correspondence with Walpole is the best source of information about eighteenth-century life in Florence. Casanova described him as 'the idol of Florence, a rich man, amiable, a great amateur of the arts and full of gout'. Mann kept open house for British Grand Tourists, and found it difficult to control the rowdier spirits. Thomas Clarke complained to his friend John Strange in 1781 that he was 'rather too old to fling chairs and tables out of the window into the Arno'.

Crossing over Ponte Santa Trinita into Piazza Frescobaldi, bear right up Via del Presto di San Martino to the Piazza Santo Spirito. This is the heart of the Oltrarno, where John Evelyn stayed in 1644. A busy market, selling everything from fruit and vegetables to second-hand clothes, forms a picturesque setting for Brunelleschi's church. The best day to visit the piazza is on 22 May, the feast of St Rita, when the church doors are thrown open and everyone in the square carries a yellow rose, blessed by the monks.

The church of **Santo Spirito** was begun in 1436 and completed in 1487, more or less to Brunelleschi's design. As at San Lorenzo, Brunelleschi used a grey and white colour scheme to create an effect of coolness and light. The ambulatory, which runs round the whole interior, enables the spectator to enjoy a constant variety of views through the arches. The concave curves of the side chapels, and the columns lining the outer walls of the aisles, create a more sculptural feel than the rectangular chapels and flat pilasters at San Lorenzo. Most of the best paintings have been sold off, although Filippino Lippi's *Madonna and Saints* still hangs in the right transept.

If you would like to have lunch, head back down Via del Presto di San Martino towards the Arno and turn left into Via di Santo Spirito. **Il Cantinone**, at no. 6, provides good, homely, country cooking. Alternatively, cross over Piazza Frescobaldi into Borgo San Jacopo and you will find **Cammillo**, a pleasant trattoria, although sometimes crowded, at no. 57. If you would like something much less formal, you can always take a picnic into the **Boboli Gardens** behind the Pitti Palace.

After lunch you are ideally placed to take a stroll in the Boboli Gardens, the best surviving example of formal gardens in Tuscany. From Il Cantinone head up Via di Santo Spirito to Piazza Frescobaldi, turn left up Via Maggio, the smartest street in the Oltrarno, and any of the streets on the left will take you to the Piazza dei Pitti. From Cammillo take any of the streets running south from the Borgo San Jacopo to the Pitti.

The Pitti Palace, originally built by the Pitti in the fifteenth century in an attempt to outdo the Medici, has always appealed to autocratic rulers. It was the main residence of all the Grand Dukes of Tuscany and used by members of the Italian royal family from the Risorgimento to the establishment of the Republic in 1946. Osbert Sitwell thought it 'the sort of residence a sea god would have erected for himself so that you could almost perceive the weed clinging to the huge rusticated buildings of the retaining walls, from which it seems that the ocean has only just receded'. Grand Tourists were very impressed by the eclectic collections of the Medici housed in the palace, now normally inundated with tourists and, since the interior is shut in the afternoons, you can head straight into the Boboli Gardens.

The Gardens were begun by Tribolo (who designed the area directly behind the palace in 1549) and continued by Ammannati and Buontalenti, and later the Parigi brothers. Just inside the entrance is Buontalenti's fantastic grotto which originally contained Michelangelo's *Prisoners* (now replaced by copies), guarding the lusty group of *Paris and Helen* in the second chamber, and Giambologna's delightful figure of *Venus Surprised by Satyrs* in the inner sanctum.

Ammannati designed the dramatic rusticated courtyard behind the palace, where the wildness of nature seems to be in conflict with the discipline of classical architecture. The amphitheatre above made a perfect setting for the festivities that the Medici loved to

56

organise. At a famous Naumachia in 1589 the amphitheatre was filled with water and Christian galleys attacked a mock Turkish castle. Nowadays the courtyard is the setting for a season of concerts in the summer.

Above the amphitheatre a series of winding paths leads up to the fountain of Neptune and the Belvedere. The most charming part of the Boboli is the Giardino del Cavaliere, a secluded spot with wonderful views over the city walls towards Arcetri. Cosimo III (1642–1723) planted it with spices from Goa and the East Indies, and built the casino which now houses the Porcelain Museum.

The gardens gradually expanded during the late sixteenth and early seventeenth centuries to cover the hillside south of the palace. Alfonso and Giulio Parigi designed the cypress avenue that sweeps down to the Isolotto, a circular fishpond inspired by the Maritime Theatre at Hadrian's Villa and dominated by a copy of Giambologna's figure of *Oceano* standing on a huge granite block.

Most eighteenth-century visitors, and particularly those who had seen how Capability Brown transformed formal gardens in England, disliked the artificial quality of the Boboli. Samuel Sharp, who visited the gardens in 1766, commented: 'They are esteemed fine by the Italians, but, in the eyes of an Englishman, they are execrable.' The gardens appealed more to the Romantics. In 1780 William Beckford loved to relax at the recently built *kaffeehaus* at the top of the garden from which he could enjoy the view 'with Florence deep beneath, and the tops of the hills which encircle it, jagged with pines.' Beckford travelled in such style that he was mistaken for the Austrian Emperor Joseph II, who was touring Italy incognito at the same time. The snobbish Horace Mann saw the emperor meet his brother, the enlightened Grand Duke Peter Leopold, in the Boboli, and was shocked at the shabbiness of his appearance. In the nineteenth century Mendelssohn refreshed himself with midnight walks in the Boboli.

Leave the gardens by the gate near the Isolotto that leads into Via Romana, where, at no. 17, you will find one of the most extraordinary leftovers of the Grand Tour, a collection of medical waxworks dating from the late eighteenth century. Set up by the Grand Duke Peter Leopold in 1771 to house the hundreds of wax models of human anatomy created by the master modeller Clemente Susini, the museum proved a great success. Joseph II ordered a special collection for the military medical school in Vienna in 1780, and Napoleon one for Paris in 1796. The Romantic era, with its emphasis on decay and death, enjoyed the macabre fascination of the museum. On his visit in 1827 the poet Henry Longfellow recorded a waxwork of the plague by a Sicilian called Zumbo: 'He [Zumbo] must have been a man of the most gloomy and saturnine imagination, and more akin to the worm than most of us, thus to have revelled night and day in the mysteries of death, corruption, and the charnel-house.'

From the museum, continue down Via Romana into Piazza Santa Felice. Many foreigners lived in this area in the nineteenth century. Robert and Elizabeth Browning held literary soirées and seances at Casa Guidi, on the corner of Via Maggio, until Elizabeth's death in 1861, and formed one of the leading circles of expatriates in the city. Dostoevsky lived at Casa Fabriani, at no. 21 Piazza dei Pitti in the 1860s and wrote part of *The Idiot* there. Almost next to his house, at no. 37, Giannio e Figlio sells excellent marbled paper, a Florentine speciality.

Passing in front of the Pitti into Via de' Guicciardini, the church of **Santa Felicità**, set back on the right, possesses one of the most beautiful paintings of the sixteenth century. The Capponi Chapel, immediately on your right inside the main door, contains the *Lamentation* (1525–8), the masterpiece of the solitary hypochondriac Pontormo. The brilliance of the blues, pinks and greens, the startled expressions of the spectators and the lack of background give the painting a strange emotional intensity.

Outside the church, follow Via de' Guicciardini up to the **Ponte Vecchio**, the only bridge to have survived both the German retreat in 1944, when all the other bridges were blown up, and the disastrous flood of 1966. Florentine medieval history, despite the romantic glow awarded to it by the Victorians, was very violent, and the assassination of Buondelmonte de' Buondelmonti at the north end of the bridge, on the way to his wedding on Easter Sunday, 1215, sparked off the conflict between the Guelphs and Ghibellines that lasted until the middle of the fourteenth century. The Ponte Vecchio has been lined with goldsmiths' and jewellers' shops since the seventeenth century, most of them very expensive. Above them runs Vasari's famous corridor, built in 1565, which connected Cosimo I's apartments in the Uffizi and the Pitti.

At the north end of the bridge, turn right up Lungarno Archibusieri and the **Uffizi** is immediately on your left. Built by Vasari for Cosimo in 1560, the Uffizi was turned into a museum by Francesco I in 1581. Ever since, it has housed the cream of the Medici paintings, antique sculpture and cabinets full of curiosities. Not everyone can cope with this abundance of culture; back in the eighteenth century, James Boswell records the flippant reaction of a Mr Damer and Captain Howe: 'They submitted quietly to be shewn a few of the pictures. But seeing the gallery so immensely long, their impatience burst forth, and they tried for a bett who should hop first to the end of it.'

The Uffizi contains enough variety to cater for the most eclectic taste. Early visitors admired the cabinets of curios and weapons quite as much as the paintings and sculpture, and many of them took a course in medals in the Grand Duke's cabinet; Lassels's account in 1670 pays as much attention to the unicorn's horn as to the Raphaels. In the eighteenth century, as the collections became organised in a more coherent way, many of these curios, including the alchemical nail, were taken out of the gallery.

Guided by Addison's influential *Voyage to Italy*, most visitors bypassed the pictures in their haste to reach the antique statues. Gibbon visited the Uffizi twelve times in 1764 before mentioning a picture. He, like many others, was amazed at the beauty of the *Venus de' Medici*, which had arrived in Florence from Rome in 1677 and was installed in the Tribuna, an octagonal room designed by Buontalenti in 1584. To the Earl-Bishop of Derry her pose was '*detestable, l'attitude d'une Coquette ou d'une Putain*', and he was not alone in finding her profoundly erotic. Thomas Apleton described his sensations to the collector Charles Townley: 'I'm greatly afraid that the sight of the Venus in the Florentine gallery will give you some yammering (according to T. Booth's phrase) after a Tuscan whore.' As late as the 1820s Mariana Starke, who awarded stars to works of art like a present-day Michelin, gave five to the *Venus de' Medici* and none to Michelangelo's *Doni Tondo*. Another sculpture much admired was the *Dancing Faun*, particularly as the restorations were thought to be the work of Michelangelo.

The account written by Jonathan Richardson and his son in 1722 was the first to challenge the undisputed supremacy of sculpture over painting. They wanted their readers to become connoisseurs. In Zoffany's *Tribuna* (1775) the Grand Tourists are examining paintings as well as sculpture, and it became fashionable to compare the respective merits of Titian's *Venus of Urbino* and the *Venus de' Medici*. William Beckford confessed that he 'ran childishly by the ample ranks of sculpture' before settling down to look at the paintings. However, the cult of the antique persisted into the nineteenth century, and the copious notes Shelley made on his daily visits to the Uffizi in 1819 mention only sculpture.

The most famous pictures in the Uffizi are the works of Botticelli, which were almost completely ignored until the middle of the last century, and condemned by Fuseli in his history of Italian art as of 'barbarous taste . . . dry minuteness . . . puerile ostentation'.

Yet by 1900 Ruskin and Walter Pater had rehabilitated Botticelli's reputation and he had become one of the most popular of all Italian painters, a position that he continues to hold today.

As Botticelli's reputation and that of other Quattrocento artists rose, so that of Michelangelo fell. The massive nudes in his paintings and sculpture were contrasted unfavourably with the purity and serenity of the Madonnas of Fra Angelico and Filippo Lippi. In 1848 Mrs Jameson boldly attacked Michelangelo's Virgin in the *Doni Tondo*, 'whose brick-dust coloured features, and muscular arms, give me the idea of a washer woman'.

By good fortune the best ice-cream shop in Florence is very near the Uffizi. From the Piazza della Signoria take Via dei Gondi down the left side of the Palazzo Vecchio into Piazza Santa Firenze. Go down Via della Vigna Vecchia behind the Bargello until you reach Via Isola della Stinche, where Vivoli's, at no. 7, has every flavour of *gelato* that you have ever heard of.

INFORMATION

Boboli Gardens: May to August 9 a.m. to 6.30 p.m., September, October, March and April 9 a.m. to 5.30 p.m., November to February 9 a.m. to 4.30 p.m.

Giardino del Cavaliere: Tuesday, Thursday and Saturday 9 a.m. to 2 p.m.

Anatomical rooms in Zoological Museum: Saturday in summer 3 p.m. to 6 p.m., in winter 2 p.m. to 5 p.m.

Uffizi: 9 a.m. to 7 p.m., Sunday 9 a.m. to 1 p.m., closed Monday

RESTAURANTS

Sostanza detto 'Il Troia'
Via del Porcellana 25, Florence
Telephone: 055 212 691, closed Saturday evening and Sunday

Il Cantinone
Via di Santo Spirito 6, Florence
Telephone: 055 218 898

Cammillo
Borgo San Jacopo 57, Florence
Telephone: 055 212 427, closed Wednesday and Thursday

If I could afford it, I really would take a Villa near
Florence, but I am afraid of its becoming a cheesecake for
all the English

Horace Mann

SANT' APPOLLONIA~SAN SALVI~FIESOLE

The Last Supper, a scene which offers great dramatic possibilities, seems to have been a favourite with Florentine artists. Two of the finest but least-known examples are hidden away in the back streets of the city.

Andrea del Castagno's *Cenacolo* (the Italian word for a painting of the Last Supper in a refectory), in the convent of **Sant' Apollonia** at Via XXVII Aprile 1 near San Marco, was painted in 1447 for the refectory of the convent. Like Leonardo fifty years later, Castagno has chosen the moment after Christ has announced his forthcoming betrayal. A sinister, malevolent atmosphere of disaster centres on Judas. Castagno, according to Vasari, resembled the character of Judas and was supposed to have been so jealous of the skill of his contemporary Domenico Veneziano that he killed him; in actual fact, Veneziano died later than Castagno.

Each disciple in the fresco is an introverted figure, contemplating the future. In a macabre gesture St Andrew, seated next to St John, shows St Bartholomew a knife with which he will be flayed. At either end of the table there is a statue of a harpy, the terrible creatures who took souls down to Hell. The extraordinary *pietra dura* panel behind Christ's head seems like a piece of modern abstract art. Above the *Last Supper* are the remains of equally powerful frescoes of the *Crucifixion*, flanked by the *Entombment* and the *Resurrection*. Castagno worked with extreme rapidity; the *Last Supper* was painted in just thirty-two days.

Andrea del Sarto's *Last Supper* in the refectory of **San Salvi** on the way to Fiesole (reachable by bus no. 10 from the station or no. 20 from Piazza San Marco) was painted from 1520 to 1525, eighty years after Castagno's work. It lacks the violence of the earlier fresco, but Sarto increased the drama by placing Judas next to Christ, from whom he receives the bread. St John leans forward to try to find out who will betray Jesus. Three of the disciples, unable to stand the tension, have risen to their feet. Shortly after it was painted Florence was besieged, and some workmen were instructed to tear del Sarto's fresco down, but they were so taken with its beauty that they refused.

If you have come to San Salvi by car, you may like to continue out of Florence up to **Fiesole**. Head due north and follow the signs to Fiesole which stands in a commanding position overlooking Florence, and is a favourite summer retreat for those trying to escape from the heat of the city. The Villa Medici, built by Michelozzo for Cosimo Il Vecchio's son Giuliano and used by Lorenzo as the setting for his Platonic Academy, stands just below the main square. In the eighteenth century it was owned by the chain-smoking Lady Orford, Horace Walpole's sister-in-law, who decorated it with Chinese wallpaper and entertained her lovers at midnight parties, scandalising Horace Mann. In the nineteenth century the collector William Blundell Spence provided a more respectable ambience, entertaining numerous artists, including Holman Hunt. At the turn of the century Sybil Cutting held intellectual soirées here, attended by the architect Geoffrey Scott and the art historian Bernard Berenson.

Fiesole contains a number of good restaurants. The **Aurora**, at Piazza Mino da Fiesole 39, is a spacious restaurant with a terrace overlooking Florence.

On the way down, below the church of San Domenico, you pass the Villa Palmieri, at Via Boccaccio 26, where Dumas wrote *The Count of Monte Cristo* in 1840.

INFORMATION

Cenacolo di Sant' Apollonia, Via XXVII Aprile 1 (Castagno): 9 a.m. to 2 p.m., Sunday 9 a.m. to 1 p.m., closed Monday

Cenacolo di San Salvi, Via San Salvi 16 (Andrea del Sarto): 9 a.m. to 2 p.m., Sunday 9 a.m. to 1 p.m., closed Monday

RESTAURANT

Aurora
Piazza Mino da Fiesole 39, Fiesole
Telephone: 055 59100, closed Sunday evening and Monday

TUSCANY
From Florence to Rome

No one has seen Italy who has missed San Gimignano
Augustus Hare

There are two routes from Florence to Siena: the old Via Cassia (SS 222) which passes through the heart of Chianti country, and the *autostrada*, a better route if you would like to see San Gimignano.

Grand Tourists followed the old scenic Roman Via Cassia through Greve and Castellina in Chianti, passing through rolling hills covered in vines and cypresses. One of the most delightful sites is the Romanesque monastery at **Badia a Coltibuono**, 20 km east of Castellina in Chianti. The church dates from the eleventh century, shortly before the monastery was taken over by the Vallombrosan order. In the nineteenth century it was owned by the Poniatowskis, one of the great families of Poland; it is now the headquarters of a flourishing vineyard, and you can enjoy an excellent wine-tasting under the wisteria-covered pergola in the monastery garden. The restaurant across the courtyard serves an excellent meal specialising in all types of game. (Make sure that you book in advance.)

On the way back to the main road it's worth stopping at the shop which sells the estate's wine, olive oil and other produce. From the Badia continue south down the SS 408 to Gaiole from where the road winds through the hills to Siena, with distant views of the skyline of the city.

San Gimignano

55 km south-west of Florence

COLLEGIATA~SANT' AGOSTINO

The alternative route to Siena follows the SS 2 *autostrada* to the wonderfully named Poggibonsi; 5 km further on take the SS 68 to Colle di Val d' Elsa and follow the signs to San Gimignano, the best-preserved medieval town in Tuscany. San Gimignano, which became the place where the Victorians soaked up the romance of medieval Tuscany, is famous for the extraordinary number of its towers, built as status symbols by the ruling families, and as vantage points from which to attack their neighbours. E. M. Forster based his novel *Where Angels Fear to Tread* (1905) on the town. To bring it into line with modern life, it is now regarded as 'the medieval Manhattan'.

No cars are allowed inside the walls, so park outside and walk through the Porta San Giovanni up Via San Giovanni which is lined with shops, many selling excellent pottery, to the Piazza della Cisterna, which leads into the Piazza del Duomo. Many of the best frescoes in the town are in the Romanesque **Collegiata** on the west side of the square.

The scenes from the New Testament in the south aisle are attributed to Barna da Siena and dateable to the mid-fourteenth century. The intense violence of the scenes of the Passion in the lower tier and the grotesque expressions of the figures seem to reflect the catastrophe of the Black Death in 1348. One of the most powerful scenes is the *Betrayal*, where a leering Judas embraces Christ, while St Peter hacks savagely at Malchus.

On the opposite wall, Bartolo di Fredi's scenes from the Old Testament, also dateable to the mid-fourteenth century, are in an altogether lighter vein. Bartolo takes a special delight in the exotic animals in the *Creation* and *Noah's Ark*, and in the dramatic trials and tribulations that befall the unfortunate Job. Benozzo Gozzoli's *St Sebastian* on the west wall, below Taddeo di Bartolo's devil-filled *Last Judgement* appears quite absurd as he nonchalantly ignores the archers who fire arrows into his body from every conceivable angle.

The elegant chapel of Santa Fina, off the right aisle, built by Giuliano da Maiano in 1468, was frescoed by Domenico Ghirlandaio in 1475 with some of the most beautiful paintings of the Quattrocento. They depict events from the *Life of Santa Fina* who lived in harsh austerity; at her death flowers grew from the towers of San Gimignano, which Ghirlandaio has portrayed on the left wall.

Outside the Collegiata turn left down Via San Matteo and after about 200 metres turn right into Via Venti Settembre and second left into Via delle Romite, which takes you to the church of **Sant' Agostino**, built from 1280 to 1298.

The best and most interesting paintings in the bare interior are Gozzoli's fresco cycle of the *Life of St Augustine* (1464–5) in the chancel, packed with a wealth of incidental detail. Gozzoli painted what amused him, even if it was of no relevance to the story, whether it is the baby's naked bottom in *St Augustine is Handed over to the*

Grammar Master at Tageste or a groom removing his spurs in *St Augustine is received by St Ambrose and the Emperor Theodosius.* On the way out of the church, notice to the right of the entrance the exquisite altar sculpted by Benedetto da Maiano in 1495.

As the church shuts at midday and San Gimignano is on the edge of the Chianti district, there is ample time before lunch to try a glass of wine at Enoteca Castello at Via del Castello 12, below Piazza della Cisterna. You can either sit in the medieval courtyard or go out into the terraced garden. The best restaurant in town is **La Cisterna** in Piazza della Cisterna, where you can sit outside and enjoy the superlative view of the Elsa valley.

If you would prefer lunch in less crowded surroundings, there are several alternatives in neighbouring hill towns and villages. The medieval Colle di Val d'Elsa is a few kilometres southeast down the valley; **Arnolfo**, at Piazza Santa Caterina 2, is an excellent restaurant specialising in *lasagnette ai funghi porcini* and *bocconcini di cinghialetto disossato in salmi* (wild boar in rich wine sauce). Nearer Siena, **Il Pozzo**, within the splendidly fortified town of Monteriggioni, overlooking the Florence–Siena *autostrada*, specialists in game dishes such as *pappardelle al cingiale* and *piccione ripieno* (stuffed pigeon).

RESTAURANTS

Badia a Coltibuono
20 km east of Castellina in Chianti
Telephone: 0577 749 498/749 300

La Cisterna
Piazza della Cisterna, San Gimignano
Telephone: 0577 940 328, closed Tuesday and Thursday lunch

Arnolfo
Piazza Santa Caterina 2, Colle di Val d' Elsa
Telephone: 0577 920 549, closed Tuesday

Il Pozzo
Piazza Roma 2, Monteriggioni
Telephone: 0577 304 127, closed Sunday evening and Monday

Siena

Very dreamy, and fantastic, and most interesting
Charles Dickens

68 km from Florence

Siena's almost perfect medieval appearance, now regarded as one of
the most delightful sights in Italy, was, for centuries, almost completely ignored. An exception was Fynes Moryson, one of the earliest
foreigners to visit the city, who wrote: 'There is no place to live in
through all Italy, than the state of Florence, and more specially the
sweet City of Sienna', but his advice went unheeded. Most Grand
Tourists, stopping overnight en route for Rome, did no more than
praise it for its beneficial climate and the purity of the Italian spoken
here. Boswell stayed for several weeks in 1765, but confessed: 'I
have been a week in Siena and have not as yet seen any *meraviglia*
(sights), as the Italians say . . . because I have been so busy with
women that I have felt no curiosity about inanimate objects.'

He managed to carry on two affairs simultaneously at a fast and
furious pace. On 10 September 1765, he recorded: 'Yesterday morning sent bold, spirited, noble letter to Porzia. At 10 1/2, Girolama.
Alone; kind, concerted. You went away . . . Then Porzia at harpsi-
chord. Was free. Got billets. Went out bold. Then Girolama. Quite
agitated. Put on condom; entered. Heart beat; fell. Quite sorry, but
said "A sign of true passion." Dined full to have courage; was fever-
ish after it and did little all day.'

Probably because of this, Boswell had a higher opinion of Siena
than most Grand Tourists. Horace Walpole dismissed the city in
1741 as 'bold, and very smug, with very few inhabitants'. In the
nineteenth century, however, with the new-found passion for the
Middle Ages, visitors came to see Siena as exquisitely beautiful.
Dickens described it as 'very dreamy and fantastic, and most interesting', and added, more prosaically, that it was 'like a bit of Venice,
without the water'.

Siena, standing on an exposed hilltop (unlike Florence, which lies
in a bowl), is a good place to visit when the climate becomes unbearable in Florence. Horace Walpole complained of the cold, and
approved of the local remedy:

> The men hang little earthen pans of coals upon their wrists,
> and the women have portable stoves under their petticoats to

warm their nakedness, and carry shovels in their pockets, with which their *cicisbeos stir* them – Hush! by them, I mean their stoves.'

THE CENTRE OF SIENA: CAMPO~PALAZZO PUBBLICO~ DUOMO~PICCOLOMINI LIBRARY~MUSEO DELL' OPERA DEL DUOMO~BAPTISTERY~SAN DOMENICO

The medieval cobbled streets winding through the city lead to the **Campo**, situated on the junction of Siena's three hills. Its romantic, curved shape, symbolically representing the Virgin's mantle, quite the opposite of Florence's Piazza della Signoria, centred on the stern Palazzo Vecchio, has inspired countless visitors to agree with Montaigne's verdict, back in 1581, that it is the most beautiful square in the world. Fynes Moryson described it in 1593: 'In the center of the City, lies a neat faire Marketplace, in the forme of an Oyster, and lying hollow as the shell thereof. And there is a stately Pallace of the Senate, built when the Citie was free.'

The Campo is the site of the Palio, a combination of medieval pageantry and a dramatic horse race between ten of the city's seventeen *contrade* (districts). It takes place annually on 2 July and 16 August. This is no tourist gimmick: the whole city takes the Palio very seriously, with its feasts, processions, choosing of the horses and jockeys (where bribery is rife), and the blessing of the horses in the church of their *contrada* on the eve of the race.

The Campo looks its best at night, with the moon rising behind the battlements of the Palazzo Pubblico, which takes on the appearance of a fairy-tale castle. The tower of La Mangia (named after a 'wastrel' bellringer) dominates the skyline, and the enormous bell installed at the top was used to warn the city's inhabitants of impending danger. The other buildings in the square echo the curved façade of the **Palazzo Pubblico** which, together with La Mangia, was built in the first half of the fourteenth century, the period of Siena's greatest power, which ended abruptly in the calamity of the Black Death in 1348.

The Palazzo was the seat of government of the Sienese Republic, and the splendid frescoes on the walls were intended to reinforce the rule of law. De Brosses, with masterly understatement, gives a typical eighteenth-century verdict on the Palazzo: 'an old building which has nothing recommendable, or at least curious, except some paintings still more antique and more ugly than itself'. The first cycle of frescoes you see, in the Sala dei Priori, was painted by

Spinello Aretino in 1407–8 with scenes from the life of the Sienese Pope Alexander III. Passing through the Cappella del Consiglio, with Trecento frescoes by Taddeo di Bartolo, and sparing a glance for Beccafumi's frescoes of the Political Virtues in the Sala del Concistoro on the right, you enter the Sala del Mappamondo.

The majestic but very damaged *Maestà* on the east wall, painted by Simone Martini in 1315–16, is dedicated, like the city of Siena, to the Virgin. Siena's greatest victory, over the vastly superior forces of Florence at Montaperti in 1260, was supposedly caused by the Virgin's divine intervention, and the idea of the Maestà (the celebration of the Virgin as Queen of Heaven) is a Sienese invention. To emphasise the legal foundation of the Sienese government, the Christ child is holding a real piece of parchment on which is inscribed the motto of justice.

On the opposite wall is the controversial fresco of the Sienese general Guidoriccio da Fogliano, with Simone Martini's signature and the date 1328. The image of Guidoriccio riding his gaily caparisoned charger across the barren landscape towards the walls of Montemassi, a town in the Maremma which he captured for Siena, epitomises the chivalric ideal of medieval Siena.

An American art historian, Gordon Moran, has, however, recently thrown doubt on the fresco by claiming that it is a fake. This has so enraged the Sienese that they have tried to ban him from the Palazzo Pubblico. Moran argues that the imprints in the gold on the horse's coat and the siege machines in front of the castle walls date from as late as the seventeenth century. His argument is supported by the discovery of a fresco attributed to Duccio beneath the *Guidoriccio*, since it is unlikely that Simone, who was Duccio's pupil, would have wanted to paint over the work of his master. Most art historians, however, find the concept of an anonymous seventeenth-century artist possessing the ability to fake a fresco of this quality inconceivable, and still maintain that it is a genuine Simone.

The room beyond, the Sala dei Nove, where the Council of the Nine sat, contains Ambrogio Lorenzetti's allegorical frescoes of *Good and Bad Government*, dating from c. 1338–40. In *Good Government*, on the left wall, Lorenzetti has depicted the prosperity of Siena, both in the city itself, with craftsmen plying their trades and women dancing in the streets, and in the surrounding countryside, where labourers till the land and a noble party sets out hawking. The figure of Securitas, flying through the sky, holds a man dangling from a gallows in one hand, to demonstrate the power of justice.

From what is left of the fresco opposite of *Bad Government*, all is confusion and violence, with the city falling into ruin and the countryside laid waste. Ironically, a decade after Lorenzetti painted the frescoes, the horrors of the Black Death reduced the prosperous Sienese Republic to a position resembling that of *Bad Government*. On the end wall a number of allegorical figures dispense justice to the burghers of Siena gathered below.

If the weather is fine and you are feeling fit, the climb to the top of the Mangia affords a magnificent panorama over the province of Siena. Before leaving the square, you might like to sit outside one of the numerous cafés; if you are hungry try a doughnut, which is much tastier in Siena than the usual cornetto.

From the Campo, turn left into Via di Città, which is full of shops selling every sort of memento of the Palio, including pottery mugs of the various *contrade*, as well as prints and other souvenirs. Follow the second sign on your right towards the Duomo. This takes you into the Piazza del Duomo, with the hospital of Santa Maria della Scala on your left.

The **Duomo**, one of the great Gothic buildings of Tuscany, was begun in the later twelfth century and completed in the following century. The elaborate façade, modelled on that of Orvieto, was begun in 1284, to the design of Giovanni Pisano who carved some of the most powerful sculptures (now replaced by copies, the originals being in the Museo dell' Opera del Duomo, although one of the heads is in the Victoria and Albert Museum in London). The Duomo did not appeal to classically minded Grand Tourists; even William Beckford, more enlightened than most, was still unable to come to terms with it, calling it 'a masterpiece of ridiculous taste and elaborate absurdity'.

In 1339 a decision was taken to build a new cathedral, using the existing structure as one transept. It was one of the most ambitious building projects in Italian history, and encapsulates the curse of Siena: an insane desire to surpass the achievements of Florence. The gigantic open arch, the only part of the new cathedral to be completed, can be seen for miles around, standing as mute testimony to the unfulfilled ambitions of the Sienese Republic.

The effect of the interior is that of 'a solemn sort of zebra, black and white', as Adam Walker described it in 1787. Its most original feature is the pavement, which is covered in wonderful sgraffito decoration (black outlines on white marble) which was done by forty Sienese artists from the fourteenth to the sixteenth centuries. The octagonal pulpit standing in the middle of the pavement, executed by Nicola Pisano and his pupils from 1265 to 1268, contains some of the most expressive Gothic sculpture in Italy. The scenes from the *Life of Christ* are treated very dramatically, particularly the *Last Judgement*, where the mass of writhing bodies being dragged down to hell gave full scope to Pisano's new-found interest in human anatomy.

The beautiful **Piccolomini Library**, on the left side of the nave, is covered in delightful frescoes by Pinturicchio of scenes from the life of the Sienese Pope Pius II. The frescoes date from 1502 to 1509, and form a magnificent decorative cycle with a wealth of naturalistic detail, such as the storm which lashes the galleys in the *Departure of Aeneas Silvius Piccolomini for Basle*, the first in the series. Below the frescoes are a series of beautiful illuminated books by Pinturicchio's contemporaries Liberale da Verona and Girolamo da Cremona. Pinturicchio's leading pupil, Raphael, almost certainly designed some of the scenes, although Grand Tourists such as Edward Wright, who attributed the frescoes to him, did so for totally spurious reasons.

Just west of the entrance to the Library is the Piccolomini altar by Andrea Bregno, with four unremarkable saints in the lower niches – the work of the youthful Michelangelo. Other notable works of art in the Duomo are Donatello's bronze statue of St John the Baptist and the tomb of Bishop Giovanni Pecci in the left transept, and the Chigi Chapel by Bernini in the right transept.

The **Museo dell' Opera del Duomo** has been constructed in a part of the unfinished new cathedral. On the ground floor are the powerful statues by Giovanni Pisano taken from the Duomo façade; they appear totally distorted since they were designed to be seen from far below. Upstairs is Duccio's *Maestà*, the masterpiece of the Sienese school of painting. Painted between 1308 and 1311, it was triumphantly installed over the high altar where it stood for two hundred years; it was dismantled in 1771.

The *Maestà* is the prototype for all later Sienese representations of the subject. Duccio chose to depict the 'Madonna in Majesty, surrounded by Saints' and scenes from the 'Life of the Virgin' and 'Christ's Ministry' on the front, and scenes from 'The Passion' on the back of the doublesided altarpiece. Duccio had a natural mastery of composition and the figure of Christ is always the focus of attention, even when he is not in the centre of the scene. The brilliant colours and graceful figures create a splendid effect.

Outside the museum, a steep flight of steps descends to the **Baptistery**, unusually sited immediately beneath the apse of the Duomo. In the centre of the early fourteenth-century interior stands a hexagonal font with a series of important bronze reliefs illustrating the *Life of St John the Baptist*. They were executed between 1417 and 1430 by the major sculptors of the early Quattrocento, including Donatello, Ghiberti and Jacopo della Quercia. Much the most complex work in the series is Donatello's *Feast of Herod*, dated c. 1425, depicting the dramatic moment when the decapitated head of the Baptist is unveiled to Herod and his courtiers, who shrink back in horror. Donatello's primary interest is the psychological reaction of the figures, but he cannot help showing off his mastery of the newly discovered art of perspective in the series of receding rooms in the background.

By now you may be wishing that you had followed the example of that avid sightseer Stendhal. 'We halted no more than ten minutes in Sienna,' he wrote, 'just time enough to glance at the Cathedral, about which I shall not permit myself to say a word.' Siena is not renowned for its food, so you can either enjoy the setting of the Campo or try to capture some local flavour somewhere less touristy. To reach the Campo, turn right up Via dei Pellegrini and follow the signs back to the Campo, where **Al Mangia** is probably the best restaurant. If your preference is for the food rather than the setting, head due north from the Baptistery up Via di Diacceto, and take the second left into Via della Galluzza; **Grotta Santa Caterina** is at no. 26, set in a handsome medieval palazzo.

After a surfeit of culture, you may want to explore some of Siena's back streets, off the main tourist route. One of Siena's most famous citizens is St Catherine (1347–80), who took the veil at the age of eight; she received the stigmata and imagined that she had been mystically married to Christ, the subject of numerous paintings. One of her greatest achievements was to persuade Gregory XI to return to Rome from Avignon. Her house is very near the Grotta Santa Caterina. Continue down Via della Galluzza, which becomes Costa San Antonio, to the bottom of the hill. The road then leads up past the Casa di Santa Caterina, which is entered through a light redbrick courtyard. If you are coming from the Campo, cross over Via di Città and head down Via della Beccheria which joins Via della Galluzza.

From the Casa di Santa Caterina, continue up the hill and turn left into Via della Sapienza which leads to the vast basilica of **San Domenico**, begun in 1226 and completed over the next two centuries. The barn-like interior, typical of so many Dominican and Franciscan churches, allowed the congregation an unimpeded view of the preacher. St Catherine performed many of her miracles in this church, and Andrea Vanni's portrait at the west end is the only authentic likeness of her. The Chapel of St Catherine, on the south side of the nave, contains dramatic frescoes by Sodoma, painted in 1526, depicting episodes from the saint's life. The melodramatic scenes of the *Fainting and Ecstasy of St Catherine* and the explicit violence of the *Execution of Niccolo di Tuldo* show a reaction to the idealised works of Raphael and Leonardo at the beginning of the sixteenth century. At the west end, Matteo di Giovanni's *St Barbara* altarpiece, with its richly dressed, heavy-lidded women and their languid gestures, is typical of late Quattrocento Sienese art.

INFORMATION

Palazzo Pubblico: April to September: Monday to Saturday 9.30 a.m. to 7.30 p.m., November to March: 9.30 a.m. to 1.30 p.m., Sunday 9.30 a.m. to 1.30 p.m., closed Monday

Piccolomini Library in the Duomo: 9 a.m. to 7 p.m., winter 9 a.m to 5 p.m.

Museo dell' Opera del Duomo: 9 a.m. to 7 p.m.

RESTAURANTS

Al Mangia
Piazza del Campo 42, Siena
Telephone: 0577 281 121, closed Monday

Grotta Santa Caterina
Via della Galluzza 26, Siena
Telephone: 0577 282 208, closed Monday

Some Sienese Paintings

A series of gaudy, gilt pictures
Joseph Forsyth

PINACOTECA~SANT' AGOSTINO~ ORATORIO DI SAN BERNARDINO

The **Pinacoteca** in Palazzo Buonsignori, in Via San Pietro, is the best place in the world to look at early Sienese painting, which is something of an acquired taste, certainly to Grand Tourists, who wrote it off as primitive and therefore bad. Even to the student of art history there is something daunting in the acres of gold ground on which obscure saints perform their miracles. Do not miss the minute Duccio of the *Madonna dei Francescani*, which has a lyrical quality reminiscent of French Gothic miniatures. The succeeding rooms are filled with works by Duccio's followers; Simone Martini's altarpiece of the *Blessed Agostino Novello*, the saint swooping down to work his miracles, Bartolo di Fredi's brilliantly coloured

Adoration of the Magi, and two charming small landscapes attributed to Sassetta, depicting a *Town by the Sea* (perhaps the port of Talamone, south of Grosseto) and a *Castle by a Lake*, possibly two of the earliest pure landscapes in the history of art.

The next rooms show how Sienese artists reacted to the revolutionary developments of the Florentine Renaissance. Some fifteenth-century artists such as Giovanni di Paolo, whom Berenson called the Sienese El Greco because of the ethereal beauty of his figures, continued to use the old-fashioned gold-leaf backgrounds, but others such as Sassetta, Matteo di Giovanni and Francesco di Giorgio attempted to make their works more realistic by using the discoveries in anatomy and perspective that Masaccio and his contemporaries made in Florence in the early Quattrocento.

The sixteenth-century works on the first floor show Siena's increasing integration into the Florentine tradition. Sodoma's *Scourging of Christ* and *Deposition*, and Beccafumi's *St Catherine Receiving the Stigmata* date from the second decade of the sixteenth century, and reflect the influence of Leonardo and Raphael.

Al Marsili, one of Siena's better restaurants, stands near the museum in an elegant fifteenth-century palazzo. Head up Via San Pietro towards the Duomo, turn right into Via di Città and Via del Castoro is the first street on your left. Try the guinea fowl *alla Medici* for some local flavour.

The other sites of interest in Siena, the churches of **Sant' Agostino** and the **Oratorio di San Bernardino**, have all been closed for several years for restoration. Should they open in the foreseeable future, Sant' Agostino, standing at the southernmost point in the city, has a number of important Renaissance paintings, including a *Crucifixion* by Perugino in the second chapel on the right, an *Epiphany* by Sodoma in the Piccolomini chapel beyond, and a violently realistic *Massacre of the Innocents* by Matteo di Giovanni, with a *Madonna and Saints* by Ambrogio Lorenzetti in the lunette above. In the Capella Bichi, off the south transept, some interesting newly discovered frescoes attributed to Francesco di Giorgio are still being restored. The Oratorio di San Bernardino, next to the basilica of San Francesco, in the northeast quarter of the city, has beautiful frescoes by Sodoma, Beccafumi and Girolamo del Pacchia in the upper chapel.

INFORMATION

Pinacoteca: Tuesday to Saturday 8.30 a.m. to 1.30 p.m. and 3 p.m. to 6 p.m., Sunday 8.30 a.m. to 1 p.m., closed Monday

Al Marsili
Via del Castoro 3, Siena
Telephone: 0577 47154, closed Monday

Arezzo

This little town belongs to the Duke of Florence, and
contains nought worth notice

Michel de Montaigne

86 km east of Florence on N 67

PIAZZA GRANDE~SAN FRANCESCO~DUOMO~
MONTERCHI~BORGO SANSEPOLCRO

A long but extremely worthwhile excursion can be made from Siena
into western Tuscany, the two most important towns of which are
Arezzo and Cortona.

It was not until the rediscovery of Piero della Francesca this century that Arezzo began to rate more than a passing mention in guidebooks. The city stands far to the east of the main route from
Florence to Rome, and Grand Tourists tended to miss it out. Those
who came here either did so by accident, like Nelson and Sir William
and Emma Hamilton, who were trying to avoid capture by the
French in 1800, or were interested in the town for its literary
connotations. Maecenas, the friend of Virgil and Horace, was born
here, as were Petrarch and Pietro Aretino, the Renaissance writer
who specialised in lampooning his famous contemporaries and is
said to have died of apoplexy after thinking up a particularly dirty
joke. Tourists had little to say about its works of art. Lady Morgan,
who came here in 1820, was not impressed by 'its narrow and dirty
streets crowded with beggars, chequered by petty vendors of fruit
and macaroni'.

The centre of Arezzo is the picturesque **Piazza Grande**, where an
antique market is held on the first Sunday of every month. This used
to be a place for bargains, but a recent spate of publicity has put

paid to the chance of making a real discovery. The square is a classic
example of the Italian genius for creating beauty out of the juxta-
position of totally separate elements. Vasari's stately Loggia, dating
from 1573, stands at the top of the Piazza next to the Palazzetto
della Fraternità dei Laici, a curious mixture of Gothic and
Renaissance architecture, and below it is the apse of the church of
the Pieve di Santa Maria.

The slope of the square adds to the excitement of the jousting that
takes place in the Giostra del Saracino on the first Sunday in September. The tournament celebrates the defeat of Saracen invaders
in the fourteenth century, when Arezzo, under a series of warrior-
bishops, was one of the strongest towns in Tuscany. Members of
Arezzo's four quarters dress up in medieval costume, parade
around the square and sing the Saracino hymn. The highlight is the
joust, where eight competitors charge in turn at the target held by
the pivoting figure of the 'Buretto Re delle Indie'. If they miss, they
are liable to be unseated by the wooden balls held in the figure's
other hand.

From the Piazza Grande go down the south side of the Pieve di Santa Maria to the Corso Italia. The blind arcades and mass of carving on the façade are typical of the Romanesque churches of Pisa and Lucca. Inside the church, which has been rather clumsily restored, make your way through the clusters of columns to the altar, above which hangs a beautiful Pietro Lorenzetti polyptych, with the Virgin clothed in a wonderful ermine-lined cloak. Outside the church, the Corso Italia, one of the main streets, is full of shops selling clothes and jewellery, a leading industry in Arezzo. Head south and take the first right into Via Cavour, which takes you to the church of **San Francesco**.

Arezzo's chief artistic glory is the magnificent fresco cycle by Piero della Francesca in the choir, depicting the *Legend of the True Cross*, painted between the 1450s and 1470s. The frescoes have recently been restored to their full glory. The legend is extremely complex, beginning at the top of the right wall with Adam, on whose grave the tree from which the cross was made was planted, and continuing with the Queen of Sheba and, at the bottom, the victory of Constantine over Maxentius. Next to this scene, on the altar wall, is the famous *Dream of Constantine*, one of the earliest night scenes in the history of painting. On the left wall are scenes of St Helena, Constantine's mother, finding the cross, and the Emperor Heraclius defeating Chosroes, who had stolen it.

Piero's statuesque figures, with their commanding presence and aloof gaze, are painted with a restrained palette of cool silvers and blues typical of the early morning light in this part of Italy. The monumentality of the figures, and the simplicity of their gestures, make it easy to understand the scenes, something that is doubly important considering their obscure subject-matter.

Piero's reputation was negligible until the mid-nineteenth century, when Lord Lindsay's *Sketches of the History of Christian Art* and James Dennistoun's *Memoirs of the Dukes of Urbino* praised his art. However, few visitors bothered to come to Arezzo until early this century, when Berenson and Longhi described his paintings as some of the most important of the entire Renaissance.

Outside the church, if you can resist the delicious ice-creams in the café in the square, and you are not yet ready for lunch, there is a beautiful *St Mary Magdalene* by Piero in the left aisle of the **Duomo** at the end of Via Cesalpino. Returning to the Piazza San Francesco, the **Buca di San Francesco**, in a vaulted fourteenth-century palace with murals covering the walls, is one of the best restaurants in Arezzo.

Three more paintings by Piero della Francesca lie within easy reach of Arezzo. Twenty-eight kilometres east of the town, following the turning towards Città di Castello off the SS 73, there is a small chapel outside the village of **Monterchi** which contains the *Madonna del Parto*, the most intimate of all his works, dating from the mid-fifteenth century. Two angels draw back a curtain to reveal the pregnant Madonna; if you look very carefully or, as a friend of mine somewhat embarrassingly did, climb on the altar, you can see that the Virgin is crying at the realisation of the tragedy to come.

Returning towards Arezzo, turn right on to the SS 73 for **Borgo Sansepolcro**, Piero's home town. The Museo Civico, in the old town hall, contains the *Madonna della Misericordia*, an early polyptych dominated by the statuesque figure of the Virgin whose outspread cloak enfolds the figures kneeling at her feet. The *Resurrection* on the wall opposite is an awe-inspiring work dateable to c. 1460. The monumental figure of Christ, one foot planted on the edge of the tomb, looks back to the hieratic images of Byzantine mosaics.

The fresco was totally ignored by early travellers. A typical reaction was that of Montaigne, who wrote of Sansepolcro: 'This little town belongs to the Duke of Florence, and contains nought worth notice.' Aldous Huxley, however, was so inspired by Piero's fresco that he wrote an article about it in the 1930s entitled 'The Greatest Painting in the World'. In 1944, when the British Eighth Army was preparing to bombard Sansepolcro, it was the memory of this article which persuaded Gunner Clark to attempt to capture the town without a preliminary bombardment. His initiative paid off, as the Germans had already retreated.

Other outstanding paintings in the museum are a *Crucifixion* by Signorelli, painted on a processional banner, and the *Martyrdom of San Quintino* by Pontormo.

INFORMATION

Chapel of the Madonna del Parto, Monterchi: 10 a.m. to 12.30 p.m. and 3 p.m. to 6 p.m.

Museo Civico, Sansepolcro: 9.30 a.m. to 1 p.m. and 2.30 p.m. to 6 p.m.

RESTAURANT

Buca di San Francesco
Piazza San Francesco 1, Arezzo
Telephone: 0575 23271, closed Monday evening and Tuesday

Cortona

There is a sleepy indolence in these Italians, that singularly
suits my humour. They seem too gentlemanlike to work, or
to be fussy, but appear disposed to make a siesta of life,
and to enjoy the passing moment

James Fenimore Cooper

117 km from Florence

MUSEO DIOCESANO~SAN NICOLÒ~
SANTA MARIA DEL CALCINAIO

Cortona (rather surprisingly twinned with Glasgow) is one of the
most appealing hill towns in Italy. Perched, like so many Etruscan
sites, on a hilltop and commanding magnificent views over the plain,
the town features on the Grand Tourists' itinerary because of its
proximity to Lake Trasimene, the site of Hannibal's decisive victory
over the Romans in 217 BC. So many legionaries were killed that two
local villages are named Ossaia (bones) and Sanguineta (blood).

In the early nineteenth century, as the cult of the picturesque
grew in popularity, travellers began to seek out the Italian hill
towns. Lady Morgan, anxious to capture every romantic nuance of
Italian history, waxed lyrical:

> The sun was setting on a drizzling rain, which fell like coloured
> gems. The dense vapour of the atmosphere obscured the
> distant prospect, until, suddenly rising above the clouds,
> appeared the forms of towers and cupolas hanging suspended
> in mid-air – the vision of a city. As the mists rolled down upon
> the valley, more definite and salient forms became visible –
> domes, and turrets, and forts, and ponderous walls, resting on
> clouds, which, as they melted into mists, gradually revealed
> the steep and rocky basis upon which these shadowy edifices
> seemed to hover, till the whole dark mass was reddened in the
> crimson light of the horizon, and the most ancient of Etruscan
> cities, CORTONA, stood full in view, crowning the summit.

The centre of Cortona is the lively and picturesque Piazza della
Repubblica, with two loggias overlooking the magnificent stairway
ascending to the thirteenth-century Palazzo Comunale. The palace
houses an assorted collection of Etruscan objects and some paintings, including – in an unlikely place to find mementoes of the Grand

Tour – self-portraits of the eighteenth-century artists Northcote and Zoffany.

The Piazza hosts an annual antique fair in September. Visitors and locals alike linger in the Bar Signorelli at the corner of the square on Via Nazionale, known as the Rugapiana, the only level street in the town. On the far side of the square, Via Casali, running behind the Palazzo Pretorio in Piazza Signorelli, leads to the **Museo Diocesano** in Piazza Trento Trieste, on the edge of the Etruscan walls.

Signorelli (c. 1441–1523), a native of Cortona, and Fra Angelico (1400–55), who lived in the monastery attached to the church of San Domenico for ten years, are both well represented in the museum. Passing a fine Roman sarcophagus and an amusing predella by Tommaso Bernabei of a naked St Benedict throwing himself among thorns to avoid the temptations of the flesh, you come to the *Lamentation over the Dead Christ* by Signorelli, an anguished scene full of suffering which becomes more explicit in the violent scenes of the *Arrest* and the *Flagellation of Christ* in the predella. Fra Angelico's works, on the other hand, are all sweetness and light. The *Annunciation* and the *Madonna of Mercy* are painted in wonderfully fresh colours, particularly the blue and red of the Virgin's robes and the predella scenes of the *Life of the Virgin* beneath the *Annunciation*. It seems extraordinary that as late as the 1850s the American Theodore B. Witmer, one of the very few to notice Fra Angelico's paintings, could find nothing 'worth wasting time over', and the *Annunciation* reduced him to uncomprehending laughter.

Returning to the Piazza della Repubblica, a steep climb up Via Santucci and Via Berrettini leads to Piazza Pescaia; bear left and take the first right down Via San Nicolò to the delightful Romanesque church of **San Nicolò**, set back in a courtyard surrounded by cypresses. The church contains a *Madonna and Child between Saints* on the left-hand wall from Signorelli's studio, and a harrowing *Entombment* painted on a processional panel over the altar by the master himself. Continuing to climb up the hill, you reach the church of Santa Margherita which commands one of my favourite panoramas in Tuscany, with a cluster of Roman roads fanning out from Cortona. On a clear day you can see far beyond Lake Trasimene towards Montepulciano, Pienza and the cone of Monte Amiata, the highest mountain in southern Tuscany.

The most well-known restaurant in Cortona is **La Loggetta** overlooking Piazza della Repubblica but a more charming alternative is **La Grotta**, off the far side of the piazza, where you can sit outside in a small courtyard.

On the way down from Cortona towards Lake Trasimene, you pass the pilgrimage church of **Santa Maria del Calcinaio**, built between 1485 and 1513, the architectural masterpiece attributed to Francesco di Giorgio. A miraculous image of the Virgin was discovered on the site by a lime-burner in 1484, and the church, erected to house the pilgrims who flocked here, was dedicated in the following year. The architectural detail is kept to a minimum to create an effect of simplicity, and the interior is flooded with light which streams through the windows in the dome.

INFORMATION

Museo Diocesano: April to September 9 a.m. to 1 p.m. and 3 p.m. to 6.30 p.m., October to March 9 a.m. to 1 p.m. and 3 p.m. to 5 p.m., closed Monday

RESTAURANTS

La Loggetta
Piazza Peschiera 3, Cortona
Telephone: 0575 603 777, closed Monday

La Grotta
Piazza Baldelli 3, Cortona
Telephone: 0575 604 834, closed Tuesday

Excursions from Siena

*I went into their Vineyards without leave to refresh myself
with some of their grapes. Which the Italians like very good
fellowes did winke at*

Thomas Coryate

SAN GALGANO~MONTE OLIVETO~SANT' ANTIMO~
PIENZA~MONTEPULCIANO

There are numerous delightful excursions into the countryside
around Siena. The most romantic of these is to the ruined Gothic
abbey of **San Galgano**, one of the two largest Cistercian foundations
in Italy. It lies 33 km from Siena on the road to Massa Marittima,
which passes, after 17 km, the hamlet of Torri with its exquisite
three-tiered Romanesque cloister. San Galgano's position, set in the
hills in the most remote corner of Tuscany, is exceptionally beautiful. The abbey was built by the Cistercian order between 1218 and
1288 and, although the order was dissolved in the seventeenth century and the roof has long since fallen in, the main body of the building has survived. In Arthurian style, the small round Romanesque
church on the hill above the ruins still has the sword which Galgano
plunged into the stone after taking his vows, in symbolic rejection of
his former career as a mercenary knight.

The most fascinating area of the Sienese countryside is south of
the city along the Via Cassia (SS 2) which runs from Siena to Rome,
a lonely road passing through a barren landscape with lines of
cypresses marching along the horizon. At Buonconvento, after
27 km, turn left and travel for 8 km to the abbey of **Monte Oliveto**,
founded in 1313 by a group of wealthy Sienese who wished to escape
to a life of rural simplicity. Their descendants managed nevertheless
to acquire some of the finest works of art in Tuscany. The intarsia
work on the wooden choir stalls, carved by Giovanni da Verona in
1505, is of the highest quality, depicting musical instruments and
views of ideal Renaissance towns, often with birds in the foreground.

The great cloister was frescoed by Signorelli and Sodoma between
1497 and 1508 with scenes from the life of St Benedict, one of the
most important cycles in Italy at this date. Signorelli prided himself
on his knowledge of anatomy and used every opportunity in the nine
scenes on the right of the entrance to portray his figures flexing their

muscles to maximum effect. Sodoma's scenes, on the other hand, are painted in a softer style, the trials and tribulations of St Benedict and his followers taking place in feathery, rolling landscapes, showing the influence of the Roman paintings in the Golden House of Nero in Rome which had only just been discovered.

If you continue along the road towards Asciano for 9 km, there is an excellent fish restaurant, **La Pievina**, with a delicious set menu which takes several hours to consume. Alternatively, you may want to continue to the Romanesque abbey of Sant' Antimo. From Monte Oliveto return to Buonconvento, turn left on to the Via Cassia and right towards Montalcino. If you are starting from Siena, take the Via Cassia and turn to the right just after Buonconvento towards the hill town of Montalcino, where the Sienese made their last stand after Cosimo de' Medici captured Siena in 1555, holding out for another four years. Montalcino's courage is commemorated every year in the Palio, when its representatives are given pride of place in the procession. The marvellous view from the castle, where you can taste the rich Brunello wine, is said to be the one Leonardo used in his famous drawing of a bird's-eye view of the earth.

The abbey of **Sant' Antimo** stands in splendid isolation 8 km south of the town. Unlike San Galgano, the early twelfth-century building is still intact. The interior is beautifully lit and has the most wonderful acoustics so that, if you are lucky enough to hear the monks chanting Gregorian plainsong, the swelling sound of the music fills the whole interior. Unfortunately, the recent installation of an organ in the left aisle has rather ruined the effect. If you find the church closed, some of the monks work as part-time shepherds and should be happy to let you in.

From Sant' Antimo it is a short journey across the lovely Orcia valley to **Pienza**. Return to the Via Cassia and turn right at San Quirico on to the SS 146. Pienza, 9 km down that road, is perhaps the most beautiful and compact of all Early Renaissance towns. Pius II renamed the town of Corsignano after himself, and summoned Bernardo Rossellino to design the Cathedral and the surrounding palaces in 1462. His courtiers, including the ambitious Cardinal Rodrigo Borgia, later the infamous Pope Alexander VI, hastened to build palaces overlooking the little piazza. Pius II, in marked contrast, was a peaceable man who loved the beauty of his native Tuscan landscape. Don't miss the stunning view from the three-storeyed loggia of his Palazzo Piccolomini, which faces towards Monte Amiata.

The centre of the town is traffic-free. **Dal Falco** is a good but simple restaurant just outside the main gate to the town; try the antipasto of pecorino cheese. An alternative restaurant is **La Chiusa** at Montefollonico, 4 km north of the road between Pienza and Montepulciano. Wherever possible the owners use local produce; try the *crespelle ai funghi porcini* or the *piccione al vinsanto*.

Montepulciano, 13 km east of Pienza on the SS 146, is renowned for its *vino nobile*, which you can sample at leisure in any of the bars in the main Piazza Poliziano. It is also worth visiting for the pilgrimage church of San Biagio which stands at the foot of the town, and is one of the most handsome Renaissance churches in Italy. The noble proportions of the interior (based on the Greek-cross plan) and the severity of the decoration testify to Antonio da Sangallo's profound study of Roman architecture. The church was built between 1518 and 1545 of white travertine, and is one of the most important religious buildings erected in Italy during this period. Sangallo also built the Canonry opposite, with a charming double-tiered loggia.

INFORMATION

Cloister at Torri: Monday and Friday 9 a.m. to 12 noon
Monte Oliveto: winter 9.15 a.m. to 12.30 p.m. and 3.15 p.m. to 5.30 p.m., summer 9.15 a.m. to 12.30 p.m. and 3.15 p.m. to 6.45 p.m.
Sant' Antimo: winter 11 a.m. to 12.30 p.m. and 3 p.m. to 5 p.m., summer 11 a.m. to 12.30 p.m. and 3 p.m. to 6 p.m., sung mass (Gregorian chant): winter 4 p.m., summer 5 p.m.
Palazzo Piccolomini, Pienza: 10 a.m. to 12.30 p.m. and 3 p.m. to 6 p.m., closed Monday

RESTAURANTS

La Pievina
Via Lauretana 9, Asciano
Telephone: 0577 718 368, closed Monday and Tuesday

Dal Falco
Pienza
Telephone: 0578 748 601, closed Friday

La Chiusa
Via della Madama 88, Montefollonico
Telephone: 0577 669 668, closed Tuesday

From Siena to Rome

A wild naked Prospect of Rocks and Hills
Joseph Addison

BOMARZO~VILLA LANTE~CAPRAROLA

From the Via Cassia, which runs south through the Orcia valley with distant views of Pienza and Montalcino, there are many interesting places to visit, including San Quirico d' Orcia, with the delightful carved portals of its Collegiata, and Bagno Vignoni, whose piazza was converted by the Medici into a heated piscina. Grand Tourists from Montaigne to Dickens broke their journey to stay in the now ruined Medici hunting lodge of La Posta at Radicofani, a hilltop eyrie across the valley from Monte Amiata. They regarded the barren landscape with horror, their fears reinforced by the limbs of executed criminals lining the roadside, and lived in constant dread of highwaymen. Joseph Forsyth, who was captured by the French on his way home from Italy in 1803 and was unable to publish his erudite guidebook until 1813, described on his journey in 1802 'a pious ruffian who held a pistol in his right hand, and a rosary in his left'. Beyond Radicofani the road winds on to the Lago di Bolsena, famous for its eels, over-consumption of which caused the death of Pope Martin IV in 1285.

Continuing south, the Via Cassia passes through Montefiascone, famous for its wine, to Viterbo, a medieval walled town where the popes retreated when they lost control of Rome. This area of northern Lazio contains three of the finest Renaissance gardens in Italy, the Parco dei Mostri at Bomarzo, the Villa Lante at Bagnaia and the Villa Farnese at Caprarola. They were all created in the middle of the sixteenth century and their owners, who knew each other well, designed them in a sense of competition.

Bomarzo lies just north of the SS 204 which runs from Viterbo to Orte; alternatively, you can reach it from the Orte junction on the A 1 *autostrada* from Rome to Florence. At the Parco dei Mostri the monstrous sculptures, best seen on an autumnal evening when the mist is rising from the valley, give the garden its unique character. The park is very run down, but it is still possible to see what Vicino Orsini, Duke of Bomarzo (an important intellectual figure of his day), was attempting to create between 1552 and his death in

87

1584. The route running anti-clockwise round the garden follows the allegorical ascent of man, from the base ignorance and madness of the monsters and the sloping house on the lower level, to the calm of the upper level with the exquisite chapel in memory of Vicino's wife, Giulia Farnese. Many of the monsters are based on creatures that appear in Ariosto's *Orlando Furioso*; they are also probably an attempt by Orsini to mock the pretensions of his friends Cardinals Gambara and Farnese.

One of the only travellers to have ventured here was the Romantic novelist Sir Walter Scott, who marvelled at the statues 'by the pale moonlight'. Appropriately enough, much of the garden's revival in popularity is due to Salvador Dali, who came here in 1949 and brought the garden back to public attention.

Cardinal Gambara's garden at the **Villa Lante** stands on a hillside above the village of Bagnaia, 5 km outside Viterbo on the SS 204. Between 1566 and 1577 the Cardinal commissioned Vignola to create one of the most enchanting formal gardens in Italy. The garden's effect is entirely dependent on Vignola's brilliantly imaginative treatment of the water flowing down the hillside so that it assumes different shapes and sounds as it passes through the garden. As at Bomarzo, the garden is an allegorical progression, from the wildness of the *bosco* at the top to the level parterre at the bottom, representing the fusion of art and nature. For the first time architecture is subservient to nature, so that the central vista of the fountains and the water-chain flowing down to the fountain of the Moors is flanked by the two casinos on either side.

Cardinal Gambara loved to entertain in the garden, and Vignola designed a stone dining table so that bottles of wine could be cooled by the water flowing down the middle. Montaigne, who came here in 1581, particularly praised Vignola's originality 'in turning water to use and beauty', and thought it surpassed both the Medici garden at Pratolino and the Villa d' Este at Tivoli, two of the most famous gardens of their time. The papacy succeeded in acquiring the garden after Cardinal Gambara's death in 1587, and gave it to Cardinal Montalto and later to the Lante della Rovere family, who continued the tradition of lavish entertainment.

The garden's fame endured into the age of the Grand Tour. The aspiring architect Robert Adam visited it in 1757, and made a drawing of the fountain of the Moors supporting the crest of Cardinal Montalto. Sacheverell Sitwell, a latter-day Grand Tourist, stressed the garden's unique appeal: 'Were I to choose the most lovely place of the physical beauty of nature in all Italy or in all the world that I have seen with my own eyes, I would name the gardens of the Villa

Lante.' The Villa has recently been lent to Prince Charles, who will hold summer schools on conservation and architectural studies there.

Cardinal Alessandro Farnese inherited the property of Caprarola from his grandfather Pope Paul III in the 1550s, and immediately set his architect Vignola to build a magnificent villa on the foundations of a fortress that Antonio da Sangallo the Younger had begun for Paul III in the 1530s. The pentagonal Villa stands in a magnificent position commanding the surrounding countryside; its approach, up a series of diagonal ramps, is the most impressive of any in Italy.

Vignola hit on the novel solution of placing a circular courtyard within the pentagon to let in the maximum amount of light. Inside, a spiral staircase on the left ascends to the *piano nobile*, where the Cardinal's rooms were divided into summer and winter quarters, frescoed by the Zuccari family with grotesque decorations and scenes glorifying exploits of the Farnese family. The most fascinating is the map room, showing a comprehensive view of the world in 1570.

Behind the Villa, Vignola designed formal summer and winter gardens with quartered parterres and box hedges, surrounded by ilexes. Further up the hill, hidden by the chestnut and fir trees and carpeted in wild orchids and cyclamen in spring, is a secret garden, where the cardinal could relax in private. A charming casino stands on a terrace at the top of a staircase, with a water-chain running down the middle. To emphasise the different nature of this section of the garden, Vignola introduced a note of frivolity by making the statues of river gods at the top of the water-chain too large for their setting. The casino beyond is set on a terrace enclosed by box hedges and cypresses, with statues of herms, pagan figures holding baskets of fruit and making music; in the corners they are holding hands and making intimate jokes to one another.

Queen Christina of Sweden, who came here in the mid-seventeenth century, was bewildered that a cardinal could have commissioned so much pagan statuary, and commented: 'I dare not speak the name of Jesus lest I break the spell.' Several eighteenth-century travellers came to Caprarola, but by then the gardens had fallen into ruin, and the contents of the palace had been removed by the Bourbons of Naples, who had inherited the Farnese properties. Only recently, since it was chosen as the private residence of the President of Italy, has the Villa been restored.

From Caprarola, follow the signs to Viterbo and turn left on to the pretty road running beside Lake Vico; the first turning on your left takes you to Ronciglione, where **Al Vecchio Mulino** is a good restaurant in a small hotel, with a terrace overlooking a dramatic gorge. After lunch you can continue south until you rejoin the Via Cassia which crosses the Campagna for 50 km to Rome.

INFORMATION

Parco dei Mostri, Bomarzo: 8.30 a.m. to sunset
Villa Lante, Bagnaia: November to February 9 a.m. to 4 p.m., March and October 9 a.m. to 5.30 p.m., April and September 9 a.m. to 6.30 p.m., May to August 9 a.m. to 7.30 p.m., guided tours every half hour
Palazzo Farnese, Caprarola: palace 9 a.m. to 4 p.m., garden 10 a.m. to 11.30 a.m. and 3 p.m. to 5 p.m., closed Monday, garden closed Sunday

RESTAURANT

Al Vecchio Mulino
Piazza del Monumento, Ronciglione
Telephone: 0761 625 011, closed Tuesday

ROME

All the dreams of my youth I now behold realised before me
                                                    Goethe

'Rome is the most glorious place in the universal world', wrote the
aspiring architect Robert Adam, known as Bob the Roman, to his
sister Peggy in 1755. To Adam and countless others, the lure of Rome
lay in the magnificence of her past, the voluptuous emperors in their
palaces on the Palatine Hill, the kings and chieftains led captive
through the cobbled streets of the Forum and the splendour of the
Renaissance and Baroque papacy, when the greatest artists in Europe
were at the pope's beck and call. Goethe felt that all his life had been
leading to the moment of his arrival in the Eternal City: 'All the
dreams of my youth I now behold realised before me', he rhapsodised.
   Aristocrats and artists alike mixed freely in the cosmopolitan
cafés and galleries with their fabulous collections, and indulged in
the brilliant social life, culminating in the mayhem of Carnival. A
century after Goethe, Henry James, losing his normally immaculate
self-control, admitted: 'I went reeling and moaning thro' the streets,
in a fever of enjoyment.'
   The sheer weight of history concentrated the attention of most
visitors on the past, and, in particular, on the Rome of antiquity. In the
seventeenth century, as religious persecution abated and Protestants
felt encouraged to visit the Papal States, a standard tour of Rome
emerged, concentrating on the most important classical ruins: the
Forum, the Colosseum, the Palatine Hill, the Roman Baths and the
major collections of antique sculpture, most of which – like Pope
Clement XII's museum on the Capitol, founded in 1733 and the first
public museum in the world (see page 106) – were easily accessible to
the public.
   The tour included the major Renaissance monuments. Almost all
the greatest sixteenth- and seventeenth-century architects played a
part in the building of St Peter's, and the frescoes of Michelangelo
and Raphael in the Vatican attracted scores of visitors. Even more
popular was Bramante's Belvedere courtyard, where the most
important antique statues in the papal collections were placed,
including the *Laocoon* and the *Apollo Belvedere*. Summing up the

powerful influence of the antique and the classical revival, it was one of the central points on the whole Grand Tour.

Grand Tourists were fascinated by the literary and historical associations of these antique statues and, to enhance their interest, gave them titles, often wildly inaccurate. They also restored them in a fanciful way. The *Dying Seneca* in the Villa Borghese was placed in a marble basin which was reddened to look like blood, so that spectators could visualise the pathos of the aging writer's suicide. It was quite acceptable to alter or add to these statues, which encouraged dealers and connoisseurs to flout the stringent export laws. All through the eighteenth century important paintings and sculpture were smuggled abroad, forming the core of many English collections, such as the purchase of the Giustiniani marbles for the Earl of Pembroke's house at Wilton.

Thomas Jenkins, the leading dealer in Rome, was an unscrupulous character who is supposed to have made turkeys eat and excrete gems to make them appear antique. According to the sculptor Nollekens, 'he followed the trade of supplying foreign visitors with Intaglios and Cameos made by his own people, that he kept in a part of the Coliseum'. Collectors were willing to turn a blind eye to obtain what they wanted. Charles Townley, who formed a famous collection of antique sculpture and bought extensively from Jenkins, remarked that 'fine things like fine Ladies must be taken when they are to be had.'

James Byres and Colin Morison, who competed with Jenkins as dealers, also acted as *ciceroni* (informed guides) to Grand Tourists. Both were distinguished classical scholars and even the indefatigable Peter Beckford, steeped in the classics from an early age, found it difficult to keep up. 'No schoolboy toiled harder or at times more unwillingly,' he complained in 1765, 'hurrying over pleasing objects to visit stones and rubbish of very little importance, for what? – to say I had visited all the antiquities of Rome.' Edward Gibbon, author of *The Decline and Fall of the Roman Empire*, who experienced Rome 'in a dream of antiquity' on his arrival in 1764, was quite exhausted by his eighteen-day tour with Byres. And James Boswell, whose diary is largely devoted to accounts of his sexual liaisons, ended by speaking in Latin after a six-week course in the study of antiquities with Morison.

In between visiting the antiquities, these energetic travellers eulogised over the paintings of Michelangelo and Raphael and admired the sculpture of Bernini. They showed little interest in Baroque architecture, although the magnificent picture gallery of the Palazzo Colonna, which Président de Brosses thought surpassed even that of Versailles, was widely imitated throughout Europe.

The paintings collected by Grand Tourists reflect the overwhelming influence of classical antiquity. The academic paintings of the Bolognese school, whose names are now largely forgotten, were prized far above those by Caravaggio and his followers, whose realism and chiaroscuro owed little to the study of antiquity. The French painter Claude Lorraine had settled in Rome in the 1620s and his Arcadian landscapes were keenly sought after; the impulsive William Beckford made one of the most spectacular purchases of the century when he paid the Irish artist Robert Fagan £6825 for a pair of Claude's landscapes which Fagan had bought for £500. They were exhibited in Beckford's house in Grosvenor Square after Nelson brought them back to England in 1799.

The most fashionable contemporary painter was Pompeo Batoni, whose aristocratic sitters pose self-consciously amid classical surroundings, a copy of Plutarch to hand, an antique bust, often of Minerva the goddess of wisdom, standing on a plinth, and Roman ruins filling the background. These portraits, the eighteenth-century equivalent of modern tourists' photographs, still hang in many of the houses for which they were commissioned. Almost as popular was Pannini, whose capriccios are filled with antique buildings and statuary. Piranesi's engravings of ancient Roman architecture were one of the prime inspirations of the neoclassical movement, which began in Rome in the 1740s and swept across Europe. The sculptor Canova's studio was also an essential stopping-point on the Grand Tour.

Most foreigners lived near the Piazza di Spagna, known by the English as 'the Westminster end of town'. Impoverished artists and rich aristocrats alike flocked to the Caffè degli Inglesi in the Piazza di Spagna, where Canova liked to play billiards. The interior was decorated in a neo-Egyptian style with sphinxes, obelisks and pyramids by Piranesi. In this Bohemian ambience, drinking, whoring and seeing the sights, and listening to the anecdotes of Justice Welch, who described himself as the head hangman in London, the young tourists felt far away from their cloistered English upbringing.

But they had to be careful of political entanglements. The Jacobites (supporters of the exiled Stuart dynasty) were a force to be reckoned with, particularly as the Papacy recognised the Old Pretender, the son of the exiled James II, as the legitimate king of Britain. James III, as he styled himself, had come to Rome shortly after the failure of the rebellion in 1715, and remained in the city until his death in 1766. The British government regarded it as a serious offence to be seen consorting with his entourage. This was very awkward since it was much easier to get official sanction for the export of works of art with Jacobite help. It is a measure of the complicated relationship between art and politics in Rome that Cardinal

Albani and Baron von Stosch, two of the leading connoisseurs in the city, were both Hanoverian spies.

After the failure of the 1745 rebellion, led by the Old Pretender's eldest son Bonnie Prince Charlie, the Jacobite threat diminished. The Stuart dynasty came to be seen in a romantic light and the British crowded into St Peter's to watch Bonnie Prince Charlie's brother Henry, the Cardinal of York, presiding at Mass. For many nineteenth-century visitors, the most moving monument in St Peter's was the simple tomb of the Old Pretender and his two sons at the foot of the left aisle, designed by Canova after the Cardinal of York's death in 1807 and paid for by the Prince Regent, later George IV.

In between visiting all the sites, most travellers led a hectic social life. Friendships were made which lasted a lifetime, and many aspiring artists and architects, like the ambitious Robert Adam and John Soane, met patrons who were to provide the most important commissions of their careers. The Dilettanti Society was founded in 1732 by Grand Tourists who had been to Italy, although the only qualification for membership, in Horace Walpole's eyes, was to have been seen drunk in Rome.

The highlight of the social round was the festivals and, of course, Carnival, which rivalled those of Venice and Naples in its licentiousness. Boswell, who caught the pox while in Rome, entered into the festivities full of his usual lust, as his diary records, on 20 February 1766: 'Went to see Gavin Hamilton's sculpture of Hector. Then to girl near Cardinal Protector of France; charming (costing 7 shillings). Sister, a nun. Mother, who sells daughters, talked of "vocation". Much enjoyment. Home.'

Everyone at Carnival wore fancy dress, and some appeared as cuckolds with bells on their horns, others in drag. In 1741 James Russell found it 'extremely difficult, if not impossible, to distinguish a lord from a lackey, or a prince from a pimp'. Goethe, who enjoyed himself hugely in 1787, witnessed a violent quarrel ending in a fight with huge knives made of silver cardboard. The night sky was illuminated by firework displays which took place from the top of the Castel Sant' Angelo, 'horribly antique and pleasing', as Robert Adam thought.

All visitors, Catholics and Protestants alike, wanted to see the Pope presiding over a service in St Peter's, particularly in Holy Week. John Chetwode Eustace thought a pontifical service in St Peter's the most majestic of all Roman ceremonies. Not all visitors were as impressed by the lavish decoration, however. The irascible Tobias Smollett condemned Bernini's cathedral as 'a heap of puerile finery, better adapted to an Indian pagod, than a temple built upon the principles of Greek architecture'.

And some visitors positively scandalised the Romans: Sir Francis Dashwood entered the Sistine Chapel in darkness with a group of penitents on Good Friday and proceeded to scourge them. Lady Morgan was shocked by the crowd of foreigners she encountered in St Peter's on Good Friday, 1820, 'laughing, flirting, chattering, and love-making, through all the philological varieties which might be supposed to make a conversazione in the Tower of Babel'.

A few tourists were lucky enough to witness a papal conclave. In 1740 Président de Brosses saw the Cardinal Chamberlain rap a small hammer on the brow of the deceased pope to ascertain if he was dead, and then take the fisherman's ring from his finger and break it, according to the ancient custom.

This idyllic phase of the Grand Tour ended with the French invasion of Italy in 1796. Under the Treaty of Tolentino, Napoleon removed to Paris one hundred of the most famous works of art in Italy, including many of the most renowned antique statues in Rome. Some of these remained in France even after Napoleon's defeat in 1815.

After the French occupation ended in 1814, Grand Tourists flocked to Rome once more. Classical art was now seen in a more romantic light, and visitors enjoyed a *frisson* of horror when looking at the busts of the more decadent Roman emperors. It became the fashion to visit galleries of antique sculpture by torchlight and to make trips into the catacombs, where early Christians were reputed to have hidden from their persecutors. Sitting in the Baths of Caracalla, Shelley, moved by the sublimity and desolation of these monuments to past glory and uplifted by the Roman climate which 'drenches the spirits even to intoxication', began *Prometheus Unbound* in 1818.

The nineteenth-century British, with their expanding empire, liked to see themselves, unlike contemporary Italians, as the heirs of the ancient Romans. They continued to congregate around the Spanish Steps, set on the Pincian Hill. The pale figure of John Keats, who lived the last months of his life during 1820–1 in an apartment at the foot of the Steps (see page 103) could be seen vainly attempting to improve his health by riding there.

The foreign community scarcely socialised with Italians. They bought their stationery at Parkinson and Gott's, their drugs at Savory and Moore's and their pickles at Crosse and Blackwell's. They dropped in at the English Club at Palazzo Lepri at Via Condotti 11, and took tea at Babington's Tea Rooms at the foot of the Spanish Steps. They banked at Packenham and Hooker's in the Piazza di Spagna because, as Murray's *Handbook* (1842) loftily explained:

It is impossible to feel, after any competent trial, how vastly different is the treatment an Englishman receives from an

English banker above an Italian one. No silly vanity should induce any traveller to afford certain grandiose Roman establishments the opportunity of fleecing him, for they will not even do it with civility, except to a duke or a great lord.

Mrs Slade, in Edith Wharton's short story 'Roman Fever', analysed the new attitude to travelling: 'I was just thinking what different things Rome stands for to each generation of travellers. To our grandmothers, Roman fever; to our mothers, sentimental dangers – how we used to be guarded – to our daughters, no more dangers than the middle of Main Street.'

The Victorians took their sightseeing very seriously and treated Murray's *Handbook* as their bible. One of Cardinal Manning's favourite stories was of the Italian sacristan who mistook the handbook for a prayer book and was very impressed by the piety of the English who spent their whole time in churches reading from it.

By the middle of the nineteenth century the study of medieval and Early Renaissance art, so ardently championed by Ruskin, had gradually replaced that of the art of antiquity. Visitors to the Sistine Chapel admired the Quattrocento frescoes which had previously attracted little attention. Florence replaced Rome as the most popular tourist attraction in Italy. However, the Victorians, like their Grand Tour predecessors, continued to neglect Baroque art. Burne-Jones dismissed St Peter's as 'pompous and empty', and it is only in this century that the originality of Borromini's architecture has been fully appreciated.

The walks in this chapter are designed to show the astonishing richness of Rome's culture and to avoid the most crowded tourist sites, although it is impossible to visit Rome without seeing St Peter's. The Piazza di Spagna and the main classical sites were both firm favourites with Grand Tourists, and you can follow in their footsteps as they experienced what was, often, the highpoint of their travels abroad. The Piazza Navona is in the heart of Baroque Rome, which reached its full flowering in the works of Caravaggio, Bernini and Borromini. Trastevere remains the most unspoilt part of the city, its winding streets and picturesque squares still inhabited by the Trasteverini, residents here for centuries. And everywhere on these walks you come across fountains, for 'consuls, emperors and popes', as Nathaniel Hawthorne noted, 'the great men of every age, have found no better way of immortalising their memories than by . . . writing their names in that unstable element and proving it a more durable record than brass or marble.'

The Westminster end of town
Allan Ramsay

PIAZZA DI SPAGNA~VILLA BORGHESE~VILLA MEDICI~ KEATS–SHELLEY MEMORIAL MUSEUM~VIA CONDOTTI~ PIAZZA DEL POPOLO~SANTA MARIA DEL POPOLO

This is a morning's walk covering the area around the Piazza di Spagna, the favourite haunt of foreigners (particularly the British) over the centuries, and the Pincian Hill, famous for its villas and gardens.

The first stop for Grand Tourists arriving in Rome was the **Piazza di Spagna**. They were more concerned with finding accommodation than with Francesco de Sanctis' spectacular staircase of 1723–5, rising to the church of Santa Trinità dei Monti, or with the Barcaccia fountain in the square, designed in the shape of a boat by Pietro Bernini (the father of Gian Lorenzo Bernini) to commemorate, so it is said, the highest point that the Tiber reached during a notorious flood in 1597. Perhaps Keats, who died in the house to the right of the Steps in 1821, was thinking of this fountain when he wrote his epitaph: 'Here lies one whose name was writ in water.'

One of the prettiest walks in Rome is up the Spanish Steps, looking their best in May when flanked by tubs of purple azaleas, and through the Borghese Gardens, threading your way between the dashing roller-skaters, exhausted joggers and unabashed courting couples, and pausing to admire the smart uniforms of the mounted *carabinieri*. Head north-west across the gardens, past the lake and the temple of Aesculapius, to the **Villa Borghese**.

The Villa, standing on the far side of the Borghese Gardens, one of the finest parks in Rome, was laid out by Cardinal Scipione Borghese at the beginning of the seventeenth century. He commissioned Giovanni Vasanzio to build a villa and Girolamo Rainaldi to lay out an enormous garden in emulation of Hadrian's Villa at Tivoli. 'An elysium of delight', concluded John Evelyn in 1644.

In the late eighteenth century the Scottish painter Jacob More redesigned the gardens in an informal English style; they became the place to be seen doing the *passeggiata* (evening promenade), particularly at sunset when the view of the dome of St Peter's is magnificent. Robert Adam, a crashing snob, liked to come here at night to watch the Roman cardinals and princes walking in disguise with their wives or mistresses.

The Cardinal was an extremely enlightened patron of the arts, and the Villa was used to house his collection of Renaissance and Baroque paintings and sculpture which ranks second only to that of the Vatican. Tobias Smollett thought it 'a complete academy for painting and sculpture'. (The sculpture is on the ground floor, paintings on the first floor.)

The entrance hall, with its highly realistic mosaics of gladiatorial combats, has the finest pieces left from the collection of classical art sold by Camillo Borghese to his brother-in-law Napoleon in 1807, including the famous *Borghese Gladiator*, and the *Dying Seneca*. Canova's provocative nude statue of Pauline Buonaparte, Camillo's wife and Napoleon's sister, stands in the first room on the right. It was the talk of Rome and gave rise to much salacious gossip since the Princess was reputed to have a string of lovers. Byron's friend Tom Moore recorded how he and the sculptor Francis Chantrey had a private viewing of the statue by candlelight in 1819 with 'Canova himself holding the light and pausing with a sort of fond lingering on all the exquisite beauties of this most perfect figure.'

Bernini's dramatic early sculptures of *David, Apollo and Daphne* and *The Rape of Persephone* dominate the next three rooms, the figures frozen in motion. The statues stood among classical sculpture and the poses are modelled on antique prototypes, the *David* being based on the *Borghese Gladiator*. Bernini loved to show off his virtuosity in marble carving and, in *The Rape of Persephone*, Pluto's fingers actually seem to be digging into Persephone's flesh. The exuberant movement of these statues influenced countless Baroque sculptors, although Dr Parkinson expressed the opinion of many eighteenth-century visitors when he declared: 'Bernini spoilt the Taste for Sculpture in Italy as Borromini did the Taste for Architecture.'

From here you make your way up to the first floor past the provocative statue of the sleeping *Hermaphrodite*, which induced certain Grand Tourists to blush with pleasure and shame simultaneously. The rooms upstairs contain a number of masterpieces from the sixteenth and seventeenth centuries. Raphael's style is based on a wide variety of sources, the muscular figures in the *Entombment* of 1506 in his most Michelangelesque style, while the *Virgin and the Unicorn* reveals his more lyrical qualities. Contemporary with the Raphaels are Andrea del Sarto's *Madonna and Child with St John the Baptist*, and, in the room off the landing, Lotto's sombre and intense portrait of a man and Savoldo's *Tobias and the Angel*, bathed in a cool, silvery light.

On the far side of the landing a large room houses Cardinal Borghese's eclectic collection of Baroque paintings and some wonderful Bernini busts of him. Domenichino's *Diana*, greatly admired for its classical beauty, hangs in the same room as several paintings by Caravaggio, including two versions of the provocative *Boy with a Basket of Fruit*, where the semi-naked youths gaze knowingly out at the spectator. In the rooms beyond, Correggio's seductive *Danae* competes with Dosso Dossi's magical *Melissa*, and Titian's *Sacred and Profane Love*. The two women in Titian's early masterpiece, one fully clothed and the other naked, and set against a ravishing landscape, still inhabit the dreamworld of the paintings of his mentor Giorgione.

Outside, you might like to linger awhile in the gardens before following the Viale della Trinita dei Monti down to the **Villa Medici**. Begun by Lippi for Cardinal Ricci in 1540, the Villa was greatly enlarged by Ammannati after Ferdinando de' Medici purchased it in 1578. The austere and fortresslike exterior makes a complete contrast with the remarkable decoration of the garden façade which Ammannati covered piecemeal with antique sculpture from the Cardinal's famous collection.

Most of the famous antique sculptures in the Medici collection were originally housed here, including the *Wrestlers* and the *Niobe Group*, which John Evelyn greatly admired. Evelyn seems to have been unaware that in 1644 Galileo had sought refuge in the Villa from the Inquisition, and had named the satellites of Jupiter 'the stars of the Medici' in gratitude for the Medici's protection.

The best surviving example of a Renaissance garden in Rome lies behind the Villa, with formal beds and covered walks set between hedges of ilex beneath the canopy of Roman pines. Velázquez captured the beauty of the site in two charming landscapes on his second visit to Rome in 1650. The garden provided a fitting setting for the beautiful Lady Spencer to crown the actor David Garrick with a wreath of bay leaves in 1763.

To the south of the Villa there is a *bosco* (wood) on a raised terrace, with a crumbling stairway leading up to a belvedere commanding a magnificent view over the city. Henry James thought it 'perhaps on the whole the most enchanting place in Rome. The part of the garden called the Boschetto has an incredible, impossible charm.'

The Villa has been the site of the French Academy since Napoleon moved it there in 1803. The neo-classical painter Ingres was one of the first directors at the Villa Medici, filling the role held in the seventeenth century by Poussin and Le Brun, earlier champions of French classicism. Many great artists studied here, including the composers Berlioz and Debussy, and the painter Corot, who possessed an unrivalled ability to capture the clarity of the Roman light.

From here it is an easy walk downhill to the top of the Spanish Steps. The eccentric and much-travelled Earl of Bristol, Bishop of

Derry, after whom the Bristol hotels are named, lived at Viale della Trinità 11 in the late eighteenth century, the same house that the painter Claude Lorraine had inhabited a century earlier. At the end of the street in the Palazzo Zuccari, the German art historian Winckelmann, who was advising Cardinal Albani on his collection of classical sculpture, was compelled to live cheek by jowl with a number of rowdy British artists, including the caricaturist Thomas Patch, who was expelled from the Papal States in 1755 for his homosexual activities, and David Allan, who took over the lodgings of Sir Joshua Reynolds and the French landscapist Claude-Joseph Vernet.

If you want to break for lunch at this point, walk down the Steps, bear right across the Piazza di Spagna and turn left to **Otello's**, at Via della Croce 81, a restaurant dating back to the mid-nineteenth century, when it was owned by Spillman Bros. The walls are covered in paintings by artists living in this neighbourhood (though my hopes of finding one by Giorgio di Chirico, who lived in the Piazza di Spagna, have yet to be fulfilled). Romans have hearty appetites, and enjoy tripe, oxtail and dishes like *saltimbocca alla romana* with a bottle of Frascati wine from the surrounding hills. An even better restaurant in the adjoining street is **Ranieri**, at Via Mario de' Fiori 26. Another possibility is **Alla Rampa** at Piazza Mignanelli 18, which adjoins the left-hand corner of the Piazza di Spagna (you cannot book in advance but rarely have to wait long for a table). The restaurant is decorated like a stage set with washing hanging from the windows.

After lunch, return to the Piazza di Spagna and, if you have sufficient energy, climb the steep stairs to the **Keats–Shelley Memorial Museum** where Keats lived during the last months of his life. Reminders of Keats's tragic early death, his death-mask and the manuscript of his poem 'Bright Star, were I as stedfast as thou art', bring his last months, spent wasting away in this apartment, vividly to life.

The flat above the museum can be let from the Landmark Trust (see Information) on a weekly basis. It has been decorated in the same style as the museum below and is one of the most atmospheric places in which to stay in Rome, although in summer it can be extremely noisy. Youthful tourists holding impromptu concerts have replaced the artists' models who posed on the steps in the nineteenth century, fascinating Dickens who recognised the sitters from paintings hanging in the Royal Academy.

This is the heart of the smart shopping area and you will find all the latest fashions in the pedestrianised **Via Condotti** and the parallel Via Frattina. You will be playing the Grand Tour role much more convincingly if you now spend an hour window shopping. Robert Adam took time off from his studies to send his mother a black and yellow tortoiseshell snuff-box so that she could 'review the folly of her son every morning and evening when she took her plug'.

If you would like a cup of coffee or an ice-cream, the Caffé Greco, at Via Condotti no. 86, decorated with views of Rome and the Campagna, dates from the early nineteenth century and was frequented by a cosmopolitan array of writers and musicians. The Romantic poets Byron and Baudelaire came here, as did the composers Liszt and Berlioz. Gogol, another habitué, drew picturesque scenes of the Campagna on the tabletops, and wrote passionate letters to his love Maria Balabina in St Petersburg, imagining that her eyes were as blue as the Roman sky (they were in fact brown).

The western limit of this smart area is the Corso, the main street of Rome, which runs from the Piazza del Popolo – the original entrance to the city for travellers coming from the north – to the Piazza Venezia.

Under the Papacy gruesome executions took place in the **Piazza del Popolo**. In 1581 Montaigne witnessed that of the famous bandit chief Catena and noticed how 'the crowd, who had not felt any pity at the hanging, cried out in lamentation at every stroke of the axe'. In 1815 Samuel Rogers saw the executioners dressed up in macabre fashion as characters from the Commedia dell' Arte.

The Piazza is the most theatrical of all the large squares in Rome. The north gate was redecorated by Bernini in 1655 to celebrate the arrival of Queen Christina of Sweden after her conversion to Catholicism. Five years later Alexander VII commissioned Rainaldi to build the two churches on the south side of the square. Rainaldi made the churches appear perfectly symmetrical by cunningly lowering the dome of the left-hand one so that you are unaware that it is actually larger than its companion.

The church of **Santa Maria del Popolo** next to the Porta del Popolo was the favourite church of Sixtus IV and his nephew Julius II, who commissioned Pinturicchio's beautiful *Adoration of the Child* in the first chapel on the right and Andrea Sansovino's della Rovere and Sforza tombs, designed as triumphal arches, on either side of the high altar. The Chigi Chapel, halfway down the left aisle, was designed by Raphael; the mosaics in the dome and two of the statues were executed to his designs; and the altarpiece is by his contemporary and rival Sebastiano del Piombo. The chapel was completed a century later by the Chigi Pope Alexander VII, who commissioned Bernini to add the statues of *Habakkuk* (on the right of the altar) and *Daniel and the Lion*. The antiquarian and cicerone James Byres typifies eighteenth-century taste in his admiration of Raphael's work, which he contrasted with the artificial theatricality of the Baroque. He felt that Bernini 'stripped tomb sculpture of its ancient, simple grandeur . . . sacrificing all that is valuable in sculpture to what he conceived a picturesque effect'.

Modern tourists rush straight to the Cerasi Chapel on the left of the altar, with its two dramatic paintings by Caravaggio. Following Michelangelo's lead in pairing the *Crucifixion of St Peter* with the *Conversion of St Paul*, Caravaggio greatly enhanced the drama of the latter by placing St Paul beneath a horse which towers over his prostrate body. Hardly anyone notices Annibale Carracci's *Assumption* which hangs on the end wall of the chapel, although Carracci was regarded until this century as a far more important artist than Caravaggio.

Emerging from the church, you might like to linger just across the piazza in Rosati's, one of the most elegant and atmospheric cafés in Rome, or look at some of the antique shops in the Via del Babuino, leading from the south side of the Piazza del Popolo to the Piazza di Spagna and the Via Margutta running parallel to the north. Under Italian law an antique is defined as something composed of a material of a certain age, so that, for example, an old piece of wood that has been turned into a modern piece of furniture qualifies as an antique. So beware!

INFORMATION

Villa Borghese: 9 a.m. to 2 p.m., Sunday 9 a.m. to 1 p.m., closed Monday

Villa Medici: garden open Sunday 10 a.m. to 1 p.m. (check with Ufficio Intendenza, Villa Medici, Viale Trinità dei Monti)

Keats–Shelley Memorial Museum: 9 a.m. to noon and 3.30 p.m. to 6 p.m., winter 9 a.m. to 1 p.m. and 2.30 p.m. to 5 p.m., closed Sunday

Landmark Trust (England) Telephone: 062882 5925

RESTAURANTS

Otello's
Via della Croce 81, Rome
Telephone: 06 679 1178/678 1454, closed Sunday

Ranieri
Via Mario de' Fiori 26, Rome
Telephone: 06 679 1592, closed Sunday

Alla Rampa
Piazza Mignanelli 18, Rome
Telephone: 06 678 2621, closed Sunday

A dream of antiquity
Edward Gibbon

SAN CLEMENTE~COLOSSEUM~PALATINE HILL~ FORUM~ARCH OF TITUS~CAPITOLINE HILL~ PROTESTANT CEMETERY

This walk is best done in the morning when all the sites are open. It covers the heart of the eighteenth-century Grand Tour, the classical sites of the Forum, the Palatine and the Capitoline Hills, the main reason that travellers made such an effort to cross the continent to Italy. It begins at the church of **San Clemente**, which is just east of the Colosseum down Via di San Giovanni in Laterano. The church is an archaeological treasure trove, with a series of layers dating back to the first century AD. The excavations were carried out by Irish friars in the 1860s, when the science of archaeology was in its infancy.

The interior is one of the most extraordinary architectural palimpsests in Rome, a bewildering mixture of Ionic columns looted from classical buildings, a beautiful medieval marble choir and ciborium, a fine Cosmatesque pavement, glittering twelfth-century mosaics in the apse, and a side chapel to St Catherine of Alexandria by the entrance door, with early fifteenth-century frescoes by Masolino and possibly Masaccio, two of the leading Florentine painters of the early Quattrocento. They are some of the first frescoes painted after Pope Martin V's return from Avignon in 1417, and were the only works of art Byron's friend the poet Samuel Rogers noticed when he visited the church at the beginning of the nineteenth century.

Across the nave a door leads into a vestibule, from which you descend into the narthex of a fourth-century church, its walls covered in fragments of columns, reliefs and inscriptions. On the left of the nave are two eleventh-century frescoes of the *Acts of St Alexis* and *St Clement*, one of the earliest popes. To the right of the nave a fine first-century sarcophagus is covered in reliefs of a huntsman and hounds attacking a savage-looking boar.

Off the left aisle of the church, steps lead down to a Mithraeum and the original house of Clemens beneath, both dating from the first century. The cult of Mithras, with its belief in death and resurrection, was very popular with soldiers, for obvious reasons, and was the chief rival of Christianity in the early centuries AD. The Mithraeum has an altar with a relief of Mithras plunging a knife into the neck of a bull, the most sacred moment in the Mithraic cult.

Outside the church, turn right into Via di San Giovanni in Laterano and you can enjoy a view of the best-preserved part of the **Colosseum,** named after the colossal statue of Nero that stood on the site. This massive amphitheatre, one of the greatest technical achievements of the ancient Romans, was built by the emperor Vespasian in 69 AD on the site of a lake which had been constructed by his sybaritic predecessor Nero. The classical rules of architecture, with the sequence of the simple Doric order at the bottom, the Ionic above it and the more ornate Corinthian on top, were first used in this building. The Colosseum is full of reminders of its bloodthirsty past; even the name of the exits (*vomitoria*) illustrate the nature of the barbarities enacted here. To assuage some of these brutal memories and to prevent its continued use as a quarry, the popes consecrated it as a church and the Pope still leads a candlelit procession here on Good Friday.

William Beckford, typical of his era in preferring classical to Christian Rome, objected to it being turned into a church, and wanted to 'break down and pulverise the whole circle of saints' nests and chapels, which disgrace the arena' and kick the lazy abbots 'such as would have made a lion's mouth water', into the Tiber. The Romantic poets, on the other hand, eulogised it and, indeed, when it was full of wild flowers in the nineteenth century it must have been delightful. Shelley, overwhelmed by his experience of Rome, thought it 'changed by time into the image of an amphitheatre of rocky hills, overgrown by the wild olive, the myrtle, and the fig-tree'.

Walking clockwise round the exterior, past the beautifully restored Arch of Constantine which dates from c. 315 AD and is covered with reliefs taken piecemeal from earlier Roman buildings, turn left down Via di San Gregorio. The entrance to the Forum and the Palatine is through the handsome Renaissance gateway to the Orti Farnesiani; make sure you take the left-hand turning towards the Palatine. For the non-specialist, the **Palatine Hill** is much more evocative of ancient Rome than the Forum, and the picturesque ruins that so captivated Claude Lorraine, Gaspard Dughet and Richard Wilson still possess 'the inexplicable solemnity and beauty' that bewitched Dr Arnold in 1827. It is best appreciated over a lengthy picnic and a bottle of Frascati.

As you ascend the hill, birdsong replaces the roar of traffic; passing underneath some spreading umbrella pines, you reach the top of the hill by the vast stadium, part of the palace of Domitian erected in c. 80 AD. Bearing left towards the south-east corner of the hill, you look down into the Domus Augustana, the private residence of the Emperor Augustus. At the very corner of the hill, you can gaze down on the Circus Maximus, where chariot races were held. Few tourists reach here; the silence is broken only by the grumbling workmen setting up their parasols for the inevitable siesta.

While wandering among these ruins Byron's friend Lady Blessington spotted Napoleon's mother shortly after the emperor's death. 'Here was the mother of a modern Caesar,' she wrote, 'walking amidst the ruins of a palace of the ancient ones, lamenting a son whose fame had filled the four quarters of the globe.'

Bearing left along the southern side of the hill you come to the so-called House of Livia, the wife of Augustus, with charming frescoes of mythological scenes and garlands of fruit and flowers. Above the house, to the northwest, a series of box hedges and Judas trees leads to the north-west corner of the hill.

You can enjoy an excellent view of the Forum from the northern side of the Palatine and, if you are feeling at all weak, leave your experiences at that. You run the risk of losing the atmosphere among the crowds below unless you go really early or linger at dusk.

Following the north-west slope of the hill overlooking the Forum, you come to the Orti Farnesiani, a series of terraces and two casinos used as aviaries, laid out by Vignola for Cardinal Alessandro Farnese in the sixteenth century. The Cardinal owned the Palatine Hill, a perfect spot for the philosophical discussions he enjoyed with his friends while wandering among the ruins. Behind the casinos he created a botanical garden for his collection of rare plants.

The Forum, which lies below the casinos, had a humble beginning 'as a refuge of shepherds and riffraff', as Goethe liked to imagine. Originally a marketplace, it was the centre of Roman life all through the Republic, the place where victories were announced and captive kings led in chains, where Cicero delivered his orations and Augustus performed his sacrifices, where the Vestal Virgins tended the sacred fire in the Temple of Vesta and were buried alive if they were found to have lost their virginity. As the emotive heart of Rome, Mark Antony could have chosen nowhere better to deliver his funeral oration over the body of Caesar in 44 BC.

Surprisingly little remains of its former glory, but the recently restored Arch of Septimius Severus, dating from the early third century AD and standing at the end of the Via Sacra beneath the Capitol, the block-like Senate House to its right, and the three enormous coffered vaults of the fourth-century Basilica of Maxentius one hundred metres to the right, have survived as potent reminders of the grandeur of Roman architecture. The scale of the Basilica's vaults, which appear in many of Piranesi's most powerful engravings, inspired Soane and Ledoux, two of the greatest neo-classical architects. A harvest festival is held here in September, with participants dressed in folk costume.

During the seventeenth and eighteenth centuries the Forum was known as the Campo Vaccino because a cattle market was held here every Thursday and Friday. De Brosses was not impressed with this pastoral scene, commenting acidly that 'Romulus must have been drunk when he thought of building a town on so ugly a site.' Gibbon, on the other hand, was in a fever of excitement and could barely sleep the night before his visit in 1764.

Below the casinos a path descends to the right towards the **Arch of Titus**, erected in celebration of Titus's capture of Jerusalem in 70 AD. After the Roman victory, graphically described by the Jewish historian Josephus, the temple of Jerusalem was destroyed and all its holiest objects were brought back to Rome. The reliefs on the inside of the arch depict Titus in his chariot leading a triumphal procession adorned with trophies from the campaign, including the Ark of the Covenant and other treasures from the temple in Jerusalem, the last surviving record of them before their disappearance following the Sack of Rome by the Goths under Alaric in 410.

The Arch of Titus stands at the top of the Sacred Way which runs through the Forum to the Arch of Septimius Severus. Halfway down, there is a sign on the right to the exit from the Forum, at about the point where Mark Antony made his famous speech.

If you need some refreshment at this point, one of the best pizza bars is at hand. Cross Via dei Fori Imperiali and take the third turning on the left down Via dei Serpenti; the Pizzeria Leonina, in Via della Leonina, the first street on the right, is justly famous among Romans. If you don't want to stop for lunch yet, turn left at the exit, walk round the edge of the Forum and turn left between the Senate House and Pietro da Cortona's splendid church of Santi Luca e Martina, built in 1640. Continue past the Arch of Septimius Severus and up the stairs on to the **Capitoline Hill**.

The Capitol was both a fortress and a sanctuary of the gods in ancient Rome. In the Middle Ages it housed the Senate and was the focus of anti-papal government. Cola di Rienzo, who set himself up as the tribune of the short-lived Roman Republic in 1347, and was the hero of an opera by Wagner, was executed here.

Michelangelo redesigned the square, focusing away from the Forum and towards the Vatican, and moved the bronze equestrian statue of Marcus Aurelius from the Lateran in 1536 in honour of Charles V's triumphal entry into Rome as Holy Roman Emperor, culminating in his arrival on the Capitol. The square was designed around the statue which dates from the mid-second century AD, and is the only equestrian statue to have survived from antiquity because it was long thought to be of Constantine, the first Christian emperor and therefore sacred. Recently brought back to the Capitol after an extensive restoration, it remains doubtful whether it will ever be returned to its original position in the centre of the piazza because of the level of pollution in modern Rome.

Michelangelo overcame the problems of the awkward, trapezoidal site by making the façades of the two **Capitoline Museums**, Palazzo dei Conservatori and the Palazzo del Museo Capitolino, which face one another, identical, to provide a sense of unity. His use of giant pilasters, the first in Renaissance architecture, emphasised the monumentality of the square.

Many visitors were inspired by the classical associations of the Capitol, none more so than Gibbon. He later recalled its impact: 'It was on the fifteenth of October, in the gloom of evening, as I sat musing on the Capitol, while the barefooted fryars were chanting their litanies in the temple of Jupiter, that the idea of writing the decline and fall of the city first started to my mind.' Goethe came here on his last night in Rome and was amazed by the way the moonlight shining on Marcus Aurelius seemed to transform him into Mozart's 'Commendatore' from *Don Giovanni*.

Since it would be impossible to see all the paintings and antique sculpture housed in Michelangelo's two palaces in one viewing, it is best to concentrate on the sculpture which is more evocative of ancient Rome. If you would like to recapture the romantic atmosphere loved by Grand Tourists, come back on a Tuesday or Saturday evening when you can emulate them by examining the sculptures by candlelight.

The museum was opened by Clement XII in 1733 to house his recent purchase of Cardinal Albani's collection of antique sculpture, and it rapidly became one of the most important sites on the Grand Tour. The Abbé Barthélemy wrote to the Comte de Caylus shortly after its opening: 'The first time I went into the Capitoline Museum I felt a shock of electricity . . . it is the dwelling-place of the gods of ancient Rome.' Many of the sculptures are rather damaged, something that would have shocked eighteenth-century connoisseurs such as Winckelmann and Cardinal Albani who believed strongly that a restored statue was far superior to an antique fragment, and commissioned their friend Cavaceppi to carry out endless restorations.

The Roman emperors seem to have increasingly suffered from delusions of grandeur. In the courtyard of the **Palazzo dei Conservatori**, on your right facing the Palazzo Senatorio, are the remains of an enormous statue of the fourth-century Emperor Constans II which would probably have stood originally beneath the gigantic vaulting of the Basilica of Maxentius. Eighteenth-century visitors, with a typical interest in associational values, disputed endlessly whether the statue was of Apollo, Augustus, Nero or Commodus.

The rooms on the first floor contain several of the most famous ancient Roman sculptures: the bronze bust of Lucius Junius Brutus, whose formidable features seem to sum up the resolution and austerity of the Roman Republic; the *Spinario*, a charming figure of a boy pulling a thorn out of his foot, an image endlessly repeated in eighteenth-century bronzes; and the *Capitoline Wolf*, the original symbol of Rome. Earlier visitors failed to notice that the figures of the infants Romulus and Remus were actually added in the fifteenth century, although Jonathan Richardson perceptively compared the *Spinario* with Quattrocento bronzes.

The **Palazzo del Museo Capitolino** opposite has a larger group of antique sculpture. In the courtyard is one of the finest of all antique river gods, a favourite subject and one that profoundly influenced Michelangelo in his design of the Medici Chapel. The first room upstairs is centred on the statue of *The Dying Gaul*, 'butcher'd to make a Roman holiday' in Byron's memorable phrase. Next door is a beautiful statue of a faun in *rosso antico*, and another which inspired Nathaniel Hawthorne's *Marble Faun*, and in the room beyond are two charming *Centaurs* from Hadrian's Villa, copies of which appeared on many a tourist's mantelpiece. The rooms further on are filled with endless busts of philosophers and ancient Romans, whose literary and historical associations inspired Grand Tourists but which now seem remarkably boring. Those that stand out are of the more insane emperors such as Caracalla, whose scowling features seem to epitomise their tyranny and megalomania.

Moving along the corridor, you come to the athletic figure of a gladiator, his right arm raised to ward off an impending blow. In an octagonal room off the left side of the corridor, the rather lumpy figure of the *Capitoline Venus* produced reams of eulogistic prose from besotted Grand Tourists. In a small room opposite, a charming mosaic of birds is yet another of the enormous number of finds made in Hadrian's Villa at Tivoli. Downstairs, there are several highly realistic sarcophagi of figures fighting and a remarkably life-like statue of an exhausted athlete.

The nearest good restaurant is in the Ghetto. Turn left out of the museum, go down the steps to Via del Teatro di Marcello, turn left and first right down Via Montanara into Piazza di Campitelli, full of handsome palaces. The **Vecchia Roma**, at no. 18, round the corner of the piazza on the left and decorated with murals of old Rome, specialises in Roman cooking, particularly seafood. Try the *filetti di baccalà* (strips of dried salt cod deep-fried in batter), a speciality of the Ghetto. Another possibility is **Piperno** at Monte de Cenci. Head south from Piazza Campitelli down Via della Tribuna di Campitelli, turn right into Via di Sant' Angelo in Pescheria, named after the fish market which survived in the portico of the church until the last century and where Cola di Rienzo and his followers gathered before marching on the Capitol in 1347. Duck under the scaffolding propping up the Porticus of Octavia, turn right, first left into Via del Tempio and first right opposite the synagogue into Via Catalana, which leads into Monte de Cenci. Piperno, at no. 9, offers *carciofi alla giudia* (crisp fried artichokes) as well as other regional dishes.

Piazza Campitelli is the heart of the Ghetto, where the Jews were segregated from 1556 until 1848. John Evelyn, as always fascinated by local customs, came here to attend a circumcision, and records that the red hats they were originally forced to wear were changed to yellow after the short-sighted Cardinal of Lyons mistook a Jew for a fellow Cardinal as he passed his coach.

The church of Santa Maria in Campitelli, which dominates the square, was the Cardinal of York's parish church, where the Jacobite court came to attend mass. Prayers are still said here for the reconversion of England to Catholicism. From the Piazza you can either take a bus or a taxi to the Protestant Cemetery. If you choose the bus, walk up Via dei Funari. This leads past the handsome façade of the church of Santa Caterina dei Funari into Piazza Mattei with its charming Fontana delle Tartarughe, executed by

Taddeo Landini to designs by della Porta. The tortoises drinking from the fountain were probably added by Bernini in the seventeenth century. From Piazza Mattei turn right up Via Paganica to Via delle Botteghe Oscure where the body of the unfortunate Prime Minister Moro was left after his murder by the Red Brigade in 1978. At the junction with the Piazza Venezia take a no. 95 bus to the Porta San Paolo. From Piperno return to Piazza Campitelli and follow similar directions. It is an easy walk past the Pyramid of Gaius Cestius, dated 12 BC, to the Protestant Cemetery, which has its entrance at no. 6 Via Caio Cestio.

At the end of the street, the **Checchino dal 1887** restaurant, at Via di Monte Testaccio 30, has been going strong for over a century. The same family still serves traditional food, including *coda alla vaccinara* (oxtail), *abbacchio alla romana* (suckling lamb) and *pajata* (small intestines). Bear in mind that the cemetery shuts at 5.30 p.m.

No description of the **Protestant Cemetery** can surpass that of Shelley, whose ashes are buried here:

> The English burying-place is a green slope near the walls, under the pyramidal tomb of Cestius, and is, I think, the most beautiful and solemn cemetery I ever beheld. To see the sun shining on its bright grass, fresh, when we first visited it, with autumnal dews, and hear the whispering wind among the leaves of the trees which have overgrown the tomb of Cestius . . . and to mark the tombs, mostly of women and young people who were buried there, one might, if one were to die, desire the sleep they seem to sleep.

The cemetery is divided into New and Old sections, Keats's grave being in the old part and Shelley's ashes in the new. The custodian will give you a map and point out how to reach Keats's grave in the far left-hand corner, where he was buried in 1822. Other notable people buried here are Keats's friend Joseph Severn (1793–1879) beside him, Shelley's friend Edward Trelawny (1792–1881), John Addington Symonds (1840–93), the historian of the Renaissance, John Gibson (1790–1886), the sculptor, and Julius Goethe (d. 1830), the only son of the writer.

INFORMATION

San Clemente: 9 a.m. to 12 noon and 3.30 p.m. to 6 p.m., Sunday 10 a.m. to 12 noon and 3.30 p.m. to 6 p.m.
Colosseum: 9 a.m. to sunset, Wednesday and Sunday 9 a.m. to 1 p.m.
Forum and Palatine: 9 a.m. to one hour before sunset, Tuesday and Sunday 9 a.m. to 1 p.m.

Capitoline Museums: 9 a.m. to 1.30 p.m. and on Tuesday 5 p.m. to 8 p.m., on Saturday in winter 5 p.m. to 8 p.m. and in summer 8 p.m. to 11 p.m., Sunday 9 a.m. to 1 p.m., closed Monday

Protestant Cemetery: 8 a.m. to 11.30 a.m. and 2.30 p.m. to 5.30 p.m.

RESTAURANTS

Da Mario
Piazza del Grillo, Rome
Telephone: 06 679 3725

Vecchia Roma
Piazza Campitelli 18, Rome
Telephone: 06 686 4604, closed Wednesday

Piperno
Monte de' Cenci 9, Rome
Telephone: 06 654 0629, closed Sunday evening and Monday

Checchino dal 1887
Via di Monte Testaccio 30, Rome
Telephone: 06 574 6318, closed Sunday and Monday

Palazzo Zuccari

The most sumptuous edifices in Rome
Joseph Forsyth

PIAZZA NAVONA~SANT' AGOSTINO~
SAN LUIGI DEI FRANCESI~SANT' IVO ALLA SAPIENZA~
PANTHEON~SANTA MARIA SOPRA MINERVA~
PALAZZO DORIA PAMPHILJ~CAMPO DE' FIORI~
PALAZZO FARNESE~PALAZZO SPADA

For many, put off by the prospect of acres of classical ruins and horrified by the queues swarming through the Vatican, one of the great
joys of visiting Rome is its magical fountains, and there is no better
place to begin a tour of Baroque Rome than in front of Bernini's
fountain of the Four Rivers in the **Piazza Navona**. 'The noble
Piazza Navona', wrote Tobias Smollett admiringly, 'is adorned with
three or four fountains, one of which is perhaps the most magnificent in Europe, and all of them discharge vast streams of water:
but,' he could not help adding, 'notwithstanding this provision, the
piazza is almost as dirty as West Smithfield.'

In the early morning this superb Baroque square is still one of the
most delightful spots in Italy, free of both tourists and traffic. The
Piazza, following the ancient plan of the stadium of Domitian, is the
creation of the Pamphili Pope Innocent X (1644–55), and is centred
on the fountain of the Four Rivers, designed by Bernini and executed by his pupils. Four allegorical figures, representing the continents of Europe, Asia, Africa and America, support an obelisk
which Domitian brought back from Egypt and which Lord Arundel
tried to buy for 60 crowns on his Grand Tour with Inigo Jones in
1613–14. The fountain was unveiled in 1651, two years before
Bernini's arch-rival Borromini began work on the church of Sant'
Agnese, which stands on the site of St Agnes's martyrdom in an
ancient Roman brothel.

The Piazza Navona is a perfect setting for festivities and was
flooded on feast days, following a custom inaugurated by Innocent X
to refresh the air in August. The Roman nobility much enjoyed driv-
ing their carriages through the water, which Lady Morgan, on her
visit in 1820, thought 'a curious sport for ladies'. Between festivals
the Piazza served as the main market-place in the city, and a children's market, full of every type of toy, is still held at New Year,
attracting locals from all over Lazio.

If you want to linger and have a *gelato*, there are numerous cafés
in the square, of which the most famous is the Tre Scalini; try the

delectable *tartufo*. For a sample of Rome's antique shops, particularly in May when there is an antiques fair, pause for a moment in Via dei Coronari, which you reach by heading north out of Piazza Navona and taking the first left out of Piazza di Tor Sanguigna. Prices here are much more reasonable than in the shops around the Spanish Steps.

Heading back to the Piazza di Tor Sanguigna, pass under an arch on the east side of the square into Piazza di Sant' Agostino. The church of **Sant' Agostino**, overlooking the square, was built from 1479 to 1483 of travertine quarried from the Colosseum, and was one of the most fashionable churches in Rome during the Renaissance. Humanists, intellectuals, penitent courtesans and artists all used to meet here, including Raphael who painted the forceful figure of the prophet *Isaiah* in 1512 over the third pillar in the nave. Beneath it is his friend Andrea Sansovino's group of the *Madonna and Child with St Anne*. Jacopo Sansovino's *Madonna del Parto* by the main door, another classical sculptural group of the High Renaissance, has become a cult object and is surrounded by lamps and votive candles.

The *Madonna of Loreto* of 1605, one of Caravaggio's most deeply religious works, hangs in the Cavalletti Chapel in the left aisle. The two peasants kneeling before the miraculous apparition of the Madonna and Child can be seen from right across the nave, so that we approach the altarpiece as participants in the miracle.

Outside the church, turn left and first right into Via della Scrofa, which passes the church of **San Luigi dei Francesi**, begun in 1523 during the reign of François I, whose emblem of the salamander decorates the façade.

Grand Tourists came here to admire Domenichino's frescoes of the *Life of St Cecilia* in the second chapel in the right aisle. They showed little enthusiasm for the early Caravaggios in the Contarelli Chapel, the last in the left aisle, which are now some of the most famous Baroque paintings in Rome.

The three canvases (painted in 1597–1602) show Caravaggio's dramatic use of chiaroscuro to intensify the psychological drama. There is a curious ambiguity in much of Caravaggio's work, and this is apparent in the *Martyrdom of Saint Matthew* on the right wall, a mixture of spirituality and violence as the executioner bends over the body of the saint. In the *Calling of Saint Matthew* opposite, Christ's arm appears out of the darkness, summoning Matthew from his friends seated round the table. The paintings were never intended to be so dimly lit, but the Palazzo Madama now cuts out the light entering the window in the chapel.

Re-emerging into Via della Scrofa, head downhill to Piazza Sant'
Eustachio, with two bars which dispute the honour of serving the
best cappuccino in Rome. On the west side of the square stands the
Old University of Rome, which now houses the National Archives.
Above it rises the extraordinary spiralling dome of Borromini's
masterpiece, the church of **Sant' Ivo alla Sapienza**, built between
1642 and 1660. The church is guarded jealously by a small custodian
recognisable by the jangling of his keys; his office is at the end of the
left arcade in the courtyard. He never admits to it being open but an
'offering' of 1500 lire may suddenly help to change his mind.

Borromini supposedly designed the ground plan in the shape of a
bee, the emblem of Urban VIII who had commissioned it. He produced an extraordinary tension between the undulating motion
around the entablature and the walls, which are broken up into a
series of convex and concave curves, and the vertical thrust of the
giant pilasters which lead into the ribs and stars in the dome. No
colour detracts from the drama of the architecture.

Borromini's architecture has always excited strong emotions.
Evelyn, who saw the church being built, greatly admired it but later
visitors, particularly in the nineteenth century, despised what they
regarded as Borromini's wilfulness. Forsyth thought him mad and
wrote dismissively: 'I am surprised that, after having built one
church, he was ever employed on a second; yet the man went on,
murdering the most sumptuous edifices in Rome, until at last he
murdered himself.'

Returning to Piazza Eustachio, leave the church of Sant'
Eustachio on your left, turn left up Via di Sant' Eustachio and the
tiny Piazza della Rotonda is immediately on your right, dominated
by the **Pantheon**, the finest of all ancient Roman monuments. The
piazza has always been a scene of bustling activity: during the sixteenth and seventeenth centuries the vast portico was used as an
exhibition space and in the nineteenth century a fish market was held
here. Lady Morgan, holding smelling salts to her nose, exclaimed disapprovingly: 'The senses are everywhere assailed; and the pavement,
sprinkled with blood and filth, exhibits the entrails of pigs, or piles of
stale fish, sold almost within the pale of the doorway.'

Despite the looting of popes and emperors, and particularly
Bernini's stripping of the bronze from the roof in the 1620s to provide cannon for the Castel Sant' Angelo, the exterior remains much
the same as when Hadrian built it in 118–28 AD. The ground level of
the city has risen a great deal since antiquity, and the entrance,
which was originally at the top of a flight of steps, is now well below
that of the square. Before the embankment was constructed at the

end of the last century this part of Rome was regularly flooded, and tourists rowed inside the Pantheon by candlelight.

Inside, the lightness and feeling of immense space are a revelation. The dome, larger than that of St Peter's, appears to float effortlessly overhead, a sensation enhanced by the view of the sky through the oculus. The exact correlation between the height and the diameter add to the sense of harmony. The massive side walls have supported the tremendous weight of the concrete dome for almost two thousand years. Robert Adam was one of many who thought the Pantheon the finest of all Roman monuments, and it was a favourite subject of Piranesi, whose etchings were hugely popular with Grand Tourists.

Unfortunately the monuments inside are dull, although a number of famous artists are buried here, notably Raphael whose tomb is still bestrewn with flowers. It also houses the tombs of several kings of Italy since the Risorgimento.

If you are tempted by Rome's ice-creams, the most famous *gelateria* in the city stands virtually next to the Pantheon. Head north out of the piazza and take the first right into Via Uffici del Vicario, where Giolitti is on your right. Just beyond is the **Piccola Roma**, an excellent restaurant where you can sample delicious *abbachio al forno*.

Directly behind the Pantheon down Via della Minerva stands the Piazza Minerva, with Bernini's delightful statue of an elephant with an obelisk on its back, an image widely reproduced in eighteenth-century bronzes and clocks. Next to the elephant is the ochre façade of the only Gothic church in Rome, **Santa Maria sopra Minerva**, built in 1280 at the same time as Santa Maria Novella, its sister church in Florence.

The interior contains the tombs of Fra Angelico, the Medici Popes Leo X and Clement VII, and (under the high altar) St Catherine of Siena, who did so much to persuade the popes to return from Avignon. To the left is Michelangelo's second-rate statue of *The Risen Christ*.

The Carafa chapel in the right transept has delightful frescoes by Filippino Lippi, painted from 1488 to 1492, depicting the *Annunciation with St Thomas Aquinas Presenting Cardinal Carafa to the Virgin* on the altar wall, and *St Thomas Aquinas Confounding the Heretics* on the right wall. The chapel also contains the tomb of the horrid Pope Paul IV Carafa, whose championship of the Inquisition during his papacy between 1555 and 1559 did so much to eradicate the humanist spirit of the Renaissance. It was in the monastery adjoining this church that the famous trial of Galileo took place in 1633, in which he was forced to recant his theory that the earth rotates around the sun.

If you feel like lunch now, the **Ristorante Santa Chiara** on the far side of Piazza della Minerva is famous for its fish and for deep-fried fresh vegetables such as *fiori di zucchi* (courgette flowers).

Alternatively, you might like to visit the grandest Baroque palace in Rome before it closes at 1 p.m. Walk down Via Santa Caterina di Siena which turns into Via Pie di Marmo, past some appetising food shops to the Piazza del Collegio Romano and the two wings of the vast **Palazzo Doria Pamphilj**, designed by Antonio del Grande in the seventeenth century, stand at the far end of the square. It contains the collections accumulated from a series of dynastic marriages between the Aldobrandini, Pamphili and Doria families.

The picture galleries surround a courtyard and are divided into separate categories. On the right-hand wall are the sixteenth- and early seventeenth-century paintings, notably a delectable Titian of *Salome*, a penetrating Raphael portrait of his friends Andrea Navagero and Agostino Beazzano, and three early Caravaggios including *Rest on the Flight into Egypt*, containing his only known landscape. The gallery beyond has more Baroque paintings, much appreciated by Grand Tourists, particularly those by Guido Reni and the Bolognese school, but now virtually ignored. In the far rooms off the courtyard are the Italian Primitives and the northern European paintings, most of mediocre quality but including a very rare Pieter Brueghel the Elder seascape.

The most famous masterpiece in the main gallery is the Velázquez portrait of the scheming Innocent X which hangs in its own room next to the Bernini bust of the same sitter. It was painted in 1650–1, on the artist's second visit to Rome as the official representative of the King of Spain. Although Velázquez was not well known in Rome, the portrait was an immediate success and the Pope showered him with honours. The wonderfully thick impasto of the Pope's red and white robes shows Velázquez's profound debt to Titian, many of whose finest paintings were in the Spanish royal collections; this marvellous freedom of brushwork strongly influenced Manet and the Impressionists. In the same section are all the best landscapes, including two ravishing views by Claude, and one by Annibale Carracci.

The sumptuous state apartments are among the grandest in Rome, with ornate gilded furniture placed beneath silk wall hangings and finely woven Flemish tapestries, and the highest quality cut-glass chandeliers hanging from the ceilings. Rare portraits of a man, supposedly Christopher Columbus by Jan Gossaert and of the

119

Genoese admiral Andrea Doria posing naked as Neptune, hang beside a beautiful Filippo Lippi *Annunciation* and a Memling *Deposition*.

Emerging from the palace, you can sample some excellent Tuscan cooking at **Il Buco**, in the far corner of the Piazza del Collegio Romano. Try the speciality of mixed pasta, particularly the *crespelle* (pancakes stuffed with ricotta cheese and spinach).

If you don't want to stop for lunch, grab a piece of pizza and you may just catch the end of the lively flower and vegetable market in the **Campo de' Fiori** by returning to the Piazza della Minerva, turning left down Via de' Cestari, right into Via Vittorio Emanuele and taking the third left after the great Baroque façade of Sant' Andrea della Valle. The Campo is named, as Fynes Moryson recounted, after the harlot Flora, in whose honour 'the harlots of Rome kept a yeerely feast, and used to runne naked into this field, with unspeakable libertie of speech and gesture'. The fruit and flower market in the square is a picturesque sight, enhanced by the piecemeal effect of the architecture, especially the extraordinary building at the east end of the square which looks as though it has been sheared in half.

The history of the square is rather grimmer than its present-day appearance would suggest. It was used as a place of execution during the Papacy, and a huge crowd watched the burning of the philosopher Giordano Bruno in 1600, against whose statue little children now play football. Six years later Caravaggio killed a man in a duel after a ball game in the square and was forced to flee Rome.

Byron was very affected by his visit in 1817. He wrote to John Murray:

> The day before I left Rome I saw three robbers guillotined – the ceremony – including the masqued priests – the half-naked executioners – the bandaged criminals – the black Christ and his banner – the scaffold – the soldiery – the slow procession – & the quick rattle and heavy fall of the axe – the splash of the blood – & the ghastliness of the exposed heads – is altogether more impressive than the vulgar and ungentlemanly dirty 'new drop' & doglike agony of infliction upon the sufferers of the English sentence . . . The first of the three died with great terror and reluctance – which was very horrible – he would not lie down – then his neck was too large for the aperture – and the priest was obliged to drown his exclamations by still louder exhortations – the head was off before the eye could trace the blow . . . The first turned me quite hot and thirsty – & made me shake so that I could hardly hold the opera-glass.

The surrounding streets are full of shops of craftsmen, many of whom continue to practise the original trades of the area, like the Via Balestra, known locally as Via de' Materassi, where mattresses are still made.

The Piazza Farnese, south of the Campo de' Fiori, has two handsome fountains constructed from ancient Roman baths, purloined from the Baths of Caracalla. The square focuses on the **Palazzo Farnese**, the largest Renaissance palace in the city. It was built in the first half of the sixteenth century by Antonio da Sangallo and Michelangelo for Cardinal Farnese, later Pope Paul III (on the proceeds, so it is said, of what his beautiful sister earned as mistress of Alexander VI, the Borgia pope). The plain façade, dominated by the large cornice Michelangelo added in 1546, is on a grandiose scale, in keeping with the Colosseum from which the stone was quarried. Since 1871 the palace has been the French Embassy; if you want to gain admittance, write in advance to the French Embassy (see Information) and remember to take your passport. It is well worth the effort.

Passing through a vestibule, whose vault is based on the ancient Roman Theatre of Marcellus, you enter a courtyard of impressive severity lightened only by Vignola's open loggia in the centre of the top storey facing towards the Tiber. Michelangelo's original plan had been to link the palace with the Villa Farnesina, which is directly across the river, but this proved beyond even his capabilities.

From the courtyard a staircase ascends to the Salon d' Hercule, a gigantic room containing a copy of the *Farnese Hercules* and two recumbent statues by the fireplace originally intended for Paul III's tomb in St Peter's. The crowning glory of the palace is the Carracci gallery, which Annibale Carracci painted between 1597 and 1603, contemporary with Caravaggio's paintings in San Luigi dei Francesi. This complex fresco cycle, with its brilliant colours and riot of movement, is a key work in the development of the Baroque. The ceiling is covered with scenes from Ovid's *Metamorphoses* depicting the amorous exploits of the gods of Olympus. It focuses on the central scene of the *Triumph of Bacchus*, where an exuberant crowd of revellers draw Bacchus and Ariadne, seated in their chariot, across the ceiling. Commissioned by a Roman Cardinal, the frescoes unashamedly proclaim the triumph of love.

In the eighteenth century the Bourbons of Naples inherited the fabulous Farnese collections and removed all the paintings and sculpture to Naples, including the *Farnese Hercules*, where they are now housed in the Capodimonte Museum and the Museo Archeologico Nazionale (see pages 168–70 and pages 162–3). In 1787

Goethe lamented: 'Rome is threatened with a great loss. The King of Naples is going to transport the *Farnese Hercules* to his palace. All the artists are in mourning,' and added bitterly: 'If they could transport the Gallery with the Carracci . . . they would.'

Emerging from the palace turn right down Vicolo de' Venti, passing several shops selling excellent reproduction sculpture and tiles, to the **Palazzo Spada** in the Piazza di Capo di Ferro, whose intricate stucco façade contrasts with the massive Palazzo Farnese. Cardinal Capodiferro built the Palazzo Spada in the mid-sixteenth century, and the lightness of the stuccowork reflects the influence of the Palace of Fontainebleau where he was ambassador to François I in the 1530s. The recent cleaning of the façade and courtyard have brought out the light, playful quality of the classical decoration. The garden on the left contains a wonderful *trompe l'oeil* colonnade designed by Borromini. As you walk through it you are trapped between the ascending floor and the descending ceiling. Early travellers' accounts of the palace almost invariably mention the classical statue of Pompey which they associated with the one at whose feet Caesar fell, and pass over the Borromini colonnade in silence. The Palazzo Spada, with its closely hung furnishings, is a splendid example of what a Roman palace must have looked like in the eighteenth century, but you will have to come back in the morning to be able to visit the gallery on the first floor.

INFORMATION

Palazzo Doria Pamphilj: Tuesday, Friday, Saturday and Sunday 9 a.m. to 1 p.m., guided tours of the state apartments every half hour

Palazzo Farnese: to gain admittance write to the French Embassy, Palazzo Farnese, Piazza Farnese

Palazzo Spada: courtyard and colonnade open all day; gallery: 9 a.m. to 2 p.m., closed Monday

RESTAURANTS

Piccola Roma
Via Uffici del Vicario 36, Rome
Telephone: 06 679 8606, closed Sunday

Il Buco
Via Sant' Ignazio 8, Rome
Telephone: 06 679 3298, closed Monday

They speak a dialect of their own, are bigoted in their wor-
ship of the Madonna, and extremely gasconading in their
manners

Lady Morgan

TRASTEVERE: SANTA CECILIA~
SANTA MARIA IN TRASTEVERE~TEMPIETTO~
VILLA FARNESINA~PIAZZA SAN PIETRO

If you would like to sample the atmosphere of old Rome, there is
nowhere better than Trastevere, a working-class area whose inhabitants have always fought for their independence, at the foot of the
Janiculum Hill across the Tiber from the Ghetto. The area remains
one of the least spoilt areas of modern Rome, full of winding streets,
crumbling stucco façades and medieval churches: in general, a good
place to recover from three days' intensive sightseeing.

If you walk through the district on a Tuesday or Thursday
morning, you can include a visit to the frescoes in the church of
Santa Cecilia, built on the site of the house of St Cecilia who was
martyred in 230. The eighteenth-century façade by Ferdinando
Fuga complements the medieval portico and the twelfth-century
brick campanile.

The interior is a less successful combination of styles, the eighteenth-century redecoration probably destroying much of Pietro Cavallini's work in the process. All that remains is his fragmentary fresco of the *Last Judgement* high up on the entrance wall, dating from the 1290s, which shows remarkable sensitivity in the treatment of light and colour on the faces and draperies of the Apostles.

Arnolfo di Cambio's Gothic ciborium (canopy) above the high altar, dating from 1283, is contemporary with Cavallini's work. Both Arnolfo and Cavallini were disregarded by Grand Tourists, who came to the church to listen to the choir (St Cecilia being the patron saint of music) and to admire Maderno's beautiful and touching statue of St Cecilia, carved shortly after the sculptor had witnessed the opening of her tomb in 1599; the saint's body was lying in the position he used for his sculpture.

Leave the church by the charming garden outside the entrance, turn left and left again into Via dei Genovesi. This leads to the hideously noisy Viale Trastevere which bisects the area. Cross over and turn right, and take the first left by the medieval campanile of San Crisogono into Via della Lungaretta, which leads to the beautiful Piazza Santa Maria in Trastevere, the heart of the district.

The church of **Santa Maria in Trastevere**, which dominates the square, dates from the fourth century and is the earliest church in Rome dedicated to the Virgin. The fine Cosmatesque pavement, the splendid Ionic columns taken from classical buildings, and the glittering twelfth- and thirteenth-century mosaics glorifying the Virgin, both on the façade and in the apse, make this the most splendid church in Trastevere. The six scenes of the *Life of the Virgin* round the apse are by the same Pietro Cavallini who painted the fresco in Santa Cecilia. Jacobite enthusiasts can admire the chapel to the right of the apse, which was restored by the Cardinal of York, who placed his royal coat-of-arms over the door.

The Early Christian antiquities in the church are one of the undiscovered joys of Rome, although dismissed by Addison as 'so embroil'd with Fable and Legend, that one receives but little Satisfaction from searching into them'. The neo-classical sculptor Flaxman, who influenced nineteenth-century artists as diverse as Blake and Ingres, was one of the few who appreciated them, and he made copies of the mosaics.

The piazza outside the church is an ideal place to stop for a cappuccino. For the more adventurous a short climb up the Janiculum Hill leads to the church of San Pietro in Montorio. Take Via della Paglia past the right wall of the church, bear right into Via della Frusta, cross over Via Garibaldi and climb the steps up to San Pietro in Montorio.

The **Tempietto** by Bramante, which adjoins the church, made his reputation and is traditionally cited as the first building of the Roman High Renaissance. It was erected on the supposed site of the crucifixion of St Peter and was commissioned by Ferdinand and Isabella of Spain in 1502. The combination of the simple Tuscan Doric order and the harmony of the proportions gives the Tempietto a feeling of grandeur out of all proportion to its size. Inigo Jones, one of many budding architects who came to visit this masterpiece while on the Grand Tour, was profoundly impressed.

The chapel on the right of the entrance door of the main church contains Sebastiano del Piombo's powerful *Flagellation*, based on drawings by Michelangelo. Until 1809 his great rival Raphael's *Transfiguration* hung over the high altar; it now hangs in the Pinacoteca in the Vatican. All visitors, British and American alike, lavished praise on Raphael's altarpiece, many considering it the greatest painting in the world. Only Tobias Smollett, as so often holding a heretical view, thought the composition disjointed and would have liked to cut it in half. Outside the church there is a wonderful view over the city if you can see round the newly married couples posing self-consciously on the terrace.

Returning down the stairs below the church, turn left and follow Via Garibaldi down the hill towards the Tiber. Via Lungara, on your left at the bottom of the street, takes you to the **Villa Farnesina**, the most charming Renaissance villa in Rome, and one that contains works by all the leading artists (except Michelangelo) who were working in the city in the second decade of the sixteenth century.

The Villa was built between 1508 and 1511 by the Sienese architect Peruzzi for his compatriot Agostino Chigi, the fabulously wealthy papal banker. The gardens of the Villa used to lead down to the Tiber into which Chigi threw his gold plate after dinner in order to impress his guests, and waited till they had departed before fishing them out of the nets concealed in the water.

A pagan scheme of decoration appealed to Chigi and his genial friend Leo X, who officiated at Chigi's wedding to his mistress Andreosia after the Pope had already baptised their four illegitimate children. The famous loggia on the ground floor was decorated by Raphael's pupils with scenes from the touching love story of Cupid and Psyche, to commemorate Chigi's wedding. Opinion has always been sharply divided over these frescoes: even before work stopped in 1517 rumours abounded that Raphael was so sated by his mistress, La Fornarina, that he was unable to paint. Michelangelo was very unimpressed with the frescoes, but by the eighteenth century they were accepted as one of Raphael's masterpieces. Goethe frequently came here with the painter Angelica Kauffmann, who was half in love with him, and thought them the most beautiful decorations he had ever seen.

The adjoining room, which was also designed as an open-air loggia facing the Tiber, was enclosed in the seventeenth century. Raphael's beautiful *Triumph of Galatea* re-emphasises the theme of love as the graceful figure of the nymph is drawn across the waves on her scallop-shell by a pair of dolphins while winged cupids fire arrows at her and her companions frolic at will. The brooding figure of *Polyphemus*, deprived of his love, in Sebastiano del Piombo's adjacent fresco, stares morosely at Galatea, reflecting the bitter rivalry between the two artists. Sebastiano also painted the scenes from Ovid's *Metamorphoses* in the lunettes. Peruzzi, who had started life as a painter, drew the colossal head in a lunette, and frescoed the ceiling with the position of the planets and stars on 1 December 1446, the date of Chigi's birth.

The first room you enter at the top of the staircase on the first floor is the Sala delle Prospettive, Peruzzi's *tour de force*. The illusionistic architecture is so carefully constructed that it appears totally realistic, giving a good idea of how Trastevere and the Borgo (the area round St Peter's) must have looked when Peruzzi painted it in 1515–17. Next door was Chigi's own bedroom, frescoed by Sodoma with scenes from the life of Alexander the Great. The *Marriage of Alexander and Roxana* is an intensely sensual painting where the gap in the balustrade appears to invite the spectator into their bedroom.

Trastevere is full of restaurants. Two of the best are in the Piazza Santa Maria in Trastevere, which lies at the end of Via della Lungara and its extension Via della Scala. **Sabatini** and **Galeassi** both specialise in typical Roman cuisine and seafood while **Da Ivo**, which is just behind the square, is the most famous pizzeria in Rome. An alternative restaurant is **Checco er Carrettiere** at Via Benedetta 10, which has a quiet and shady eating area. From the Farnesina head down Via della Lungara through the fortified Porta Settimiana, and turn left into Via Santa Dorotea and bear right into Via Benedetta.

After lunch, if you can resist a siesta, you should visit St Peter's. Cross over the pedestrianised Ponte Sisto, which stands next to Checco er Carrettiere, and just down Via del Moro from Piazza Santa Maria. On the far side of the Tiber, take a no. 65 bus to the Porta Cavallegeri, which is just south of the **Piazza San Pietro**.

The enormous oval forecourt of St Peter's was built by Bernini between 1656 and 1667. The two arms of the oval, surmounted by a forest of statues, encompass the pilgrims who come here for papal audiences and to witness the Pope's appearance on the balcony of

St Peter's on Christmas Day and Easter morning. It is still possible to have a papal audience in the Piazza on a Wednesday morning.

The history of the present basilica begins with Bramante's destruction of the Constantinian basilica in the early sixteenth century, and his commencement of a vast domed building based on a Greek cross plan, inspired by his study of the ancient Roman baths. Bramante's death in 1514 was followed by a hiatus until Michelangelo took over in 1547. He reverted to a simplified version of Bramante's plan and increased the sense of scale by introducing a giant order of Corinthian pilasters around the walls of the exterior. Before Michelangelo's death in 1564 much of the apse, transepts and nave had been completed, and his pupil Giacomo della Porta erected the dome to his design in 1590. In the early seventeenth century Maderno completed the destruction of Constantine's basilica, lengthened the nave and built the façade. The basilica was consecrated in 1626, thirteen hundred years after the initial consecration.

Early visitors were amazed at the scale of St Peter's. John Evelyn, coming here in 1644, rhapsodised over 'that most stupendous and incomparable Basilicum, far surpassing any now extant in the world, and perhaps, Solomon's temple excepted, any that was ever built'. The only criticism of the exterior was directed at Maderno's lengthening of the nave which has ruined the view of the dome from the front and becomes more apparent as you approach the façade.

The splendid decoration of the interior is in large measure the creation of Bernini, who worked on the monuments in St Peter's from 1624 until his death in 1680, and epitomises the triumph of the Catholic Church in the age of the Baroque. In the first chapel in the right aisle stands Michelangelo's *Pietà*. Executed in 1499 when Michelangelo was only twenty-four, it is one of his most beautiful works and the only sculpture that he ever signed. It has been miraculously repaired after a madman attacked it with an axe some twenty years ago. It is entirely fitting that it should stand in his greatest work of architecture.

The nave leads to Bernini's huge Baldacchino, an extraordinary fusion of sculpture and architecture. Cast from bronze stripped from the roof of the Pantheon, it is supported by barley-sugar columns which hark back to the original Constantinian basilica. It was unveiled by Urban VIII in 1633. Notice the agonised female faces entwined with the Barberini bees on the reliefs at the foot of the columns. They are said to represent the pain the Pope's niece suffered giving birth, while the placid face looking towards the nave represents her safe delivery.

Bernini's second major work in St Peter's is the Cathedra of St Peter (1657–65) which stands in the tribune. The ancient wooden chair, supposedly used by St Peter himself, is hidden from view, but Bernini's substitute, surrounded by a halo of light, hovers above statues of the Four Fathers of the Church. The enormous scale of the basilica compelled Bernini to adopt theatrical devices; in the Cathedra he displayed the full mastery of dramatic effects so that it appears as a theatrical *tableau vivant*, inviting the participation of the spectator.

INFORMATION

Santa Cecilia (Cavallini fresco): Tuesday and Thursday 10 a.m. to 12 noon
Villa Farnesina: 9 a.m. to 1 p.m., closed Sunday
Papal Audience: for tickets apply to Prefettura della Casa Pontifica, Città del Vaticano 00120 6982

RESTAURANTS

Checco er Carrettiere
Via Benedetta 10, Rome
Telephone: 06 581 7018, closed Sunday evening and Monday

Galeassi
Piazza di Santa Maria in Trastevere 3, Rome
Telephone: 06 580 3775, closed Monday

Sabatini
two branches, either Piazza di Santa Maria in Trastevere 13, Rome
Telephone: 06 582 026, closed Wednesday
or Vicolo Santa Maria in Trastevere, Rome
Telephone: 06 581 8307, closed Tuesday

I ate my midday meal there and took my siesta on the papal throne

Goethe

THE VATICAN: THE SISTINE CHAPEL~THE STANZE

The Vatican State, the remnant of the Papal States, where the Papacy has resided since the Unification of Italy in 1870, is unsurpassed in its collection of art. During the whole period of the Grand Tour, the popes preferred to live in their palace on the Quirinal Hill; consequently, the rooms decorated by the Renaissance popes after their return from Avignon in 1417 have been almost perfectly preserved. The most celebrated of these are the Sistine Chapel and the Stanze.

During the Grand Tour visitors flocked to the **Sistine Chapel**, primarily for the excitement of seeing the Pope conduct a service and to listen to the Papal Choir, which included a number of famous *castrati*, the last of whom, Alessandro Moreschi, retired as recently as 1913. Lady Morgan described the scene on Maundy Thursday, 1821, when the crowd entered without tickets:

> A scene of indescribable confusion ensues. The guards get mingled with the multitude. English peers are overturned by Roman canons. Irish friars batter the old armour of the mailed halberdiers with fists more formidable than the iron they attack. Italian priests tumble over tight-laced dandies; and the 'Via Via' of the Roman guard, and the 'Fous ne restez pas issi'

of the Swiss, mingle with screams, supplications, reproofs, and the English 'God-dam', long after the solemn service of the church has begun. The Viceregent of God on earth in vain represents, the cross of peace in vain shines above the high altar: tranquillity is only restored when suffocation begins.

A visit to the Vatican Museums today tends to assume the same manic chaos. If you can face the crowds, an early morning visit to see the newly restored Michelangelo frescoes on the Sistine ceiling is one of the most exciting experiences Rome can offer. The Chapel is far and away the most popular site in the Vatican and it is essential to arrive at the entrance to the museum before 9 a.m. There is little chance of your emulating Goethe, who recorded: 'I ate my midday meal there and took my siesta on the papal throne.'

The masterpieces in the Sistine Chapel date from three different eras of the Renaissance. The scenes from the lives of Moses and Christ on the walls are by Perugino and his Florentine contemporaries, and were commissioned by Sixtus IV when the chapel was built in the 1480s; the Michelangelo frescoes on the vault date from 1508–12; and his *Last Judgement* was painted from 1536 to 1541.

Visitors have varied widely in their appreciation of these frescoes. In the seventeenth century the overpowering nudes of the *Last Judgement* appealed most, and some writers, such as Richard Lassels, ignored the ceiling altogether. During the eighteenth century, however, the Sistine ceiling was regarded as the highest point to which painting could aspire. Goethe, like many others, came here numerous times, and felt that until you had seen it 'you can have no adequate conception of what man is capable of accomplishing'. The scale of Michelangelo's achievement, the power of the figures and the complexity of their movements were regarded as the summit of human artistic achievement. Some admired the *Last Judgement*, but in general it was felt to lack the sublimity of the vault.

Those few who noticed the frescoes on the walls attributed them to Perugino, but made no attempt to separate the works of the various artists involved. As late as 1831 the painter Fuseli thought the walls of the chapel 'a monument of puerile ostentation'. Taste only changed in the middle of the nineteenth century, when Perugino, Signorelli and Botticelli replaced Michelangelo as the most favoured artists. Ruskin referred to Michelangelo as the 'captain of evil' and Lady Eastlake, the wife of the first director of the National Gallery, thought the Sistine ceiling 'coarse and ungraceful' and the *Last Judgement* 'a daub'.

The **Stanze**, the official apartments of Julius II and later

Renaissance popes, stand next to the Sistine Chapel. Evelyn thought them 'one of the most Superb and royall Appartments in the world, much too beautifull for a guard of gigantic Swizzers who do nothing but drinke, and play at Cards in it'. The rooms were frescoed by Raphael at the same time as Michelangelo was working in the Sistine Chapel. The earliest frescoes, in the Stanza della Segnatura, are static compositions, full of harmony and beauty. In the next rooms, the Stanza d' Eliodoro and the Stanza dell' Incendio, Raphael introduced greater drama and movement, particularly the wonderful night scene of the *Liberation of St Peter*. The final room, the Sala di Costantino, is the work of Raphael and his pupils, particularly Giulio Romano, and tends to be regarded as of inferior quality and is often ignored. Grand Tourists, on the other hand, made little distinction in quality between the work of Raphael and his followers, and many of them preferred the Sala di Costantino.

The chapel of Nicholas V is a minute room frescoed by Fra Angelico and Gozzoli between 1447 and 1449 with charming scenes from the lives of St Stephen and St Lawrence. The frescoes have retained their purity of colour and reflect the optimism of this pope, the founder of the Vatican library, who did so much to re-establish Rome as the artistic centre of Italy. Fra Angelico's devoutness exactly suited the Victorians, who contrasted it with the paganism of the later Renaissance popes.

On the way out of the Vatican, you will be following closely in Grand Tourist footsteps if you glance in at the Pinacoteca, a collection composed of the paintings brought back to Italy from France in 1815. Chief among these are Raphael's *Transfiguration*, 'justly considered the first oil painting in existence' in Murray's *Handbook*, and valued so highly by the French (who removed it from the church of San Pietro in Montorio in 1809) that they did not dare to transfer it from panel to canvas. Raphael's *Madonna di Foligno* and Domenichino's *Communion of St Jerome* were rated almost as highly as the *Transfiguration*, and far above Giotto's *Crucifixion* or Caravaggio's *Entombment*, which was condemned by Murray as 'deficient in religious expression'.

A final stop in the Vatican is the Belvedere court, designed by Bramante at the beginning of the sixteenth century, and the setting for some of the most famous antique sculptures in the world. Indeed, seventeenth and eighteenth-century visitors rated the statues here and in the Museo Pio-Clementino, which houses the collections formed in the eighteenth century by Pius VI and Clement XIV, far more highly than the Michelangelos and Raphaels.

The group of *Laocoon and His Sons*, which had been highly

praised by Pliny the Elder, was dug up in 1506, one of the most thrilling discoveries of the Renaissance. By chance, Michelangelo was one of the first on the site, and the agonised expressions of the figures and contortions of their bodies as they attempt to escape from the grasp of the pursuing serpents were to be extremely influential on his painting and sculpture.

Seventeenth- and eighteenth-century visitors were immensely impressed by the group but, with characteristic disregard for archaeological purity, praised the way that the sculpture was completed in the sixteenth century by the inaccurate replacement of the missing arm. The beauty of the *Apollo Belvedere*, in a neighbouring niche, was eulogised by countless visitors and widely copied by artists. Both Reynolds and Ramsay, two of the leading eighteenth-century British painters, used the pose in their portraits.

Roman society was fascinated by the impact these classical statues would make on the American painter Benjamin West, who was thought to resemble Rousseau's noble savage, a fresh mind untainted by the associations of European civilisation. He was followed to the Vatican by thirty carriages full of inquisitive Romans; he came straight to see the *Apollo Belvedere* and exclaimed: 'My God, a young Mohawk warrior.' Byron, as usual, took a more frivolous line. He wrote to Thomas Moore on 12 May 1817: 'The *Apollo Belvedere* is the image of Lady Adelaide Forbes – I think I never saw such a likeness.'

By now you will almost certainly be in need of a break, and **Pierdonati's** is a good restaurant near the entrance to the museums. Follow the signs for St Peter's, and Pierdonati's is 150 metres on the right down Via della Conciliazione, the avenue Mussolini cut through the middle of the Borgo in the 1930s. Here you will eat well in a cool haven, a welcome relief from the surfeit of souvenir shops.

INFORMATION

Vatican Museums: October to June, Monday to Saturday 9 a.m. to 2 p.m., July to September 9 a.m. to 4 p.m., Saturday 9 a.m. to 1 p.m., closed Sunday except last Sunday of the month

RESTAURANT

Pierdonati
Via della Conciliazione 39, Rome
Telephone: 06 654 3557, closed Thursday

ENVIRONS
OF ROME

The desolation of the Campagna assumed a smile, the amiability of a wilderness in an eighteenth-century park
Edmond de Goncourt

When the pressure of life in Rome becomes too much, you can emulate generations of travellers by escaping into the surrounding countryside. For centuries Roman cardinals and nobles retreated into the Alban Hills 25 km south-east of Rome, and relaxed at their villas in Frascati and Tivoli. The eighteenth-century traveller's nerves were frayed by the same combination of overpowering heat and appalling noise that afflicts the modern visitor. Thomas Mansel Talbot described the effect of the heat to his uncle William Beach:

> However the smallpox has not made such ravages as last summer when above 5,000 persons, mostly children, were taken off by that cruel disease. You know that the Italians are revengefull & much given to stabbing with stilettos or knives: this cool season has not prevented this diversion. Above 25 persons have been struck within 2 months . . . We expect great sport, this month of August particularly, as the weather begins to be insufferably hot. In the time of the vintage, September, 'tis incredible the number, as they then aledge the new wine for an excuse.

Artists were inspired by the beauty of the landscape, dotted with Roman ruins and the Claudian aqueduct running south from the city formed the backdrop to many a landscape by painters aspiring to emulate the genius of Claude Lorraine whose works were so popular with Grand Tourists. Thomas Jones, a follower of the landscape painter Richard Wilson, was entranced by the scenery, and eulogised: 'Every scene seemed anticipated in some dream, it appeared Magick land.'

For the more enterprising there was always the possibility of making a fortune. The painter, archaeologist and dealer Gavin

135

Hamilton organised digs at Ostia, down the Appian Way and at Hadrian's Villa, where he made spectacular finds including the Warwick Vase. His clients included the Pope, Catherine the Great, the Duke of Dorset, the Earl of Warwick, Lord Shelburne and Charles Townley, all of them avid collectors.

You can either sample the delights of the villas at Tivoli and Frascati or the impressive Roman ruins at Ostia Antica, or simply head into the beautiful Alban Hills to explore the towns and villages clustered around the lakes.

Tivoli

A terrestrial paradise
Fynes Moryson

31 km east of Rome on the Via Tiburtina (SS 5)

VILLA ADRIANA~MARITIME TEMPLE~PIAZZO D' ORO~ CANOPUS~VILLA D' ESTE~CASTELLO DI LUNGHEZZA

Tivoli, a fashionable retreat from Rome since the days of the Emperor Hadrian, stands on a hill just beyond the city's suburban limits. To the Grand Tourist, steeped in classical antiquity, there could be no more fascinating excursion than to inspect the extensive ruins of Hadrian's magnificent Villa followed by a visit to the Villa d' Este, the most famous of all Renaissance gardens and directly influenced by Hadrian's creation. Anyone with a penchant for the romantic or the formal garden will find the villas still make a thoroughly rewarding day out from Rome.

Leave Rome on the Via Tiburtina and follow the sign to the **Villa Adriana** (Hadrian's Villa) just below the town. Hadrian's extensive building programme between 118 and 138 AD created the most splendid villa in the world, but it has remained derelict ever since his death, although centuries of looting have only served to enhance its atmosphere of decayed grandeur.

Hadrian himself was a proto-Grand Tourist who travelled all over his empire. His recreation of the classical buildings which had impressed him most on his travels was similar to that of the English Milord who erected classical follies in his park on his return from his travels. He used many of the buildings as architectural experiments

136

before he began work on the Pantheon in Rome. The Romans had only recently discovered the use of concrete and the inherent strength of this new material enabled Hadrian to vault enormous spaces. There are acres of ruins to explore and it takes several hours to wander round the whole site.

The discovery of antique sculptures in the Villa excited tremendous interest during the Renaissance, and induced Raphael to make a visit in April 1516 with his friends Castiglione, the author of *The Courtier*, and Cardinal Bembo. The first systematic excavations were carried out by Pirro Ligorio in the middle of the sixteenth century; he moved many of the statues found on the site to the garden of the Villa d' Este which he was building for Cardinal Ippolito d' Este. The publication of his researches encouraged excavators, and a series of spectacular finds were made throughout the eighteenth century. Many famous sculptures in Clement XII's new museum on the Capitol, opened in 1733, came from the Villa, including several statues of Antinous, two *Centaurs*, and the *Faun in Rosso Antico*. They were particularly admired for their association with the Emperor Hadrian, who spent much of his reign erecting monuments to his lover Antinous who had tragically drowned in the Nile.

A large amount of the sculpture dug up appeared on the art market, since the popes only kept one-third of the finds made in the Papal States. Thomas Jenkins and Gavin Hamilton, two of the leading dealers in eighteenth-century Rome, exported much of this sculpture to England, including the *Discobolus*, dug up in 1791, and sold by Jenkins to the collector Charles Townley for £400, who proceeded to make it the centrepiece of his famous collection; it is now in the British Museum. Even more important was Gavin Hamilton's discovery of the Warwick Vase in 1771, which was bought by the leading antiquarian Sir William Hamilton, who sold it to the Earl of Warwick. Its fame was so great that Napoleon placed it first on the list of works of art to be taken to France after his conquest of Britain; it now resides in the British Museum.

Many architects were inspired by the extensive ruins of the Villa. Borromini, the most daring Baroque architect, made measured drawings of them, and Piranesi, who signed his name in the cryptoporticus a century later, made a series of engravings which influenced neo-classical architects such as Robert Adam and Clérisseau, who came here in April 1756 with their friend Mr Hervey. Hervey read *Tom Jones* to them while they were sketching and so keen were their sensibilities that they 'hugged the lovely Sophia amidst the ruins of that ancient palace'. Adam later bought Pirro Ligorio's plan of the Villa.

Hubert Robert and Fragonard, who spent many hours sketching here, were the most famous of many artists inspired by the ruins, their picturesque quality greatly enhanced by the cypress trees Count Fede planted throughout the site in 1730. Casanova spent six hours looking at the site in 1743, but was more interested in sleeping with two sisters, one a betrothed virgin.

The model of the Villa in the room next to the coffee shop gives you some idea of the vast scale of the original although scholars are still arguing over the functions of the various buildings. The Villa's size was greater than that of many towns in the empire, with baths, theatres, libraries and barracks as well as the quarters of the emperor and his household. There was no unified plan, an informal feature that was to influence seventeenth-century Baroque gardens such as the Borghese Gardens in Rome.

The most attractive building is the **Maritime Temple**, which sits on a little island to the left of the entrance. The movable bridges spanning the pool enabled Hadrian to isolate himself from his courtiers. The little house contained its own dining-room, library and bath. The idea of an island in the middle of a pool inspired imitations at the Villa Lante and the Boboli Gardens, two of the most famous Renaissance gardens.

The Maritime Temple stands on the edge of the Imperial Palace, a complex of buildings, probably used for the emperor's private quarters. At the south-eastern corner the splendid **Piazza d' Oro** is named after the wealth of sculpture that was excavated here. South of the Imperial Palace there is a Nymphaeum, flanked by some majestic cypresses. The two bath-houses beyond are roofed with a series of complex vaults which revolutionised Borromini's ideas on architecture.

At the very far end of the site is the **Canopus**, a beautiful pool surrounded by copies of Greek statuary and designed to imitate the sanctuary of Serapis at Alexandria. Hadrian used it for lavish entertainment and it is easy to imagine the emperor and his friends reclining beside the water. On a fine day, with the wild cyclamen flowering among the ruins, this is one of the most romantic sites in all Italy.

To reach the town of Tivoli, drive back to the main road and turn right. Once you get to the main square, follow the signs to the Villa Gregoriana. The **Ristorante Sibilla**, an old inn where travellers lodged in the eighteenth century, stands next to the Temple of the Sibyl in a spectacular setting overlooking the ancient Falls of Tivoli. It is the classic view that artists loved to depict and was admired by visitors ranging from Evelyn to Thomas Gray, Chateaubriand and Florence Nightingale, although the cascade is much less spectacular since the falls have been dammed. The eccentric Earl-Bishop of Derry is reputed to have tried to buy the temple in 1828 so that he could transport it back to his home in Ireland.

After lunch, follow the signs to the **Villa d' Este**, park in the main piazza and walk down to the entrance past the numerous stalls selling tourist souvenirs. The Villa can be inundated with tourists; try to avoid going on a Sunday when most of the population of Rome seems to have the same idea.

The Villa is the creation of Cardinal Ippolito d' Este, the son of the infamous Lucrezia Borgia. Having three times missed the Papacy, he used his position as governor of Tivoli to acquire the most favourable site in the town and employed the eminent archaeologist Pirro Ligorio as his architect until the Cardinal's death in 1572.

Ligorio designed a formal town garden, laid out in a series of ramped terraces which criss-cross the hillside. His design was probably inspired by the classical temple of Praeneste near by and by Bramante's design for the Belvedere in the Vatican, which Ligorio completed. As at the Belvedere court, the garden was intended as a framework for the important sculptures unearthed in Hadrian's Villa. The Cardinal's collection was dispersed shortly after his death, and much of it now resides in the Capitoline Museum.

The sombre courtyard of the Villa d' Este, originally the cloister of a Benedictine convent, gives little idea of the splendours beyond. After passing through a series of rooms frescoed by Taddeo and Federico Zuccari in the 1560s, you emerge on to a balcony overlooking the spectacular fountains, created by the Cardinal's fountain-maker Macaroni, taking maximum advantage of the awkward, precipitous slope and the abundant supply of water from the river Aniene near by.

Begun in 1550, the garden's complex iconography centres on Hercules, from whom the Este family claimed descent. The entire garden glorifies Cardinal d' Este's virtues and his ability to transform nature into art. There are three main cross-axes, the first running from the Oval Fountain on the right, from which the water runs through the garden, to the Rometta Fountain on the left, with miniature representations of famous buildings in Rome. Much of this fountain collapsed down the hillside in the nineteenth century. Next to this fountain are those of Persephone and the Owl, which once made noises imitating birds.

From here a diagonal path leads down to the second cross-axis, the Path of the Hundred Fountains. Directly beneath it is the Dragon Fountain, erected in honour of Gregory XIII's visit in 1572.

On the level ground beneath, three fish ponds are flanked by the mightiest fountains of all, whose roar drowns every other noise. The Organ Fountain, above them, was much admired for the musical noises it made. The lowest part of the garden was originally laid out with flower beds and fruit trees but the whole is now dominated by great cypresses, planted in the eighteenth century, enhancing its romantic attraction but blocking many of the views, particularly on the central axis, and making it difficult to visualise the original plan. Ligorio intended the Villa to form the culmination of the central vista and therefore wanted visitors to enter the gate at the bottom of the garden, and to ascend the hillside.

Early visitors were amazed at the garden. Fynes Moryson, who came here in the 1590s, thought it a terrestrial paradise, with nightingales flying among the groves and fountains. A decade earlier, Montaigne had been very impressed by the statuary and fountains, and took a hearty delight in the water jokes with which the garden abounded, designed to soak the unwary. John Evelyn, sixty years later, was fascinated by the ingenuity of the Owl Fountain, where statues of songbirds created a variety of musical noises, which were silenced by the appearance of a stone owl.

Eighteenth-century tourists disliked the artifice of some of the fountains. Président de Brosses thought the Hundred Fountains 'wretched little squirts, only fit to amuse children', and the poet Thomas Gray complained in May 1740, of the garden 'containing two millions of superfine laurel hedges, a clump of cypress trees and half the river Teverone, that pisses into two thousand several chamberpots'. Later travellers preferred the romantic qualities of the garden; Dickens saw it as 'deserted and decaying among groves of melancholy pine and cypress-trees'.

Artists have always loved the Villa. Hubert Robert and Fragonard lived here for a whole summer in 1760 and countless painters have followed in their steps including Hackert, who came here with his friend Goethe, in the summer of 1787. In the nineteenth century Corot was inspired by the magical quality of the light and Liszt, who lived here periodically from 1865 to 1886, composed *Les Jeaux d' Eaux à la Villa d' Este* as a tribute to the garden's beauty.

Returning to Rome on the A 24 *autostrada*, follow the sign to Lunghezza after 15 km. The **Castello di Lunghezza**, somewhat off the beaten track, is traditionally said to be the site of the Rape of Lucretia. Centuries later Catherine de' Medici, orphaned at the age of three weeks, was brought up here before being sent to France to marry Henry II. From the Medici it passed to the Strozzi, who sold it in 1880 to the Swedish doctor Axel Munthe, the author of *The Story of San Michele*.

Upstairs the sitting-room is dominated by a powerful portrait of Eleanor of Toledo, the wife of the Grand Duke Cosimo I, attributed to Bronzino. The low doorway at the far end of the room was specially designed as the entrance to the young Catherine de' Medici's bedroom with its famous scalloped basin with a real pearl for a plug. The chapel, with a rather creepy statue of Axel Munthe's wife Hilda under the altar, leads to the great hall, with its intricate Cosmatesque seat, where bridal couples sat during the marriage feasts of the Strozzi and the Medici. Some of the most fascinating antique sculptures collected by Axel Munthe on his travels are displayed in the corner tower. For special groups, the descendants of Munthe will kindly display their best pictures, including a magical *Flight into Egypt*, attributed to Rembrandt and the pearl plug that Catherine de' Medici used, so it is worth enquiring in advance.

From Lunghezza, follow the signs to the A 24 *autostrada*, which leads to Rome.

INFORMATION

Hadrian's Villa: 9 a.m. to dusk, closed Monday
Villa d' Este: 9 a.m. to dusk, fountains play 10 a.m. to 1 p.m. and 2 p.m. to dusk, closed Monday
Castello di Lunghezza: Wednesday and Saturday guided tours at 11 a.m., 12 noon, 2 p m. and 3 p.m. For guided tours ring 06 618 0518

RESTAURANT

La Sibilla
Via Sibilla 50, Tivoli
Telephone: 0774 20281/ 292913, closed Monday

Appian Way~Castel Gandolfo~ Ariccia~Lake Nemi~Frascati

A noble prospect, beset with sepulchres and antiquities
John Evelyn

This day's excursion into the Alban hills south-east of Rome is favoured by Romans and foreigners alike. It begins on the **Appian Way**, rich with classical and Early Christian associations and runs from the Porta San Sebastiano down to Naples and on to Brindisi, the gateway to the eastern part of the empire.

The first part of the road passes the most extensive catacombs in Rome (St Calixtus, St Domitilla and St Sebastian), which have exerted a macabre fascination on generations of travellers exploring their labyrinthine passages by candlelight. The theory that the early Christians used them to escape from their persecutors has now been disproved, but they remain immensely popular. Those suffering from claustrophobia should definitely give them a miss.

Beyond the catacombs, the Appian Way, still partly paved with ancient Roman cobbles, is lined with Roman funerary monuments, the largest of which, such as the Tomb of Cecilia Metella, were turned into fortresses in the Middle Ages. After the great slave revolt led by Spartacus was crushed by Crassus in 63 BC, the Senate, terrified out of its wits, ordered the slaves to be crucified at intervals the whole way down this road from Rome to Naples.

Grand Tourists, particularly artists, revelling in the wealth of the classical associations, loved to take this route out of the city. The dapper Robert Adam, wearing a green silk short coat and waistcoat, and his stockings ungartered, walked out to sketch the ruins with his friend Piranesi; John Robert Cozens, who was taken on the Grand Tour as the personal artist of William Beckford, preferred to ride a jackass. Dickens walked all the way to Albano down the Appian Way, clambering over the remains of tombs and temples.

Eventually the old cobbled road joins the Via Appia Nuova. After about 16 km there is a sign on the left to **Castel Gandolfo**, the summer residence of the Pope, and the only part of the Papal States apart from the Vatican that was not incorporated in the Italian State in 1870. The simple church overlooking the village square is by Bernini.

In the eighteenth century Castel Gandolfo was in the depths of the countryside and the primitive locals were as yet unused to tourism. The artist Paul Sandby recorded how Richard Wilson, out sketching, was taken to be a spy and almost put to death. Wealthy foreigners, such as the dealer Thomas Jenkins, invested in property in the village. Angelica Kauffmann entertained her compatriots Hackert and Tischbein, who came to paint the local beauty spots, and it was at her house that Goethe fell hopelessly in love with Maddalena Ricci.

From Castel Gandolfo the road runs south-east for 6 km, through Albano to the picturesque village of **Ariccia**, dominated by the Chigi palace of Pope Alexander VII, who commissioned Bernini to restore it and to build the beautiful church of Santa Maria dell' Assunzione, modelled on the Pantheon, opposite. Hendrik Ibsen, one of a stream of Scandinavians to draw inspiration from the Campagna in the nineteenth century, settled here with his family in 1864. Hans Andersen, in his *Improvisatore*, waxed lyrical over the olive trees and the golden cistus growing wild by the roadside.

The next village is Genzano where the famous flower festival is held on the first Sunday after Corpus Domini. Beyond Genzano turn left to **Lake Nemi**, which lies in a volcanic crater. It is a beautifully secluded spot, known as Diana's looking-glass because of the stillness of the water; Byron described it in *Childe Harold's Pilgrimage* (1812–18) as 'navell'd in the woody hills'. Sir James Frazer begins his *Golden Bough* (1890) with a graphic account of the sacred grove of mistletoe beside the lake, guarded by a priest who qualified for the job by killing his predecessor. The little village of Nemi is an excellent place to stop for a picnic lunch and to enjoy the lovely view over the lake. John Robert Cozens, perhaps the most talented watercolourist to embark on the Grand Tour, painted an exquisite picture of this view.

An alternative route back to Rome passes through **Frascati**. Head north-west from Nemi and turn right through the Alban Hills to Rocca di Papa and Grottaferrata and on to Frascati, home of the famous white wine. In antiquity Frascati was the site of Tusculum where many of the rich and famous had villas, including Pliny the Younger, Cicero and the Emperor Nero. During the late sixteenth and seventeenth centuries, it became the favourite retreat for the Roman nobility who wished to escape from the heat of the city, and the whole hillside is covered with their villas.

In the eighteenth century Frascati was the see of the Cardinal of York, the younger brother of Bonnie Prince Charlie. He was a big attraction for Grand Tourists who were fascinated to meet the last

surviving male member of the house of Stuart. Boswell had the luck to see him presiding at mass in May 1765, and thought him 'majestic and elegant with the face of an angel'. In 1790 Thomas Coutts, the banker, came with his family to visit the Cardinal, who let Coutts's daughter try on the ring which his great-grandfather Charles I had worn at his coronation.

The **Villa Aldobrandini** overlooks the main square, where you can obtain permission to visit the park from the Azienda Autonoma di Soggiorno e Turismo. You reach the entrance by climbing up Via Massaia from the top left-hand corner of the square.

Designed by della Porta in 1598–1602 for Cardinal Pietro Aldobrandini, the nephew of Pope Clement VIII, and completed by Maderno, the Villa is the grandest in Frascati. From the terrace there is a wonderful distant view of Rome. The Villa is set on a steep slope which enabled the Cardinal to commission an extensive chain of fountains and cascades. Unlike those at the Villa d' Este, these are set behind the Villa and are meant to merge with the surrounding woodland. Water pours down the hillside in a series of cascades before passing between two Doric columns and tumbling into the nympheum below, centred on a globe supported by Atlas, flanked by statues of Pan and a centaur. The surrounding rooms were designed to protect guests from the heat of the Roman summer.

The way that the upper part of the garden merges with the

surrounding woods is typical of the Baroque desire for informality. John Evelyn, who visited the gardens of the Villa d' Este and the Villa Aldobrandini in 1644, much preferred the latter, describing them as 'full of elegance, groves, ascents and prospects surpassing in my opinion the most delicious places that my eyes ever beheld.' He was particularly taken with the way that water could be made to imitate musical instruments and songbirds.

A century later the sophisticated de Brosses objected to the statues but hugely enjoyed the water jokes. Having soaked themselves at the neighbouring Villa Mondragone, his friends repeated the process in the theatre and on the cascade. De Brosses was most amused when his friend Legouz turned on yet another valve and only succeeded in soaking himself: 'He fled with his breeches full of water running out into his shoes.' Goethe, who had a less hearty sense of humour, preferred the view, and commissioned a painting of it by Kaiserman which still hangs in his bedroom in Weimar. Frascati was badly bombed during the war, when it was the German headquarters.

Two restaurants worth trying, both with terraces, are Cacciani, in Via Diaz, and Spartaco in Via Letizia Bonaparte.

From Frascati it is 20 km back to Rome on the SS 215.

INFORMATION

Villa Aldobrandini, Frascati: Monday to Friday 9 a.m. to 1 p.m. Tickets available from Azienda di Soggiorno, Piazza Marconi 1, Frascati. Telephone: 06 942 0331

RESTAURANTS

Cacciani
Via Diaz 13, Frascati
Telephone: 06 942 0378, closed Tuesday

Spartaco
Via Letizia Bonaparte 1, Frascati
Telephone: 06 942 0431, closed Tuesday

Ostia Antica

*But nothing remains of the stately buildings of that City, but
some poore houses*

Fynes Moryson

*23 km from Rome on the Via del Mare (S 8) or the Via Ostiense.
Trains run frequently from Termini station.*

Ostia Antica, the ancient port of Rome near Fiumicino airport,
should not be confused with the hideous modern town of Ostia. The
ancient Roman port, through which all the capital's imports and
exports passed, played an immensely influential role right down to
the sack of Rome in 410 AD. Thereafter, it fell into decline and
became uninhabitable when the area became infected with malaria.
Much of the city has survived, and in spring is carpeted with wild
flowers, giving a delightful sense of the atmosphere of ancient Rome.

Despite its proximity to Rome, Ostia remains off the main
tourist's itinerary. After the grandeur of the palaces on the Palatine
Hill and the Baths of Caracalla and Diocletian, Ostia provides a
more modest example of how people actually lived. In the Forum,
now almost denuded of buildings, you need to use your imagination
to visualise Cicero, Caesar and all the other great Roman figures. In
Ostia, on the other hand, the buildings themselves, with their plain
brick façades and shop fronts where traders sold their wares, bring
the place to life. In the spacious Piazzale delle Corporazioni, where
the various guilds were housed, and overlooked by the Theatre, the
pavement is composed of a series of fascinating, well-preserved
mosaics showing the functions of the dockers, sailors, customs officials and foreign corporations who had offices here.

One of the main centres of urban society in ancient Rome was the
baths, of which there are a large number scattered throughout the
town. One of the most complete is the Baths of Neptune, which were
carefully constructed, with underground heating systems, glass in
the windows, and all the social amenities. The entrance hall has a
fine mosaic of Neptune in his chariot, surrounded by tritons,
nereids and dolphins.

Ostia has been excavated several times, most notably in the
1930s, when about half the ancient city was uncovered. Before

Mussolini drained the Pontine Marshes and eradicated the threat of malaria, it was hardly ever visited and did not feature on the Grand Tour itinerary. Montaigne came to Ostia in 1580, but only to look at the saltworks. Those who came, did so for profit. The neo-classical painters and dealers Gavin Hamilton and Robert Fagan organised digs here in the late eighteenth century; they were rash enough to risk catching malaria in order to get their hands on the mass of sculpture which lay scattered throughout the site.

Just outside the entrance to the site, **Allo Sbarco di Aenea** offers a selection of fish dishes beneath a pergola, served by bizarre waiters dressed up in togas and sandals.

INFORMATION

Ostia: 9 a.m. to one hour before sunset, closed Monday
Museum: 9 a.m. to 1 p.m.

RESTAURANT

Allo Sbarco di Aenea
Via dei Romagnoli 675, Ostia Antica
Telephone: 06 565 0034, closed Monday

NAPLES

Naples is a paradise: everyone lives in a state of intoxicated self-forgetfulness, myself included

Goethe

Naples, 'A City swelling with all Delight, Gallantry and Wealth', was, perhaps, the most idyllic spot on the whole Grand Tour. After the intellectual effort of visiting the sites of Rome, most travellers came here to enjoy 'A little bit of heaven fallen upon the earth', as the Neapolitans referred to their kingdom. The beauty of the scenery remained a constant inspiration. Goethe waxed lyrical on his arrival in 1787: 'Then we came to the top of a ridge and a grand panorama unfolded before us: Naples in all its glory, rows of houses for miles along the flat coastline of the Gulf, promontories, headlands, cliffs, then the islands and, beyond them, the sea. A breathtaking sight!'

The atmosphere affected even the most industrious traveller, particularly during Carnival. In 1644 Evelyn spent much of his time escaping the attention of the swarms of courtesans who sought to inveigle him, and a century later Gibbon, who had been overwhelmed by the antiquities in Rome, wrote: 'We are at present in the midst of a most brilliant carnival, and shall scarce be able to breathe between balls', and Goethe, who was a successful, middle-aged writer when he set out for Italy, confessed: 'Naples is a paradise; everyone lives in a state of intoxicated self-forgetfulness, myself included. I seem to be a completely different person whom I hardly recognise.'

The heyday of the Grand Tour in Naples was the late eighteenth century. Important finds were being dug up in Pompeii and Herculaneum, many of them now on display in the Archaeological Museum in Naples, and the Greek temples at Paestum on the Gulf of Salerno were one of the prime sources of the Greek Revival. The newly built Teatro San Carlo, which housed the largest opera house in Europe, was packed every night, and the countryside, which had been regarded as a rich man's playground during the Roman Empire and had been eulogised by Virgil in his *Georgics*, was regarded as a paradise. In the city itself gambling and womanising were the most popular pastimes, the women 'generally well featur'd, but excessively libidinous', as many a visitor found to his cost.

From 1764 to 1800 the British ambassador was the cultured Sir William Hamilton, a great patron of the arts. His home at Palazzo Sessa was an essential visiting point for all Grand Tourists. Mozart was entertained here, as was the actor David Garrick and the fabulously wealthy William Beckford, who struck up an intimate friendship with Hamilton's first wife. Hamilton himself was a noted antiquarian, a voracious collector and an expert on volcanoes, but was not above laughing at his intellectual pursuits and trained his pet monkey to study a vase through a magnifying glass in mockery of aesthetes. One of the sights of the Grand Tour was of his beautiful second wife Emma performing her 'Attitudes', a semi-erotic *tableau vivant* in which she displayed herself scantily clad in classical costume. Emma's ample charms captivated Nelson when he visited Naples after the Battle of the Nile in 1798 and their tempestuous affair became the talk of Europe.

During the period of Hamilton's ambassadorship Naples was ruled by the house of Bourbon, which took over in 1734 from the Austrians who had, in turn, succeeded the Spanish. Naples was one of the most important ports on the Mediterranean and, during the seventeenth and eighteenth centuries, larger and richer than Rome.

The Neapolitan Baroque, which lasted from about 1600 to 1750, is characterised by great exuberance and vitality. Caravaggio, one of the most important early Baroque painters, fled to Naples in 1606 after committing manslaughter in Rome, and painted several of his most influential works in the city, including the dramatic *Seven Acts of Mercy* and *Flagellation*, both of which are in the Capodimonte Museum (see page 168). His followers, including Ribera and Mattia Preti, were extremely prolific and versatile, and you can see many of their finest works in the Certosa di San Martino. The sense of drama in Caravaggio's paintings is characteristic of Neapolitan Baroque sculpture whose swirling figures decorate countless churches in the city. The greatest sculptor of this period was Cosimo Fanzago (1591–1678), who, like his great contemporary Bernini, working in Rome but a Neapolitan by birth, was both a sculptor and an architect.

Charles III, the first Bourbon king of Naples, was an able ruler who introduced many social reforms, built the Teatro San Carlo and instigated excavations at Herculaneum and Pompeii, installing the finds in his new palace at Portici (later transferred to the Museo Archeologico Nazionale, see page 162). He also built a palace at Capodimonte, and set up the famous Capodimonte porcelain works in the park near the palace in order to keep safe the secret of making porcelain, a process only recently discovered in Europe at Meissen in Saxony. The palace now houses the royal apartments with the Salottino di Porcellana, a room covered in Capodimonte porcelain, perhaps the most elegant rococo room in Naples, and the wonderful collection of paintings of the kings of Naples.

Charles III was succeeded in 1759 by Ferdinand IV who was more interested in hunting and shooting than in ruling his kingdom, a task which he left to his wife Maria Carolina and her favourite and lover Sir John Acton. Ferdinand related closely with the poorest of his subjects, the *lazzaroni*, who loyally supported his regime, unlike his regular troops about whom he commented: 'Signori, dress them as you please, they will run away.' During the momentous events of 1798–9, when the French invaded Naples, ousting Ferdinand and setting up the short-lived Parthenopean Republic, the *lazzaroni* fought ferociously for the house of Bourbon. Although Ferdinand regained Naples in 1799, British tourists regarded it as too unsafe to visit the kingdom until the end of the Napoleonic Wars in 1815.

During the eighteenth century little interest was paid to the medieval art in the city. Travellers concentrated instead on the excavations carried out at Pompeii and Herculaneum, and the equestrian statues of *Balbus* and the bronze figure of the *Seated Mercury* became famous throughout Europe. Pompeii is a more extensive site in an incomparable setting against the dramatic backdrop of Vesuvius, although the houses at Herculaneum are better preserved.

The excavations in the eighteenth century were carried out in the most haphazard way, with convicts used as workmen. The Bourbons forbade the sale of works of art, but this did not prevent collectors from buying or stealing what they wanted. Even Sir William Hamilton took advantage of this cavalier approach to archaeology.

Goethe records dining with him and inspecting his secret treasure vault: 'Out of curiosity I lifted the lid of a long case which lay on the floor and in it were two magnificent candelabra. I nudged Hackert [the painter] and asked him in a whisper if they were not like the candelabra in the Portici museum. He silenced me with a look. No doubt they somehow strayed here from the cellars of Pompeii.'

Dominating the whole bay was the active volcano of Mount Vesuvius, adding a *frisson* of danger to the beauty of the landscape so that, in Gibbon's words, the Neapolitans 'seem to dwell on the confines of paradise and hell-fire'. Hamilton conducted dozens of parties up the volcano, and delivered learned papers to the Royal Society on his findings. He gave a vivid description of one of the many eruptions he witnessed: 'The mountain split; and, with much noise, from this new mouth a fountain of liquid fire shot up many feet high and then, like a torrent, rolled on directly towards us. The earth shook, at the same time that a volley of pumice stones fell thick upon us; in an instant clouds of black smoke and ashes caused almost total darkness; the explosions from the top of the mountain were much louder than any thunder I ever heard and the smell of sulphur was very offensive. My guide, alarmed, took to his heels.' The volcano has never been silent for more than fifty years and last erupted in 1944, causing havoc in Naples which had just been liberated by the Allied forces.

The Neapolitans themselves, particularly the *lazzaroni*, amazed visitors with their antics. The Irish singer Michael Kelly watched spellbound as one of them picked a handkerchief out of a gentleman's pocket at one end of the Largo di Castello and offered it to him for sale at the other end. His contemporary Dr Moore was shocked at them 'walking and sporting on the shore perfectly naked, and with no more idea of shame than Adam felt in his state of innocence; while the ladies from their coaches and the servant maids and young girls contemplate this singular spectacle with as little apparent emotion as the ladies of Hyde Park behold a review of the Horse Guards.'

Most visitors willingly succumbed to the relaxed atmosphere; women were in plentiful supply and the experiences of Michael Kelly, who met a pretty widow with whom he 'scored and spared not', were far from rare. Nelson, coming to Naples in 1798 after his victory at the battle of the Nile, was overwhelmed by the solicitous attentions of Emma Hamilton, and was soon to be seen rowing her round the bay by moonlight. Fortunes were won and lost at the gaming tables, particularly that of the Irishwoman Sarah Goudar whose exquisite beauty captivated Casanova. Charles James Fox, the future Whig politician, lost £16,000 at the gaming tables of Naples in the 1760s. The novelist Tobias Smollett, writing in 1765, lampooned the naivety of contemporary Grand Tourists who gambled away their fortunes and let themselves be 'poxed and pillaged' by the prostitutes who filled the city.

Nevertheless, despite the pox and pillage, there were many who profited from the artistic wealth of Naples and its environs. The neo-classical movement, which looked back to the art of antiquity for inspiration, was profoundly influenced by the discoveries at Pompeii and Herculaneum, which showed, for the first time, the way of life, art and decoration of an ancient Roman town. The fashion of painting rooms in Pompeian red swept across Europe.

Naples was one of the most important places to purchase antiques and many foreigners were inspired by what they found. Greek and Etruscan vases, a totally neglected subject, were championed by Sir William Hamilton who published a volume on them, one of the most beautiful of all eighteenth-century books. He also formed two important collections, the first of which was purchased by the British Museum in 1772. The second collection was lost when the ship bringing it home was shipwrecked in the Scilly Isles, although some pieces have been recovered in the last twenty years. Hamilton's first collection was greatly admired, and motifs from the vases were used in furniture and ceramics, particularly in the work of Josiah Wedgwood. Robert Adam's Etruscan room at Osterley Park in Middlesex is one of many rooms to be decorated in the new style.

The rediscovery of the magnificent Greek temples at Paestum, following the opening of a new coach road along the Bay of Salerno in the middle of the eighteenth century, was one of the main sources for the Greek Revival, since mainland Greece was under Turkish rule and therefore virtually inaccessible. The Greek Revival was inspired by the German art historian Winckelmann, who thought that the art of classical Greece was purer and nobler than that of ancient Rome. Goethe, one of many tourists to visit Paestum, was deeply impressed on his visit in 1787, and Shelley, thirty years later, thought the temples 'inexpressibly grand'.

The Napoleonic Wars brought an era of the Grand Tour to an end. When travellers flocked to Italy once more after 1815, it was the beauty of the landscape and the Neapolitans themselves, rather than their works of art, that appealed to them. Lady Morgan, in 1820, firmly instructed her readers that 'it is a relief, rather than a disappointment, to learn that Naples contains few if any of those objects worthy to arrest the attention on which Florence and Rome have so deeply drawn'. But she rhapsodised about the Neapolitans, claiming that 'The fires of Vesuvius seem to circulate in their veins and the brilliancy of their skies to be reflected in their imagination.'

Chateaubriand saw the Bay of Naples at dawn: 'Flowers and fruit moist with dew are not as suave or as fresh as the Neapolitan landscape emerging from the shadows of night.' The catastrophic destruction of Pompeii and Herculaneum was seen as an example of the dominance of nature over man.

The British, with their innate dislike of anything foreign, were almost universally damning of the locals, endorsing Nelson's verdict that Naples was 'a country of fiddlers and poets, whores and scoundrels'. They objected strongly to the natural religiousness of the Neapolitans. Theodore Witmer, whose *Wild Oats, Sown Abroad* was one of the racier American accounts of nineteenth-century Italy, was appalled at the fresco of the Virgin in the leading bordello in Naples, and the care with which the courtesans removed the rosary from their wrists before making love.

To avoid this sort of temptation, the small English colony, largely composed of those seeking to benefit from the mildness of the climate, kept very much to themselves, shopping at Durst the chemist and Smith and Codrington's grocery stores, and booking their holidays at Thomas Cook and Sons' office in the Piazza dei Martiri. But there were still some who fell for the city's sensual charm. Cardinal Newman, in 1833, noted disapprovingly 'the wealthy English adulterers who are the attraction of the place', and Oscar Wilde, at the end of the century, wrote provocatively: 'It is not for pleasure that I come here, though pleasure, I am glad to say, walks all round.'

The countryside around Naples, particularly the resorts of Sorrento, Amalfi and Ravello, and the island of Capri, continued to increase in popularity throughout the nineteenth century. The nearest that visitors to these resorts came to Naples was when they bought pretty views from painters of the School of Posilippo. Many foreign artists and writers came to live here, including Ibsen, who finished *Peer Gynt* in Sorrento in 1867, and Wagner who was inspired by the gardens of the Palazzo Rufolo in Ravello for Act II of *Parsifal*. Sorrento, Amalfi and Capri are now inundated by tourists, but Ravello, which lies inland, still retains great charm.

Naples today is full of the cocktail-party atmosphere that so enthralled eighteenth-century Grand Tourists, perhaps most evident at the festival of Piedigrotta on 7 September, when the whole city is imbued with a carnival atmosphere, the streets full of music and colourful processions. Neapolitans possess the quick wit and exuberance which the English tend to associate with Cockneys, and their infectious humour helps you to survive the noise and traffic jams which are such a feature of the city.

The following walks, which are designed to include the most interesting parts of the city and the surrounding sites, show Naples'

extraordinary cultural richness and how the past is jumbled up with the present: Gothic churches filled with Renaissance tombs and covered with sumptuous Baroque decoration overlook tenement blocks; washing flutters in the breeze from every window, and grandiose doorways offer tantalising glimpses of spiralling staircases. No wonder John Evelyn, who came here in 1645, declared the city 'the most magnificent in Europe'.

Neapolitans take all this for granted. No mention is made in guidebooks of a perfectly preserved eighteenth-century Apothecary's Shop in the Ospedale degli Incurabili in Via Longo. Naples appears to live in a world of its own, content to accept any misgivings with which the rest of the world views it. Perhaps it is as well to remember the advice of Cavour, the architect of the Unification of Italy, on his deathbed: 'We are all Italians – but there are still the Neapolitans.'

North of Naples

*The vines, climbing to the summit of the trees, reach in fes-
toons and fruitages from one tree to another, planted at
exact distances, forming a more delightful picture than
painting can describe*

John Evelyn

NINFA~ABBEY OF FOSSANOVA

If you are approaching Naples from Rome, the most interesting
route, and one taken by most Grand Tourists, follows the Via Appia,
the most important road in Roman antiquity. The early part of the
route up to the Alban Hills is included in the previous section.
Beyond the Alban Hills the Via Appia runs across the Pontine
Marshes, an area which used to be infested with malaria and much
feared by travellers.

Ninfa, just to the left of Doganella, 9 km beyond Cori, is the site
of a luxuriant garden set in the ruins of a medieval town. The
property was owned by the powerful Caetani family, and Pope
Alexander III was crowned here in 1159. The nineteenth-century
German historian Gregorovius thought the ruins of the medieval
town more enchanting than Pompeii, and Augustus Hare was enrap-
tured by its sylvan beauty and the altars of the churches covered in
'flame-coloured valerian'. The garden as you see it today is largely
the creation of the Duchess of Sermoneta and her son Prince Gelasio
Caetani, who began work on it in 1922. They were great admirers of
the English garden and planted many roses, which thrive in the
fertile soil. The Duchess's daughter Lelia and her husband Hubert
Howard continued to improve the garden so that it is now the finest
example of an informal English-style garden in Italy.

Continuing for a short way down the Via Appia, follow the sign to
the left to the Cistercian **Abbey of Fossanova**. Built in 1187–1208
and recently cleaned, this is one of the finest early Gothic churches
in Europe, with scarcely any ornamentation to detract from the simplicity of the architecture. The cloister off the right aisle is a combination of solid Romanesque arches and graceful Gothic columns.

Returning to the Via Appia, the road reaches the coast at
Terracina and follows it all the way to Naples. John Evelyn was one
of many Grand Tourists entranced by the richness of the vegetation,
which flourished in the mild climate, and by the amount of Roman

ruins. Evelyn, and the Grand Tourists who followed in his path, particularly enjoyed seeing the countryside described by the classical authors. It is fascinating to speculate on the effect that the ruins must have had on the architects James Stuart and Nicholas Revett, the pioneers of the Greek Revival, who walked down the Appian Way from Rome to Naples, accompanied by the Palladian architect Matthew Brettingham and the antiquarian Gavin Hamilton, in April 1748. Sadly, many of the ruins that so inspired these travellers have now disappeared.

INFORMATION

Ninfa: April to October, 1st Saturday and Sunday of the month 9 a.m. to 12 noon and 2.30 p.m. to 6 p.m., July to September, 3 p.m. to 6 p.m. Tickets are limited, but you can buy them in advance from the Fondazione Roffredo Caetani, Via delle Bottcghe Oscure 32, Rome (telephone: 06 654 3231), open 8 a.m. to 6 p.m., or from the World Wildlife Fund for Nature, Via Mercadante 10, Rome (telephone: 06 844 0108), open 5 p.m. to 7 p.m.

A paradise inhabited by devils
Joseph Forsyth

CERTOSA DI SAN MARTINO~VIA TOLEDO~ GESÙ NUOVO~SANTA CHIARA~ SAN DOMENICO MAGGIORE~CAPPELLA SANSEVERO

The Certosa di San Martino is a Carthusian monastery founded in the fourteenth century and enlarged in the late sixteenth and early seventeenth centuries. Its splendid setting, overlooking the Bay of Naples, is a perfect place to view the museum of Neapolitan art housed here.

It is best reached on the Funicolare Centrale from Via Toledo, the Funicolare di Chiaia from Via Crispi in Chiaia, or the Funicolare di Montesanto from Montesanto station. If you travel on the Centrale or the Chiaia Funicolare, head north out of the station into Via Cimarosa and turn right. Bear left into Via Caccavello and right into Via Tito Angelini which takes you to the entrance to the Certosa. From Montesanto station, head east into Cammarano Maestro Colantonio and left into Via Caccavello where you join the same route.

The Gothic church to the left of the entrance was completely redecorated in a light Baroque style in the seventeenth and eighteenth centuries. The interior is Baroque at its most exuberant, the walls entirely covered in frescoes, sculpture and coloured marble, a speciality of Cosimo Fanzago who decorated several of the side-chapels in the 1630s. Neapolitan painting was inspired by the arrival of Caravaggio in 1606, escaping the authorities in Rome, who wanted him on a charge of manslaughter. Two of his leading followers, Stanzione and Ribera, competed for the honour of painting a Pietà for the church. So excellent was their work that both paintings were accepted, Stanzione's hanging above the main door and Ribera's in the Treasury to the left of the choir. The rooms off the choir are in contrasting styles, some filled with intarsia work, others covered in brilliantly coloured frescoes by Luca Giordano, known as 'Fa Presto' from the speed at which he worked.

Emerging from the church, turn left and go through the Chiostrino dei Procuratori, a simple late sixteenth-century courtyard by Dosio, and past the magnificent gilded carriages belonging to the Bourbon royal family to the terrace beyond, which enjoys a commanding view over the Bay of Naples. Below it is a charming garden with a vine-covered pergola.

Re-entering the monastery, the rooms on the right, with their collection of *presepi* (cribs), are enjoyed by locals and tourists alike. The elaboration of these representations of the Nativity is quite astounding, the Holy Family surrounded by a mass of intricately carved food, exotic animals and negro attendants. Some of the polychrome statues date back to as early as the fifteenth century.

The heart of the monastery is the Chiostro Grande, a masterpiece of restrained Baroque architecture. Cosimo Fanzago, who built the upper storey in the 1620s and organised the sculptural programme of the niches over the doors, took great care to integrate his work with Dosio's simple grey and white marble arcade. Notice the monks' cemetery on the right with skulls on the balustrade. The rooms around the cloister house works by Neapolitan artists including a number of dark, violent Caravaggesque canvases so typical of the Baroque.

Outside the monastery a picturesque flight of steps winds down into the heart of the city. At the bottom, turn right and continue descending down Via Santa Lucia and bear left into Via Scura. This area of the city is known as the Tavoliere (chessboard) because the streets still adhere to the original Roman grid plan. The high tenement blocks flanking the narrow streets filled with vegetable stalls are very characteristic of nineteenth-century Naples. Via Scura descends to Via Roma, known as **Via Toledo**.

Built by the Spanish Viceroy Don Pedro de Toledo in the sixteenth century and lined with palaces, Via Toledo was one of the most magnificent streets in Europe. Sixteenth- and seventeenth-century travellers were most impressed, not only by the architecture but also by the splendour of the inhabitants who 'ruffle in Silks and Satins'. It is now the commercial heart of Naples, full of shops and businesses and so crowded that it is difficult to look at the architecture properly.

One of the finest palaces just off the street is Palazzo Gravina in Via Monteoliveto. Cross over Via Toledo into Via Capitelli, known as Spaccanapoli (literally split Naples) and take the first right down Via Sant' Anna dei Lombardi. The street enters Piazza Monteoliveto and on the left of the square stands Palazzo Gravina, now the university Faculty of Architecture, one of the most handsome Renaissance buildings in Naples. On the far side of the square the church of Monteoliveto, with its wealth of Renaissance sculpture, is, unfortunately, closed for an extensive period of restoration.

This area is full of vignettes of Neapolitan life: a man chatting as a barber trims his hair, a policeman adjusting his hair in the wing mirror of his motorbike, an old woman hauling up her shopping in a bucket, a grandiose coat-of-arms in a courtyard festooned with washing.

From Piazza Monteoliveto, head north up Calata Trinità Maggiore to Piazza del Gesù Nuovo, a meeting-place for students from the nearby university. In the centre of the piazza stands the Guglia dell'Immacolata, an eighteenth-century Baroque column covered in statuary. It is one of three guglie in the city, unique to Naples and allowing full scope for the Neapolitan love of extravagant decoration.

To the left of the square is the truncated façade of the church of the **Gesù Nuovo**, originally the façade of the Palazzo Sanseverino; the rusticated stones, cut in diamond shapes, date from the late fifteenth century. The interior, as so often in Naples, is in complete contrast. The architect Valeriano intended the church to be filled with light and open-planned so that the congregation could see as much as possible (the Jesuits, who commissioned him to build the church, valued this very highly). Over the main door is Solimena's *Expulsion of Heliodorus*, a brilliantly coloured, swirling Baroque composition, concentrating worshippers' minds on the fate of non-believers.

Almost directly opposite the façade is the church of **Santa Chiara**, badly damaged when an incendiary bomb fell on it on 4 August 1943, destroying almost all the Angevin royal tombs. Fortunately, the wonderful fourteenth-century cloister, turned into a rustic garden by Domenico Antonio Vaccaro in 1742, has survived. The lemon trees and pergolas, covered in vines and wisteria beneath which you can sit on seats decorated with brightly coloured maiolica tiles depicting rustic scenes, make this an oasis of calm in this busy part of the city.

If it is still before midday, you may like to glance in at the church of **San Domenico Maggiore**. Emerging into Piazza del Gesù Nuovo, continue up Via Benedetto Croce, a continuation of Via Capitelli, until you reach Piazza San Domenico Maggiore. Before entering the church, Scaturchio, on the opposite side of the square, serves some of the best snacks in the city, particularly rum babas (a type of doughnut), a great favourite with Neapolitans.

The church of San Domenico actually faces away from the piazza. At the foot of the octagonal apse, with its semi-Arabic crenellations, you ascend a flight of stairs and emerge beside the high altar, an extravaganza of coloured marble decoration designed by Cosimo Fanzago in the 1640s. The church is a typical Neapolitan palimpsest, a Gothic structure filled with Renaissance and Baroque monuments. It was very popular with the Aragonese kings, who are buried in the Sacristy. The tombs of the Aragonese nobility, following their lead, are ranged round the walls of the nave.

Facing away from the high altar, the Cappellone del Crocifisso in the left aisle contains a painting of the Crucifixion which is said to have spoken to St Thomas Aquinas when he lived in the adjacent monastery. The Cappella Saluzzo on the left of the main door, with its beautiful Renaissance arch, has a handsome monument by Romolo Balsimelli to the nobleman Andrea Carafa, built between 1507 and 1515. On the left of the chapel is a neo-classical tomb to

Filippo Saluzzo, his bust resting, in thoroughly military fashion, on five drums flanked by cannon, cannonballs and muskets.

Heading out of the main entrance, turn right and first left into the Via de' Sanctis, which contains the most extraordinary creation of the Neapolitan Baroque. The **Cappella Sansevero** was decorated in the eighteenth century on the instructions of Prince Raimondo di Sangro, a famous alchemist and the head of the Freemasons in Naples. He commissioned a series of allegorical statues for the chapel, many of them possessing masonic symbolism. They are some of the most complex figures ever carved in marble, particularly Francesco Queirolo's *Disillusion*, a figure caught up in a fishing-net and Sammartino's *Cristo Velato*, completely encased in a transparent veil. This extravagant virtuosity is what the Victorians most detested about the Baroque. In the crypt are some perfectly preserved corpses; the victims were reputed to have died after swallowing an embalmer's substance.

Naples, of course, is pizza heaven, and **Pizzeria Lombardi** at Via Benedetto Croce 57 is one of the best and specialises in *calzone* (stuffed pizzas). If you don't fancy a pizza, why not try the **Ciro a Santa Brigida** restaurant at Via Santa Brigida, one of the best in town, where the conductor Toscanini and the author Pirandello used to eat. Return to the church of San Domenico, turn left into the Piazza San Domenico Maggiore, and right into Via Benedetto Croce. When the street reaches Via Roma, turn left and continue for five minutes until you reach Via Santa Brigida on your left; Ciro a Santa Brigida is at no. 71. Try the *zucchini cacio e uova* (made with courgettes, cheese and eggs), or the *timballo di maccheroni in bianco con polpettine*. One of the best main dishes is *pignatiello e vavella* (shellfish casserole) one of many Spanish dishes that have entered Neapolitan cuisine.

INFORMATION

The **Certosa di San Martino**: 9 a.m. to 2 p.m., Sunday 9 a.m. to 1 p.m., closed Monday
Cappella Sansevero: 10 a.m. to 1.30 p.m., Sunday 11 a.m. to 1.30 p.m.

RESTAURANTS

Pizzeria Lombardi
Via Benedetto Croce 57, Naples

Ciro a Santa Brigida
Via Santa Brigida 71, Naples
Telephone: 081 552 4072, closed Sunday

I was extremely delighted with the Museum of the things
taken out of Herculaneum, but could steal nothing for you
Earl of Carlisle

MUSEO ARCHEOLOGICO NAZIONALE~DUOMO~
SAN LORENZO MAGGIORE~SAN GREGORIO ARMENO~
CASTEL DELL' OVO~TEATRO SAN CARLO~CASTEL NUOVO

The exhibits from Pompeii and Herculaneum, and the sculpture
from the Farnese collections, inherited by Charles III from his
mother Elizabeth Farnese, make the **Museo Archeologico
Nazionale** one of the most important museums in the world. The
palace in which the collection is housed was the seat of the university
in the seventeenth and eighteenth centuries, and remodelled in 1790
to incorporate the finds from Pompeii and Herculaneum and the
Farnese collections. Unfortunately, the collection was badly damaged in the earthquake in 1980, and much of it is often closed to the
public. Indeed, the priceless collection of gems, which had originally
belonged to the Medici, has never been open to the public.

The ground floor is devoted to sculpture, much of it good Roman
copies of Greek originals, including the two equestrian statues of
Balbus excavated in Herculaneum in 1746, and compared, somewhat
optimistically by Grand Tourists, to that of Marcus Aurelius. There
are also several fine statues of Aphrodite, the *Tyrannicides*, a copy of
two statues that stood in the Agora at Athens, and the *Doryphorus*
from Pompeii, the famous spear-carrier after Polycleitus.

The two finest sculptures from the Farnese collection, the
Farnese Bull and the *Farnese Hercules*, were both excavated in the
Baths of Caracalla in the early sixteenth century. The *Farnese Bull*
was widely admired by eighteenth-century travellers because it had
been described by Pliny, and because it was the largest sculptural
group to have survived from antiquity. The *Farnese Hercules*, for
which a special room had been built in the Palazzo Farnese in Rome,
was regarded by Napoleon as the single most important omission
from the art that he removed from Italy in 1797.

The best of the mosaics preserved from Pompeii and
Herculaneum, with their realistic depictions of animals and birds,
are housed halfway up the stairs on the left. The large set-piece at
the end is a psychologically acute depiction of the turning-point of
the Battle of Issus, at the moment when Darius turns to flee, urging
his panic-stricken charioteer to whip up his black horses to escape
from the wrath of Alexander. This dramatic mosaic was much

admired by Sir Walter Scott on his visit to Pompeii in 1832. Across the stairs on the right are a number of Roman bronzes including a wonderfully debauched *Silenus*.

Upstairs, you can obtain a vivid glimpse of life in antiquity from a whole series of rooms filled with exhibits from Pompeii. In the first section of murals actors rehearse, sacrifices are enacted, and one of the landscapes depicts a bloody brawl in the amphitheatre at Pompeii. Even the mythological scenes come to life so that you can feel the emotion of Achilles as he is taken off to the Trojan War, and sympathise with Hercules' humiliation at the hands of Omphale. The last rooms show a change of style and content, with elaborate still lifes and ornate architectural scenes.

Emerging from the museum, cross over the street and walk down the impressive Galleria Principe di Napoli. At the bottom continue down Via Bellini and take the first left into Via Conte di Ruvo. Crossing over the busy Via Santa Maria di Costantinopoli, with a number of bars and pizzerias should you need some refreshment, head down Via Sapienza. This street reaches Via del Duomo, which was cut through this crowded section of the city in the late nineteenth century in an attempt to clear away some of the slums.

Turn right and the **Duomo**, built between 1294 and 1323 and dedicated to San Gennaro, the patron saint of Naples, is immediately on your right; the unremarkable neo-Gothic façade was not completed until the late nineteenth-century.

The cathedral has always been a popular tourist site because of the extraordinary ceremony of the liquefaction of the blood of St Januarius (San Gennaro) which occurs on 19 September and 16 December in the Chapel of St Januarius, the third chapel on the right (the other occurrence taking place on the first Saturday of May in Santa Chiara). St Januarius was martyred by the Romans and his blood is kept in two phials in a tabernacle behind the altar, along with his head. The blood is meant to have first liquefied in the hands of St Severus, one of the first bishops of Naples. Neapolitans regard the ceremony, which dates back to at least 1389, as a vital sign

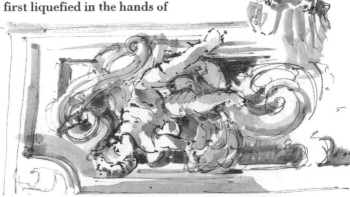

of the saint's continued interest in the welfare of the city and, in particular, his ability to safeguard them from volcanoes.

Grand Tourists flocked to witness the ceremony of liquefaction but were often regarded with grave suspicion in case they interfered in the proceedings, and a Frenchman was torn to pieces at the event in 1750. Michael Kelly, who witnessed the ceremony in 1780, noticed that the crowd's exclamations of 'Blessed Madonna' rapidly changed to 'You pig of a Saint' when there was some delay in the occurrence of the miracle.

In 1799, in protest against the occupying French forces, a priest announced that the miracle would not occur, whereupon the populace rioted, and order was only restored after a French officer threatened to shoot the priest if the miracle did not take place in the next ten minutes, which it duly did. The Neapolitans, in disgust, threw the image of San Gennaro into the sea and rededicated Naples to St Antony Abbot, well known for his ability to prevent fires. However, as soon as Vesuvius erupted again, St Antony's powers were deemed insufficient, and San Gennaro, his image safely retrieved from the sea, was restored to his rightful place as the patron saint of the city.

In the nineteenth century the Reverend Buckland, an eccentric don of Corpus Christi College, Oxford, and an expert on every form of gastronomic experience, tasted a drop of the blood spilt on the floor and proclaimed it to be bat's urine.

As recently as 1944 the author Norman Lewis went to the village of San Sebastiano under Mount Vesuvius to watch it being slowly engulfed by the flow of lava from an eruption. He witnessed a crowd kneeling in the street and praying for the lava to stop. They had borrowed the image of San Gennaro from Naples and, as a last resort, were just preparing to show it to the volcano when the flow of lava ceased.

The decoration of the Chapel of St Januarius was one of the prize commissions in early seventeenth-century Naples. There was vicious in-fighting among artists, and Domenichino, who painted some of the altarpieces, was driven from the city by his jealous rivals, led by the painter Ribera. Domenichino's friend and compatriot Guido Reni was almost killed when the scaffolding in the Gesù Nuovo collapsed over his head.

On the opposite side of the nave the Basilica of Santa Restituta is another Neapolitan palimpsest: Baroque decoration superimposed on Roman Corinthian columns, probably from a temple of Apollo, with a fourteenth-century Byzantine-style mosaic in the left aisle, flanked by Gothic bas reliefs depicting the stories of Joseph and Samson. At the far end of the right aisle there is a fifth-century Baptistery.

The finest work of art in the cathedral is the Crypt of St Januarius beneath the high altar. Executed by Tommaso Malvito in 1497–1506, the bronze doors and walls, with their shell-headed niches are carved in delicate relief with putti, birds and grotesque motifs. The striking statue of the kneeling Cardinal Oliviero Carafa, the founder of the chapel, faces the altar.

Outside the cathedral, turn left and first right into Via Tribunali, one of the most picturesque streets in the city. It is renowned for its snacks: pizzas, croquette potatoes and *timballi* are on sale at a number of stalls; they must be followed by a cup of very strong expresso coffee. Heading down Via Tribunali, immediately on your right is the handsome grey and white façade of the church of the Gerolomini, designed by Fuga in the late eighteenth century.

Just beyond the Gerolomini, in Via Tribunali, is the side entrance to the splendid Gothic church of **San Lorenzo Maggiore**, begun by Charles of Anjou to commemorate his victory at Benevento in 1266. A great favourite of the Angevin nobility, this was where, at a service on Easter Saturday, 1336, Boccaccio, who spent many years in Naples working for the Bardi family bank, was first smitten with love for Maria, the natural daughter of Robert of Anjou whom he immortalised as Fiammetta. After she betrayed him he was never again able to enter the church without weeping.

Tombs of the Angevin nobility are ranged all round the walls of the interior, posing as soldiers, propped on their helmets, or men of letters resting an elbow on a book, or courtiers, in suitably toadying fashion, hat in hand. To emphasise their lineage, these nobles plastered the walls of the cloister with their coats-of-arms. Petrarch experienced a terrible storm in this cloister in 1344 and his graphic description of it and his desire to understand the workings of nature look forward to the humanism of the Renaissance.

To the left of the main entrance of the church, Via San Gregorio runs downhill beneath a campanile built on an arch over the street. The whole street is filled with shops selling *presepi*, Neapolitan cribs crammed with every sort of character and food, carved in the most painstaking detail. In December, when demand for *presepi* is at its height, they are also sold in the surrounding streets. Near the top of the street a flight of broad steps on the right leads up to the charming, secluded cloister of **San Gregorio Armeno**, fragrant with lemon trees. Back down the steps, the Church of San Gregorio Armeno further down the street on the right, begun in 1574, has an ornate gilded wooden ceiling dating from the 1580s, one of the most splendid in Naples, and two excellent Baroque paintings of the *Life of St Gregory* by Fracanzano in the third chapel on the right.

At the end of Via San Gregorio, turn right into Via San Biagio dei

Librai, full of shops selling jewellery and religious objects, which leads into Piazzetta Nilo, named after the antique statue of the river god of the Nile reclining in the corner. The busy square is a picturesque jumble of vegetable and bric-à-brac stall-holders peddling their wares, and students frequenting bookshops. The little church of Sant' Angelo a Nilo with its tomb of Cardinal Rinaldo Brancacci by Michelozzo and Donatello, erected in 1428 and the first Renaissance monument in Naples, is, unfortunately, closed for restoration.

If you want a change from the endless pizzerias in this part of Naples, take a taxi down to La Cantinella, at Via Cuma 42, near Castel dell' Ovo. One of the specialities is fish cooked in *acqua pazza* (literally mad water, flavoured with olive oil, bay leaves, chilli pepper and anchovy). An alternative is Il Pulchinella at Vico Ischitella 4 off the gardens of the Villa Comunale overlooking the bay, an unpretentious restaurant where you are made to feel at home by Signora Mussa. Both these restaurants are in the thriving Santa Lucia area, one that was laid out in the late nineteenth century when the government made a major effort to clear away some of the slums, rife with cholera.

From Il Pulchinella a short walk through the Villa Comunale leads to the waterfront with the Castel dell' Ovo on your left. If you are setting out from La Cantinella, walk down Via Cuma to the waterfront, turn left and the castle is straight in front of you. The twelfth-century Castel dell' Ovo, named after Master Virgil (a mythical recreation of the poet Virgil), who was said to have balanced it on an egg, was built on the site of a Roman villa. Conradin and Beatrice, the last of the Hohenstaufen dynasty, were imprisoned here after their defeat by Charles of Anjou in 1268, and it was from here that Conradin was led to his execution.

Following the waterfront to the north for 300 metres, turn inland up Via Cesario Console to Piazza del Plebiscito, an impressive if soulless square constructed by Ferdinand IV after his restoration in 1815. On one side of the square an enormous Doric colonnade is centred on the church of San Francesco di Paolo, an early nineteenth-century copy of the Pantheon. Opposite stands the Palazzo Reale, begun in 1600, its façade decorated with eight statues of the founders of the various dynasties to rule Naples. Starting on the left with Roger the Norman, the next statue is of the Emperor Frederick II, followed by Charles I of Anjou, Alfonso of Aragon, the Emperor Charles V, Charles III of Bourbon, Napoleon's General Murat and Victor Emmanuel II. Like so much late nineteenth-century statuary the heroic poses of the figures appear operatic and slightly ridiculous.

The Piazza Trento e Trieste leads out of the north side of the square. Bear right down Via San Carlo past the **Teatro San Carlo**, founded by Charles III in 1734 and the largest opera house in Italy. Président de Brosses, who came here in 1740, used to play draughts and sip chocolate while waiting for the recitative to finish. Ferdinand IV loved to eat macaroni in his box, a sight surpassing anything on stage. 'He seized it in his fingers,' to Michael Kelly's amazement, 'twisting and pulling it about, and cramming it voraciously into his mouth, most magnanimously disdaining the use of either knife, fork, or spoon.'

Naples' reputation as a musical centre continued into the nineteenth century. Rossini became musical director of the San Carlo Theatre in 1815 and Stendhal, who attended the re-opening of the theatre in 1817 following a disastrous fire and had his coat torn in the crush, thought it unrivalled in Europe, the auditorium 'a symphony in silver and gold'. It is possible to visit the interior in the morning. The Caffé Gambrinus, in the Piazza Trento e Trieste in front of the opera house, is the place to go after seeing an opera.

The Via San Carlo leads off the piazza to the Piazza del Municipio in front of the **Castel Nuovo**, built for Charles of Anjou between 1279 and 1282, and reconstructed by Alfonso of Aragon. The entrance to the castle is a handsome Triumphal Arch, an intentional evocation of the triumphal arches of antiquity, celebrating Alfonso's entry into Naples in 1443. The arch itself, with its wealth of sculptural detail, is one of the most important Renaissance monuments of the mid-fifteenth century in Italy. The pure white of the marble, startlingly bright against the grey stone of the castle walls, symbolises the introduction of the Renaissance into Naples.

INFORMATION

Museo Nazionale Archeologico: 9 a.m. to 2 p.m., Sunday 9 a.m. to 1 p.m., closed Monday
Teatro San Carlo: 9 a.m. to 12 noon

RESTAURANTS

La Cantinella
Via Nazario Sauro 23, Naples
Telephone: 081 404 884, closed Sunday

Il Pulchinella
Vico Ischitella 4, Naples
Telephone: 081 764 2216, closed Monday

Capodimonte

After dinner the king bows and retires and immediately drives away to a Palace near the town where he shoots every Sparrow he can find

William Blackett

The Palazzo Reale di Capodimonte, begun in 1738 for Charles III as a hunting-lodge, and gradually enlarged over the next century, houses the National Gallery of Naples. If you do not want to take a taxi, take the no. 24 bus from Piazza Vittoria, or no. 110 or 127, both of which go from Piazza Garibaldi to the Tondo di Capodimonte. From here you climb up the steps, turn right at the top and right into Via di Miano until you reach the entrance to the Capodimonte park. The palace stands in the middle of the large park, one of all too few in Naples, and commands wonderful views over the city.

The fantastic Salottino di Porcellana on the first floor, designed in 1757 by Johann Sigismund Fischer who had trained at Meissen, is almost entirely composed of Capodimonte porcelain, made in kilns in the park. The collection of paintings is housed on the second floor. A magnificent series of tapestries, after designs by Bernard van Orley, vividly depicting Charles V's defeat and capture of Francis I at the battle of Pavia in 1525, are in the first room on the right, surrounding cases containing a number of Renaissance bronzes, including figures by Giambologna.

The next rooms are devoted to early Italian painting. Simone Martini's *St Louis of Toulouse crowning Robert of Anjou King of Naples*, a regal image covered in gold, Masaccio's emotional *Crucifixion*, the prostrate Magdalen lying with arms outstretched at the foot of the cross, Filippino Lippi's *Annunciation with Saints* and Botticelli's beautiful *Madonna and Child with Angels* show Naples' link with Tuscany.

The room beyond has paintings from other Italian schools, two intense paintings by Lorenzo Lotto, a fascinating portrait attributed to Jacob de Barbari of Fra Luca Pacioli and his assistant, surrounded by mathematical instruments, a delightful portrait by Mantegna of Francesco Gonzaga, a charming fifteenth-century *View of Naples*, and Giovanni Bellini's *Transfiguration*, suffused with the light of early morning. To the left of the room is Michelangelo's cartoon fragment for the *Crucifixion of St Peter*, which he painted for the Farnese Pope Paul III in the Pauline Chapel in the Vatican. The beautiful face of the soldier turning back shows how strong was Michelangelo's response to male beauty even in old age.

Contemporary Neapolitan paintings cannot match this quality, although various renderings of the *Adoration of the Magi*, with particularly vivid depictions of Balthazar, the black king, who is always shown wearing the most outrageous costume, possess great charm.

One of the strengths of the collection is its wonderful High Renaissance portraits, especially Sebastiano del Piombo's forceful image of Clement VII, his head cast in shadow, Salviati's virile portrait of a man, Maso da San Friano's double portrait of two architects poring over a drawing, a study in black, and two masterly works by Parmigianino. Best of all are Titian's portrait of Charles V, holding the spectator with his mesmeric gaze, and two portraits of Paul III, a wizened figure clutching the arm of his chair. Next to them is Titian's *Danae* with her 'warm yet passive limbs', as Shelley imagined.

The Neapolitan kings inherited an eclectic collection from the Farnese, including El Greco's famous *Boy Blowing on a Hot Coal*, Holbein's penetrating portrait of Erasmus, Joos van Cleve's *Adoration of the Magi*, and Pieter Brueghel the Elder's *The Blind Leading the Blind*, a masterly allegory of human folly as the different characters, symbolising the military, the church and the law, tumble headlong into the stream.

The second half of the collection concentrates on the seventeenth and eighteenth centuries. Two charming Panninis of *Charles III's Visit to Rome* and some excellent still lifes provide a brief interlude before you plunge into the violence of the Neapolitan Baroque. Caravaggio's *Seven Acts of Mercy*, originally housed in the church of the Madonna della Misericordia, and his fearsome *Flagellation of Christ* dominate the next room, their sombre mood reinforced by Artemisia Gentileschi's gruesome *Judith and Holofernes*, where Holofernes is still struggling for life as his throat is cut. On a lighter note Guido Reni's *Atalanta and Hippomenes*, their drapery fluttering in the breeze, and the idyllic landscapes of Claude Lorraine and Carlo Saraceni were the sort of works that appealed strongly to Grand Tourists.

Caravaggio's dramatic use of chiaroscuro profoundly influenced Neapolitan painting. Two of his most successful followers were

Mattia Preti and Cavallino, whose canvases are filled with tension and mystery. Other artists tried to create a sense of theatrical drama so characteristic of Neapolitan Baroque sculpture and architecture, a good example being the *Annunciation to the Shepherds* by the Master of the Annunciation to the Shepherds, where the shepherds are just waking from a deep sleep. These Neapolitan painters were extremely versatile and prolific, and Ribera, who seems to have shared Caravaggio's mercurial temperament, was able to switch seemingly at will from religious subjects to an orgiastic depiction of the drunken Silenus.

The park at Capodimonte is an excellent place to take a picnic. If you would like to visit another part of Naples, take a taxi to **La Sacrestia** at Via Orazo 116, one of the best restaurants in the city, with a wonderful terrace overlooking the Bay of Naples.

INFORMATION

Museo e Gallerie Nazionale di Capodimonte: 9 a.m. to 2 p.m., Sunday 9 a.m. to 1 p.m., closed Monday

RESTAURANT

La Sacrestia
Via Orazo 116, Naples
Telephone: 081 664 186, closed Wednesday

Palazzo Fernandes

Pompeii

*No other sight on earth can furnish such understanding of
antiquity*

Stendhal

One of the highlights of a visit to the kingdom of Naples while on the
Grand Tour was the chance to see Pompeii and Herculaneum.
Herculaneum was discovered in 1709 and serious excavations begun
in 1738, a decade before Pompeii was uncovered, and the two sites
gave eighteenth-century travellers a unique opportunity to purchase
important antiques. After some marble statues of Vestal Virgins had
been secretly exported to Vienna as a present to Prince Eugene, the
kings of Naples did their utmost to stop foreigners buying antiquities.
The finds continued into the nineteenth century: the delightful
bronze *Dancing Faun* was dug up in 1830, and the *Narcissus* thirty
years later, and both were widely copied.

Contemporary accounts are full of a sense of wonder, and even
the blasé Old Etonian Horace Walpole was amazed by his visit to
Herculaneum. Stendhal summed up the appeal of Pompeii to countless Grand Tourists, reared on classical literature, on his visit in
1817: 'no other sight on earth can furnish such understanding of
antiquity'. Other travellers were fascinated by the suddenness of
the catastrophe, and tried to visualise the fate of the victims. Of
the two sites, Pompeii is the more atmospheric, because, unlike
Herculaneum, it is not enclosed by apartment blocks.

If you have time, make a preliminary visit to the Villa of
Oplontis, near the Torre Annunziata exit on the Naples–Salerno
autostrada (follow the yellow signs to Scavi Oplonti). This extensive
and well-preserved villa gives an excellent idea of life in the ancient
world. It may have belonged to Poppaea, the wife of Nero. The
bright, almost gaudy, murals emphasise the functions of the architecture: the spacious colonnade in the atrium, the vases of delicately
painted fruit in the dining room, and the animals and birds on the
walls of the smaller bedrooms. The communal latrines, with their
continually flowing water, testify to the cleanliness of the inhabitants. The garden, which was intended for enjoyment, has been
replanted with original Roman species; bay, laurel, oleander and
assorted fruit trees.

Returning to the *autostrada*, **Pompeii** is the next exit on the way back to Naples. The site is very large and takes three to four hours to walk round. If you are pressed for time, concentrate on the more picturesque southern section of the town, with its two intimate overgrown theatres surrounded by cypresses, and the Quadriporticus, where gladiatorial combats were held.

A preliminary visit to the Museo Nazionale in Naples, with its fascinating collection of artefacts and paintings, helps to recreate life in Pompeii. The catastrophe following the eruption of Vesuvius in 79 AD struck with incredible swiftness and the ruins are littered with the corpses of the unfortunate victims, condemned to an agonising death.

The major public buildings near the entrance – the Forum, the Basilica, and the Temples of Apollo and Jupiter – are of less interest than the individual houses of the inhabitants. The buildings flanking Via dell' Abondanza, running east from the Forum down to the Porta di Sarno, have many interesting features: the elegant atrium in the house of Menander and the mural of wild animals fighting one another, including a leopard and wild boar, in the house of L. Ceius Secundus. At the end of the street, the garden in the house of Loreius Tiburtinus opens out of the villa and is laid out on axis with it, two ideas taken up by Renaissance architects who could not have seen Pompeii but were well versed in classical literature. A line of fountains, now sadly disused, leads down to a row of tall cypresses. Notice the dramatic mural of Actaeon being torn apart by his own hounds.

In true Grand Tourist fashion, do not miss the brothel (Lupinare) in Vico del Lupinare, running north from Via dell' Abondanza, with its crude erotic paintings in the corridor. The rooms on either side in which the prostitutes performed must have left little room for manoeuvre. Pompeii has always been famous for the number of phallic symbols on the outside of its houses, devices to ward off the evil eye and ever popular as tourist attractions.

In the northern section of the city, much of which is closed to the public, make for the house of the Vettii, on Vicolo del Vettii, with its excellent murals. Just inside the entrance is a shameless figure of Priapus weighing his member on a pair of scales. On both sides of the atrium there are mythological scenes of amorous gods interspersed with *trompe l'oeil* architecture. The central courtyard has been laid out with a typical Pompeian garden in which flowers are planted between little yews and box hedges.

At the northernmost point of the site go through the Porto Ercolano down the Via delle Tombe, where Shelley sensed 'the late leaves of autumn shiver and rustle in the stream of the inconstant wind like the footsteps of ghosts'. The Villa of the Mysteries has a room frescoed with scenes connected to Dionysiac rites; all round the walls figures recline at a banquet and are entertained by musicians and dancers, while a woman has her hair done by a servant.

Outside the site there are a number of small restaurants and pizzerias catering for the tourist trade. You might like to try the Pizzeria Tiberio near the railway station, where you can wash down the pasta with some good local Lacrima Christi.

INFORMATION

Villa of Oplontis: 9 a.m. to 3 p.m.
Pompeii: 9 a.m. to one hour before sunset, closed Monday

Bay of Naples

A little bit of heaven fallen upon the earth
Neapolitan saying

POSILIPPO~PHLEGREAEN FIELDS~SOLFATARA DI POZZUOLI~LAKE AVERNUS~CUMAE

Naples is set in the Campagna Felice, some of the most beautiful countryside in Europe, rich in classical associations and full of interesting natural phenomena. For the eighteenth-century tourist weaned on the classics, the combination proved irresistible. He could visualise the landscape through the eyes of Virgil, who had composed his *Georgics* and *Aeneid* in Naples, and imagine the excesses of the Roman emperors, particularly Tiberius with his boys on Capri and Caligula building a bridge of boats across the Bay of Naples.

During the seventeenth and eighteenth centuries the area to the west of Naples was particularly popular. Many tourists visited Sir William Hamilton's villa at **Posilippo** and bought a copy of his *Campi Phlegraei*, a series of views of the Bay of Naples illustrated by Pietro Fabris. Near Hamilton's villa was Virgil's tomb, a mythical site of great importance; it stood at the entrance to the Grotta di Posilippo which led to the **Phlegreaen Fields**, an area full of volcanic activity and regarded as the site of the Elysian Fields and Tarturus.

Another natural curiosity was the Grotta del Cane whose poisonous fumes stunned unfortunate dogs, to the amusement of passing

173

tourists. The more inquisitive visitors such as Joseph Addison attempted to discover the origin of the phenomenon. By the early nineteenth century romantics such as Shelley sympathised with the plight of the dogs and refused to let them be dragged into the cave.

Nearby, on the coast, is the **Solfatara di Pozzuoli**, still an active volcano; the Temple of Serapis, in the town of Pozzuoli, has moved considerably during volcanic eruptions and in 1970 the floor was raised by as much as 90 cm. Further west lies **Lake Avernus**, the supposed entrance to Hades and over which it was meant to be impossible for a bird to fly, a myth repeated in countless descriptions of the area. Just west of Lake Avernus is the Cave of the Cumaen Sybil at **Cumae**, where Aeneas came to consult the Sibyl in the *Aeneid*. The long, dark corridor, the walls sloping inwards as they rise to the roof, looks back to the Mycenaean architecture of ancient Greece. The cave itself and the Temple of Jupiter at the end of the Via Sacra overlooking the sea are two of the most evocative sites in the Campagna.

Today the most attractive part of the Campagna west of Naples is around Baia and Cape Misenum, looking towards the islands of Procida and Ischia. You can enjoy an excellent view of the bay from **Il Gabbiano** in Baia, which serves a good selection of seafood dishes.

CASERTA

Apart from the main classical sites and an ascent of Vesuvius, Grand Tourists enjoyed the novelty of the palace at Caserta, begun for Charles III by Vanvitelli in 1752, the Neapolitan answer to Versailles. The palace became the new centre for the Court, well away from the twin dangers of Vesuvius and the British navy which had bombarded Naples in 1742. Ferdinand IV and his queen Maria Carolina spent much of their time here, indulging in theatricals to the amusement of visitors, who were surprised at their enthusiastic participation, normally playing the comic parts of Buffo and Buffa.

The exterior of the palace was much criticised for its lack of variety (Stendhal compared it to a barracks in 1817), but the Bourbons never had the means to complete the façade to Vanvitelli's design. The main staircase, however, one of the most imposing in Italy, the vistas gradually unfolding as you ascend, was universally admired. Vanvitelli's use of classical statues and a restrained colour for the decoration, a reaction to the extravagances of the Neapolitan Baroque, mark the beginnings of neo-classicism (although James Adam, who was to become one of the leading neo-classical architects in England, thought the decoration execrable on his visit in 1762). The apartments upstairs are rather dull, apart from some moderate neo-classical furniture and some good paintings by Hackert, particularly his delightful views of the English Garden in the park, laid out on Hamilton's advice in 1786.

The gigantic formal garden which stretches from the palace to the hills 3 km away is not easily viewable on foot. It is over 1.5 km before you reach the cascades and the grotto of Diana and Actaeon, a wonderfully lively group of freestanding statues carved by Paolo Persico in 1785–9. To the east of the cascade is the entrance to the charming English garden. The long stretches of formal parterres, the static canals, the groups of statuary and the central vista centred on the royal palace all echo the design of the gardens at Versailles, the epitome of royal splendour.

In the nearby village of San Leuccio Ferdinand IV founded a silk factory which produced some of the finest silk fabrics in Italy. The locals, however, thought the colony was the king's private harem and the children born in the village were known, to their parents' annoyance, as 'king's children'.

RAVELLO

Nowadays, Caserta is less appealing than the resorts of the Sorrento peninsula, the spectacular drive along the Amalfi coast, and the islands of Capri and Ischia. Ravello, lying slightly inland from Amalfi, is the most appealing spot on the Sorrento peninsula, relatively free of tourists. The Palazzo Rufolo, a fine eleventh-century building in a Norman–Saracenic style, leads to an enchanting semi-tropical garden which gave Wagner the idea for Klingsor's magic garden in *Parsifal*. The Belvedere Cimbrone, set on a cliff looking out to sea, is in an even more stunning setting. For some good, inexpensive, local food, try the **Cumpa Cosima**, named after Signora Bottone's father Cosimo, in Via Roma. The artichokes baked in parmesan cheese are quite delicious.

PAESTUM

At the most southerly point on the standard Grand Tour are the three Doric temples of Paestum, dating from the fifth century BC and the best examples of classical Greek architecture on mainland Italy. They caused a sensation when they were rediscovered during the building of a new coaching road along the Gulf of Salerno. Eighteenth-century tourists were overwhelmed by their majesty, Goethe declaring himself instantly cured of 'the distorted saints and tobaccopipe columns of Gothic art' on his visit in 1787. The fame of the temples increased in the nineteenth century, Shelley being one of a flood of tourists to visit them after the Napoleonic Wars. Many visitors felt humbled by their age; Fenimore Cooper exclaimed: 'What a speck does the history of America become in this long vista of events.'

From Paestum some travellers ventured further south, a few, like Goethe, as far as Sicily, but the majority of Grand Tourists headed back north.

INFORMATION

Solfatara di Pozzuoli: 7 a.m. to sunset
Cave of the Sibyl, Cumae: 9 a.m. to one hour before sunset, closed Monday
Palazzo Reale, Caserta: 9 a.m. to 12.30 p.m.; park 9 a.m. to 3 p.m.
Paestum: 9 a.m. to two hours before sunset, the museum: 9 a.m. to 2 p.m., closed Monday

RESTAURANTS

Il Gabbiano
Baia
Telephone: 081 868 7969, closed Tuesday

Cumpa Cosima
Via Roma, Ravello
Telephone: 089 857 156, closed Monday

UMBRIA AND
THE MARCHE

It realised all my dreams of Italy
Samuel Rogers

The picturesque hill towns, the fresco cycles in obscure churches
and the rolling hills so evocative of early Italian painting make a trip
to Umbria and the Marche one of the most exciting visits in Italy.
Apart from the hordes of pilgrims and art lovers who descend on
Assisi, the two provinces are still largely neglected, and their distance from major airports makes it likely that the remoter towns
such as Urbino, with its exquisite Ducal Palace built for the
legendary *condottiere* Federico da Montefeltro, will retain their
unique atmosphere.

It was the Victorians, with their fascination for all things medieval and their passion for natural beauty, who first began to visit
Umbria in any numbers. As the home of St Francis, whom they
revered for his love of the natural world, and of Perugino, whose
Madonnas express a profound purity of emotion, the province provided a wonderful contrast with the material degradation of Rome
and Naples. The Victorians steeped themselves in the drama of
Umbria's medieval history, the bloody internecine feuds between the
various city states, Perugia constantly warring with Assisi and
Spoleto with Foligno, which only ended when the province became a
part of the Papal States in the fourteenth and fifteenth centuries.
During the Renaissance, at a time when all Europe trembled at the
mention of Alexander VI Borgia and Julius II della Rovere, this
remote corner of Italy produced artists of the calibre of Perugino,
Raphael and Bramante, and Frederico da Montefeltro's court at
Urbino was one of the most cultured in Europe.

Throughout the seventeenth and eighteenth centuries, however,
these achievements counted for nothing to Grand Tourists, their
heads firmly buried in the study of antiquity. They dismissed the
picturesque hill towns for their 'crooked towers and conundrum
staircases', and hurried through the 'tedious, dreadful and dangerous' Apennines, sticking closely to the Via Flaminia, the only decent

road in this part of Italy. They admired the Roman ruins at Spoleto and Ancona, searched diligently for the River Rubicon where Caesar made his famous statement 'The Die is cast', before marching on Rome, and approved of the lilliputian Republic of San Marino, a sturdy bastion of freedom.

By the middle of the eighteenth century, travellers were beginning to appreciate the charm of the countryside. Wherever possible they drew classical associations, though few went as far as the sculptor Nollekens and the painter Gavin Hamilton, who had themselves shaved at Augustus' bridge at Narni in 1748 'by way of remembrance of so famous a situation'. In 1776 the painter Thomas Jones, whose arcadian views of the Campagna are full of classical ruins, crossed the Apennines in 1776, 'almost in rapture at getting among Rocks, Precipices and Picturesque Mountains'.

But even those who admired the countryside ignored the hill towns with all the wonderful works of art hidden away in their churches and palaces. In 1748 James Forrester, with his friends Hamilton and Nollekens, reached Spello with its beautiful Pinturicchio frescoes, and recorded: 'The appearance was romantic, but not hearing of anything remarkable in it we passed by.' Goethe walked from Assisi to Foligno in 1787 in order to enjoy the view, behaviour regarded as so extraordinary that he was taken for a smuggler and arrested. In Assisi his interest in art extended only as far as the Temple of Minerva, 'the first complete classical monument I have seen', and he 'turned away in distaste' from the church of San Francesco, with its marvellous treasure of paintings by Giotto and his contemporaries.

Umbria and the Marche, well off the beaten track, were not places in which to travel in comfort or meet people of rank, two prerequisites of the Grand Tour. Tobias Smollett thought the inns 'dismal and dirty beyond all description; the bedclothes filthy enough to turn the stomach of a muleteer: and the victuals cooked in such a manner that even a Hottentot could not have beheld them without loathing'. He was incensed by his innkeeper at Foligno, who insulted him for being a German and then confessed that his room had not been cleaned since it had been profaned by a heretical Englishman.

The backwardness of the two provinces led to the survival of some nasty old-fashioned customs. Norcia was famous for its castrati; a boy's good voice was an investment and parents in the region cashed in. He would be 'drugged with opium or some other narcotic, placed in a very hot bath, until he was in a state of virtual insensibility. Then the ducts leading to the testicles were severed, so that the latter in course of time shrivelled and disappeared.' Castrati were often attractive primadonnas, and Casanova frequently had trouble avoiding succumbing to their charms (or what was left of them). The last castrato in the Vatican Choir retired early this century.

Visitors, particularly Protestants, reacted strongly against the major pilgrimage centre at Loreto in the Marche, often in the most bigoted terms. Fynes Moryson disapproved so strongly that he stole some coins from the almsbox on his visit in 1593. He noticed a priest exorcising a woman and was disgusted by the 'truly conjuring words he used . . . If he had eaten a bushell of salt in hell, if he had been an inhabitant thereof, surely this Art could never have been more familiar to him.'

Président de Brosses in the eighteenth century was equally scathing, ridiculing the figure known as the *Beatissima Madonna di Loreto*, 'the work, like so many others, of St Luke', on his visit in 1740. The locals retaliated by making fun of foreigners. Boswell enjoyed it all, and recorded: 'I made him [his companion Lord Mountstuart] laugh by showing him the sign-board of a barber who had the impudence to put outside his shop a very crudely drawn, ugly figure standing beside a wig, with the inscription, "Al Milordo Inglese".'

By the early nineteenth century the Romantics came to view Umbria and the Marche in a golden light. Samuel Rogers, a friend of Byron, confessed that 'It realised all my dreams of Italy', and Shelley declaimed: 'Spoleto, I think, the most romantic city I ever saw'. But they continued to show little interest in Umbrian art. Byron stopped at Perugia in April 1817, en route from Venice to Rome, with an entourage of five carriages embossed with his coat-of-arms, seven servants, nine horses, a monkey, a bulldog, two cats, a bed, a library and his own set of china, but disdained to look at any of the sights.

Umbria continued to attract off-beat travellers. The most frequent foreign visitor to Perugia was the lecherous Ludwig I of Bavaria, the mad Ludwig's father, who came here twenty-two times in the first half of the nineteenth century, invariably in hot pursuit of the lovely Marchesa Florenzi, for whom he had fallen at the Carnival in Rome in 1821. The elder Dumas stayed in Perugia in 1835, after his expulsion from the Papal States for Jacobinism, but only after persuading his escorts, 'with the help of several bottles of Orvieto', to stop off for the night.

The Nazarenes, a group of early nineteenth-century German painters, were the first to champion Perugino and his school. In the 1820s the French artist Valéry illustrated the Trecento frescoes in Assisi, the Peruginos in Città della Pieve and Panicale, and the

Pinturicchios in Spello. Medieval art and literature came into fashion, and the church of San Francesco in Assisi became one of the sights of Italy. The French art historian Taine stated: 'I would give all the churches in Rome for this cave.' Urbino, its Renaissance treasures hidden away in the hills of the Marche, began to be visited after James Dennistoun published his *Memoirs of the Dukes of Urbino* in 1851. The French historian Ampère preferred Gubbio to the other towns in Umbria because it reminded him most of Dante. Visitors espousing Ruskin's championship of the Gothic flocked to Orvieto to admire its magnificent Duomo.

Umbria's provincialism became one of its main attractions, and the fact that 'the very fashions date back three hundred years' added to its charm. Modern tourists are drawn to Umbria and the Marche for the same reasons: a love of picturesque scenery and of the Italian Primitives, enhanced by a bottle of good Orvieto wine. Many of the festivals date back to the Middle Ages, and, apart from those in Assisi, are seldom inundated with tourists. One of the most spectacular is the Corsa dei Ceri, celebrated every 15 May in Gubbio, where the statues of three saints, attached to wooden towers, are raced up the hill to the church of San Ubaldo.

You need perseverance to dig out Umbria's masterpieces. In the picturesque red-brick village of Panicale, 7 km north of the SS 220 which runs between Perugia and Città della Pieve, the whole altar wall of the Chapel of San Sebastiano, 200 metres east of the main square, is covered by the *Martyrdom of St Sebastian*, one of Perugino's greatest paintings. Collect the key from the woman who lives at Piazza Mercato 13 at the bottom of the steps to the right of the entrance. Four athletic archers, in brilliantly coloured costumes and enormous codpieces, strain every muscle as they loosen off their arrows into the saint's body. Perugino's effortless mastery of the problems of human anatomy and perspective, inherited by his pupil Raphael, earned him the prize commission of leading a team of the greatest artists in Italy, including Botticelli and Ghirlandaio, in the decoration of the walls of the Sistine Chapel for Sixtus IV.

Even the Adriatic coast of the Marche, almost ruined by industrialisation and tourism, still possesses one Renaissance masterpiece, Giovanni Bellini's *Coronation of the Virgin* in the museum in Pesaro, radiant with colour and light. The rest of the coast is definitely worth avoiding; the most interesting towns of Loreto and Urbino stand inland. Ancona, a major stopping point on the Grand Tour where the Via Flaminia reaches the coast, now justifies James Joyce's description: 'Filthy hole: like rotten Cabbage. Thrice swindled.'

Perugia

The most consistently ancient city I ever saw
Mrs Elliott

CORSO VANNUCCI~COLLEGIO DEL CAMBIO~ NATIONAL GALLERY OF UMBRIA~CONVENTO DI SANT' AGNESE

Perugia, the capital of Umbria set on a commanding hilltop, is a curious mixture of the sacred and the profane. The city's violent medieval history, culminating in the fifteenth-century vendetta between the Oddi and the Baglioni, rife with assassination, incest and intrigue, coincided with the emergence of a school of painting monopolised by religious pictures verging on the sentimental. Perugia today is a mixture of the cosmopolitan and the provincial. The University for Foreigners, the jazz festival in July and the sacred music festival in September attract people from all over the world, although fashions lag way behind those in Rome and Florence.

The city, like so many of the larger Italian hill towns, has preserved its historic centre, now free of traffic, although the suburbs, seen from the *autostrada*, are sprawling and pretty hideous. The centre of town is the **Corso Vannucci** (named after Vannucci, better known as Pietro Perugino, the town's most famous painter), a pedestrian precinct which leads from the Piazza Italia, with splendid views over Lake Trasimene, to the Duomo. It passes the Della Posta hotel, where Grand Tourists including Goethe and the elder Dumas stayed. Hans Christian Andersen, highly critical of the snobbishness of the Italians, noted disapprovingly in 1833 that the Posta was 'decorated with coats-of-arms, one for each prince who had stayed a night there'.

Almost everything of note is within easy walking distance of the Posta, although the rabbit warren of surrounding streets makes it all too easy to get lost. These streets show the extraordinary feat of engineering needed to construct a town on this hilltop, one house facing the street on one side and extending down five stories on the other. The ornately panelled and frescoed Café Sandri, at Corso Vannucci 32, is an excellent place to stop for a cappuccino or a cake.

Continuing down Corso Vannucci towards the Duomo, the walls of the tiny **Collegio del Cambio** are covered in paintings by

Perugino and his pupils. The Bankers' Guild commissioned Perugino to fresco the walls of the hall in 1496 with a mixture of elegant classical and religious figures, symbolising the harmony of knowledge. Art historians are much vexed over how much of the painting should be ascribed to the youthful Raphael. The lively paintings on the ceiling depict Apollo and other gods and goddesses in chariots drawn by mythical beasts. Do not miss Perugino's fierce *Self-portrait* on the left wall.

Just to the north the Gothic Palazzo dei Priori, with its glistening white Travertine façade, houses the **National Gallery of Umbria**. The collection, with its endless paintings by Perugino and his pupils of the miracles of obscure local saints, reflects the church's monopoly on the patronage of the arts in Umbria in the Quattrocento. Some of these scenes are extremely decorative, such as the series of panels of the life of St Bernardino by Perugino and his school, where gaily clad figures pose in front of capriccio landscapes, full of extravagant architecture, showing off the artist's knowledge of perspective. Two major Tuscan altarpieces by Fra Angelico and Piero della Francesca were commissioned for churches in Perugia. Fra Angelico's polyptych of the *Madonna and Saints* is painted in his bright, primary colours, whereas Piero preferred a cool, silvery palette redolent of early morning for his serene *Annunciation*.

Below the Gallery the Sala dei Notari on the ground floor is decorated with an eclectic mixture of biblical scenes and Aesop's fables interspersed with coats-of-arms, painted in the last decade of the thirteenth century and heavily restored in 1860.

The Corso Vannucci ends in the Piazza Quattro Novembre in front of the Duomo. The Fontana Maggiore, designed by Fra Bevignate in 1277–80 to designs by Nicola and Giovanni Pisano who carved the reliefs representing the months, is a triumph of late medieval sculpture, particularly the vivid depictions of peasants sowing, harvesting and making wine, and nobles setting out hawking.

On the east side of the piazza the quirky house at the top of Via Pinella was cut in half, in order to help an idle eighteenth-century Jesuit bishop walk from the Duomo to the Gesù at the bottom of the street. The Duomo itself is disappointing, apart from Barocci's fine *Descent from the Cross*, painted in 1569, on the right of the west door and Signorelli's exquisite *Madonna and Saints* in the Duomo Museum.

Just north of the Duomo is the Piazza Danti; bear left down Via Ulisse Rocchi and turn left by the La Lanterna restaurant into Via della Cantina. The street turns into Via Appia and heads sharply downhill, but don't miss the extraordinary narrow Via dell' Acquedotto, set on top of the old Roman aqueduct, with a sheer drop on both sides and views into a number of the prettiest gardens in the town. At the far end take the Via Fagiano, then turn right into Via Benedetta and left into Via Garibaldi. This takes you to the **Convento di Sant' Agnese** which is run by the Poor Clares, a closed order of nuns. Despite the forbidding exterior, the nuns will let you in to see their pride and joy, a beautiful Perugino of the *Crowned Madonna* with two kneeling donors, the nuns Verasia and Eustochia, cousins of Perugino, for whom he painted this fresco as a dowry. The two figures in the side niches are St Antony Abbot and St Antony of Padua. The exquisite Umbrian landscape in the background is still just visible beneath heavy layers of dirt.

From the convent a leisurely walk up Via Garibaldi takes you to Piazza Fortebraccio, named after a celebrated fifteenth-century *condottiere* (*fortebraccio* meaning strong arm in Italian). The Palazzo Gallenga Stuart, the home of Mary Stuart Gallenga who was one of the first to revive interest in Perugino in the mid-nineteenth century, overlooks the piazza and now houses the University of Foreigners, founded in 1921. Across the piazza stands the Arch of Augustus on its massive Etruscan foundations 'frowning down on the pigmy erections of later ages', in the eyes of one romantic visitor. Behind it Via Ulisse Rocchi climbs towards the Duomo; **La Lanterna**, at no. 6, is an excellent restaurant, or, if you are happy with a glass of wine, try the Enoteca next door. Alternatively, climb the steps on the north side of Piazza Fortebraccio and turn right into Via Bartolo and the **Ristorante Falchetto** is at no. 20.

INFORMATION

Sala dei Notari, Palazzo dei Priori: 9 a.m. to 1 p.m. and 3 p.m. to 6 p.m.

Collegio del Cambio: March to October 9 a.m. to 12.30 p.m. and 2.30 p.m. to 5.30 p.m., November to February 8 a.m. to 2 p.m.

Galleria Nazionale: 9 a.m. to 2 p.m., Sunday 9 a.m. to 1 p.m., closed Monday

Convento di Sant' Agnese: 9 a.m. to 11.30 a.m. and 3 p.m. to 6 p.m.

RESTAURANTS

La Lanterna
Via Rocchi 6, Perugia
Telephone: 075 66064, closed Sunday

Falchetto
Via Bartolo 20, Perugia
Telephone: 075 61875, closed Monday

Assisi

I would give all the churches in Rome for this cave
Hippolyte Taine

SAN FRANCESCO~SAN DAMIANO

Assisi, the home of St Francis, the eminently likeable patron saint of Italy, stands on a hilltop 26 km east of Perugia, and can be reached by following the SS 75 and the SS 147. A beautiful, almost too perfect, medieval town in a wonderful position, Assisi can, however, be ruined by hordes of pilgrims and art lovers descending on the basilica of San Francesco.

The town's reputation as a centre of art stems from the middle of the nineteenth century, when there was a popular revival of interest in the Middle Ages and the art of Giotto. Ruskin, who once dreamt that he had become a Franciscan monk, ecstatically praised the purity of the frescoes in San Francesco, which he saw as a product of the religious age in which the artists lived.

Unless you are inspired by large crowds of worshippers, avoid coming to Assisi during Easter, the festival of 3–4 October, to celebrate the saint's canonisation, or that of Corpus Domini in November when the streets are strewn with flowers. Instead, the festivals on 22 June and 31 June–2 July, when the locals dress up in medieval costume, and the old pagan festival on 1 May, preserve more of the characteristic atmosphere of Umbria.

It is imperative to see the basilica of **San Francesco** without the crowds, so make sure that you go early in the morning or wait until late in the afternoon. Precious little survives of Henry James's impression that 'The tone of the place is a triumph of mystery, the richest harmony of lurking shadows and dusky corners, all relieved by scattered images and scintillations'. However much the caretakers of the faith insist on correct clothing, the atmosphere tends to resemble more that of a football stadium than a church.

The building, actually two churches superimposed on one another, stands at the edge of the town. It was built under Brother Elias's direction in just two years after the death of St Francis in 1228 and over the next century the walls and ceilings of both churches were decorated with scenes from the life of St Francis. The body of the saint was stolen by Elias during the canonisation ceremony and buried secretly in the foundations of the lower church where it remained undiscovered until 1818.

The frescoes in the lower church include major works by Giotto, Simone Martini, Cimabue and Pietro Lorenzetti, Sienese and Florentine near-contemporaries of St Francis. Over the high altar the *Mystic Marriage of St Francis with his Vows of Poverty, Chastity and Obedience* and *St Francis in Glory* were formerly attributed to Giotto, but, although the individual figures are excellent, the compositions are crowded and difficult to understand. Better examples of Giotto's school, and very possibly by the master himself, are in the Chapel of the Maddalena on the right of the nave. The *Noli me Tangere* and the *Raising of Lazarus* have all the qualities of simplicity and naturalism associated with St Francis himself. Even more beautiful are the Simone Martini frescoes of the *Life of St Martin* in the first chapel on the left side of the nave.

The upper church, a wonderfully light structure which was to influence all subsequent Franciscan churches, has a series of frescoes by contemporaries of Giotto of the *Life of St Francis*, the episodes designed, like so much of medieval art, to be read like a continuous narrative. The charming image of *St Francis's Sermon to the Birds* by the main door epitomises the love of nature that has made him such an immensely popular saint. Above the St Francis

Basilica S. Francesco, Assisi

cycle there is a series of stories from the Old Testament starting with the *Creation of Adam* where Adam appears like an astronaut in a bubble.

After leaving the church, head up Via San Francesco to the Piazza del Comune. A feature of the street, and many others in the town, are the numerous 'doors of death', narrow bricked-up entrances raised slightly above street level which were only opened to carry corpses out of the house. They were designed to be just wide enough to let the body out of the house leaving the spirit behind as a household god.

The Piazza del Comune contains the Temple of Minerva with its Corinthian columns so admired by Goethe. Just below it, in Via Arco dei Priori, is the **Medio Evo**, the best restaurant in town. A good alternative is the **Umbra** at Via degli Archi 6, also just off the south side of Piazza del Comune.

Outside the town are several shrines closely connected with St Francis, of which only **San Damiano** has managed to preserve the feeling of peace and quiet so incompatible with modern tourism. From the Piazza del Comune walk down Corso Mazzini past the church of Santa Chiara, enjoying a magnificent view over the Umbrian countryside. Continue down Via Borgo Aretino through the Porta Nuova and follow the well-signposted road downhill for 1 km to the secluded church of San Damiano, set in a grove of olives and cypresses, where St Francis renounced the world in 1212 and brought his disciple St Clare to live.

When the Papal States became a part of the kingdom of Italy in 1870, the monasteries were dissolved and their property was seized by the state. In order to prevent this, Lord Ripon, a latter-day Grand Tourist who had been converted to Catholicism, bought San Damiano and let it back to the monks on condition that it never be restored. Since his children remained stout Anglicans he left it to another Catholic convert, his friend Annabel Cooper, whose descendants have, in turn, recently returned it to the Franciscans.

INFORMATION

San Damiano: summer 10 a.m. to 12.30 p.m. and 2 p.m. to 6 p.m., winter 10 a.m. to 12.30 p.m. and 2 p.m. to 4.45 p.m.

RESTAURANTS

Medio Evo
Via Arco dei Priori 4, Assisi
Telephone: 075 813 068, closed Wednesday

Umbra
Via degli Archi 6, Assisi
Telephone: 075 812 240, closed Tuesday

Spoleto

The most romantic city I ever saw
                              Shelley

PONTE DELLE TORRI~ROCCA~DUOMO~SANT' EUFEMIA~ SAN PIETRO~TEMPIETTO DI CLITUNNO

Spoleto is 65 km from Perugia and 48 km from Assisi following the SS 75 and the SS 3. The road passes a number of splendidly situated hill towns evoking Umbria's medieval past. Approaching the town from the south, with the fortress dominating the hilltop and the magnificent aqueduct bestriding the narrow valley beneath, it is hard to disagree with Shelley's verdict.

The town is made up of a series of narrow, steeply climbing streets up which Fiat Unos hurtle at impossible speeds. The decision by the conductor Giancarlo Menotti to choose Spoleto as the setting for his music Festival of Two Worlds has given the town a new lease of life, and it is inundated with visitors at the end of June and beginning of July. The festival tends to attract the jet set, but there are enough fringe activities for all comers.

Spoleto's Roman ruins and its position on the Via Flaminia appealed to Grand Tourists, though they remained nervous of the dangers of the Apennines. Montaigne's visit in 1581 was spoiled by stories he heard of a local brigand who was terrorising the neighbourhood. The town was renowned for its lavish hospitality: both Queen Christina of Sweden in 1655, and Maria Casimira (widow of the Polish hero John Sobieski) in 1699 had sumptuous banquets given in their honour. Nineteenth-century travellers wallowed in Spoleto's picturesque qualities; Lady Morgan entered the 'terrible walls' by night in 1819, 'and as we wound slowly between the high dark double vallum, or caught glimpses of the lofty, black, and ruinous houses, (made visible by the lighted shrines of the Madonna), it appeared to us a mass of prisons; the air seemed close, and all looked fearful'.

The most spectacular site is the **Ponte delle Torri**, a triumph of Trecento engineering built by the *condottiere* Gattapone on Roman foundations. Grand Tourists, with their lack of interest in historical accuracy, made no distinction between Roman and Romanesque architecture, and praised the aqueduct for being Roman although it was actually built in the fourteenth century. The setting is magnificent: the aqueduct spans a ravine and a stream trickles far beneath its monumental arches.

At the east end of the aqueduct the path to the right follows the edge of the town, giving marvellous views over the River Tessino. Standing above the path is the awe-inspiring **Rocca**, built by Gattapone for Cardinal Albornoz out of stone looted from the Roman amphitheatre. The Cardinal, a stalwart champion of the Papacy, reconquered the neighbouring province of the Marche in the fourteenth century. For many years the Rocca was used as a prison, its most famous inmate being the attempted assassin of the present Pope. At the point where the path re-enters the city walls, you can glimpse the **Duomo** below on your right.

The Piazza del Duomo is one of the most arresting pieces of town planning in Italy, a long, shallow flight of steps descending into the square and focusing on the Duomo. Thomas Schippers, the co-founder of the Spoleto festival, loved this piazza so much that he was buried here in 1978. The beautiful Romanesque façade of the Duomo, punctured by eight rose windows and a mosaic dated 1207, has an elegant Renaissance portico dating from 1491, its symmetry enhanced by two charming little pulpits at either end.

The seventeenth-century Baroque interior makes a cold contrast with the warmth of the façade. The frescoes in the apse of the *Life of the Virgin* are some of the finest in all Umbria, particularly the exquisite *Annunciation*. Painted by Filippo Lippi and Fra Diamante, they have recently been restored to their original brilliant colours and are visible from far down the nave. The delightful frescoes by Pinturicchio and his pupil Jacopo Siculo in the first chapel off the right aisle help to lighten the atmosphere, particularly the background of *St Jerome* where the lion is vastly enjoying chasing some donkeys round the landscape.

Emerging out of the Piazza del Duomo, take the first left out of Via del Duomo into Via Saffi to the twelfth-century church of **Sant' Eufemia**. The spartan interior, devoid of decoration, gives a feeling of great antiquity. This, one feels, is how the early Christians liked to worship, building their churches from whatever came to hand, in this case taking the capitals and the plain altar from ancient Roman buildings.

The picturesque streets around Sant' Eufemia are filled with antique shops. After an inevitable browse, particularly in the delightful Piazza del Mercato, the ancient Roman Forum, with its bustling fruit market, make your way downhill to Corso Mazzini. Sabatini, a rather trendy restaurant at no. 52–4 where you can eat outside in summer, serves excellent pasta at a reasonable price.

After lunch, a ten-minute walk down the Viale Matteotti past the Roman amphitheatre and left into Via Roma takes you outside the town and across the river to the church of **San Pietro**, splendidly sited at the top of a steep flight of steps. It is best visited in the late afternoon when the sun shines directly on to the west front. The Romanesque façade is covered with a profusion of naturalistic carving depicting an aggressive free-for-all. The human figures, despite their heavy armour, are by no means having the best of it, a number of them being devoured by an extraordinary collection of animals, who are, in turn, devouring each other.

Just off the SS 3 back to Perugia 14 km north of Spoleto is the jewel-like **Tempietto di Clitunno** below the hill town of Trevi. The miniature classical temple, actually a church, was probably built in the fourth century AD and is said to be the oldest in Umbria. Four Corinthian columns support a pediment decorated with grapes, the symbol of the God Bacchus. The plain altar-slab, in wonderfully haphazard fashion, sits on a section of a fluted column. The Fonti del Clitunno nearby is an idyllic spot, painted by Richard Wilson and eulogised by Byron, who imagined the white oxen described by Ovid grazing here.

INFORMATION

Tempietto di Clitunno: 9 a.m. to 12 noon and summer 4 p.m. to 7 p.m., winter 3 p.m. to 6 p.m.

RESTAURANT

Sabatini
Corso Mazzini 52–4, Spoleto
Telephone: 0743 37233, closed Monday

Hill Towns of Southern Umbria

It is the most beautiful countryside in the world. I do not exaggerate

Abbé Barthélemy

SPELLO~FOLIGNO~BEVAGNA~MONTEFALCO~TODI

Spello, 31 km from Perugia on the SS 75, is an almost perfectly preserved medieval town nestling on its hilltop, and offers two essential elements guaranteed to attract the discerning traveller: some exquisite Quattrocento frescoes and a first-rate restaurant. The town looks its prettiest on the feast of Corpus Domini, when the streets are carpeted with flowers.

You enter through the Roman gate and follow the road sharply uphill to the church of Santa Maria Maggiore. The Pinturicchio frescoes of the *Annunciation,* the *Adoration of the Shepherds* and *Christ Disputing with the Elders* in the Cappella Baglioni on the left of the nave, painted in c. 1501, have been sensitively restored to their original brilliant colouring. They fully justify Pinturicchio's nickname of 'rich painter'. A local inhabitant jokingly told me that, prior to the restoration, the frescoes had been rather more picturesque, with real flowers growing out of the mould to match those that bestrew Pinturicchio's landscapes.

A little further up the hill on the right, beyond the church of

Sant' Andrea, is the excellent **Il Molino**, a formal restaurant in a former eighteenth-century mill with a large, open fire over which Umbrian game specialities are grilled or spit-roasted and served with polenta.

The next town south, **Foligno**, is 5 km further on and situated at a strategic point on the Via Flaminia. Even the most hurried Grand Tourist stopped to admire Raphael's *Madonna di Foligno*. Queen Christina of Sweden failed to buy it on her triumphant procession to Rome in 1655. The revolutionary French had fewer qualms and removed it, something that the writer Chateaubriand deeply regretted. It is now safely in the Vatican, and escaped the air raids which all but destroyed Foligno in the last war.

Apart from the Raphael there was little to detain the eighteenth-century traveller. Should you want to stop for lunch at this point, the restaurant of the **Hotel Villa Roncalli** at Viale Roma 25 offers an imaginative menu making good use of local ingredients, and washed down by good regional wines.

A short distance west of Foligno, the charmingly theatrical Piazza Silvestri in the centre of **Bevagna** is ideally suited to performances of Shakespeare's Italian plays. Two fine Romanesque churches face each other across the piazza, each with a dramatic flight of steps leading up to the altar. Both façades look as though they have suffered from an earthquake; one is very ruined and the other appears lopsided with its single tower. The interior of the former is entirely free of decoration, concentrating your attention on the purity of the architecture.

Don't miss the vivid second-century Roman mosaic of tritons, seahorses and a variety of fish in the old baths in Via Porta Guelfa; from Piazza Silvestri head up Corso Matteotti, turn left into Via Crescimbeni and first left into Via Porta Guelfa.

To the south-east of Bevagna (and 47 kms from Perugia) lies **Montefalco**, yet another supremely picturesque hill town. The church of San Francesco below the circular Piazza della Repubblica has been turned into a small but select museum of Umbrian painting including an atmospheric Perugino *Adoration of the Shepherds*. Benozzo Gozzoli, one of the most appealing painters of the Quattrocento, left Florence to come and work in the more rarefied atmosphere of Umbria. His major work in the province is the fresco cycle of the *Life of St Francis* in the apse of San Francesco. Gozzoli's charm lies in his wealth of incidental detail and his love of the Tuscan and Umbrian landscape, and if Montefalco was more accessible, this series would be almost as famous as his frescoes in the Medici–Riccardi palace in Florence. No Grand Tourist would have

dreamt of visiting Montefalco, although, curiously enough, in 1586 four Japanese converts to Catholicism who were making a visit to Europe were given a lavish welcome in Perugia, and travelled on to Montefalco to see the body of the Blessed Chiara.

If you follow the old road from Montefalco across the rolling hills southwest past Bastardo for 25 km, you come to **Todi**, perched like an eagle's nest on its hilltop. Alternatively you can come south down the SS 3 *bis* from Perugia along the upper Tiber valley. The most lively events in the town's calendar are the antiques fair in April–May and an exhibition of wood and metal crafts in August–September.

The main piazza, laid out in the thirteenth century on the site of the Roman Forum, is a wonderful example of the Italian genius for architectural drama. The Duomo, with its truncated façade, stands at the top of a flight of steps and overlooks the surrounding Romanesque and Gothic palaces. On the east side, the battlemented Palazzo Comunale and the Palazzo del Capitano are linked by a monumental stairway, from which medieval heralds read out proclamations.

Inside the Duomo the pretty Gothic arcade off the right aisle is in rather surprising contrast to the severity of the palaces in the piazza. The inlaid choir stalls in the apse, with their sensitive depiction of architecture and *trompe l'oeil* still lifes, are some of the best examples in Umbria. The *Last Judgement* on the west wall, by Ferrau da Faenza, is a poor pastiche of Michelangelo's masterpiece in the Sistine Chapel. On every side of the square there are superb views over the surrounding countryside. San Fortunato, off the south-west side of the piazza, has a soaring Gothic interior and a *Madonna and Child* by Masolino in the second chapel in the right aisle.

The **Umbria** restaurant at Via San Bonaventura just off the Piazza del Popolo serves excellent wild game and has a blazing log fire if the weather is cool.

On the way down the precipitous hill, you pass Santa Maria della Consolazione, one of the most beautiful centrally planned churches of the Renaissance, of which there are several in the area. Designed by Cola da Caprarola in 1508, and strongly influenced by Bramante, whose rebuilding of St Peter's began two years earlier, the church was erected during the following century; it is prettier but less imposing than Sangallo's San Biagio at Montepulciano. It is best seen on a fine day when light streams through the windows into the interior.

For a contrast to all the culture in Umbria's southern hill towns, you might like to stop at the Locanda **Le Tre Vasselle** at Torgiano just to the right of the SS 3 *bis* 10 km south-west of Perugia. There is an excellent restaurant, though certainly not cheap by Umbrian standards. I would suggest instead a tour of the wine museum, followed by a tasting.

INFORMATION

Terme Romane, Bevagna: ring at no. 2 Via Porta Guelfa
Wine Museum, Via Garibaldi 48, Torgiano: 9 a.m. to 12 noon and 3 p.m. to 7 p.m.

RESTAURANTS

Il Molino
Piazza Matteotti 6/7, Spello
Telephone: 0742 651 305, closed Tuesday

Hotel Villa Roncalli
Viale Roma 25, Foligno
Telephone: 0742 670 291, closed Monday

Umbria
Via San Bonaventura 13, Todi
Telephone: 075 882 737, closed Tuesday

Le Tre Vasselle
Via Garibaldi 48, Torgiano
Telephone: 075 982 447

Orvieto

The greatest polychrome monument in the world
Jacob Burckhart

Orvieto, an ancient Etruscan town steeped in history, the scene of a feud of such violence between the Monaldeschi and the Filippeschi that Dante included it in his *Purgatorio*, is perched on a hilltop overlooking the *autostrada del sole*. At the very summit of the town stands the black and white striped Duomo, like a wonderful humbug sweet, dominating the view from all directions. Neglected by Grand Tourists who preferred to follow the Via Cassia from Radicofani through Viterbo to Rome, Orvieto's Duomo became one of the most famous buildings in Italy in the nineteenth century, admired for its magnificent medieval sculpture and for its cycle of frescoes by Signorelli.

The Duomo, begun in 1290 by Arnolfo di Cambio but not completed until the seventeenth century, was built to commemorate the Miracle at Bolsena, when the wafer held by a heretical priest began to bleed while he was celebrating Mass, an event Urban IV commemorated in the feast of Corpus Christi, first celebrated in 1264. This is still Orvieto's largest festival, with processions winding through the town, although rivalled by the Festa della Palombella on Whit Sunday, when a mechanical dove explodes into a group of fireworks representing the Virgin and the Disciples, a glorious example of the Italian love of drama.

The Duomo has one of the most complex façades in Italy, an intricate ensemble of mosaics, sculpture and tracery. It has recently been repaired following the damage from the 1982 earthquake. The design is attributed to Lorenzo Maitani, who executed many of the finest sculptures including a series of powerful bas reliefs depicting biblical scenes ranging from the *Creation* to the *Last Judgement*.

Signorelli's frescoes in the Cappella della Madonna di San Brizio in the right transept overshadow everything else in the interior, even the lovely fourteenth-century frescoes in the Cappella del Corporale opposite and a delicate *Madonna and Child* by Gentile da Fabriano.

Fra Angelico began work on the chapel in 1447 but was almost immediately summoned to decorate Nicholas V's chapel in the Vatican, and it was not until 1499 that Signorelli was asked to undertake the commission. Signorelli chose to depict the *Last Judgement* and, like Michelangelo after him, used the subject matter as an excuse to portray the male nude in all its vigour. In the *Resurrection of the Dead* the Elect wrench themselves out of the ground, while the Damned on the opposite wall writhe in agony as they are consigned to Hell. But perhaps the most disturbing scene of all is the *Preaching of the Antichrist* on the left wall, where Signorelli has depicted himself and his predecessor Fra Angelico watching impassively as society appears to disintegrate before their eyes.

To recover from the violence of Signorelli's frescoes, you might like to try some excellent Orvieto wine in a small wine cellar in the piazza. If you would prefer something to eat, **Maurizio**, at Via del Duomo 78, is a perfectly acceptable, if uninspired restaurant. A more enterprising alternative is **Le Grotte del Funaro** at Via Ripa Serancia 41, set in tufa caves. Go down Via del Duomo, turn left into Corso Cavour and turn left just past the church of Sant Andrea into Via Ripa Serancia. You can enjoy one of the most spectacular views in all Italy from **La Badia**, a twelfth-century monastery 5 km south of Orvieto.

RESTAURANTS

Maurizio
Via del Duomo 78, Orvieto
Telephone: 0763 41114, closed Tuesday

Le Grotte del Funaro
Via Ripa Serancia 41, Orvieto
Telephone: 0763 43276, closed Monday

La Badia
Orvieto
Telephone: 0763 90359, closed Wednesday

Into the Southern Marche

*Something like population was visible, in the swollen,
squalid, hollow figures, who steal from straw sheds, or
appear at work in the pestilential marshes; many of them
were ghastly spectres, with nothing of humanity but its sen-
sibility to suffering*

Lady Morgan

NORCIA~ASCOLI PICENO

Spoleto is a good base from which to make a tour of the southern
Marche. Head east on the SS 395 for 19 km on a lonely, winding road
to Piedipaterno, turn left on to the SS 209 for 10 km until you reach
Triponzo where you turn right for **Norcia**. St Benedict came from
this attractive town set in the heart of the Apennines, and the determination with which he set about establishing his monastic order is
typical of the resolute character of the Norcians. St Benedict's
statue dominates the main square and is surrounded by massively
constructed buildings designed to withstand the earthquakes which
occur frequently in this part of Italy. Nowadays, Norcia is famous
for its salami festival in September.

Beyond Norcia to the south the road climbs steeply out of the valley and continues through some of the most spectacular scenery in
central Italy. If you grow tired of the winding road, turn left after
18 km and follow an easier route through the Piano Grande, a verdant plateau lost in the mountains. Zeffirelli used it as a location for
his film *Brother Sun and Sister Moon* on the life of St Francis.

Emerging from the stillness of the Piano Grande, you rejoin the
SS 4 at Arquata, turn left and after 30 km reach **Ascoli Piceno**. If
you arrive before 1 p.m. make for the Palazzo Comunale opposite
the Duomo, which has a surprisingly good picture collection with
works by Crivelli, Titian, Reni, Ribera and Bellotto. The
Tornasacco restaurant at Via Tornasacco 29 is behind the western
side of the palace. Local specialities are *olivi ripieni*, intricately
stuffed olives, and pasta enriched with whole hunks of lamb.

On the far side of the Palazzo Comunale the elegant façade of the
Duomo, added by Cola dell' Amatrice to the twelfth-century building in the 1530s, gives no idea of the extraordinary interior, decorated with dozens of glass chandeliers which look as though they

have just been imported from Murano. To add to the bizarre effect the side chapels are designed like scallop shells. There is a beautiful polyptych in the south aisle by Carlo Crivelli, a Venetian painter who came to work in this remote province in the latter part of the fifteenth century.

A short walk from the Duomo down Via Venti Settembre and Via Trieste takes you to the pedestrianised Piazza del Popolo. This delightful square, with its travertine floor resembling a skating-rink, is the haunt of the young blades of Ascoli Piceno, who lounge on the steps of Cola dell' Amatrice's Palazzo del Popolo scrutinising passers-by.

Ascoli, like Norcia, has suffered from a number of earthquakes through the centuries and many of the most impressive buildings, although built in a most robust style, show signs of damage. This gives an eclectic feel to the architecture, with its haphazard mixture of the Romanesque, the Renaissance and the Baroque. Before you leave, have a look at San Marco Evangelista, a hospital annexed to the neighbouring church, with a façade designed, yet again, by Cola dell' Amatrice. It is known as 'the Broom', since the brothers who ran the hospital used to flagellate themselves with a scourge shaped like a broom.

INFORMATION

Palazzo Comunale, Ascoli Piceno: summer 10 a.m. to 1 p.m. and 4.30 p.m. to 6.30 p.m., winter 9 a.m. to 1 p.m., Sunday 10 a.m. to 12 noon

RESTAURANTS

Tornasacco
Via Tornasacco 29, Ascoli Piceno
Telephone: 0736 54151, closed Friday

Loreto

Loreto has been an important pilgrimage site ever since the Virgin's house, which had unexpectedly flown from the Holy Land to Istria in 1291, took wing again in 1294, and landed here, like a sacred flying saucer. As a result of this miraculous and uniquely trouble-free house move, it is full of tourist shops selling religious trinkets. The architecture is, however, of the highest quality and the Piazza della Madonna is one of the finest Renaissance squares in Italy. The beautiful façade of the Sanctuary, an understated work of the late Renaissance, provides the focal point of the square; its three bronze doors are decorated with dramatic scenes from the Old and New Testaments from the school of Giambologna.

In front of the Sanctuary stands a charming Baroque fountain by Carlo Maderno bearing the unusual motif of boys with tridents spearing dolphins. The Palazzo Apostolico running round two sides of the square is an impressive work of the High Renaissance, the stately arcades reflecting the influence of the monumental architecture of the Roman baths. Many of the leading Italian artists of the late Quattrocento and the early Cinquecento worked on the interior of the Sanctuary. They include Bramante, who designed the exquisite marble screen in front of the Santa Casa, Andrea Sansovino, who sculpted some of the bas reliefs around its exterior, and Melozzo da Forli and Signorelli, who painted the ceilings of two of the side chapels with a series of beautiful angels.

Loreto is not famous for its cuisine but there are any number of restaurants catering for the pilgrims, one of the pleasantest being the **Giardinetto** at Corso Boccalini 10, out of the south-west corner of Piazza della Madonna.

After lunch, you may like to explore Recanati, the first town on the SS 77 south-west of Loreto, and one of the prettiest hill towns in the whole Marche, enjoying splendid views over the countryside in all directions. The town is built in a mellow red brick, and has various memorabilia to honour its two most famous sons, the poet Leopardi (1798–1837) and the opera singer Gigli, who is buried here. As so often in this remote corner of Italy, the museum contains some unexpectedly fine paintings, including two intensely emotional and richly coloured paintings by Lorenzo Lotto, an artist from the Veneto who found it easier to gain commissions here in the Marche.

RESTAURANT

Giardinetto
Corso Boccalini, Loreto
Telephone: 071 977 135

Urbino

Is it possible that into yonder hall, where now the lion of St Mark looks down on staring desolation, strode the Borgia in all his panoply of war, a gilded glittering dragon, and from the dais tore the Montefeltri's throne, and from the arras stripped their ensigns, replacing these with his own Bull and Valentinus Dux?

John Addington Symonds

PALAZZO DUCALE~DUOMO~ORATORIO DI SAN GIUSEPPE~ORATORIO DI SAN GIOVANNI

Urbino is one of the most attractive towns in Italy, still remarkably unscathed by the ravages of mass tourism. It owes its fame to the genius of Federico da Montefeltro, one of the most enlightened rulers of the Renaissance. A ruthless general with a hooked nose and one eye, Federico devoted his time between campaigns to culture and managed to attract Alberti and Piero della Francesco to his remote duchy. He built himself one of the finest palaces in Quattrocento Italy and filled it with magnificent works of art. Raphael, the son of the court painter in Urbino, was born here, as was Bramante, who was to become the leading architect of the High Renaissance.

Federico's reputation was so high that Baldassare Castiglione based *The Courtier* (1528), his manual of civilised behaviour, in Urbino. A few enterprising travellers such as William Thomas came to see for themselves the achievements. Then, quite suddenly, Urbino disappeared from the tourist map. Between 1600 and 1850

virtually no one visited the town, no account of Italy gives more than a passing mention to Federico, and Grand Tourists in the area were far more interested in looking at the Rubicon. It was not until 1851, with the publication of James Dennistoun's *Memoirs of the Dukes of Urbino*, that scores of tourists descended almost overnight on this corner of the Marche, revelling in the dramatic life of the illustrious *condottiere*.

Federico's reputation as a patron of the arts resides primarily in the **Palazzo Ducale** he commissioned the Dalmatian Luciano Laurana to build for him between 1465 and 1474. Perhaps its most appealing aspect is the lightness and harmony of the elevations that surround the courtyard, which were to be extremely influential on later Renaissance architecture.

Inside the palace every room possesses beautifully modelled door-ways and chimney-pieces, and the walls of Federico's study are covered in delicate *trompe l'oeil* intarsia work depicting musical instruments, armour, books and other attributes of Federico's remarkable personality. From this side you can enjoy the view over the rolling hills of the Marche, one of Federico's prime reasons for siting the palace high above the rooftops of the town on the summit of the hill.

Next door is Piero della Francesca's enigmatic *Flagellation*, in which the three figures in the foreground apparently totally ignore the scourging of Christ taking place in the palace behind them. In the room beyond, the architect Laurana has painted a view of an ideal city which may well have influenced the young Bramante. Raphael's serene portrait of *La Muta*, her expression as remote as Piero's figures, is the only work by the youthful master still in the town.

Despite the lack of furniture, the palace possesses plenty of atmosphere. John Addington Symonds, the prolific Victorian art historian, waxed lyrical in his description of it:

Are these chambers really those where Emilia Pia held debate with Bembo and Castiglione; where Bibbiena's witticisms and Fra Serafino's pranks raised smiles on courtly lips; where Bernardo Accolti, 'the Unique', declaimed his verses to admiring crowds? Is it possible that into yonder hall, where now the lion of St Mark looks down alone in staring desolation, strode the Borgia in all his panoply of war, a gilded glittering dragon, and from the dais tore Montefeltri's throne, and from the arras stripped their ensigns, replacing these with his own Bull and Valentinus Dux? Here Tasso tuned his lyre for Francesco Maria's wedding-feast, and read 'Aminta' to Lucrezia d' Este. Here Guidobaldo listened to the jests and whispered scandals of the Aretine. Here Titian set his easel up to paint; here the boy Raphael, cap in hand, took signed and sealed credentials from his Dutchess to the Gonfalonier of Florence. Somewhere in these huge chambers, the courtiers sat before a torchlit stage, where Bibbiena's 'Calandria' and Castiglione's 'Tirsi,' with their miracles of masques and mummers, whirled the night away. Somewhere, we know not where, Giuliano de' Medici made love in these bare rooms to that mysterious mother of ill-fated Cardinal Ippolito; somewhere, in some darker nook, the bastard Alessandro sprang to his strange-fortuned life of tyranny and license, which Brutus Lorenzino cut short with a traitor's poignard-thrust in Via Larga. How many men, illustrious for arts and letters, memorable by their virtues or their crimes, from the great Pope Julius down to James III, self-styled King of England, who tarried here with Clementine Sobieski through some twelve months of his ex-royal exile!

Outside the palace, turn left and in the **Duomo**, look at the beautiful colouring of Barocci's *St Sebastian* and the *Last Supper*. Barocci was court painter in Urbino in the sixteenth century, the last major artist to work here before the town reverted to its provincial origins. Behind the Cathedral **Il Nuovo Coppiere** in Via Porta Maja is a friendly up-market trattoria.

After lunch, continue down Via Puccinotti to Piazza Repubblica, cross the square and head up the narrow Via Barocci. The **Oratorio di San Giuseppe** on the right-hand side was covered by Federico Brandini in the sixteenth century in an illusionistic *tour de force* of stuccowork. On the wall is a portrait inscribed Giacomo III Stuart, Re d' Inghilterra, who came here shortly after his marriage to Clementina Sobieski in 1717.

At the end of the street, the **Oratorio di San Giovanni** was frescoed by Giacomo and Lorenzo Salimbeni in 1416, with a series of scenes from the *Life of the Baptist*. Salimbeni's figures are very reluctant participants in the drama, not at all keen to shed their wonderful costumes to bathe in the Jordan, and taking not the slightest bit of notice of the earnest preaching of St John the Baptist.

INFORMATION

Palazzo Ducale: 9 a.m. to 2 p.m., Sunday 9 a.m. to 1 p.m., closed Monday

Oratorio di San Giuseppe and **Oratorio di San Giovanni**: 10 a.m. to 12 noon and 3 p.m. to 5 p.m., Sunday 10 a.m. to 12.30 p.m. and 3 p.m. to 5 p.m.

RESTAURANT

Il Nuovo Coppiere
Via Porta Maja 20, Urbino
Telephone: 0722 320 092, closed Wednesday

EMILIA-ROMAGNA

Here all the cities are capitals, and have not that provincial
tone of the secondary towns of other kingdoms

Byron

Although filled with bustling cities and, to some extent, spoilt by industrialisation, Emilia's culture is among the richest in Italy, and the province merits far more than the cursory glance most twentieth-century tourists devote to it, hurrying from Florence to Venice. A visit to Emilia is a chance to enjoy the creature comforts in life, eat the best food in Italy, enjoy the wealth of goods displayed in every shop window, listen to the wonderful operas staged in Parma, and admire the paintings in the galleries and churches of Bologna, Parma and Modena and the exquisite mosaics in Ravenna.

The cities of Emilia, with their widely varied histories, give the area its peculiar character. Bologna, the province's capital and its cultural centre, a fiercely independent member of the Lombard League in the Middle Ages, became the second city in the Papal States after it succumbed to Pope Julius II in 1506. Parma was the seat of the Farnese family from 1545 to 1801, and was then ruled by Marie Louise, the second wife of Napoleon, and her family until the Risorgimento in 1859. The Este family, who rivalled the Farnese as patrons of the arts, held court at Ferrara and Modena, and attracted a glittering array of artists, including Tasso, Ariosto and Titian. And Ravenna, lost in the marshes on the shores of the Adriatic, enjoyed the most glorious history of all, ruling the rump of the Roman Empire in the west long after Rome herself had fallen.

Bologna was one of the most important stopping points on the Grand Tour because of the extraordinary popularity of the Bolognese School of painting, regarded as the height of academic excellence. The style of the leading masters, Annibale Carracci, Guido Reni and Guercino, combined the two elements that most appealed to eighteenth-century visitors, namely a close study of classical sculpture and the art of Raphael. Horace Walpole summed up contemporary opinion by declaring that 'All the qualities of a perfect painter, are never met but in Raphael, Guido and Annibale

Carracci', and almost a century later Jacques Galiffe, in his guide-book declared: 'Whenever I think of paintings, the name of Guido Reni is the first that occurs to me.' It seems incredible to us to imagine Stendhal claiming, with no more than a hint of irony, that he found Bologna one hundred times more interesting than Florence.

Bologna was renowned as a centre of learning. Its university, specialising in law and medicine, dates back to the eleventh century and is the oldest in Italy, earning the city the nickname of 'La Dotta' (the Learned). One of the stock figures in the commedia dell' arte is the Dottore, a cunning lawyer from Bologna. The university numbered among its students Ignatius Loyola, the founder of the Jesuits, and Bologna was famed as a centre of the dreaded Inquisition. Before the eighteenth century many Protestants gave the city a wide berth and there was no question of attending the university, unlike that in Padua.

Grand Tourists, when they were not lost in rapture before the altarpieces of the Carracci, went to Parma to admire the paintings of Correggio and Parmigianino, the city's two great High Renaissance artists, whose graceful figures earned them a reputation almost as exalted as Raphael himself. With their determination not to miss any remnant of antiquity, these tourists headed for Rimini to study the Roman Arch of Augustus, on the junction of the Via Flaminia and the Via Aemilia. But they showed minimal interest in any art between the Sack of Rome in 410 AD and the High Renaissance, including the marvellous mosaics in nearby Ravenna and Alberti's fascinating Tempio Malatestiano in Rimini, even though Alberti was consciously trying to recreate an antique temple. Addison, whose influential guidebook concentrates almost exclusively on classical art, wrote dismissively: 'Rimini has nothing modern to boast of.'

Emilia's popularity lasted into the early nineteenth century, with the Romantics continuing to praise the Bolognese school of painting which they now viewed in a literary light. Guido Reni's portrait of Beatrice Cenci, who had been executed in 1589 for murdering her incestuous father, became as famous as the *Mona Lisa*, and was particularly admired by Balzac and Dickens (both the attribution of the sitter and the painter are now extremely doubtful). Ferrara, where the Estes had established one of the most brilliant courts of the Renaissance, was visited by literary enthusiasts, who copied the example of Byron and his friends Rogers and Hobhouse in carving their names in Tasso's cell.

Ferrara had fallen into decay since the days of the Estes, adding to its romantic allure. Hazlitt waxed lyrical on his visit in 1826: 'Of all the places I have seen in Italy, it is the one by far I should most covet to live in. It is the ideal of an Italian city, once great, now a shadow of itself . . . nothing is to be seen of Ferrara but the remains, graceful and romantic, of what it was.' Dickens was similarly enthusiastic, revelling in the melancholic atmosphere of the palaces 'where rank weeds are slowly creeping up the long-untrodden stairs'.

A dramatic change in artistic taste occurred around the middle of the nineteenth century, and the sophistication of the Bolognese painters, with their carefully composed groups based on the study of antique and High Renaissance art, lost its appeal. It was now the Middle Ages, the time of Dante, Giotto and St Francis, instead of antiquity, which inspired travellers. Victorians heading to Italy, full of religious fervour, were spiritually uplifted by the Madonnas and saints of Giotto and Fra Angelico and avidly read descriptions by art critics such as Ruskin and Lord Lindsay of how the Middle Ages was an age of faith.

The simplicity and purity of the paintings of the Trecento and Quattrocento masters, painted in strong primary colours and easily understandable, were contrasted with the darkened saints of Lodovico Carracci, the pagan nudes of Guido Reni and the classical gods of Domenichino. Ruskin dismissed the Bolognese painters as 'Eclectics', a phrase he coined to describe their lack of originality. By the end of the century virtually no one was interested in visiting Bologna to look at its art. As George Bernard Shaw stated: 'Nowadays ten acres of Carracci, Giulio Romano, Guido, Domenichino and Pietro da Cortona will not buy an inch of Botticelli, or Lippi, or John Bellini.'

Correggio and Parmigianino suffered a similar fall from grace. Their elegant elongated figures, so admired in the eighteenth century, now attracted ridicule. Charles Dickens, writing in 1846, was very dismissive of the Duomo in Parma:

> This cathedral is odorous with the rotting of Correggio's frescoes in the cupola. Heaven knows how beautiful they may have been at one time. Connoisseurs fall into raptures with them now; but such a labyrinth of arms and legs: such heaps of foreshortened limbs, entangled and involved and jumbled together: no operative surgeon, gone mad, could imagine in his wildest delirium.

Together with the change in artistic taste, the Victorians wanted to escape from the larger cities and explore the dramatic countryside of Tuscany and Umbria, with their spectacularly sited medieval hill towns filled with obscure Quattrocento masterpieces. Emilia, dominated by cities strung along the Po valley, offered little competition.

Bologna's and Parma's reputations have yet to recover from the severe criticism they received from the Victorian critics. Most foreigners regard them as no more than the homes of Bolognese sauce and Parma ham. This makes them very good value for the discerning tourist before they are ruined by the hordes who now descend on Florence and Venice.

The province is full of neglected treasures like the evocative Romanesque Abbey of Pomposa, standing in splendid isolation on the shores of the Adriatic. A similar disregard is paid to the fresco cycle by Francesco del Cossa and Ercole de' Roberti in the Palazzo Schifanoia, at Via Scandiana 23 in Ferrara, one of the decorative masterpieces of the Renaissance. All round the walls are delightful depictions of the months, with classical gods and goddesses being paraded in triumph. Even in Modena, a sombre city devoted to the motor-racing industry, the Romanesque Duomo has some of the best medieval sculpture in Italy, with mythological creatures crawling over every pillar. And the Galleria Estense, housed in the Palazzo dei Musei in Via Santa Eufemia, has a superb collection of Renaissance and Baroque masterpieces, ranging from pictures by Hans Baldung Grien, Cosimo Tura and Dosso Dossi to a wealth of Bolognese paintings, a series of delightful landscapes by Salvator Rosa and a masterly overmantel by Grinling Gibbons, given to the Este family on the marriage of James II to Mary of Modena. The collection was largely formed by Francesco d' Este, who commissioned, in the best possible taste, Velázquez to paint his portrait and Bernini to sculpt his bust, a masterpiece of Baroque movement. And around Parma the fairy-tale castle of Fontanellato, the perfect Renaissance town of Sabbioneta and the dramatic setting of the castle of Torrechiara against the backdrop of the Apennines all show the diversity of Emilia's appeal, and prove the Victorians to have been every bit as blinkered in their sightseeing as their Grand Tour predecessors.

Bologna

That celebrated mart of lapdogs and sausages
William Beckford

*PIAZZA MAGGIORE~SAN PETRONIO~ARCHIGINNASIO~
SANTO STEFANO~SAN GIACOMO MAGGIORE~
PINACOTECA NAZIONALE~PALAZZO BEVILACQUA~
COLLEGIO DI SPAGNA*

Bologna's characteristic arcaded streets, dating back to the city's independent heyday in the Middle Ages, are some of the most handsome in northern Italy. Historically, the city is 'celebrated for the producing of Popes – painters – & sausages' as Byron noted on his visit in 1817. Bologna is a city where tourists feel free of pressure. There are no crowds thronging the churches and galleries, no obligation to tick off all the famous sights, and shops and restaurants on every side to offer welcome distractions. The university continues to enjoy a high academic reputation, making Bologna a fitting setting for the annual book fair which is held here every spring. And the city has always been one of the gastronomic centres in Italy, earning it the nickname of *La Grassa* (the Fat).

Bologna's centre is the **Piazza Maggiore** and the adjoining Piazza Nettuno, off which the major shops and restaurants radiate. Giambologna's fountain, standing in the centre of the Piazza Nettuno and executed in 1566 to a design by the Sicilian Tommaso Laureti, was the forerunner of much free-standing Baroque statuary. Evelyn, who responded enthusiastically to Baroque art, much admired it, unlike later Grand Tourists who thought Neptune's stylised pose too contrived.

On the east side of the square is the thirteenth-century Palazzo di Re Enzo, where the unfortunate son of the Emperor Frederick II was incarcerated for the last twenty-two years of his life after the Bolognese captured him at the battle of Fossalta in 1249. The Emperor Charles V lodged in the Palazzo Comunale on the west side of Piazza Maggiore when he came to Bologna for his coronation in 1530. On the second floor of the palace there is a good collection of Baroque paintings, including an excellent portrait of a *Cavaliere* in armour by Artemisia Gentileschi.

The windows of the palace open on to the Piazza Maggiore, dominated by the massive unfinished red-brick façade of **San Petronio**, the largest and most impressive church in Bologna. The powerful sculptures of scenes from the book of Genesis and of the *Infancy of Christ* by Jacopo della Quercia round the main portal, dating from 1425 to 1438, exerted a profound influence on Michelangelo.

In a magnificent ceremony in 1530 Clement VII crowned Charles V emperor in the vast vaulted interior. The most striking of the numerous works of art in the side-chapels are the attractive early fifteenth-century frescoes of *Heaven* and *Hell* by Jacopo di Paolo in the third chapel on the left, and a brightly coloured decorative altarpiece of the *Martyrdom of St Sebastian* attributed to a late fifteenth-century Ferrarese artist in the fourth chapel. In the seventh chapel hangs a *St Roch* by Parmigianino, much admired in the eighteenth century. What really fascinated Grand Tourists, products of an age of scientific curiosity, however, was the meridian line which runs down the nave.

Emerging from the basilica, turn right down Via dell' Archiginnasio, named after the **Archiginnasio** on the left, where the university was housed until 1800. Every available inch of the cloister and staircase is covered with coats-of-arms in fresco and relief of former rectors and professors. One of the most renowned faculties was that of medicine, and anatomical dissection first took place in the anatomical theatre, destroyed in the last war and rebuilt on the first floor, one of its less salubrious specialities being the performing of castrations.

Byron, as ever, found some titillation in the Archiginnasio, and recorded his impressions:

> I saw an anatomical gallery, where there is a deal of waxwork in which the parts of shame of both sexes are exhibited to the life – all made and moulded by a female professor . . . I thought the male part of her performance not very favourable to her imagination or at least to the Italian originals . . . more particularly as the feminine display was a little in the other extreme.

Outside the Archiginnasio, head left down Piazza Galvani, turn left into Via Farini and left again into Via Castiglione. Via Pepoli, the first street on the right, takes you past some of the finest palaces in Bologna to the basilica of **Santo Stefano**, a complex of three of the earliest churches in the city. This group of churches, with its different layers of architectural history, is one of the most interesting survivals of early Christianity in Europe. The first of these, the Crocifisso, is on a split level, an unhappy mixture of a Baroque choir with a Romanesque nave and vault. Adjoining it is the centrally planned church of San Sepolcro which may once have been an Early Christian Baptistery.

The church of Santi Vitale e Agricola beyond is the oldest church of the three. The early Christians were indiscriminate in treating antique monuments as quarries, and the capitals, slabs of porphyry and other details are all stripped from ancient Roman buildings; the tombs of the martyred saints Vitale and Agricola in the side-apses are original Roman sarcophagi. The extraordinary windows in the apse are made of alabaster. Behind the churches is a courtyard and a cloister with the bowl where Pilate is supposed to have washed his hands (the bowl was actually made in the eighth century AD).

From Santo Stefano bear right down Via Santo Stefano to Piazza Mercanzia, overlooked by the fine Gothic Palazzo della Mercanzia and the eccentric leaning towers which are the most famous landmark in the city and mentioned by Dante. Evelyn remarked of Bologna: "'Tis built like a ship, whereof the Torre d' Asinello may go for the mainmast.' The two towers were built by the rival Asinelli and Garisenda families in the early eleventh century, but the Torre Garisenda had to be left unfinished (and indeed was shortened in the fourteenth century) when the foundations began to subside.

If you are ready for lunch, there are numerous excellent trattorias and restaurants in the surrounding streets, the best of which, and one of the oldest in the city, is Il Papagallo at Piazza della Mercanzia 3c. After an unsuccessful experiment with *nouvelle cuisine* Il Papagallo has reverted to typical Bolognese food, with a range of pasta dishes followed by *misto, zampone* and *cotechino* (different ways of preparing pork). An alternative is Taverna Tre Frecce at Strada Maggiore 19 off the east side Piazza della Mercanzia. The atmospheric medieval interior, with beamed ceilings and paintings of the Bolognese School, is a worthy setting for the Salsini's excellent cooking. The menu changes every month but there are certain constants such as the delicious fizzy Lambrusco, which helps to digest the richness of Bolognese cooking. A much less exotic restaurant, full of students, is the Birreria Lamma at Via de' Giudei 4 just off the north side of the Piazza di Porta Revegnana. It gives a good idea of the rich standard of Bolognese cuisine, even in the cheaper restaurants, and bears out Dr Burney's view, in 1770, that: 'The trade here is chiefly that of the belly.'

If you would like to press on, take the Via Zamboni off the northeast side of the Piazza di Porta Ravegnana. The Romanesque church of San Giacomo Maggiore on your right contains charming frescoes by the Renaissance painters Francia and Lorenzo Costa, both in the Cappella Bentivoglio at the end of the north aisle and behind the apse in the Oratory of St Cecilia.

Continue down Via Zamponi and, just past the eighteenth-century Teatro Comunale overlooking Piazza Verdi, and the univer-

sity opposite which has been housed here since 1803, is the
Pinacoteca Nazionale, where the acres of Bolognese paintings may
well cause you to doubt Sir Robert Walpole's judgement, typical of
the taste of his era, that 'next to Rome Bologna boasts the most capital paintings in the world'.

The most striking exhibit in the first rooms is Nicola dell' Arca's
terracotta *Entombment*, an emotional group of grief-stricken figures
verging on hysteria, not the sort of art designed to appeal to puritan-
ical visitors. The pick of the Renaissance paintings in the following
rooms are a *Madonna and Child* by Cima da Conegliano and a
charming *Madonna of the Rose Garden* by Schongauer. You may
well want to emulate Grand Tourists, who tended to ignore the sweet,
sometimes sentimental Madonnas of Francia and Perugino and saved
their admiration for Raphael's famous painting of *St Cecilia*, one of
the paintings Napoleon took to Paris in 1797. Until the middle of the
nineteenth century this altarpiece inspired reams of praise. It was
Ruskin, as much as anyone, who lowered Raphael's reputation in
favour of earlier and, in his view, purer painters. He recorded his
decision in 1845: 'So much the worse for Raffaelle. I have been a long
time hesitating, but I have given him up today, before the St Cecilia.
I shall knock him down, and put up Perugino in his niche'.

The vast altarpieces of the Carracci and their followers, so inspi-
rational to Grand Tourists, now seem rather overwhelming. Perhaps

214

the most easily appreciated are the early works of Guercino, such as *St Sebastian Cured by Irene* with its dramatic use of light and shade, and the landscapes of Annibale Carracci and Domenichino. In the eighteenth century, as taste changed, genre scenes replaced religious works, those by the Bolognese Crespi being some of the finest in Italy.

If you have managed to hold out this long without sampling the delights of Bolognese cooking, head back up Via Zamponi. Cross the Piazza di Porta Ravegnana, bear right down Via Rizzoli and take the fourth right down Via dell' Indipendenza, the smartest shopping street in Bologna. **Ristorante Diana** at no. 24 is heavily patronised by locals and serves some of the best pasta and meat dishes in Bologna. An excellent starter is the salad made of rocket, parmesan cheese and truffles. A grander restaurant with a sumptuous dining-room decorated with sixteenth-century grotesques is **I Carracci** at Via Manzoni 2, the second street on the left down Via dell' Indipendenza. Many of the recipes are traditional ones which have been used in Bolognese cuisine for centuries and include *tortellini in brodo di cappone* (pasta in chicken broth) and *pappardelle al sugo di coniglio* (pasta strips with rabbit sauce.)

After lunch, if you can resist the tantalising goods cramming every shop window, return to Via Rizzoli and turn down Via di Archiginnasio. At the bottom of Piazza Galvani turn right into Via Farini and left into Via d'Azeglio. The **Palazzo Bevilacqua**, at nos. 31–3, with a splendid double colonnade in the courtyard, is a handsome Renaissance palace where the Council of Trent, the spearhead of the Counter Reformation, was housed in 1547.

The next turning on the right, into Via Urbana, passes, on the right, the **Collegio di Spagna**, the last survivor in Bologna of the medieval collegiate system which once resembled that at Oxford and Cambridge. Two of the more famous students of this college were Ignatius Loyola and Cervantes, the author of *Don Quixote*. The main building dates from the time of Cardinal Albornoz, who founded the college in 1365 and placed his arms and his Cardinal's hat all over the walls. The beautiful Gothic chapel, its vault decorated with stars, is reminiscent of the Sainte Chapelle in Paris. Behind the chapel is a charming secluded garden ending in a pergola. The complex of buildings still conveys something of the atmosphere of the medieval university.

INFORMATION

Pinacoteca Nazionale: 9 a.m. to 2 p.m., Sunday 9 a.m. to 1 p.m., closed Monday

RESTAURANTS

Il Papagallo
Piazza della Mercanzia 3c, Bologna
Telephone: 051 232 807, closed Sunday evening and Monday

Taverna Tre Frecce
Strada Maggiore 19, Bologna
Telephone: 051 231 200, closed Sunday evening and Monday

Birreria Lamma
Via de' Giudei 4, Bologna
Telephone: 051 236 537, closed Wednesday

Ristorante Diana
Via dell' Indipendenza 24, Bologna
Telephone: 051 231 302, closed Monday

I Carracci
Via Manzoni 2, Bologna
Telephone: 051 270 815, closed Sunday

Parma

At Parma I know nothing half as curious as the Arch Duchess. I had rather see her than all the paintings of Correggio put together

Lord Pembroke

SAN GIOVANNI EVANGELISTA~DUOMO~BAPTISTERY~ CAMERA DEL CORREGGIO~GALLERIA NAZIONALE~ MADONNA DELLA STECCATA

The golden era of Parma's history was the sixteenth century, when Pope Paul III carved out the duchy for his illegitimate son Pier Luigi Farnese, the beginning of a long and flourishing rule by the family coinciding with the careers of Correggio and Parmigianino, Parma's two most famous artists. Perhaps the most remarkable of all the Farnese was the third duke, Alexander, the hero of the seventeenth-century Grand Tourist Richard Lassels, who described his career:

Indeed his leaping the first man into the Turk's galley in the battle of Lepanto, with sword in hand, and in the eighteenth year only of his age, was such a prognostic of his future worth; his reducing of Flanders again, with the prodigious actions done by him at the taking of Antwerp, was such a making good of the prognostic; and his coming into France in his slippers and sedan to succour Rouen besieged by Henry the IV, was such a crowning of all his other actions, that his history begets belief in Quintus Curitus, and makes men believe, that Alexanders can do anything.

If Parma ranks slightly below Bologna in terms of works of art, there is no doubt that its cuisine rivals that of the provincial capital. And so high is Parma's standard of opera, particularly in performances of works by Verdi who was born at Roncole Verdi, 33 km north of the city, that aspiring singers only progress to La Scala in Milan after being sanctioned here first.

You can view the major sights in this handsome red-brick city in a morning, concentrating on the works of Correggio and Parmigianino. Correggio's two great fresco cycles are in San Giovanni Evangelista and the Duomo. He painted the splendid fresco of the *Vision of St John the Evangelist* in the dome of San Giovanni Evangelista between 1520 and 1524, increasing the effect of movement by depicting Christ in sharp foreshortening as he descends from heaven, watched by the twelve Apostles. The swirl of movement, which was to be so influential on Baroque painting, is even more pronounced in Correggio's next work, the fresco of the *Assumption* in the dome of the eleventh-century **Duomo**, which stands directly in front of San Giovanni Evangelista. The central figure of the Virgin sweeps up to heaven bearing a whole host of figures in her train.

Correggio's frescoes were much admired by Grand Tourists, particularly by artists. Even the American painter John Singleton Copley, hurrying home to his young wife in 1775 on hearing of the outbreak of war, could not resist stopping in Parma to copy the Correggios. But neither Copley nor any other Grand Tourist commented on Antelami's magnificent *Deposition* in the south transept of the Duomo.

Emerging from the Duomo, the octagonal **Baptistery**, built in Verona marble, stands on your left. It was begun in 1196 by the architect Antelami, who also carved the charming frieze of animals running round the exterior, the three portals depicting scenes from the *Life of the Virgin* and the *Last Judgement*, and the reliefs of the months in the interior.

217

Despite the praise lavished on the Correggio frescoes in the Duomo, Grand Tourists, with their dislike of medieval art, generally ignored the Baptistery. When they did choose to comment on it it was in the most derogatory terms. Lady Morgan's guidebook, published in 1819, described the thirteenth-century frescoes in the vault: 'The Virgin is always painted like a large female baboon, feeding her young. The eyes meet, the nose is long, the lower part of the face retreats, the complexion is ebony, and the expression a mixture of ferocity and cunning.'

Beyond the Baptistery, take the second right off Strada al Duomo into Strada Cavour. Take the first left into Via Melloni and the first right to the **Camera del Correggio** at the end of the street. Correggio painted this small room, originally the refectory of the convent of San Paolo, with sensuous mythological scenes which scandalised the Victorians, especially as the abbess, Giovanna Piacenza, seems to be posing as Diana. The next room is covered in amusing grotesques by Correggio's contemporary Araldi.

Returning to Via Melloni, turn right and cross Strada Garibaldi into Piazza Marconi. If you need a break from culture, **La Greppia**, at Strada Garibaldi 39, is a first-class restaurant with all sorts of delectable dishes on the menu. Try the *nocciole di semolina con carciofi* and the *tournedos di maiale in salsa berbera*.

If you would rather wait for lunch, the finest collection of paintings in Parma (only a remnant of the Farnese collections removed by the Bourbons of Naples in the eighteenth century after they inherited the Farnese properties) is housed in the **Galleria Nazionale**, across Piazza Marconi. The gallery adjoins the enormous wooden Teatro Farnese, an early seventeenth-century pastiche of Palladio's Teatro Olimpico in Vicenza. Parma was renowned for its theatre, and it was probably here that David Garrick, the greatest English actor of the eighteenth century, performed the dagger scene from *Macbeth* before the Duke of Parma in 1764. The duke was so pleased that he invited Garrick to stay in his palace, and gave him a gold snuff-box. The Italian interpretation of Shakespeare was not always as correct as Garrick's. John Owen saw a production of *Amletto (Hamlet)* in 1791. He was amazed to find that the play was taken for a burlesque with the audience constantly breaking into 'tremendous peals of applause'. The theatre was almost totally destroyed in the last war, but has been carefully restored.

Among the finest works are Correggio's famous *Marriage of St Jerome*, some beautiful Cimas, Holbein's portrait of Erasmus and Sebastiano del Piombo's penetrating portrait of Clement VII, the Medici pope who was unfortunate enough to fall victim of the sack of Rome in 1527.

Outside the museum, cross Piazza Marconi and turn left down Strada Garibaldi. The first large building on your right is the Teatro Regio, built by the ex-Empress Marie Louise in 1829. She employed Paganini as her musical director and the Teatro opened with a performance of Bellini's *Zaira*. The high standard of music has continued into this century. The conductor Toscanini, who was born in Parma in 1867, began his career playing in the orchestra here.

If you would like an alternative to La Greppia restaurant, continue down Strada Garibaldi and turn left into Strada Mazzini. Cross Piazza Garibaldi and continue down Strada Repubblica where **Parizzi**, at no. 71 on the ground floor of an old palace, is famous for its *delizie di Parma* and its delicious sparkling Lambrusco.

After lunch you may like to visit some of the fashionable clothes shops based around the Piazza Garibaldi or some good antique shops south of the square. The economy in Emilia is thriving, so do not expect to find many bargains.

If you would like to visit one further sight, return to the Strada Garibaldi and the **Madonna della Steccata**, a handsome sixteenth-century church filled with Renaissance paintings including frescoes by Parmigianino, Anselmi and Bedoli.

INFORMATION

Galleria Nazionale: 9 a.m. to 2 p.m., Sunday 9 a.m. to 1 p.m., closed Monday

RESTAURANTS

La Greppia
Strada Garibaldi 39, Parma
Telephone: 0521 33686, closed Thursday and Friday

Parizzi
Strada della Repubblica 71, Parma
Telephone: 0521 285 952, closed Sunday evening and Monday

Environs of Parma

SABBIONETA~FONTANELLATO~TORRECHIARA

The most interesting excursion from Parma is to Mantua (see pages 12–15). On the way, some 29 km north of Parma, make a brief stop at **Sabbioneta**, a perfect example of an ideal Renaissance town laid out on a grid pattern. It has hardly changed since its creator Vespasiano Gonzaga died in 1591. The theatre, built by Scamozzi in 1588, is yet another example of the profound influence exerted by Palladio's theatre in Vicenza which Scamozzi completed after Palladio's death. The Palazzo Ducale, unfortunately denuded of its furniture, has some frescoes of various members of the Gonzaga family, and four splendid equestrian statues of Vespasiano and his male kinsmen. Sadly, after Vespasiano's death and reflecting the failure of his ideas, his successors let the town and the chapel fall into disrepair.

Another interesting excursion is to the fairy-tale moated castle of **Fontanellato** which lies 20 km west of Parma just off the A 1 *autostrada*. It was built by the Sanvitale family in the thirteenth century. One of the smaller rooms on the ground floor was delightfully frescoed by Parmigianino in 1524 with scenes from the story of Diana and Actaeon with Paola Gonzaga, the wife of Galeazzo Sanvitale, portrayed as Diana.

Roncole Verdi 13 km further west is the birthplace of Verdi, and 5 km beyond **I Due Foscari**, in the small town of Busseto, is one of the best restaurants in Italy, owned, fittingly enough, by Carlo Bregonzi, the well-known tenor.

The most exciting castle to visit near Parma is **Torrechiara** which lies to the south in a most impressive site on the edge of the Apennines. Despite the forbidding exterior, the interior is filled with delightful frescoes by Cesare Baglione (1540–1615). The ground-floor rooms are covered with grotesques, ruined architecture and pergolas with birds. The Sala d'Oro has frescoes of lively figures and animals, including athletes performing acrobatics over the fireplace. Upstairs, there are fifteenth-century frescoes by Benedetto Bembo in the Camera d'Oro.

INFORMATION

Castello Sanvitale, Fontanellato: summer 10 a.m. to 12.30 p.m. and 3.30 p.m. to 7 p.m., winter 9 a.m. to 12.30 p.m. and 3 p.m. to 6 p.m., closed Monday

Torrechiara: 9 a.m. to 1 p.m., closed Monday

I Due Foscari
Piazza Rossi 15, Busseto
Telephone: 0524 92337, closed Monday

Ravenna

They make love a good deal, – and assassinate a little
                                                            Byron

SAN VITALE~MAUSOLEUM OF GALLA PLACIDIA~
PALAZZO GUICCIOLI~NEONIAN BAPTISTERY~
MUSEO ARCIVESCOVILE~SANT' APOLLINARE NUOVO~
SANT' APOLLINARE IN CLASSE

Ravenna is a romantic misfit, a town that reached its heyday after the sack of Rome when it became the Roman capital of the west long before Bologna and Parma were established, and then lapsed into total decay. For centuries the name of Theodoric, Ravenna's greatest ruler and King of the Goths, meant nothing, and almost all Grand Tourists ignored the magnificent mosaics. During the nineteenth century, as interest grew in the Middle Ages, discerning travellers began to visit Ravenna, and, with the revival of Byzantine studies this century, the splendid churches and mosaics are now seen as one of the crucial links between eastern and western civilisations in the early Middle Ages.

Byron, the most famous traveller to come to Ravenna, and very conscious of following in the exiled Dante's footsteps, did so for love and not to see Ravenna's culture, as he explained to his mistress Teresa Guiccioli in a letter dated 11 June 1819:

> I have tried to distract myself with this farce of visiting antiquities – it seems quite intolerably tedious . . . The little that interests me – Dante's tomb and a few things in the library – I have already seen with an indifference made pardonable by the state of my heart.

Byron prided himself on his originality but his neglect of Ravenna's culture was typical of contemporary Grand Tourist taste.

Shelley, who came to visit Byron, thought Ravenna 'a miserable place, the people are barbarous and wild, and their language the most infernal patois that you can imagine'.

Byron was, however, original in his desire to enter into the life of provincial Italian society. He grew very fond of the town and wrote approvingly:

> Ravenna itself preserves more of the old Italian manners than any city in Italy – it is more out of the way of travellers and armies – and thus they have retained more of their originality. – They make love a good deal, – and assassinate a little.

Begin a tour of the town at **San Vitale**, the octagonal church begun in 525 by Theodoric and completed in 548 when Ravenna had come under the rule of the Byzantine Emperor Justinian. The centrally planned space, surrounded by a screen of eight arches, gives the spectator a succession of changing views as he walks around the church, and provided a crucial influence on Justinian's vast cathedral of Hagia Sofia in Constantinople, built shortly afterwards. The apse is decorated with brilliantly coloured mosaics depicting Justinian and Theodora and their attendants, flanking a central mosaic of Christ and two angels on the semi-dome. In the **Mausoleum of Galla Placidia**, adjoining the church, Christ is portrayed as the Good Shepherd against a brilliant blue sky, while his flock browse in a meadow and stags drink from the fountain of life in the side lunettes.

From the Mausoleum take the Via Carlo Cattaneo down to Via Cavour, turn left to reach the rather grim **Palazzo Guiccioli** at no. 54, where Byron settled in 1820, paying Count Guiccioli a substantial rent for the privilege of making love to his wife. Perhaps he recalled his initial observation on his arrival in Italy, that 'a woman is virtuous (according to the code) who limits herself to her husband and one lover'.

Shelley came to visit Byron in August 1821 and recorded the extraordinary set-up in the palace:

> Lord B.'s establishment consists, besides servants, of ten horses, eight enormous dogs, three monkies, five cats, an eagle, a crow, and a falcon, and all these, except the horses, walk about the house, which every now and then resounds with their unarbitrated quarrels, as if they were masters of it . . .
>
> After I have sealed my letter, I find that my enumeration of the animals in this Circean Palace was defective, and that in a material point. I have just met on the grand staircase five peacocks, two guinea hens, and an Egyptian crane.

Heading down Via Cavour, turn right into Via Matteotti and bear right into Via Nino Bixio which passes the Duomo. The **Neonian Baptistery** (as opposed to the rival Arian Baptistery) to the left of the Duomo was converted from a Roman bathhouse in the fifth century, and is covered with mosaics and sculpture. The mosaics depict the Twelve Apostles standing out against the deep blue background, arranged around the central scene of the Baptism, with the river Jordan personified as an old man holding a reed.

The **Museo Arcivescovile** behind the Duomo is a picturesque jumble of mosaics, inscriptions, sculpture and sarcophagi with no labels or dates. The Oratorio di Sant' Andrea has a delightful early sixth-century mosaic in the barrel vault of the vestibule, covered with a profusion of brightly coloured birds. The ivory Chair of the Emperor Maximian, in the far room, probably made by craftsmen from Alexandria in the sixth century, may have been given by the Emperor Justinian to the Archbishop of Ravenna. The carving, both of the main scenes of the lives of Joseph and of Christ, and of the animals and foliage between the scenes, is of the highest quality.

Outside the museum, head north-east up Via Gasperi to Piazza Caduti. To the left of the church of San Francesco, which stands back from the square, is the tomb of Dante who died in exile in Ravenna in 1321. The locals have always fiercely rejected Florence's attempts to reclaim the remains of one of her most famous sons.

The basilica of **Sant' Apollinare Nuovo** stands directly behind Dante's tomb; go up Via Dante into Piazza Garibaldi, turn right into Via Mariani and right again into Via di Roma. It was built by Theodoric in the early sixth century and dedicated to the saint when his body was transferred from the coastal basilica of Sant' Apollinare in Classe in the ninth century, due to the danger of pirate raids.

The interior glitters with the brilliant colours of the mosaics which cover the walls of the nave. Two elaborate processions of Martyrs and Virgins move in a stately rhythm towards the altar; the two lines culminate in the figures of Christ and the Virgin seated enthroned among angels. Above the Martyrs and Virgins are figures of Saints and Prophets, and at the top a series of scenes of the *Miracles* and the *Passion of Christ*. At the west end two fascinating views of the harbour of Classe and of Theodoric's palace in Ravenna give an idea of Ravenna's former greatness. The finest mosaic of all depicts the three Magi, with their spotted trousers and red Phrygian caps, at the front of the procession presenting their gifts to the Christ child. Even today scholars are undecided over the attributions of the mosaics, but it seems probable the figures in the upper two sections, with their individual characterisation, were made by local craftsmen in the early sixth century, whereas the hierarchical lines of Martyrs and Virgins were made slightly later by Byzantine artists imported into Ravenna during the reign of Justinian.

It is now time for lunch. The best restaurants in Ravenna are the **Tre Spade** and the **Bella Venezia**. From the church turn right up Via Roma and take the second left down Via Diaz to Piazza del Popolo, and the Bella Venezia is at Via 4 Novembre 16 off the north side of the square. Or, take the first left off Via Roma into Via Mariani and, crossing Piazza Garibaldi, take the fourth right down Via Guerrini and the Tre Spade is on the corner of Piazza Kennedy at Via Rasponi 35. Both serve excellent seafood. If you would like to eat outside the town, **Trattoria Casa delle Aie** in an eighteenth-century house at Via delle Aie 4, Cervia, some 24 km south of Ravenna on the Adriatic, serves local dishes such as rabbit, duck, pork and beef, grilled over a wood fire.

After lunch, either take a taxi or follow the signs towards the sea for 5 km, and you reach the basilica of **Sant' Apollinare in Classe** on the site of Ravenna's ancient port, long since silted up. As at Sant' Apollinare Nuovo, the impressive late tenth-century campanile is cylindrical, a typical feature of Ravenna's churches. The excellently preserved basilica dates from the first half of the sixth century.

The solemn interior is dominated by the two lines of Greek marble columns which lead the eye up to the mosaics in the apse. The central mosaic depicts St Apollinare attending the Transfiguration, set against a vivid green and gold background. The sheep flanking the saint represent the Apostles. The seventh-century mosaics on the side walls of the apse show the sacrifices of Abel, Melchisedech and Abraham on the right, and on the left the Emperor Constantine IV with his brothers giving Archbishop Reparatus privileges for the church in Ravenna.

The surroundings of Ravenna have unfortunately become very built up, particularly the industrial area around the port. This was where Byron loved to ride in the pine woods and where he plotted with the Italian patriots against the Austrian army who occupied this part of Italy. He recorded his feelings in one of the most beautiful passages of *Don Juan*:

> Sweet hour of twilight! – in the solitude
> Of the pine forest, and the silent shore
> Which bounds Ravenna's immemorial wood,
> Rooted where once the Adrian wave flow'd o'er,
> To where the last Caesarean fortress stood,
> Evergreen forest! which Boccaccio's lore
> And Dryden's lay made haunted ground to me,
> How have I loved the twilight hour and thee.

INFORMATION

Museo Archivescovile: winter 9 a.m. to 12 noon and 2.30 pm. to 5 p.m., summer 9 a.m. to 12 noon and 2.30 p.m. to 6 p.m., Sunday 9 a.m. to 1 p.m.

RESTAURANTS

Tre Spade
Via Rasponi 35, Ravenna
Telephone: 0544 32382, closed Monday

Bella Venezia
Via 4 Novembre 16, Ravenna
Telephone: 0544 22746, closed Sunday and from October to March on Saturday

Trattoria Casa delle Aie
Via delle Aie 4, Cervia
Telephone: 0544 927 631, closed Wednesday from mid-September to mid-May

VENICE

The Queene of Christendom
Thomas Coryate

Venice, 'the richest Paragon and Queene of Christendom', has always prided herself on being the most exotic and alluring city in Europe. Her whole history is tinged with myth, from her humble beginnings after the collapse of the Roman Empire, as groups of refugees fled from the invading Huns and Goths into the fastness of the lagoon, to her ruthless rise to greatness, most evident in the notorious Fourth Crusade of 1204. The Venetian forces were commanded by the blind, ninety-five-year-old doge, Enrico Dandolo, who persuaded his allies to sack Constantinople and return home laden with spoil which included the bronze horses of St Mark. Venice's Arsenal, in which the navy was built, was the most magnificent in Europe (and the origin of the word in sixteen languages). Foreigners marvelled, and when the French King Henry III visited the Arsenal in 1574 the Venetians, in order to impress him, built a whole galley while he was eating dinner. Lost in admiration, Henry vowed that he would give three of his best towns for such a boatyard.

The massive wealth accumulated by the Venetians in the Middle Ages, when they controlled the Dalmatian coast, much of mainland Greece and the islands of Crete and Corfu, cushioned the city's gradual decline. Even after new trade routes to America and the East, discovered in the fifteenth century, had bypassed Venice, and despite the strain of fighting an endless war with the Turks, the splendour of Venice's magnificent palaces and churches remained the envy of Europe until the fall of the Republic in 1797.

Early travellers such as the eccentric Thomas Coryate, the court jester of Prince Henry (the eldest son of James I), who came to Venice on an extensive visit in 1608, were fascinated by the civilised lifestyle of the Venetians. Coryate had never eaten with a fork, rarely seen glass windows, and was amazed by women acting in the theatre. He spent a considerable time studying the habits of the Venetian courtesans who wore masks and were given the best seats at the theatre. He reckoned there were 'at least twenty thousand, whereof many are esteemed so loose, that they are said to open their quivers to every arrow'. Coryate's inquisitiveness took him up to the Ghetto, the first such institution in Europe (originally a foundry and named after the Italian word *gettare* – to cast), where he marvelled at the beauty of the heavily bejewelled women.

The diarist John Evelyn was entranced by Venice's beauty on his visit in 1645–6, calling it 'this miraculous citty, lying in the bosome of the sea, in the shape of a lute'. He came, like many others, to see the Feast of the Ascension, a ceremony that dated back to 997, when the doge, the elected ruler of Venice, cast a ring into the waters of the lagoon, symbolically marrying Venice to the sea. One of the most surprising aspects of the delectable lifestyle enjoyed by these visitors was the efficiency of the Venetian government. Coryate and Evelyn were fascinated by the intricacies of the Republic's constitution, a complex system of checks and balances designed to limit power and to prevent any one individual seizing control, and in which the doge was no more than a titular head of state. This system proved highly effective and ensured that the Republic had political stability.

These early travellers visited Venice at the end of a golden age of artistic creativity. The brilliant colours and dazzling effects of light characteristic of the works of Bellini, Giorgione, Titian, Veronese and Tintoretto, and their originality in developing the use of oil paint and the art of landscape painting were unmatched throughout Europe. It is no coincidence that the idea of placing a picture on an easel, where its sole purpose is to please the spectator, should have originated with Giorgione. This artistic flowering extended to the fields of sculpture and architecture, where the works of Jacopo Sansovino and Andrea Palladio introduced the High Renaissance into Venice.

The second great flowering of Venetian painting took place in the eighteenth century, the classic age of the Grand Tour, when Venice became the playground of Europe. As Venice's trade declined, the Venetians adapted instinctively to tourism and visitors flocked to enjoy the delights on offer. Venetian women were renowned for their sexual charms and Boswell, who had only just recovered from catching the pox in Rome, fell for an opera dancer and succumbed once more. Many Grand Tourists took lovers since, in the words of the French Président de Brosses, who was here in 1739, 'it would be a disgrace were a lady known to be without one'. In the first palace the self-indulgent millionaire William Beckford visited in 1780, he noted 'a great many ladies negligently dressed, their hair falling very freely about, and innumerable adventures written in their eyes'.

Carnival, which lasted six months of the year, from 1 October to the beginning of Lent with a short break between Christmas and Epiphany, was a time of great excitement and encouraged every form of licentiousness, courtesans standing in their doorways 'with their breasts open and their faces all bedaubed with paint'. Venetian noblemen, who were compelled to wear black for the rest of the year and forbidden to talk to foreigners, cast aside their inhibitions. Even the most solemn magistrate, as Beckford observed, emerged from the lawcourts after a day's work, donned his domino, a black and white masked costume, and indulged his whims. Lorenzo da Ponte, who wrote the librettos for Mozart's *Don Giovanni* and *The Marriage of Figaro*, was a Venetian and the atmosphere of intrigue and sexual dalliance he evoked must have been very similar to that of Carnival. In 1733 Joseph Spence records seeing two gentlemen walking together with fishing-rods baited with sugar almonds, and a mass of boys following behind, nibbling at them like fish. A shorter two-week Carnival was revived in Venice in the 1970s, and is now one of the main tourist attractions in the winter.

Part of Venice's charm was its cosmopolitan atmosphere, which affected even the most sanguine travellers. Dr Moore, who came here in 1775, could hardly believe the crowd of 'Jews, Turks and Christians; lawyers, knaves, and pick-pockets; mountebanks, old women and physicians; women of quality, with masks; and strumpets bare-faced' he came across in the Piazza San Marco. Free spirits thrived in this environment. Lady Mary Wortley Montagu, who was widely travelled and reputed to have slept with the Sultan of Turkey, was the object of much gossip. Even more scandalous was her son Edward, who claimed to have been born in the Turkish Sultan's harem, committed bigamy, became a Muslim, and took to wearing an iron wig.

Venice was famous for her music, and the first public opera house in the world was opened at San Cassiano in 1637. A visit to the church of La Pietà, where Vivaldi was violin-master and later concert-master in the early eighteenth century, was virtually obligatory. As Beckford, an ardent music lover, commented: 'Here were no cackling old women, or groaning Methodists, such as infest our English tabernacles, and scare one's ears with hoarse coughs accompanied by the nase obligato.' Goethe was inspired by the gondoliers' singing on his visit in 1786, and was moved to tears when he heard two of them chanting verses of Tasso and Ariosto to each other across the waters of the lagoon.

In between the hectic social round, Grand Tourists went to look at many of the sites, particularly Palladio's churches and the paintings of Titian and Veronese. The Venetian school of painting was extremely popular, and the spate of commissions encouraged Venetian painters to work abroad. Canaletto spent many fruitful years in England, as did Sebastiano Ricci and Pellegrini, Rosalba

Carriera's pastels were immensely popular in both London and Paris, Canaletto's nephew Bellotto travelled to Warsaw and Dresden, and Tiepolo executed one of his most sumptuous frescoes in the Archbishop's palace at Wurzburg.

Few visitors showed any sympathy for Byzantine or medieval art. Goethe wrote dismissively of Gothic art: 'Thank God, I am done with all that junk for good and all.' The eighteenth-century traveller, brought up to admire a standard of beauty based on the classical orders and rules of proportion, showed little appreciation of St Mark's, the Doge's Palace or the Gothic palaces on the Grand Canal.

A few visitors remained unmoved by Venice's beauty. Venice possessed no antique ruins and Edward Gibbon, one of the more fervent antiquarians and the author of *The Decline and Fall of the Roman Empire*, wrote a highly critical account of his visit in 1765. He complained bitterly of 'old and in general ill-built houses, ruined pictures, and stinking ditches dignified with the pompous denomination of Canals'. Other critics took a moral line. The aptly named Dr Warner raged to his friend Selwyn: 'Venice is a stink-pot, charged with the very virus of hell', but his words fell on deaf ears. Samuel Sharp, who took a very jaundiced view of the Italians, was horrified at the free-for-all in the Piazza San Marco and particularly the way that 'the nasty fellows . . . let down their breeches wherever and before whomsoever they please; accordingly all St Mark's Place, and many parts of that sumptuous building, the Doge's palace, are dedicated to Cloacina, and you may see Votaries at their devotions every hour of the day'.

Even after the fall of the Republic, Venice continued to exert a melancholy fascination. Byron, the most romantic figure of his age, settled here in 1816 and indulged in a wild succession of affairs with all sorts of women: 'Some of them are countesses, some are cobblers' wives, some noble, some middling, some low – and all whores.' Shelley, who visited him two years later, described him as 'practising aphrodisiacs at a great rate'. Byron, like all well-to-do Venetians, owned a gondola and enjoyed drifting effortlessly along the canals, while his friend Samuel Rogers marvelled at how 'the salt seaweed clings to the marble of her palaces'. Byron described his feelings to his publisher John Murray: 'I like the gloomy gaiety of their gondolas – & the silence of their canals – I do not even dislike the evident decay of the city'. Shelley took a melancholic view of the gondola, comparing it to a coffin, whereas Goethe felt uplifted and thought himself lord of the Adriatic. Foreign artists attempted to capture the peculiar clarity of the Venetian light. Turner, the most successful of

these, described Venice as 'a city of rose and white, rising out of an emerald sea against a sky of sapphire blue'.

Byron was one of very few nineteenth-century visitors to immerse himself in the life of the city. His sybaritic lifestyle shocked most foreigners who showed little inclination to mix in Venetian society. Victorian sightseers followed in the footsteps of John Ruskin, whose *Stones of Venice*, published from 1849 to 1853, proved immensely influential. Ruskin's championship of the Venetian Gothic and his violent attack on Palladio completely changed people's perceptions of Venetian architecture. He also eulogised the paintings of Carpaccio and Tintoretto, both of whom had been neglected by earlier visitors.

The walks and boat trips in this chapter are designed to show you a selection of the most interesting sites in Venice, combining those most admired by Grand Tourists with those that inspired the Victorians. Venice has changed less than anywhere else in Italy over the centuries, and this is where you can most easily relive the experiences of generations of visitors who have fallen in love with the city.

This miraculous citty, lying in the bosome of the sea
John Evelyn

PIAZZA SAN MARCO~ST MARK'S~PIAZZETTA~ DOGE'S PALACE~SAN ZACCARIA~SCUOLA DI SAN GIORGIO~SANTI GIOVANNI E PAOLO~SANTA MARIA DEI MIRACOLI~RIALTO BRIDGE~PALAZZO LABIA

This walk takes in the heart of Venice: the Piazza San Marco, the social centre, the Doge's Palace where the government sat during the Republic, and the commercial centre around the Rialto. The best place to begin is in the **Piazza San Marco**, regarded by Napoleon as the finest drawing-room in Europe. Much of its cosmopolitan liveliness disappeared with the fall of the Republic. The Austrian government, which took control of Venice in 1815, was so uninterested in the city that the new Patriarch, appointed in 1818, was ordered to proceed to St Mark's in a coach and horses. The Piazza is a wonderful place to watch the world go by at one of the outdoor cafés, either Florian's on the south side, the café traditionally patronised by the Venetians, or Quadri's on the north side, which was patronised by the occupying Austrians in the nineteenth century. You will have to pay for the privilege, but in the afternoon and evening you can enjoy a band playing stirring Strauss waltzes.

Napoleon, with a typical French passion for order, rebuilt the west end of the Piazza (now housing the Correr Museum), destroying Sansovino's church of San Giminiano in the process, in order to provide a continuous façade all round the Piazza. The loggias around the square now contain greatly overpriced shops.

The trapezoidal square was designed to focus on the basilica of **St Mark's**, the doge's private chapel where the doges were crowned and, in many cases, are buried. It was built to rival Hagia Sofia in Constantinople and consecrated in 1094, after the first building had been burnt down in an uprising in 976. Venice showered her newfound wealth on the basilica until it was crammed with silver, gold, precious stones and mosaics, including the fabulous Pala d' Oro standing behind the high altar. Climb up to the gallery above the central door which affords an excellent view of the interior and where you can see the four horses taken from the Hippodrome in Constantinople in 1204. Together with the equestrian statue of Marcus Aurelius in Rome, these are the finest animal bronzes to have survived from antiquity. They were removed by Napoleon after he dissolved the Republic in 1797, but were returned in 1815.

Grand Tourists were less than ecstatic about St Mark's which they felt to be in bad taste. Président de Brosses, typical of his age's preference for order and harmonious proportion, criticised it for being 'in the Greek style, low, impenetrable to the light, in wretched taste both within and without', and compared the cupolas to copper kettles. In 1802, Eustace took a more romantic view of the interior, praising 'its gloomy, barbaric magnificence', and forty years later Dickens described it as

> A grand and dreamy structure, of immense proportions; golden with old mosaics; redolent of perfumes; dim with the smoke of incense; costly in treasure of precious stones and metals, glittering through iron bars; holy with the bodies of deceased saints; rainbow-hued with windows of stained glass; dark with carved woods and coloured marbles; obscure in its vast heights and lengthened distances, shining with silver lamps and winking lights; unreal, fantastic, solemn, inconceivable throughout.

On the left of St Mark's is the clock tower, built by Mauro Coducci in 1499, with the statues of two Moors who strike the bell hourly. Thomas Coryate met a merchant who had seen a man killed when he was hit on the head by one of the Moors, causing him to fall from the tower to his death. The road behind the clock tower, which leads through the Merceria to the Rialto, is the main shopping street in the city, described by Evelyn as 'one of the most delicious streetes in the world'.

On the other side of the square the **Piazzetta** leads from the Piazza to the waterfront, passing Sansovino's Loggetta, beautifully restored in the 1970s, at the foot of the campanile. During the fifteenth century, clerics convicted of immorality were hung in cages from the campanile. Goethe hastened to climb it as soon as he arrived in the city in 1786 to obtain his first view of the sea. The original campanile was over one thousand years old when it collapsed on 14 July 1902, causing miraculously little damage. It was rebuilt exactly as before. On the right side of the Piazzetta is Sansovino's Biblioteca Marciana, begun in 1537, the first High Renaissance building in Venice, with a new emphasis on classical proportion. Palladio pronounced it the most beautiful building to be erected since antiquity.

During the Republic the two columns at the bottom of the Piazzetta, surmounted by statues of St Theodore and the lion of St Mark, were the site of executions of prominent criminals. Coryate, who lived in constant fear of being arrested by the dreaded Inquisition, saw a man so horribly tortured here that 'his face and hands doe looke as red as fire'.

The **Doge's Palace** faces the Biblioteca Marciana across the Piazzetta. The fourteenth- and early fifteenth-century façades facing the Piazzetta and the lagoon defy all architectural logic in the way that the delicate Gothic arcade on the ground floor supports the solid mass of masonry above, creating a wonderful effect of lightness, 'no doubt an unfortunate afterthought' as one early guidebook scathingly commented. The interior is a poor reflection of the exterior, partly because it is so difficult to disentangle the different functions of all the rooms, and partly because so many of the best paintings have been destroyed in the numerous fires that the building has suffered.

The palace was not admired by eighteenth-century visitors. De Brosses described it as 'an ugly sort of building, heavy, sombre, and in the worst gothic style'. Forsyth, on his visit in 1803, criticised the palace for not appearing durable, a comment that could be applied to almost all Venetian Gothic palaces. Ruskin, on the other hand, thought it the most beautiful building in the world.

Turn left along the Riva degli Schiavoni, and from the Ponte della Paglia (where barges loaded with straw used to moor) there is an excellent view of the infamous 'Bridge of Sighs' across which prisoners were led to the dungeons. The Romantics' imagination was fired by the idea. Beckford relished the horror of 'damp and gloomy caverns, whose inhabitants waste away by painful degrees, and feel themselves whole years a-dying.'

The most famous inmate of the prisons was Casanova, who made a spectacular escape over the roof of the palace on the eve of All Saints' Day 1756. When his escape route was blocked by a locked door, with typical sang-froid he resorted to bluff. Changing into his smartest clothes, his hat trimmed with Spanish lace and adorned with a white feather, he signalled down to the courtyard for help. As soon as the door was unlocked and before he and his companion could be challenged, the two prisoners marched down the stairs and out of the palace. Hiring a gondola, they made good their escape to the mainland.

Just beyond the Bridge of Sighs is the Danieli Hotel, still one of the best in the city, where Ruskin, Wagner and Proust stayed. Cross the Ponte del Vin and take the second left which leads to the Campo San Zaccaria. The church of **San Zaccaria** has an unusual façade, marking the transition from the Gothic lozenge pattern of the base to the elegant Renaissance proportions of the upper storeys. The convent attached to the church was a hotbed of scandal in the eighteenth century. De Brosses objected to its being one of the convents which competed for the honour of bestowing a mistress on the Papal Nuncio. The candidate would, presumably, have received excellent instruction from her Mother Superior, who was later to carry on a torrid affair with Casanova.

Inside the church one of Giovanni Bellini's most beautiful altarpieces hangs in the left aisle. The monumentality of the composition of the *Madonna and Child with Saints* dating from 1505, marks a new development in Venetian art, bringing Bellini into line with the Florentine High Renaissance. The dazzling colours are typically Venetian but the introspective mood of the figures betrays the influence of Bellini's enigmatic pupil Giorgione. This Venetian painting was highly prized by Napoleon, who removed it to Paris in 1797.

From the Campo, bear right into Campo San Provolo which leads into Fondamenta dell' Osmarin, a pretty street which passes the fine Palazzo Priuli. Turn left into Fondamenta di San Lorenzo, away from the leaning campanile of the Greek church, and cross the second bridge into Calle del Lion. The first building on your left over the next canal is the **Scuola di San Giorgio degli Schiavoni**. The ground floor is decorated with a series of enchanting paintings by Carpaccio, scenes from the lives of St George, St Tryphon and St Jerome set in fanciful landscapes and possessing all the charm of a fairy-tale. On the right wall a group of panic-stricken monks flee from St Jerome's harmless-looking lion. By the door St Augustine sits in his study, his books cluttered on his desk and his little dog gazing up at him with rapt attention. Ruskin was the first to decipher the subject-matter of this scene; previously it was assumed to be of St Jerome.

This naive charm held little appeal to Grand Tourists, although Edward Wright, in 1720, commented on Carpaccio's style: 'Tis a dry manner, according to that age; but an excellent close pursuit of nature.' It was Carpaccio's love of anecdotal detail and the delightful figures and animals that fill the background of his canvases which so enchanted Ruskin.

From the Scuola San Giorgio head back down Calle del Lion and turn right over the second canal into Fondamenta di San Lorenzo, left at the end into Calle Larga San Lorenzo and first right into Calle Cappello, with a picturesque Gothic arch standing at the end of the street. Continuing in a straight line, you come to Barbaria delle Tole, turn left and, passing a series of cake shops and vegetable stalls interspersed with souvenirs of the Carnival, you reach the Campo dei Santi Giovanni e Paolo (known as San Zanipolo).

There are two excellent cafés in the square, the Bar Colleoni and the Caffé al Cavallo, set right next to the magnificent Verrocchio statue of the *condottiere* Colleoni, executed between 1479 and 1496. Colleoni was a formidable warrior 'who had his name from having three stones, for the Italian word Coglione doth signifie a testicle', as Thomas Coryate wryly explained. This was a favourite spot for

Casanova's assignations, from where he would proceed with his mistress to an apartment decorated with erotic prints near the San Moisè theatre. Casanova later discovered that his mistress's other lover, Monsieur de Bernis, a future Cardinal, used to spy on him through a peephole throughout the affair.

The church of **Santi Giovanni e Paolo**, begun in 1246 for the Dominicans, rivals the Frari as the largest Gothic church in Venice. In the Middle Ages there was such a strong rivalry between the Dominicans and the Franciscans, the two main preaching orders, that their principal churches tended to be in different parts of a city. In Venice the Dominican church of Santi Giovanni e Paolo stands on one side of the Grand Canal, while the Franciscan church of the Frari dominates the far side.

The austere brick interior with its soaring Gothic arches is a veritable Pantheon to the Republic, the walls covered in tombs of doges, including three members of the illustrious Mocenigo family. Unfortunately, the church's most famous artistic treasure, Titian's painting of *St Peter Martyr*, much admired by Grand Tourists, was burnt in the nineteenth century, although a fragment has recently emerged in a private Italian collection. Beside the first altar on the right is the Bragadin monument, with an urn containing the skin of the unfortunate Marcantonio Bragadin, the Venetian commander of Cyprus who was flayed alive by the Turks in 1571, a savage reminder of the ferocity of the wars between the two nations. Over the next altar the polyptych by Giovanni Bellini of *St Vincent Ferrar* is the finest surviving altarpiece in the church.

Outside the main door, pause for a moment to admire the elegant façade of the Scuola di San Marco, designed by Pietro Lombardo and Mauro Coducci, the two leading Venetian architects of the early Renaissance. Behind the Colleoni monument, follow the signs to the Rialto, cross two canals, turn right and immediately left beneath a statue of the Virgin and Child. The door beyond the statue has one of the best of all door-knockers in the city, a bronze gondola carved in the shape of a dolphin.

Calle Castelli leads up to the small church of **Santa Maria dei Miracoli**, built by Pietro Lombardo in 1489. Lombardo, with a characteristic Venetian love of beautiful materials, encrusted the façade in porphyry and other marble, creating an effect closer to the exotic splendour of Byzantium than to contemporary Renaissance architecture in Florence. The steep flight of steps leading up to the beautifully sculpted altar makes the interior a perfect setting for weddings, and the church is often garlanded in flowers.

Coryate thought the exterior the fairest of any he saw on his travels. Fynes Moryson, with typical historical inaccuracy, expressed his admiration for the statues under the organ by attributing them to Praxiteles (they are actually fifteenth-century).

From the Miracoli it is a short walk to the Rialto. Cross the canal by the façade, take the fourth left down Salizzada San Canciano and follow the signs for the **Rialto Bridge**, where the founders of Venice made their original settlement. The bridge, lined with booths selling Murano glass and every sort of trinket, affords a magnificent panorama over the Grand Canal. In a star-studded competition the Venetian authorities opted for the unspectacular design of the little-known but aptly-named Antonio da Ponte, and rejected those of his far more famous rivals Michelangelo, Palladio, Vignola, Sansovino and Scamozzi, probably the most surprising result in architectural history. The bridge was erected from 1588 to 1591; the far side is devoted to a large fruit and vegetable market (see page 244). If you would like to stop for lunch, cross over the bridge and turn left; the **Trattoria alla Madonna**, highly popular with locals, at Calle della Madonna 594 on the right, serves some of the best seafood in Venice.

After lunch cross back over the Rialto to the vaporetto stop and take the no. 1 up the Grand Canal to San Marcuola. From the vaporetto stop, head away from the Grand Canal and follow the signs to the Ferrovia (railway station) past a busy fruit and vegetable market. Crossing the Ponte Guglie you will find the **Palazzo Labia**, one of the grandest eighteenth-century palaces in Venice, on the left in Campo San Geremia. Provided there is no conference going on, you can usually get in without telephoning first to make an appointment. Upstairs, Tiepolo, inspired no doubt by the fabulous wealth of his patrons, excelled himself in the magnificent cycle of frescoes of the story of Antony and Cleopatra. At the lavish Bestegui fancy-dress ball held here in 1951 when the guests dressed as famous Venetian characters, Lady Diana Cooper outshone everyone dressed as Tiepolo's Cleopatra.

INFORMATION

Scuola San Giorgio degli Schiavoni: 9.30 a.m. to 12.30 p.m. and 3.30 p.m. to 6.30 p.m., Sunday 9.30 a.m. to 12.30 p.m., closed Monday
Palazzo Labia: Wednesday, Thursday and Friday 3 p.m. to 4 p.m.
  (Telephone: 041 781 204)

RESTAURANT

Trattoria alla Madonna
Calle della Madonna 594, Venice
Telephone: 041 522 3824, closed Wednesday

Titian was assuredly a mighty poet, but Tintoret – well,
Tintoret was almost a prophet

Henry James

THE FRARI~SCUOLA DI SAN ROCCO~CA' REZZONICO

This walk takes you to some of the greatest works of art in Venice and, in particular, the paintings of Titian and Tintoretto. Not to be outdone by the Dominicans at Santi Giovanni e Paolo, the Franciscans built the magnificent red-brick church of Santa Maria Gloriosa dei Frari, commonly known as the **Frari**, between 1350 and 1430. It is best reached by following the signs from the San Tomà stop, taking the no. 1 vaporetto.

The paintings by Titian and Bellini here are unsurpassed in any other church in Venice. Titian's *Assumption* above the high altar, with the Virgin in her red robe set against a golden background, is visible from far down the nave, and was acknowledged as a masterpiece from the moment it was unveiled in 1518. It immediately established Titian's reputation as the foremost painter in Venice. The triumphant soaring composition was to exercise a profound influence on Baroque religious art. Goethe declared that, after seeing it, he could not understand why anyone else needed to paint the subject.

The acclaim accorded to the *Assumption* persuaded the Pesaro family to commission an altarpiece from Titian in the left aisle. The Franciscan friars were shocked by Titian's daring diagonal composition which gives the Pesaro family equal prominence with the Holy Family who are placed off the central axis. The third of the great Renaissance paintings, Giovanni Bellini's *Sacra Conversazione*, hangs in the Sacristy off the right transept, past Donatello's harrowing *St John the Baptist* in the chapel on the right of the high altar. Dürer visited Venice in 1506, and was so impressed that he later copied Bellini's four saints in the *Four Evangelists*, now in Munich.

Grand Tourists flocked to admire the Titians but paid scant regard to the splendid Gothic architecture, or to the Bellini or the Donatello. By the late nineteenth century the trend had been reversed, and Henry James, directing his readers straight to the Bellini, wrote:

Nothing in Venice is more perfect than this. It is one of those things that sum up the genius of a painter, the experience of life, the teaching of a school. It seems painted with molten gems, which have only been clarified by time, and it is as solemn as it is gorgeous and as simple as it is deep.

Emerging from the Frari, follow the signs round the corner to the **Scuola di San Rocco**, the most famous of the six major *scuole* in Venice (originally charitable institutions), because it houses Tintoretto's great cycle of paintings executed between 1564 and 1587. The scenes from the *Life of Christ* on the ground floor, which Tintoretto painted last, are shrouded in a mystical light; the most beautiful are the two vertical moonlit landscapes with saints at the far end whose poetic mood seems to prefigure nineteenth-century Romanticism.

Upstairs, the walls and ceiling of the large hall are covered in scenes from the Old and New Testaments, demonstrating Tintoretto's love of violent movement and his use of artificial light and unreal colours to enhance the spiritual content of the paintings. The ceiling panels show his mastery of foreshortening and tricks of perspective so that, in *Jacob's Dream*, the ladder really does appear to ascend up to heaven. Round the walls are a series of ingenious wooden sculptures by the seventeenth-century sculptor Pianta, one of them of a spy, peering out beneath his hat which is crammed low over his face. Tintoretto saved his masterpiece for the Sala dell' Albergo off the hall, where his vast *Crucifixion* covering the far wall depicts a whole range of figures enveloped in a mystical light and subordinate to the central figure of Christ on the cross.

Seventeenth- and eighteenth-century visitors to Venice, with their admiration for the High Renaissance canon of beauty, were baffled by Tintoretto's distorted figures and tricks of perspective. They tended to prefer other painters of the sixteenth century and it may not be entirely accidental that Harry's Bar, in Calle Vallaresso off St Mark's Square, which preserves something of the self-indulgent atmosphere of the Grand Tour, should have cocktails named after Titian, Bellini and Giorgione but not Tintoretto.

Tintoretto's works evoked a very strong response from the religious-minded Victorians, particularly John Ruskin. Ruskin, himself something of a prophet, admired the visionary nature of Tintoretto's art, all 'clouds, and whirlwinds and fire and infinity of earth', and the profound effect of these paintings on him was one of the reasons he decided to study Venetian history, which led him to write *The Stones of Venice*.

A few years ago I had the luck to witness the filming of a scene from the film on Carlo Goldoni, the eighteenth-century Venetian playwright, in the *Scuola*. In a break during filming, the director explained to me the intricate way in which the pictures were lit, while all around us a throng of extras pressed forward to listen, oblivious to their extraordinary appearance in senatorial robes, with powdered cheeks and wearing full eighteenth-century wigs.

After leaving the Scuola di San Rocco, have a quick look at the bizarre collection of windmills in the house across the canal directly behind the building. If you would like to browse in the shops nearby, follow the signs to the San Tomà vaporetto which will take you past some good antique shops specialising in ironwork and smaller pieces of furniture.

Venice is a maze of interconnecting streets and alleys and it is easy to get lost on the way to the Ca' Rezzonico. Either take the no. 1 vaporetto from the San Tomà stop towards San Marco and get off at the next stop, or walk down the Calle della Scuola to the left of the Scuola San Rocco, turn left into Calle dei Preti and right into Calle San Pantalon. This leads into Campo San Pantalon, from where you can cross the canal into Campo di Santa Margherita. At the far end of the Campo, turn left, and left again into Rio Terra Canal. At the end of the street, turn left and follow the edge of the canal to the Ca' **Rezzonico**.

The Ca' Rezzonico is one of the most splendid palaces on the Grand Canal, now transformed into a delightful museum of Venetian eighteenth-century art. It was designed for the Priuli Bon family by Longhena, the architect of the Salute, in the late seventeenth century, and completed by Massari in the next century to honour the Rezzonico family's success in bribing their way into the nobility for 100,000 ducats. No expense was spared. Most Venetian palaces were built largely of brick with floors made of crushed marble, the lightest and cheapest materials available. The Ca' Rezzonico, in deliberate contrast, with its massive stone staircase ascending to the *piano nobile*, must have been astronomically expensive. After the Rezzonicos had been compelled to sell up, the palace was for a while the home of Pen Browning, the son of the poet Robert Browning who died here in 1889.

The interior gives the best idea of how a Venetian palace would have looked during the eighteenth century. The rooms are decorated with ceilings by Giam Battista Tiepolo and Crosato, lacquered furniture and carved wood frames of the highest quality, the best of them by Antonio Corradini, and hideous glass chandeliers from Murano. The most curious objects are some extraordinary ebony and boxwood chairs and vase stands by the sculptor Andrea Brustolon. The arms of the chairs and the vases are supported by carved figures of

240

negroes, many of them with chains round their necks. Président de Brosses, not surprisingly, imagined that the chairs must have been extremely uncomfortable.

The *portego* (main hall) on the top floor is hung with paintings by all the main eighteenth-century Venetian painters, including two atmospheric early Canalettos. In the rooms on either side there are a series of charming genre scenes of Venetian life by Longhi, some beautiful Guardis and frescoes by Gian Domenico Tiepolo originally painted for his own house at Zianigo near Mestre, depicting a peepshow and masquerading figures enjoying the Venetian Carnival.

Emerging from the palace and returning to the Campo San Barnabà, you might like to look at some of the excellent shops selling gilded woodwork and custom-made shoes off the square. For a quiet lunch spot, follow the Sotoportego e Calle San Barnabà out of the far side of the square, turn right over the next canal and first left into Fondamenta di Borgo. **Locanda Montin** at no. 1147 is an extremely pleasant spot where you can sit outside under a pergola.

This is the heart of the Dorsoduro, one of the most picturesque areas of Venice. Turning left out of the restaurant and left again into Fondamenta Bonlini, you reach Campo San Trovaso which has one of the two surviving boatyards where gondolas are built and repaired.

INFORMATION

Scuola di San Rocco: 9 a.m. to 1 p.m. and 3.30 p.m. to 6 p.m., closed Monday

Ca' Rezzonico: 10 a.m. to 4 p.m., Sunday 9 a.m. to 12 noon, closed Friday

RESTAURANT

Locanda Montin
Fondamento di Borgo
Dorsoduro 1147, Venice
Telephone: 041 522 7151, closed Tuesday evening and Wednesday

A veritable Golden Book on whose monumental façade the
entire Venetian nobility has signed its name
Théophile Gautier

THE GRAND CANAL: SANTA MARIA DELLA SALUTE~ ACCADEMIA GALLERY~CA' FOSCARI~PALAZZO MOCENIGO~ RIALTO BRIDGE/ CA' DA MOSTO~CA' D' ORO~PALAZZO GUSSONI~PALAZZO VENDRAMIN-CALERGI

If you can't afford a gondola, the best way to see the Grand Canal is to take the no. 1 vaporetto from outside Harry's Bar in Via Valleresso near St Mark's Square. (Byron's successful attempt to swim the length of the canal for a bet is not to be encouraged.) The vaporetto plies the length of the Grand Canal. Try to avoid peak hours and make sure that you get a seat right at the front of the boat.

The first two Gothic palaces on your right are Il Ridotto, which was the most famous casino in Venice in the 1770s, and Ca' Giustinian, now the headquarters of the Biennale. Verdi stayed here while producing his operas at the Fenice, including first performances of *Rigoletto*, which was a great success in 1851, and *La Traviata*, which was roundly booed two years later. The vaporetto crosses over to the church of **Santa Maria della Salute**, the seventeenth-century Baroque masterpiece of Baldassare Longhena. The church was built to commemorate Venice's delivery from the plague, and on 21 November there is a procession of boats across the Grand Canal and through the main entrance of the church, whose doors are thrown open only on that day.

A series of beautiful palaces lines the Grand Canal between the Salute and the Accademia bridge. Most exquisite of all is the asymmetrical Palazzo Dario, its façade encrusted with slabs of porphyry, on the left just before the Guggenheim Museum. The single storey Guggenheim Museum, known colloquially as Palazzo Nonfinito, contains the collection of the voracious collector Peggy Guggenheim including many works by her former lovers. Almost opposite, the Casetta Rossa (little red house) was the studio of the neo-classical sculptor Canova in the 1770s. The penultimate palace on the right before the Accademia bridge is the Palazzo Barbaro, where the American Curtis family entertained Henry James, Whistler, Sargent, Browning and Monet.

The **Accademia Gallery,** housed in the old Scuola di Santa Maria della Carità on the left of the bridge, possesses the finest collection of Venetian paintings in the world. You will need more than one visit to take in the beautiful Bellini Madonnas, Giorgione's enigmatic *Tempesta*, Titian's charming *Presentation of the Virgin*, Carpaccio's *Legend of St Ursula* series, which inspired Ruskin to some of his richest prose, and some of the greatest Tintorettos and Veroneses. The Scuola, together with the neighbouring church and convent, was transformed into an art gallery in the early nineteenth century.

The next landmark on the left is the massive block of the Ca' Rezzonico (see pages 240–1). Opposite is the church of San Samuele beyond which is the Palazzo Grassi, owned by the Agnelli Foundation and used for major exhibitions. Just before the bend in the Grand Canal, as you first catch a glimpse of the Rialto Bridge, you pass the long façade of Palazzo Giustinian, where Wagner wrote the first two acts of *Tristan and Isolde* in 1858–9. The Ca' Foscari beyond was decorated in the most extravagant style for Henry III's visit in 1574, the walls hung with cloth of gold and pictures by Titian, Tintoretto and Veronese; even the sheets were of crimson silk. The palace was the finishing post in the regattas so vividly depicted by Canaletto.

The long, low **Palazzo Mocenigo** on the right was the residence of Lady Arundel in 1621, when she came to Venice to clear the reputation of her alleged lover Antonio Foscarini, who had been executed for treason (it was illegal for a Venetian nobleman even to meet a foreigner). Byron began *Don Juan* here in 1818 and recorded how he returned one evening in a storm to find his mistress La Fornarina waiting for him on the steps 'with her great black eyes flashing through her tears, and her long dark hair, which was streaming, drenched with rain, over her brows and breast'. Byron, a great lover of animals as well as women, kept a menagerie on the ground floor of the palace. It included, as his friend Hanson noted 'his lordship's carriages, two or three kinds of dogs, birds, monkeys, a fox, a wolf, in different cages, and, as his lordship passed to his gondola, he used to stop and amuse himself with watching their antics, or would feed them occasionally himself'.

The Palazzo Benzon, the fourth on the right past the Sant' Angelo vaporetto stop, was where the Contessa Querini-Benzon entertained Canova and Byron. She was extremely greedy and famous for the pieces of hot polenta she used to carry about between her breasts. Opposite the San Silvestro vaporetto stop is the little, orange Palazzo Corner–Martinengo where Turner and Sir Thomas Lawrence stayed in 1819. Turner's late style, where light and colour dissolve forms, was ideally suited to the mirage-like quality of the

Venetian lagoon and his views of Venice capture the peculiar clarity of the light.

The boat now passes beneath the **Rialto Bridge**, designed to fit a dismasted galley beneath it. On the left is the Erberia, a fruit and vegetable market where Casanova used to come at dawn to meet fellow sybarites 'who have been spending the night in the excesses of Venus or Bacchus, or who have lost all hope at the gaming-table'.

The dilapidated Byzantine **Ca' da Mosto** opposite was the White Lion hotel in the eighteenth century, where the Emperor Joseph II lodged incognito in 1769, and where William Beckford, who had been mistaken for the Austrian Emperor, arrived by night in 1780. He was quite overwhelmed and wrote:

> As night approached, innumerable tapers glimmered through the awnings before the windows. Every boat had its lantern, and the gondolas moving rapidly along were followed by tracks of light, which gleamed and played upon the waters. I was gazing at these dancing fires when the sounds of music were wafted along the canals, and as they grew louder and louder, an illuminated barge, filled with musicians, issued from the Rialto, and stopping under one of the palaces, began a serenade, which stilled every clamour and suspended all conversation in the galleries and porticoes; till, rowing slowly away, it was heard no more. The gondoliers catching the air, imitated its cadences, and were answered by others at a distance, whose voices, echoed by the arch of the bridge, acquired a plaintive and interesting tone. I retired to rest, full of the sound, and long after I was asleep, the melody seemed to vibrate in my ear.

The palace beyond the canal on the right, with triangular pediments over the windows, is the Palazzo Mangilli–Valmarana where Consul Smith, the great patron of Canaletto, lived. A little further on is the magnificent **Ca' d' Oro**, built for the Contarini family between 1424 and 1430. Despite the ravages it suffered in the last century at the hands of the ballet dancer Marie Taglioni, who stripped the gilding from the intricate gold tracery on the façade and sold the grand staircase piecemeal (now in the Isabella Stewart Gardner Museum), it remains the most beautiful Gothic palace in Venice and houses an interesting collection, formed by Baron Franchetti at the beginning of this century, including Mantegna's *St Sebastian*, two lovely Guardi views of Venice, and some of the finest Renaissance sculpture in the city.

The far side of the canal is dominated by the enormous Ca' Pesaro, which houses the Gallery of Modern Art and the Gallery of

Oriental Art. Opposite is the pale yellow **Palazzo Gussoni**, where Sir Henry Wotton lived when he was appointed British ambassador for the second time in 1614. During Wotton's first ambassadorship a decade earlier, Paolo Sarpi, a free-thinking monk and the defender and champion of Venice, had been excommunicated by the Papacy and Wotton had high hopes of encouraging the Republic to adopt Protestantism. In the event, the Papacy eventually gave way and Venice remained in the Catholic fold.

A little further up the Grand Canal on the right is the imposing early Renaissance **Palazzo Vendramin-Calergi** with blue awnings outside, which is used as a casino in winter. Wagner died in the mezzanine of the palace in 1883. Opposite the San Marcuola stop is the Fondaco dei Turchi, where the Turkish merchants lived. Even when Venice was at war with Turkey, the Turks were still allowed to have Turkish baths, a harem and a mosque inside the Fondaco. You may want to disembark at the San Marcuola stop as the rest of the palaces facing the Grand Canal are of less interest. The vaporetto continues to the railway station.

INFORMATION

Guggenheim Museum: April to October 12 noon to 6 p.m., Saturday 6 p.m. to 9 p.m., closed Tuesday

Accademia Gallery: 9 a.m. to 4 p.m., Sunday 9 a.m. to 1 p.m., closed Monday

Ca' d' Oro: Tuesday to Saturday 9 a.m. to 7 p.m., Monday 1.30 p.m. to 7 p.m., Sunday 9 a.m. to 1 p.m.

I planted my umbrella on the margin of the sea, and reclining under its shade, my feet dangling over the waters, viewed the vast range of palaces, of porticos, of towers, opening on every side, and extending out of sight

William Beckford

ARSENAL~SAN FRANCESCO DELLA VIGNA~GESUITI~ MADONNA DELL' ORTO~GHETTO~SAN SEBASTIANO~ REDENTORE~SAN GIORGIO MAGGIORE

The other vaporetto worth taking is the no. 5, which goes right round the city. Embarking at San Zaccaria, the anti-clockwise route begins by taking you through the heart of the **Arsenal**, still impressively guarded by crenellated fortifications. This was once the greatest naval dockyard in the world, where the Republic's fleet was built and repaired. The frenetic scenes of activity, of tarring, caulking and building galleys, provided the inspiration for Dante's *Seventh Circle of Hell*. During an emergency in 1597, one hundred galleys were built here in sixty days. Napoleon, who wanted to eradicate all trace of the Republic, burnt the galleys, including the Bucintoro, the doge's state barge and the symbol of the power of the Venetian Republic.

The main entrance is through an impressive triumphal arch which was erected in 1460, the first Renaissance structure in Venice. The two stone lions guarding it were brought from Athens by Francesco Morosini; the one on the left is carved in Nordic runes, the peculiar script of the Varangian guard who protected the Byzantine emperors.

Beyond the Arsenal the vaporetto turns towards the northern waterfront facing the mainland. Celestia, the first stop, stands next to the church of **San Francesco della Vigna**, begun by Sansovino in 1534, with a façade composed of two superimposed temple fronts added by Palladio between 1568 and 1572. Unfortunately the buildings surrounding the church make it almost impossible to see the façade properly. In the right transept there is one of the great Gothic paintings in Venice, a *Madonna and Child* by Antonio da Negroponte, richly decorated with garlands of flowers and surrounded by pheasants, peacocks and partridges, giving the effect of a medieval tapestry. On the left of the high altar the Giustiniani Chapel has some fine sculpture by Pietro Lombardo. The fifteenth-century cloister, reached through the Sacristy, is one of the most charming in Venice.

If you continue on the vaporetto, the Fondamenta Nuove two stops further on is just across the canal from the church of the **Gesuiti**. Built by Domenico Rossi between 1714 and 1729, fifty years after the return of the Jesuit order to Venice, the Gesuiti is a Baroque extravaganza. The interior is covered with inlaid green marble curtains which look like damask. Titian's *Martyrdom of St Lawrence* in the first chapel on the left, one of the few important paintings by him still in Venice, is a violent nocturnal scene whose dramatic light effects were an important influence on Caravaggio and his followers.

The next stop is the **Madonna dell' Orto**, whose onion-domed campanile dominates the northern skyline of Venice and is visible from far across the lagoon. The church was Tintoretto's parish church and is where he is buried. It has one of the best examples of a red-brick Gothic façade in Venice.

Some of Tintoretto's greatest paintings hang in the church, including his dramatic *Presentation of the Virgin* in the right aisle, the tiny figure of the Madonna dramatically silhouetted against the sky halfway up a steep flight of steps. In the apse two vast Tintorettos, the *Worship of the Golden Calf* and the *Last Judgement*, have been carefully restored by the Venice in Peril Fund, one of the first programmes to be carried out after the disastrous flood of 1966. A luminous altarpiece by Cima da Conegliano (1460–1518) of *St John the Baptist and Four Saints* hangs in the first chapel on the right and a good Giovanni Bellini *Madonna and Child* hangs in the Valier Chapel at the foot of the left aisle.

Around the church is a poor working-class area untouched by tourism. No gondolas venture this far from the Grand Canal and the canals are full of workmen's barges plying their trades, some of them carrying piles of stakes which are still used as the foundation of buildings in Venice. If you are ready for lunch, cross the bridge over the canal and follow the street through the Campo dei Mori, with figures of Moors – probably Levantine merchants called Mastelli, who built the palace – carved into the walls, until you reach the Fondamenta della Misericordia. Turn right into Fondamenta degli Ormesini, and you'll find **Antica Mola** on your right, a local restaurant patronised by workmen, which serves good seafood.

Next to the restaurant, across the elegant iron bridge erected by the Austrians, is the **Ghetto**, a place of great historical and literary interest. Every night Shylock and his co-religionists were locked up on the island, and the impossible restrictions the Republic imposed on the purchase of land meant that they were compelled to build houses much higher than elsewhere in Venice because of the shortage of space. The idea of the Ghetto, with none of the terrible modern connotations of persecution, intrigued early visitors to Venice. Evelyn went to a Jewish wedding on 24 March 1646 and was fascinated by the moment in the ceremony where the Rabbi let fall a glass of wine 'the breaking whereof was to signify the frailty of our nature, and that we must expect disasters and crosses amidst all enjoyments'.

You can return to the no. 5 vaporetto by crossing back on to the Fondamenta degli Ormesini, turning right and second left into Calle della Malvasia, which leads up to the Sant' Alvise stop. The vaporetto continues past the station and the docks to the Giudecca Canal. Just behind the San Basilio stop on the Zattere is the church of **San Sebastiano**, Veronese's parish church and the place where he is buried. The interior is filled with his opulent paintings, the most dramatic being the scenes from the *Life of Esther* on the ceiling, depicted in dramatic foreshortening.

The vaporetto now crosses to the Giudecca. You may like to stop at the great Palladian church of the **Redentore**, built from 1577 to 1592 to commemorate Venice's delivery from the plague. The façade, a compact recreation of an antique temple front, was enormously admired by eighteenth-century visitors such as Goethe, who thought it 'strongly imbued with the spirit of the Ancients'.

Palladio united the interior by a series of giant Corinthian columns surmounted by an entablature, which form a continuous sequence down the sides of the nave and around a semicircular screen at the west end. The sense of movement is enhanced by the side-chapels leading off the nave, which look forward to the drama and movement of Baroque architecture. Some of this effect has been obscured by the heavy red curtains that prevent light from entering the nave. On the feast of the Redentore on the third Sunday in July, Venetians still process across a bridge of boats from the Zattere to the church, and the ceremony is followed by a dazzling display of fireworks.

Harry's Dolci, just along the waterfront, is an excellent restaurant at half the price of Harry's Bar; it serves a delicious risotto and excellent *dolci della casa*.

The final stop on the circumnavigation of Venice is the island of San Giorgio, dominated by the Palladian church of **San Giorgio Maggiore** which stands in a prime position opposite the Doge's Palace and the entrance to the Grand Canal. Palladio had been commissioned by the Benedictine monks to build a refectory in 1560, and work was begun on the interior of the church in 1566 and completed in 1591; the façade was finished in 1616. The importance of the site, which made it essential for the façade to be visible from across the water and particularly from the Doge's Palace, made

Palladio erect a more dramatic temple front than at the Redentore, with the pediment supported by giant Corinthian columns.

The spacious interior, with massive, Composite piers in the nave supporting a barrel vault, is strongly influenced by Palladio's study of the ancient Roman baths. Light floods in through the dome which appears to float above the cross-axis of the nave and transepts. Palladio's obvious debt to antiquity and his obsession with harmonious proportions exactly suited eighteenth-century taste. In 1780 William Beckford thought it 'by far the most perfect and beautiful edifice my eyes ever beheld', a position upheld by Eustace and Forsyth's popular guidebooks, published in the early nineteenth century. To Ruskin this all smacked of paganism and stood in direct contrast to the ideals that he attributed to the Gothic.

The interior has some wonderful sixteenth-century Venetian paintings: an atmospheric night scene of the *Nativity* by Jacopo Bassano in the first chapel in the right aisle, and two late Tintorettos in the choir, the *Gathering of Manna* and the *Last Supper* where Christ and the Apostles are seen through a mysterious smoke-filled light. In the eighteenth century the most admired painting was Veronese's *Marriage at Cana*, which used to hang in Palladio's monumental refectory. De Brosses thought it 'not only a painting of the highest merit but among the greatest that exist'. Napoleon agreed with de Brosses's verdict and took the painting back to Paris where it is now one of the chief attractions of the Louvre. You can enjoy the best view in all Venice from the top of the campanile, rebuilt in 1790 after the original bell-tower collapsed in 1774, killing a monk.

The monastic buildings adjoining the church are now the site of the Cini Foundation, founded in 1951 and dedicated to Giorgio Cini, the son of Count Vittorio Cini, one of Italy's leading industrialists and the finance minister of Mussolini. Concerts, plays and exhibitions are held in the two cloisters, the first of which is by Palladio. The refectory to the right of the cloisters is, perhaps, the grandest room built by Palladio. The splendid double staircase by the entrance to the first cloister and the library on the first floor are the work of Longhena.

INFORMATION

Gesuiti: 10 a.m. to 12 noon and 5 p.m. to 7 p.m.

San Sebastiano: 10 a.m. to 12 noon and 2 p.m. to 4 p.m., Sunday 12 noon to 1 p.m. and 2 p.m. to 4 p.m.

Cini Foundation: Write to Cini Foundation, San Giorgio Maggiore, Venice (telephone: 041 528 9900)

RESTAURANTS

Antica Mola
Fondamenta degli Ormesini
Cannaregio 2800, Venice
Telephone: 041 717 492, closed Saturday

Harry's Dolci
Fondamenta San Biagio
Giudecca 773, Venice
Telephone: 041 522 1175, closed Sunday evening and Monday

I stepped into my boat, and instead of encouraging the speed of the gondoliers, begged them to abate their ardour, and row me lazily home

William Beckford

THE LAGOON: MURANO~TORCELLO~BURANO

The Venetian lagoon, a shallow expanse of water 8 km wide and some 50 km long, and extending from the Lido di Jesolo in the north to Chioggia in the south, has played a vital role in Venetian history. After the fall of the Roman Empire in the fifth century and the subsequent invasions by the Huns and Goths, refugees fled to the lagoon for safety. At first settlements were made on the islands, including Torcello, which lay nearest to the mainland. Over the centuries these settlers penetrated further into the lagoon, Venice itself being founded in the eighth century. The treacherous shallowness of the water protected Venice from attack from the sea, the only two forces rash enough to attempt an invasion, the Franks under Pepin in 809, and the Genoese in 1380, being utterly defeated.

Early visitors to Venice tended to omit the lagoon. They knew of Murano's famous glassworks by repute, but such was the secrecy surrounding the process that only the more enterprising such as John Evelyn were fortunate enough to make a visit. The lagoon appealed more to the Romantics, who felt inspired by its sense of silence and desolation. Beckford, in 1780, imagined he was in a dream as his gondola drifted among the outer islands. Byron liked the isolation of San Lazzaro, which lies just before the Lido, and retired to the Armenian monastery to learn the language. He wrote to Douglas Kinnaird: 'Venice & I agree very well – in the mornings I study Armenian – & in the evenings I go out sometimes – & indulge in coition always.'

Beckford, always happy to leave the beaten path, was one of the very few Grand Tourists to venture to Torcello, where he criticised the mosaics for being quaint. The Victorians, at the beginning of mass tourism, liked to escape the crowds in Venice and take picnics to Torcello. Even Ruskin, who had written some of his noblest prose about the island and whose study of Byzantine architecture revived interest in the buildings on Torcello, could not resist running round the island after a heavy lunch to show that the champagne had not gone to his head.

Many of the outlying islands still carry on the specialised industries which have been their trademark for centuries. Murano is famous for its glassworks, Burano for its lace, Chioggia for its fishing industry, and the Lido, once almost deserted and where Byron used to ride for miles along the beach, is now one of the most famous pleasure resorts in Europe, immortalised in Thomas Mann's novel and Visconti's film *Death in Venice*.

A visit to the outer islands is one of the most evocative experiences Venice has to offer, and the best way of understanding the city's origins. The most interesting day's trip in the lagoon takes in Murano, Burano and Torcello, which once rivalled Venice itself in importance.

The no. 5 vaporetto leaves the Fondamenta Nuove and passes the cypress-clad island cemetery of San Michele, where Stravinsky, Diaghelev and Ezra Pound are buried, en route for **Murano**. Because of the danger of fire, Venice's glassworks were removed to Murano in 1291 and have remained on the island ever since. During the Republic, glass blowing was one of Venice's most prized secrets, and the island of Murano was seldom visited. So secretive were the Venetians that, after Ducal banquets, for which the glass blowers of Murano competed, all the prize exhibits were smashed. The Murano glass industry fell into a decline in the seventeenth century when the island lost its monopoly for making crystal glass.

There were a number of convents on the island, which fascinated Casanova, who seduced two of the prettiest nuns. His desires were aroused by the thought of forbidden fruit, 'and who does not know', he confessed, 'that, from Eve down to our days, it was that fruit which has always appeared the most delicious!' One of the nuns responded ardently to Casanova's advances and presented him with a gold snuff-box with a portrait of herself in nun's habit, which revealed her, when a secret spring was pressed, lying naked on a mattress of black satin, posing as the Magdalen.

Murano's Glass Museum, housed in a former bishop's palace, has a display of Roman glass on the ground floor and a number of examples of glass produced locally upstairs. Much of it is technically brilliant, but the coloured chandeliers, in particular, are unbelievably hideous. If you want to purchase some glass, the best factories on the island are Barovier and Toso at Fondamenta Vetrai 28 or Nason and Moretti at Fondamenta Serenella 12, but be warned that prices are lower in Venice itself, either in the shops around Piazza San Marco (Cenedese at no. 40 and 139, or Pauly at nos. 76 and 316), or at L'Isola, San Marco 1468, near the church of San Moisè. Further down the street from the Glass Museum is the Romanesque basilica of Santa Maria e Donato, with an intricate, undulating, mosaic floor covered in peacocks and other birds, and a splendid twelfth-century mosaic of the Madonna in the apse.

To visit Burano and Torcello, change to the no. 12 vaporetto. To avoid the crowds it is best to bypass Burano and go straight to **Torcello**. The imposing campanile is visible for miles across the lagoon, an evocative image of decayed grandeur.

Torcello was probably first inhabited in the fifth or sixth centuries by refugees from the mainland city of Altinum. At one point it had a population of 20,000, the largest settlement in the lagoon. But the canals dried up and malaria made the island uninhabitable. The Cathedral, begun in 639 and rebuilt in the eleventh century, is the oldest and finest building on the island. The austere stone exterior has a fortified appearance, enhanced by the extraordinary stone shutters outside the windows on the south side of the nave.

The dignified interior, its handsome columns taken from Roman buildings on the mainland, goes back to the very beginning of Venetian history. The atmosphere, like that of the churches at Ravenna further down the Adriatic coast, is strongly influenced by that of Byzantium. The superb mosaic of the *Last Judgement* at the west end, dating from c. 1100, creates an overwhelming effect with the brilliance of its colouring. As so often in representations of the subject, the artist's imagination was fired by the vision of hell, as kings and commoners alike are consigned to the flames. In the apse the majestic image of the Madonna is portrayed as an aloof, Byzantine Empress.

The adjoining church of Santa Fosca, built of the same mellow brick as the Cathedral, is a simple, centrally planned building surmounted by a dome. Its most attractive feature is the fourteenth-century relief, on the south side of the exterior, of the Virgin and Child being worshipped by a Confraternity of monks.

Resist the temptation to stop at the overpriced Cipriani restaurant and follow the path back towards the vaporetto which leads past **Ostaria al Ponte del Diavolo**, a more reasonably priced restaurant where you can eat outside.

After lunch, take the boat to **Burano**. The gaily painted houses alongside the canals give this fishing village a festive atmosphere. Much of life takes place out of doors: women sit outside their front doors, chatting and knitting, children play in the barges moored in the canals, and everywhere washing flutters in the breeze. The small scale of its streets and canals resembles Venice in miniature. Above the village looms a massive campanile, leaning over at an alarming angle. There are many small fish restaurants in which to have lunch if you have resisted those on Torcello.

INFORMATION

Glass Museum, Murano: 10 a.m. to 4 p.m., Sunday 9 a.m. to 12.30 p.m., closed Wednesday

Cathedral, Torcello: April to September 10 a.m. to 12.30 p.m. and 2 p.m. to 6.30 p.m., October to March 10 a.m. to 12.30 p.m. and 2 p.m. to 5 p.m.

RESTAURANT

Ostaria al Ponte del Diavolo
Torcello
Telephone: 041 730 401, closed Thursday and evenings except Saturday

THE VENETO

THE VENETO

Were a modern architect to build a palace in Lapland, or
the West Indies, Palladio would be his guide, nor would he
dare to stir a step without his book

William Hogarth

The Veneto, an area of extraordinary cultural richness, comprises
the part of north-east Italy controlled by Venice from the early fifteenth century to the fall of the Venetian Republic in 1797. Venetian
rule was on the whole beneficial and the area benefited greatly from
the peace that the Republic imposed. Many of Venice's leading
artists came from the mainland: Titian from Cadore, Giorgione from
Castelfranco, Veronese from Verona, Palladio from Padua and
Canova from Possagno. But perhaps an even stronger influence on
the Veneto was that of antiquity. Verona, with its Roman Bridge
and magnificent amphitheatre, the most complete in existence,
and Padua, where Donatello and Mantegna, perhaps the two
Quattrocento artists most deeply influenced by the art of antiquity,
came to work, show this influence very clearly. It is even more
apparent walking around the streets and squares of Vicenza, where
the Renaissance palaces of Andrea Palladio are a deliberate attempt
to recreate the classical world.

Generations of visitors felt this all-pervasive classical influence.
Palladio's villas and palaces were enormously influential on Anglo-
American architecture from Inigo Jones up to the American Civil
War. As William Hogarth described it: 'Were a modern architect to
build a palace in Lapland, or the West Indies, Palladio would be his
guide, nor would he dare to stir a step without his book.' Two centuries after Palladio, Canova, the leading neo-classical sculptor and
favourite artist of Napoleon and royalty throughout Europe, was
born in Possagno in the foothills of the Dolomites.

Seventeenth- and eighteenth-century Grand Tourists, well versed
in the classics, noted how many classical authors came from this part
of Italy: Livy from Padua, Catullus and Vitruvius from Verona and
Virgil from nearby Mantua. In contrast, they felt that the Middle
Ages was a time of ignorance and therefore not worth studying. They
spent hours in the amphitheatre at Verona but neglected the city's
Romanesque churches. In Padua, where many of them attended the
university, they admired the basilica of Santa Giustina, erroneously

attributed to Palladio, and the equestrian statue of the *condottiere* Gattamelata because of its connection with that of Marcus Aurelius, and paid homage at the tomb of Antenor, the mythical founder of Padua, ignoring the frescoes in the Arena Chapel by Giotto, whom Président de Brosses thought 'would not now be allowed to paint a tennis court'. In Vicenza, many imagined, like William Beckford in 1780, that Palladio's Olympic Theatre in Vicenza was 'a real and perfect monument of antiquity, which till this moment had remained undiscovered'.

Byron and his contemporaries, at the beginning of the nineteenth century, looked at the same places that had fascinated their predecessors, but also included Shakespearean sites, in particular Juliet's tomb in Verona, where Byron, typically, took away a few pieces in his pocket. This generation of tourists studied the cult of the picturesque and liked to observe the habits of the Italians. The German poet Heine was fascinated by the inhabitants of the Piazza delle Erbe in Verona. 'This is the vegetable market, and that day it was alive with delightful figures of women and girls, with faces from which gazed great languid eyes, with soft appetising bodies, marvellously golden and unashamedly dirty, made for the night far more than the day.'

Despite Napoleon, who had rated Mantegna's San Zeno altarpiece in Verona sufficiently highly to remove it to Paris between 1797 and 1815, it was not till the publication of Pugin's *Contrasts* in 1836 and Lord Lindsay's *Sketches of the History of Christian Art* a decade later, with their championship of 'Christian art', by which they meant the art of the Middle Ages, that people began to be convinced of the worth of Verona's medieval churches and Giotto and Mantegna's frescoes in Padua. Lindsay and Ruskin, whose *Modern Painters* was published in 1846, attacked what they regarded as the paganism of the Renaissance and the Baroque which lasted from the sixteenth to the eighteenth centuries.

At the same time, travellers were fascinated by the medieval history of the Veneto before it fell under Venetian rule. They were thrilled by the legendary cruelty of Ezzelino da Romano, who tyrannised Padua from 1237 to 1254, and the achievements of the Scaligers of Verona, during whose glorious rule many of Verona's most beautiful monuments were constructed. And Browning, who spent most of his life living in self-imposed exile in Italy, composed a volume of poems entitled *Asolando* in honour of Caterina Cornaro, the dethroned Queen of Cyprus, who gathered around her a cultured group of humanists in the little hill town of Asolo.

Nowadays the most attractive part of the Veneto is off the beaten track. Much of the landscape has been industrialised, the mainland opposite Venice has been ruined, including much of the Brenta Canal, and even Padua, with all its masterpieces, has become a nightmare of traffic, and the Arena Chapel is often inundated with tourists. Far better to escape into the countryside, spend days searching out the more remote Palladian villas, such as Maser with its wonderfully decorative Veronese frescoes, discover for yourself Giorgione's ravishing altarpiece hidden away in the Duomo at Castelfranco, and enjoy an excellent lunch in the complete walled town of Montagnana, somewhere that not even the most intrepid sightseer has reached. The city centre of Vicenza is still as ravishing as ever, many of Palladio's buildings recently restored to their original pristine colour, with only the occasional earnest architectural student intruding on the scene.

From Ferrara to Venice

The situation is very beautiful, indeed, among the Euganean hills and the house very fair. The vines are luxuriant to a great degree, and all the fruits of the earth abundant

Byron

ARQUA PETRARCHA~VILLA BARBARIGO, VALSANZIBIO

Most Grand Tourists visited the Veneto at the end of their stay in Italy, usually after a visit to Venice for the feast of the Ascension. They normally approached from Ferrara, many, like Evelyn and Goethe, sailing down the Brenta Canal.

The Romantics made a detour to **Arqua Petrarcha**, a small village beautifully positioned in the Euganean Hills, to visit Petrarch's house where the poet lived from 1370 until his death in 1374. The village is best reached from Monselice, which lies just off the A 13 *autostrada* running between Bologna and Padua. It is about 8 km north-west of Monselice, beyond the hamlet of Bignago. Byron came here with Teresa Guiccioli in 1818 and signed his name in the visitor's book. He himself rented a villa (now called the Villa De Kunkler) 9 km south-west at Este in 1817–18, where Shelley composed 'Lines written among the Euganean Hills'. Both poets waxed lyrical over the beauty of the landscape, and the sky, 'all golden magnificence of autumnal clouds', as Shelley described it to his friend Thomas Peacock. Next to the Villa De Kunkler is the Villa Benvenuti, with a beautiful park.

The finest garden in this part of the Veneto is at the **Villa Barbarigo** at Valsanzibio. From Este return to Monselice and head north for 10 km via the tiny village of Costa on the edge of the Lago di Arqua. The garden, set in an enclosed valley, was laid out in the seventeenth century and aligned on two cross-axes, with avenues of cypresses rising to the summits of the surrounding hills. The original entrance was by an ornate watergate representing Diana's bath, with statues of Diana and Actaeon accompanied by stags and dogs, a suitable subject for a hunting estate. Unfortunately the watergate now faces the main road, but still frames the dramatic vista which leads the eye, via a series of pools and cascades, to the amphitheatre of the hills beyond. The waterfall is very similar to that at Rousham, and it is very probable that William Kent, its architect, visited Valsanzibio on his tour of the Veneto in the early eighteenth century. The most famous feature of the garden is the rabbit island, now rather dilapidated but still containing its original domed aviary. The garden also has a maze in which it is all too easy to get hopelessly lost.

The best place to have lunch nearby is at the restaurant **San Benedetto** in the walled town of Montagnana, 24 km west of Monselice on the SS 10. From the main piazza head north-west to the right of the Loggia restaurant and the first right, down Via Andronalecca, takes you to San Benedetto at no.11. A surprisingly sophisticated restaurant for such a sleepy town, the garden offers an excellent view of the medieval walls. As you leave, glance at Palladio's Villa Pisani outside the east gate. After lunch, take the SS 10 back to Monselice, and continue on the A 13 to Padua.

INFORMATION

Petrarch's house, Arqua Petrarcha: winter, 9.30 a.m. to 12.30 p.m. and 2.30 p.m. to 5 p.m., summer, 9.30 a.m. to 1.30 p.m. and 2.30 p.m. to 7 p.m.

Villa Barbarigo, Valsanzibio: March to October 10 a.m. to 12 noon and 2 p.m. to 6.30 pm., closed Monday morning

RESTAURANT

San Benedetto
Via Andronalecca 11, Montagnana
Telephone: 0429 81566, closed Wednesday

Along the Brenta Canal

As we talked, we sailed down the lovely Brenta, leaving behind us many wonderful gardens and magnificent palaces

Goethe

VILLA MALCONTENTA~MIRA~VILLA PISANI, STRA

For centuries the easiest and most pleasant way of travelling from Venice to Padua was along the Brenta Canal. The villas on the Brenta were designed as summer retreats for the Venetian aristocracy escaping from the heat of the city. In the sixteenth century the Venetian empire in the eastern Mediterranean crumbled in the face of the Turkish onslaught and her prosperity, based on the old overland trade routes to the east, was gradually undermined by the new Spanish and Portuguese discoveries of routes to India via the Cape of Good Hope and to America. As a result the Venetians turned their attention to the Italian mainland, which until that point they had virtually neglected. In the course of the century a new Venetian empire, much closer to home, was created on the Italian terrafirma. The Venetian grandees poured their wealth into the creation of a veritable riviera along the banks of the Brenta Canal.

Grand Tourists regarded the boat trip along the canal as the most delightful approach to Venice. John Evelyn, in 1645, was entranced by the flying glow-worms, some of which he caught and used to read a book at night. Eighteenth-century travellers, such as Beckford and Goethe, with their passion for Palladian architecture, were overwhelmed by the palatial villas.

It is still possible to take the Burchiello from Venice to Padua, stopping at the Villa Malcontenta, the Villa Widman at Oriago, where you have lunch, and the Villa Pisani at Stra. A bus takes you back from Padua to Venice. The first half of the journey is much the more interesting since, as you approach Padua, the banks of the canal become too high to see the villas. If you want to take the boat, leave it after lunch and continue by car.

An even better way to view the villas is to follow the canal by car on the SS 11 which runs through the villages of Mira, Dolo and Stra en route to Padua. Leaving Venice, you pass through the industrial wasteland of Mestre before reaching the Villa Malcontenta. It was not always so. Beckford, who sailed down the Brenta in 1780, formed a very different impression:

This river [the Brenta Canal] flows calmly through banks of verdure, crowned by poplars, with vines twining around every stalk, and depending from tree to tree in beautiful festoons ... As yet, I had not perceived an habitation, nor any other objects than green inclosures and fields of Turkish corn, shaded with vine and poplars.

Joseph Smith, the British Consul in Venice in the middle of the eighteenth century and the great patron of Canaletto, retired to an elegant villa on the mainland. He was eighty-two when he married John Murray's sister, a virgin at forty; Smith sold his wonderful collections of books and works of art to George III in 1762.

From Mestre take the SS 309 south and turn left after 5 km to the **Villa Malcontenta**. The Villa, shrouded behind a screen of weeping willows, is haunted by the mysterious legend of the beautiful Foscarina, who is said to have been confined here after her voluptuous and dissolute youth and from whose unhappiness the Villa derives its name. An alternative theory claims that the inhabitants' unhappiness was caused by swarms of mosquitoes, which breed in the semi-stagnant water of the Brenta. The Malcontenta is best seen in the melancholy of a misty autumnal Veneto morning.

Palladio built the Villa in 1559–60 and its commanding portico and monumental hall, taken from the ancient baths he had studied in Rome, was his idea of a recreation of a Roman temple. It is his only work on the Brenta and the grandiose façades, together with the symmetrical arrangement of rooms around a central axis, proved immensely influential on Grand Tourists when they came to modernise their country houses back in England.

The house has suffered many vicissitudes, but recent owners have taken a great deal of trouble to restore it and, by good fortune, it is now owned by a Foscari, a descendant of the original two brothers who commissioned it. The frescoes by Franco and Zelotti, pupils of Veronese, have been lovingly restored and help to temper the austerity of the interior.

Leaving the Villa Malcontenta, cross over the SS 309 and follow the Brenta Canal for 3 km to Oriago, where Casanova, ever-hopeful of a liaison, saw a chaise upset in 1753 and was delighted to prevent a woman falling in, at 'the indiscretion of her petticoats, which had exposed in all their nakedness certain parts which an honest woman never shews to a stranger'.

The village of **Mira** is 4 km beyond Oriago and Byron lived here in the Villa Foscarini (now the Post Office in the main street) from 1817 to 1819. He was in mental anguish at the time over his recent divorce and the sale of his family home at Newstead Abbey, both of which were attempts to rid himself of any remaining ties with England. Nevertheless, in this villa he was able to compose the Fourth Canto of *Childe Harold*, 'with a black-eyed Venetian girl before me, reading Boccaccio', and to draw the locals, gondoliers and waiters alike, under his spell, as Shelley noted on his visit in August 1818.

The English tended to be less impressed than the Italians by Byron's lifestyle. Shelley wrote disapprovingly to Peacock later in the year:

> The fact is, the Italian women with whom he associates are perhaps the most contemptible of all who exist under the moon — the most ignorant, the most disgusting, the most bigoted; Countesses smell so strongly of garlic, that an ordinary Englishman cannot approach them.

Nalin's is the best restaurant on the Brenta, at Via Argine 29, on the right (south) side of the canal in the middle of Mira. It specialises in excellent fish dishes but is rather expensive. If you want something cheaper, **Alla Vida** at Via Don Manzoni 31, at the far end of the same village, is frequented by the locals and specialises in game. I was once fortunate enough to witness a singing contest by a whole team of gondoliers who had rowed here from Venice after winning the regatta.

From Mira the road winds on for 10 km, past the village of Dolo, to Stra, dominated by the **Villa Pisani**, the most grandiose villa on the Brenta and one of the grandest in the whole of Italy. When Alvise Pisani became Doge in 1735, his family already owned a series of villas in the Veneto as well as many of the grandest palaces in Venice. Nevertheless, he celebrated his election by enormously enlarging the Villa here and by adding a vast stable block in the park.

The Villa is an interesting example of the Grand Tour working in reverse. Pisani had been the Venetian ambassador at both the English and French courts and the influence of each country can be seen in the park and Villa respectively. The original, rather simple, Villa was turned by Frigimelica Preti into a neo-classical palace, inspired by Versailles. The park, which was originally designed with formal parterres surrounding a canal linking the Villa with the stables, was transformed into an informal landscape garden in the English manner in the nineteenth century. Président de Brosses, who came here in 1739 shortly after Pisani had begun work on the Villa, thought the gardens magnificent but complained of the number of pavilions scattered throughout them. These pavilions are now hidden by the elms and limes planted in the last century. The poet

Gabriele D' Annunzio used the garden as the setting for his autobio-graphical novel *Il Fuoco*. Do not miss the maze, so complex that it needs an attendant who stands on top of a central tower directing the more hopeless tourists in the right direction.

The Villa's chief artistic glory is the magnificent Tiepolo fresco in the ballroom, depicting *The Apotheosis of the Pisani Family*. Painted from 1760 to 1762, the fresco represents the culmination of Giam Battista Tiepolo's work in Italy, and was the last project he undertook before leaving to work for the King of Spain in Madrid. Members of the Pisani family are depicted seated on the clouds, sur-rounded by allegorical figures of the continents and Good triumph-ing over Evil. Considering the actual insignificance of the Pisani, and indeed of Venice, at this period in world affairs, one can only marvel at the pomposity of the subject matter.

The vastness of the Villa has always appealed to megalomaniacs. It was bought by Napoleon in 1807 and given to his stepson Eugène de Beauharnais. It was also the place chosen for the first meeting between Hitler and Mussolini in June 1934. This was the Führer's first visit abroad after coming to power and he proved no match for Il Duce, then at the height of his reputation, swaggering about the colonnades in his uniform and dagger. They talked about Austria and Mussolini gave avuncular advice on how to deal with socialists. Hitler left for home very gloomy.

Beyond Stra, the SS 11 continues 8 km to Padua.

INFORMATION

The Burchiello: leaves from the no.1 vaporetto stop outside Harry's
    Bar on Tuesday, Thursday and Saturday at 9 a.m.
Villa Malcontenta: 1 May to 30 October on Tuesday, Thursday and
    the 1st Sunday of the month, 9 a.m. to 12 noon
Villa Pisani, Stra: 9 a.m. to 4 p.m., Sunday 9 a.m. to 12.30 p.m.,
    closed Monday

RESTAURANTS

Trattoria Nalin
Via Novissimo, Mira
Telephone: 041 420 083, closed Sunday and Monday

Alla Vida
Via Don Manzoni 31, Mira
Telephone: 041 422 143, closed Monday

Padua

*Oh sir, you must come to Padua! There are a thousand
things worth seeing*

Dr Warner

*SCROVEGNI CHAPEL~EREMITANI CHURCH~UNIVERSITY~
PALAZZO DELLA RAGIONE~BASILICA OF SANT' ANTONIO~
PRATO DELLA VALLE*

Ever since the founding of the university in 1222, Padua has been
the intellectual centre of the Veneto. After Venice conquered the city
in 1405, Padua's university served the whole Venetian Republic,
and became famous throughout Europe for its faculties of science
and medicine, earning the city the title of 'La Dotta' (the Learned).
Early visitors, anxious to benefit from its excellent reputation,
enrolled in large numbers. William Harvey, later famous as the dis-
coverer of the circulation of blood, took his degree there in 1602.
From 1592 to 1610 Galileo taught physics there and numbered
among his pupils Gustavus Adolphus of Sweden, the hero of the
Protestant cause in the Thirty Years' War. Students included many
of the leading figures of seventeenth-century England: the diarist
John Evelyn, the poets Edmund Waller, Thomas Killigrew and the
Earl of Rochester, and the Royalist generals Montrose and Bonnie
Dundee.

The students of the university were known for their wild
behaviour, taking the law into their own hands whenever necessary,
and Sir Julius Caesar's son was one of several to be killed fighting
duels. They were also famed for their loose morals, 'making songs,
and singing sonnets of the beauty and pleasure of their Bardassu, or
buggered boys', as William Lithgow, who had travelled widely and
been tortured by the Inquisition in Spain, was surprised to note in
1609. During the annual fair, which still takes place at the beginning
of June, everyone was amused by races of running footmen.

Grand Tourist accounts make constant references to Livy, the
Roman historian who was born here, and to the city's founding by
the Trojan Antenor, making it as old as Rome itself. Accounts of the
sites that they visited show their extraordinarily blinkered vision.
Padua is one of the most important centres of Quattrocento art outside Tuscany, but the majority of eighteenth-century visitors passed

265

over it in silence, regarding it as too primitive to be worth commenting on, certainly compared with the art of the sixteenth and seventeenth centuries. They mentioned Donatello's equestrian statue of Gattamelata in passing, because it was modelled on that of the Emperor Marcus Aurelius, but ignored his marvellous bronzes inside the basilica of Sant' Antonio. And Richard Lassels, visiting the church of the Eremitani, mentions two paintings by Guido Reni whose classical style, modelled on that of Raphael and the antique, was immensely popular with Grand Tourists, and completely ignores the Mantegnas, and the Giottos in the Arena Chapel next door.

Unfortunately, Padua today has not preserved the charm of the other major cities of the Veneto. The traffic can be horrendous and it is some distance on foot between the main monuments. For those in a hurry, either head for the Giottos and the Mantegnas, or the Donatellos.

The city's greatest work of art, despite the opinion of Grand Tourists, is the **Scrovegni Chapel** (Arena Chapel) off the Corso Garibaldi, by the main Post Office. Painted for Enrico Scrovegni to assuage his guilt over his father's usury, Giotto's frescoes have traditionally been cited as the dawn of the Italian Renaissance. The fresco cycle marks a dramatic break from the stiff formality and lack of realism of the Byzantine school of painting in the Veneto. Each scene is easily understandable, the figures modelled in a clear light, and painted in strong, primary colours. Giotto's strength lies in his ability, not only to give his figures a solid presence, something greatly admired by Berenson, but also to imbue them with psychological insight.

Beneath the bright blue of the vault, symbolising heaven, the scenes on the walls of the chapel are devoted to the lives of the Virgin and of Christ. They form a continuous narrative sequence, each of the three sections beginning on the right wall by the chancel arch and continuing on the left wall. The top section is devoted to scenes from the lives of Joachim and Anna, the Virgin's parents, and of the Virgin herself, the middle section to the Infancy of Christ, continuing on the left wall with his Mission, and the bottom section to the Passion of Christ, culminating in the Crucifixion and Resurrection. The sequence ends with the Last Judgement on the entrance wall.

In the *Meeting at the Golden Gate* in the upper section of the right wall, Giotto gives the central figures of Joachim and Anna an intensity in their embrace which is almost tangible. In the *Raising of Lazarus* on the left wall our attention is drawn to the startled reactions of the spectators as they realise the miracle that has just occurred. Not everything in the frescoes is totally realistic. The primitive landscapes and box-like architecture, often, as in the

266

Meeting at the Golden Gate, totally out of proportion, show that Giotto had not fully mastered the complexities of perspective.

A few Grand Tourists admired the Arena Chapel, including Thomas Coke and the architect William Kent on their visit in 1714, but in general it remained virtually unknown until the nineteenth century. Mariana Starke's influential guidebook omitted the Giottos, and it was not until Mrs Graham's monograph of 1833, followed by Murray's *Handbook* of 1842, that Giotto's frescoes were finally given their rightful place in the history of Italian painting.

The building directly to the south of the chapel, the church of the **Eremitani**, contains fragments of the Mantegna frescoes which survived the bomb which fell through the roof in 1944. The scene on the right wall of the *Martyrdom of St Christopher* shows how well the young Mantegna had grasped the problem of perspective to define a real space in which the figures stand. The frescoes also show Mantegna's profound interest in classical architecture.

Goethe was virtually the only eighteenth-century critic to understand their importance:

> In the church of the Eremitani I saw some astonishing paintings by Mantegna, one of the older masters. What a sharp, assured actuality they have! It was from this actuality, which does not merely appeal to the imagination, but is solid, lucid, scrupulously exact and has something austere, even laborious about it, that the later painters drew their strength, as I observed in Titian's pictures. It was thanks to this that their genius and energy were able to rise above the earth and create heavenly forms which are still real. It was thus that art developed after the Dark Ages.

Returning to Corso Garibaldi, turn left and continue through Piazza Garibaldi to Piazza Cavour where, at Japelli's palatial Caffè Pedrocchi, built in 1831 in a neo-Egyptian style, you can enjoy a cappuccino in some of the most sumptuous surroundings in Italy.

On the south side of the café just across Via Otto Febbraio stands the ancient **University**, housed in the sixteenth-century Palazzo del Bo, named after a tavern sign of an ox that stood on the site. You can capture a flavour of Padua's importance as an intellectual centre from the wooden pulpit from which Galileo delivered his lectures, and from the claustrophobic Anatomical Theatre dating from 1594, probably the first of its kind in Europe.

From the University cross over Via Otto Febbraio to Piazza delle Erbe, the heart of historic Padua. The piazza is dominated by the **Palazzo della Ragione**, an enormous medieval hall and the seat of justice in the Middle Ages. Coryate, in 1608, never one to miss out on a quirky local custom, recorded the round stone inserted in the floor 'on the which if any bankerout [bankrupt] doth set with his naked buttocks three times in some public assembly, all his debts are ipso facto remitted'. The hall was originally frescoed by Giotto, but his work was destroyed in a fire in 1756. The main exhibit left is a fifteenth-century wooden horse built for jousting, chiefly memorable for its enormous balls.

Returning to Via Otto Febbraio, cross over and continue down Via San Francesco on the south side of the University, and take the second right down Via del Santo, which leads to the **Basilica of Sant' Antonio**, an oriental fantasy whose domes rival those of St Mark's in Venice. The basilica was begun in 1232, the year in which St Antony was canonised.

The lavishly decorated interior makes this one of the most splendid churches in the Veneto, although it is often difficult to see the works of art because of the throngs of pilgrims, who touch or kiss St Antony's sarcophagus in his chapel in the north transept, particularly on 13 June, the patron saint's day. St Antony rivals St Francis as the most popular saint in Italy, and it is therefore rare that you can have a proper look at Tullio Lombardo's handsome reliefs, on the sides of the sarcophagus dating from c. 1500 which were much admired in the eighteenth century.

Fynes Moryson, who came here in 1593, was as fascinated as Coryate by local customs, and noted all the miracles attributed to the saint, 'at whose feast day they use to present for great gifts the hallowed girdles of this St, which they tie about their loynes, and attribute strange effects thereunto'. Even William Beckford, not renowned for the strength of his religious convictions, came here in 1780 and prayed to be relieved of his passion for a young male of the Cornaro family. St Antony, however, was deaf to his entreaties, suspecting, no doubt, the Englishman's sincerity, and Beckford 'found myself a frail, infatuated mortal'. Lady Morgan, whose book is full of observations on Italian society, noted how the elegantly dressed women 'yawned, pointed their glasses, and looked about them with such an air of fashionable ennui that I almost fancied myself in an English Protestant church'.

The Chapel of St Felix in the south transept contains some dramatic frescoes by Altichiero, a leading follower of Giotto. The four reliefs around the high altar are extremely complex works by Donatello of the *Life of St Antony*, beneath the statues of the Crucifixion, the Virgin and Four Saints. Each relief has some fifty or more figures and is set within an intricate architectural framework.

Donatello's mastery of perspective and sense of drama were to have an immense influence on later Renaissance art.

Outside the basilica, Donatello's bronze equestrian statue of the *condottiere* Gattamelata was the first equestrian bronze to be cast since antiquity. Lassels, who came here in the middle of the seventeenth century, comments on the statue but makes no mention of the Donatello bronzes inside the church, and most eighteenth-century guidebooks endorsed his view.

From the square, a short walk south-west down Via Belludi leads to the **Prato della Valle**, an eighteenth-century hall of fame ringed by a canal, with statues of famous Paduans and eminent professors and students from the university round the oval canal in the centre of the enormous piazza. The Prato is the centre of outdoor entertainment in Padua and the site of a large market on Saturday mornings. The east side of the square is overlooked by the Benedictine church of Santa Giustina, its exotic domes echoing those of Sant' Antonio. Next to it is the Botanic Garden, the oldest in Europe, founded in 1545.

The best place to eat in Padua is **Dotto's**. From the north side of the Prato della Valle head up Via Umberto 1 and beyond the church of Santa Maria dei Servi, then turn left into Via Solferino. Dotto's is on the corner where the street changes its name to Via dei Songin.

INFORMATION

Scrovegni Chapel: 9 a.m. to 7 p.m., closed Monday
Eremitani Church: 8.15 a.m. to 12 noon and 3.30 p.m. to 6.30 p.m.
University: 9 a.m. to 1 p.m. and 3 p.m. to 5 p.m., closed Saturday afternoon and Sunday
Palazzo della Ragione: 9.30 a.m. to 12.30 p.m. and 2.30 p.m. to 5.30 p.m., closed Sunday afternoon and Monday

RESTAURANT

Dotto
Via Squarcione 23, Padua
Telephone: 049 25055, closed Sunday evening and Monday

From Venice to Vicenza

*The roofs of the town (Asolo) are red, darkened and mottled
by centuries of sunlight and rain, for this is the dampest and
greenest corner of Italy*

Freya Stark

*CASTELFRANCO~VILLA EMO, FANZOLO~
VILLA BARBARO, MASER~ASOLO/
CANOVA MUSEUM, POSSAGNO~MAROSTICA*

The most attractive route between Venice and Vicenza runs up into
the foothills of the Dolomites through the hill towns of Castelfranco,
Asolo and Marostica. It makes an easy day's journey through some
of the most beautiful countryside in the Veneto. Despite the number
of Palladian villas in this area, few Grand Tourists dared to venture
this far off the beaten track, since most of the locals, as Coryate ner-
vously noted, 'were furnished with muskets ready charged, and
touch-boxes hanging by their sides full of gunpowder, together with
little pouches of bullets'.

Follow the SS 245 north-west from Venice for 35 km until you
reach **Castelfranco**. The town is surrounded by a massive fortified
wall and moat, built to protect the inhabitants from their aggressive
neighbours in Padua. Originally founded by the town of Treviso in
1199 to guard the frontier with Paduan territory, it came under
Venetian domination at the end of the fourteenth century.

The town is famous for the altarpiece by Giorgione in the Duomo.
Park your car outside the main gate and wander through the narrow
streets to the central square, where a welcome cappuccino in the
café will give you time to digest the eighteenth-century façade of the
cathedral opposite. Built between 1723 and 1745 by Frigimelica
Preti in a sober, neo-classical style, it is exactly contemporary with
his work on the Villa Pisani at Stra.

Inside the cathedral, Giorgione's masterpiece stands in a chapel
at the end of the right aisle. It depicts the Madonna and Child,
seated on a throne above St Francis and St Liberalis (the patron
saint of Castelfranco) who stand on either side. The pyramidal composition leads up to the Virgin. The figures are withdrawn and
remain totally detached, both from us and from each other, so that
they appear to inhabit a dreamworld. The several signs of war in

this painting, not only in St Liberalis's armour and standard, but also in the tower and men-at-arms in the background, may have a contemporary relevance to the uneasy political situation in the Veneto at the time. The altarpiece was painted in about 1504.

Giorgione himself remains as enigmatic as his paintings. All we know is that Giorgio Barbarelli, known as Giorgione (Big George in Italian) was probably born c. 1475–7 and came to Venice when very young, probably to study under the ageing Giovanni Bellini, the most important Venetian painter of his generation. Giorgione appeared to show a zest for life, and Vasari, the gossipy sixteenth-century art historian, records him as being the life and soul of parties and a great lover. He also had a deep love of nature and a passion for music. He died young, of the plague, in 1510.

Of all the major European artists, Giorgione is the most difficult to assess, and the dispute over which paintings are his (rather than by his chief pupil Titian or Titian's followers) remains as unresolved as ever. The Castelfranco altarpiece was brought to the world's attention in the most dramatic fashion when it was stolen, as part of a series of fine-art robberies, in the 1970s. After a string of ransom demands for large amounts of money had been refused, the altarpiece was abandoned by the thieves following a gunbattle with the police.

One of Palladio's finest villas lies 7 km north-east of Castelfranco at Fanzolo. The Villa Emo was built by Palladio between 1550 and 1560. Its most unusual feature is the long ramp leading up to the portico, allowing those arriving on horseback to ride right up to the front door. Two arcaded wings stretch out on either side, integrating the house with the farm buildings, a typical feature of Palladio's buildings. If you would like to see Zelotti's frescoes extolling civic and moral virtues, you will have to come back after lunch, when the interior of the Villa is open.

Beyond the villages of Caselle and Altivole 14 km north-west of the Villa, lies Robert Browning's 'delicious Asolo', the charming hill town he fell in love with on his first trip to Italy in 1838. A large English colony settled here in the footsteps of the Brownings, whose love affair blossomed in the mountain air and the beautiful surroundings. The Brownings were originally inspired by Asolo's romantic past. Caterina Cornaro, the last Queen of Cyprus, was persuaded or, to be more accurate, compelled to hand over her kingdom to Venice in 1489, and given the hill town of Asolo in exchange. The verb *asolare*, meaning to pass the time in an agreeable, purposeless way, was coined by her friend Cardinal Bembo with poor Caterina in mind. Browning named his last volume of poems *Asolando* (1899) 'for the love of the place'.

Browning's son Pen owned five houses in the town, the grandest of which is next to the Cipriani hotel and which he referred to as 'Palazzo Pigsty'. He virtually ruled the town, restarted the silk weaving industry and was referred to by Henry James as the 'Asolan Kaiser Wilhelm', or, for those less impressed by his industry, 'Halfpenny Browning'. Asolo's most notable inhabitant in recent times has been the travel writer Freya Stark, whose parents were persuaded to move here by Pen Browning. She writes in *A Traveller's Prelude* of how the happiest times of her life have been spent here, and describes the town:

> There are two castles – Queen Cornaro's with a square tower at the head of a cobbled curve, and the medieval keep with pre-Roman foundations, which encircles the top of the hill where the town walls end. The roofs of the town are red, darkened and mottled by centuries of sunlight and rain, for this is the dampest and greenest corner of Italy. The piazza is shaded with chestnut trees . . . and the church – which possesses one Lorenzo Lotto picture – has a slim straight tower washed bright pink, in whose open top the bells can be seen ringing for even the most insignificant saint's day in the year.

Asolo possesses two excellent restaurants, the vastly overpriced **Cipriani** and **Charly's One**, a good alternative in the main piazza.

From Asolo a short detour east for 8 km takes you to the village of Maser, with one of the finest of all Palladian villas, the **Villa Barbaro**, whose long, low, yellow stucco façade blends with the landscape. Daniele and his brother Marcantonio Barbaro, who commissioned the Villa in 1557, epitomised a new type of patron. As Venetian aristocrats who owned a large villa in the provinces, they needed the income from the land to sustain their elaborate lifestyle. Daniele edited Vitruvius, wrote on mathematics and the science of perspective, and served the Republic as ambassador and Patriarch of Aquilea. It is not surprising to find that Maser is the most highly decorated of all sixteenth-century villas in the Veneto.

The Villa represents a miraculous fusion of the talents of Palladio and Veronese, although it is fascinating to note that Palladio may have felt that Veronese had destroyed his carefully calculated proportions and made no mention of him in his *Quattro Libri*. The *piano nobile* of the central block contains a whole series of *trompe l'oeil* frescoes by Veronese with imaginary views over the surrounding countryside, filled with classical ruins. Members of the Barbaro family and their servants, returning from hunting, gaze down over a fictive balustrade into the hall. Marcantonio Barbaro is depicted at one end of the side-axis returning from hunting, with his wife at the far end waiting to receive him. The spectator is intended to feel that not only does the Villa open on to the countryside but that the pergolas painted on the ceilings open on to the sky, inhabited by the gods of Olympus, fitting subjects for the two humanist Barbaro brothers. The central hall opens out on to the landscape. At the other end there is a classical nympheum, intended to reproduce an antique prototype, and influenced by the Villa Giulia in Rome; it is filled with statues of the gods of Olympus by Alessandro Vittoria, who also worked with Palladio at the Villa Rotonda.

At the foot of the hill stands a small circular chapel, given a festive atmosphere by swags of fruit suspended between columns in the porch, and continued all round the walls of the interior. The harmonious proportions and the ring of balustrading at the foot of the dome pay homage to Bramante's Tempietto in Rome, which Palladio admired above all other Renaissance buildings. Unfortunately the chapel is rarely open to the public. Jean de la Lande, one of the few Grand Tourists to reach Maser, thought it a masterpiece on his visit in 1766.

Another detour from Asolo, this one for the real Grand Tour enthusiast, takes you to **Possagno**, where Canova was born in 1757. His birthplace is now a museum and overflowing with casts of his sculptures. Canova was a great favourite of royalty and aristocracy all over Europe, who felt that his work was a brilliant recreation of the spirit of antique sculpture.

Bassano, the home of the famous family of Renaissance painters, lies 18 km south-west of Possagno. Jacopo Bassano (1510–92) and his two sons Francesco and Leandro specialised in painting religious and genre scenes filled with labourers and animals. Based on a close study of nature, these paintings were to have a strong influence on landscape and genre painting in the seventeenth century. Bassano itself is a pretty town which suffered severely during a prolonged period of fighting between the Italians and the Austrians in the mountains nearby during 1917–18. The town is famous for its ceramics and you might like to look round one of the factories or admire the bridge built after a design by Palladio, or sample the famous Grappa, a brand of delectable firewater.

From Bassano follow the SS 248 towards Vicenza. After 7 km, you pass the picturesque fortified hilltown of **Marostica**. The piazza, tucked beneath the ramparts, is laid out in the form of a chessboard. Every alternate September a match is played with human pieces to commemorate a contest between Rinaldo da Angarona and Vieri da

Vallonara for the hand of Lionara Parisio, the daughter of a six-teenth-century Venetian governor. The 'pieces' dress up in medieval costume and heralds announce the moves in Venetian dialect. The match tends to degenerate into a farce as the commands are given in an archaic dialect which is frequently misunderstood by the pieces, who then move into the wrong square.

From Marostica it is an easy 25 km down the SS 248 to Vicenza.

INFORMATION

Villa Emo, Fanzolo: Saturday and Sunday, summer 3 p.m. to 6 p.m., winter 2 p.m. to 5 p.m.
Villa Barbaro, Maser: Tuesday, Saturday, Sunday, April to September 3 p.m. to 6 p.m., October to March 2 p.m. to 5 p.m. Telephone: 0423 565 002
Gipsoteca and Casa di Canova, Possagno: summer, Tuesday to Saturday 3 p.m. to 6 p.m., Sunday 3 p.m. to 7 p.m., winter, Tuesday to Sunday 9 a.m. to 12 noon and 2 p.m. to 5 p.m., closed Monday

RESTAURANTS

Villa Cipriani
Via Canova 298, Asolo
Telephone: 0423 55444

Charly's One
Via Roma 55, Asolo
Telephone: 0423 52201, closed Friday

Vicenza

A new architectural religion was born, with Palladio as Mahomet, his Four Books of Architecture as the sacred text, and Inigo Jones as a major prophet. Of the new cult Lord Burlington was to be high priest and Chiswick the temple

John Charlton

TEATRO OLIMPICO~PALAZZO CHIERICATI~ SANTA CORONA~PALAZZO THIENE~CONTRÀ PORTI~ BASILICA~LOGGIA DEL CAPITANIATO~PALAZZO PORTO BREGANZE

Vicenza, a provincial town set on the edge of the Venetian plain against the backdrop of the Dolomites, might never have attracted travellers hurrying from Venice to Milan had it not been for the architecture of Andrea Palladio. His career (1535–80) exactly coincided with the resurgence of Venetian power in northern Italy. Vicenza had placed itself under Venetian dominion in 1404 but revolted in the early sixteenth century, and the ensuing fighting led to the sacking of the city by both Venetian and Imperial troops.

The scene was set for a major rebuilding programme. Andrea di Pietro, a humble stonemason from Padua, was chosen by his patron, Gian Giorgio Trissino, an enlightened nobleman with a passion for antiquity, as the architect who would fill the city with Renaissance palaces. Trissino took his protégé to Rome to study the classical remains and renamed him Palladio to evoke the image of Pallas Athene, the Greek goddess of wisdom. On their return in 1541, Palladio began to build a series of palaces in the town, and villas in the surrounding countryside. These are the three-dimensional blueprints for the architecture of eighteenth-century England and America.

The fame of these buildings, illustrated in Palladio's *Quattro Libri*, brought Grand Tourists flocking to the town. Inigo Jones, who introduced Palladian architecture into England, came here in 1614, as did Lord Burlington, whose villa at Chiswick is perhaps the finest Palladian building in England. They bought every Palladio drawing they could acquire.

The most remarkable of all the Palladian buildings in Vicenza is

the extraordinary **Teatro Olimpico** off the Piazza Matteotti. It
formed part of the building complex that housed the Accademia
Olimpica, an Academy founded in 1555 by a collection of local
Vicentine scholars, mathematicians and aristocrats interested in
pursuing classical studies.

The theatre, on the site of an ancient prison, was designed by
Palladio (but executed after Palladio's death in 1580 by his pupil
Scamozzi) according to his own interpretation of Vitruvian principles of theatre design. It was first used in a production of *Oedipus
Rex* in 1585. It was the first indoor theatre to revive the antique
tradition of providing a permanent stage and is the oldest playhouse
in Europe to have been continually in use. Palladio intended the
stage to consist of a screen resembling a triumphal arch, with statues
of classical heroes in the window frames, and architectural sets providing a backdrop. Scamozzi, however, changed the design and built
a series of wooden streets in sharp perspective behind the screen.
The heroic statues surmounting the screen that runs around the

back of the seats are of the Academicians themselves, with Trissino in the centre.

The idea of rebuilding a perfect piece of architecture after the antique fired the imagination of Grand Tourists. Beckford, on his visit in 1780, recited Aeschylus on stage and fancied he 'had penetrated into a real and perfect monument of antiquity, which till this moment had remained undiscovered'. Goethe, six years later, thought it 'indescribably beautiful', and Napoleon, on entering the theatre, exclaimed in amazement: 'Madame, we are in Greece.'

The theatre has been recently restored and if there is a performance on, particularly a ballet, you should not miss it. The most dramatic moment in its recent history occurred during the Queen Mother's visit in 1987, when one of her bodyguards fell off the stage into the orchestra pit. A crazy guide will explain the theatre's complexities in five languages.

Across the Piazza Matteotti, which used to serve as a public market, is the **Palazzo Chiericati** which dates from 1551, unique among Palladio's palaces in its position overlooking an open space. The colonnade on the ground floor served as a covered walkway for pedestrians. The central five bays of the *piano nobile* are set forward and surmounted by statues in order to counteract the length of the façade. The Museo Civico inside the palace houses a minor collection of local paintings.

From the piazza go up the Corso Palladio, the main shopping street in Vicenza. Contrà Santa Corona, the second turning on the right, leads to the church of **Santa Corona** which contains the two finest Renaissance paintings in the town. In the fifth chapel on the left stands a large altarpiece of the *Baptism* by Giovanni Bellini, painted c. 1501 near the end of his career. The feeling of monumentality in the figures represents a new departure in Venetian painting. The third chapel in the south aisle contains an *Adoration of the Kings* by Veronese, dominated by the resplendent red and yellow of the kings' robes.

Turning right out of the church, take the first left down Contrà Santo Stefano into Piazza Santo Stefano. In the left transept of the church hangs one of Palma Vecchio's most beautiful paintings, painted in the sumptuous colours typical of the Venetian High Renaissance. Outside the church you have an acute angled view, to your left, of Palladio's **Palazzo Thiene**, with its heavy rustication and sculptural windows, harking back to High Renaissance Rome and Giulio Romano's buildings in nearby Mantua, and forming such a startling contrast to the Venetian Gothic palaces flanking it.

Lord Burlington, who made a careful study of Palladio's buildings in Vicenza, considered it the most beautiful modern building in the world. Unfortunately for Palladio the building boom which had served him so well came to an end in the late 1560s, and none of these palaces was completed as he had intended. The effect of visiting the Palazzo Thiene is somewhat similar to that of Nash's terraces surrounding Regent's Park in London, where the grandeur of the façades hides the shallowness of the interiors.

Follow Stradella Banco Popolare down the right side of Palazzo Thiene. **Contrà Porti**, at the end, is a narrow street full of interesting Gothic and Renaissance palaces. Unfortunately this narrowness makes it extremely difficult to gain a good view of their façades. Even Palladio, with his passion for symmetry, found it difficult to impose some order on the cramped sites he was allocated. In the façade of the Palazzo Barbarana Da Porto, at no. 11, he achieved this by providing a strong contrast between the vertical columns and the horizontal entablature. The Contrà Porti leads down to the Corso Palladio, and beyond it you catch a glimpse of the **Basilica** in Piazza dei Signori.

Palladio's design for the outer shell, dating from 1546–9 and built over the next fifty years, was his first public commission. He placed a two-storey loggia on the existing medieval building, giving an impression of classical symmetry to what was, in fact, an irregular trapezoidal plan. The repetitive nature of the Serlian arches helped to unify the surrounding squares which are all on different levels. Palladio himself felt he had done a good job. He wrote: 'This building may be compared with the ancient edifices and ranked among the most noble and most beautiful fabrics that have been made since the ancient times.'

Facing the Basilica on the north side of the piazza stands the **Loggia del Capitaniato**, from where the Venetian captain could address the people. A much later work by Palladio, it has giant composite brick columns rising the whole height of the façade, reflecting the increasing grandeur of his architectural vocabulary. The east façade celebrates Vicenza's part in the great naval victory over the Turks at Lepanto in 1571. It is covered in sculptured panels of trophies surmounted by statues of Peace (Vicenza) and War (Venice). You can enjoy an excellent view of the Basilica from the Gran Caffè Garibaldi beside the loggia.

The Contrà del Monte on the east side of the loggia leads to the Corso Palladio. Turn left, and the second palace on your left, the Palazzo Trissino–Baston, its handsome first storey rising above a screen of columns, is the masterpiece of Palladio's pupil Scamozzi. Continue down Corso Palladio, and just before you reach the Porta

Castello turn left into Piazza del Castello. Straight ahead is the **Palazzo Porto Breganze**, dating from the 1570s, the strangest of all Palladio's buildings. The unfinished Palazzo is only two bays wide and this narrowness, combined with the three enormous Corinthian columns whose bases rise the whole height of the ground floor, gives an overpowering effect, as though the palace had been designed for a race of giants.

It is now time for lunch. Almost directly opposite the palace is **Agli Schioppi**, which specialises in game. An alternative is the **Scudo di Francia**, the best restaurant in Vicenza. Take the Contrà Vescovado out of the east side of Piazza del Castello, pass the right side of the graceful, honey-coloured façade of the Duomo, continue down Corso Garibaldi and turn right into Strada dei Tre Scodini by the statue of two children on a swing. Turn left into Contrà Giampietro di Proti, and, near the bottom of the street, you pass the exquisite Palazzo Pigafetta, named after Antonio Pigafetta, who circumnavigated the world with Magellan. With its beautiful curved balconies, this is one of the gems of Venetian Gothic, and stands comparison with any of Palladio's palaces in Vicenza. Beyond the palace, turn right and left into Contrà San Paolo and Allo Scudo di Francia, an old palace where many Grand Tourists lodged, including Goethe, is at the junction of Corso San Paolo and Contrà Piancoli. Napoleon billeted his troops in the lofty vaulted rooms during his lightning campaign of 1796–7.

INFORMATION

Teatro Olimpico: 16 March to 15 October 9.30 a.m. to 12.20 p.m. and 3 p.m. to 5.30 p.m., 16 October to 15 March 9.30 a.m. to 12.20 p.m. and 2 p.m. to 4.30 p.m, Sunday 9.30 a.m. to 12.20 p.m.

RESTAURANTS

Agli Schioppi
Via del Castello 26/28, Vicenza
Telephone: 0444 543 701, closed Sunday

Scudo di Francia
Contrà Piancoli 4, Vicenza
Telephone: 0444 320 898, closed Sunday evening and Monday

Today I went to see a magnificent house called the Rotonda . . . Architecture has never, perhaps, achieved a greater degree of luxury

Goethe

VILLA ROTONDA~VILLA VALMARANA~ VILLA ROCCA PISANA

The **Villa Rotonda** lies just outside Vicenza at the foot of Monte Berico. You can reach it on a bus which leaves from the Piazza Castello at the west end of the Corso Palladio, or you can walk to it, following the yellow signs, although it is advisable to take a map (obtained from the tourist office in Piazza Matteotti).

The Villa was built by Palladio from 1566 to 1570 as a suburban retreat for Monsignor Almerico, who used to have picnics and hold musical evenings here. Standing just outside the town, it is unique among Palladio's villas for its lack of any farm buildings. This enabled Palladio to plan it symmetrically around four axes.

The fame of the Villa and of the entertainments given here soon spread. Most budding architects and their patrons would have studied it in Palladio's *Quattri Libri*, but those who came to Vicenza were anxious to see the Villa for themselves. Inigo Jones attended an evening's entertainment in 1613 and made a careful study of the building, unlike the Bohemian Thomas Coryate twenty years earlier, who was more interested in being offered a glass of wine. John Evelyn was most upset by the surliness of one of his companions which prevented him from seeing it when he passed through Vicenza in 1646.

Eighteenth-century Grand Tourists were even more enthusiastic, and Lord Burlington, who spent six months in Vicenza on his second Grand Tour in 1719, designed his villa in Chiswick as a close variant of Palladio's Villa. Goethe thought it a magnificent folly, and wrote: 'Architecture has never, perhaps, achieved a greater degree of luxury.' The Rotonda, with its four porticoes, allows maximum opportunities to enjoy the view and to escape from the summer heat.

This open plan, whose details Robert Adam had criticised as 'but poorly adjusted', was all very well in the warm Italian climate but proved considerably less successful when transposed to the draughty north, and many a Grand Tourist must have cursed his devotion to Palladio while freezing through a British winter. Pope jibed at their folly:

'tis very fine,
But where d'ye sleep, or where d'ye dine?
I find by all you have been telling
That 'tis a house, but not a dwelling.

The Villa is approached up a ramp, now planted with pink roses, and stands on a knoll, with views in all directions; unfortunately the sprawl of Vicenza's suburbs has ruined the view to the east. Purists tend to disapprove of the overpowering frescoes by the seventeenth-century artist Dorigny in the circular hall.

From the Villa, turn right and first left up the Stradella Valmarana to the **Villa Valmarana**, which contains some of the finest frescoes by Giam Battista and his son Gian Domenico Tiepolo. The ground floor of the main Villa, a seventeenth-century exercise in Palladianism by Muttoni, was completely frescoed by the elder Tiepolo with scenes from the literary epics of Homer, Ariosto, Virgil and Tasso. Mengozzi Colonna provided a theatrical setting of fictive architecture in which Tiepolo could bring the classical texts vividly to life.

On entering the Villa you are immediately plunged into the drama of the Trojan War. Agamemnon, the king of the Greeks, his face hidden in his cloak, cannot bear to watch the sacrifice of his daughter Iphigenia which the gods have demanded so that the Greek fleet can set sail for Troy. At the last moment, on Artemis's instructions, a deer floats down on a cloud to replace the wretched Iphigenia, and cupids, flying across the ceiling, blow with all their might to send a ripple of wind through the sails of the Greek fleet, heralding its departure for Troy.

The conflicting themes of love and duty, so apparent in this scene, dominate all the frescoes in the Villa. In the room to the right the poignant figure of Achilles mourns alone on the seashore as his mistress Briseis, in the fresco opposite, is dragged away to be presented as a trophy to Agamemnon. The frescoes in the other three rooms take up the idea of the reluctant hero deserting his lady-love to pursue his destiny. In each case Tiepolo's sympathies seem to lie with the luckless Armida, Angelica and Dido. Tiepolo was most interested in the portrayal of realistic emotions and it is this that gives the frescoes their power; the historical accuracy of the costumes, so vital to neo-classical artists, was of lesser importance.

The Foresteria (an outhouse used as an all-purpose agricultural building) contains the masterpieces of Gian Domenico Tiepolo, a painter who spent most of his life working in his father's studio. For once he was allowed a free hand and painted a series of rustic idylls where nothing intrudes to spoil the charming semi-artificial lifestyle of the labourers, enjoying the fruits of the countryside. One room is frescoed in a Chinese style, bringing Tiepolo into line with the contemporary stylistic innovations of Chambers and Chippendale in England. Goethe, despite his classical upbringing and love of mythology, much preferred these informal genre scenes.

Outside the Villa, notice the statues of dwarfs on the outer wall of the garden, the ancestors of all garden gnomes. From the Villa turn left and follow the road downhill to Vicenza.

For those with a car, and who would like to compare the Rotonda with Scamozzi's attempt to improve on it, take the SS 11 towards Verona and turn left after 11 km at Alte Ceccato. After 13 km you reach Lonigo and, on the hilltop above the town stands the **Villa Rocca Pisana** in an even more spectacular setting than the Rotonda. Scamozzi designed his Villa to be symmetrical around only one axis and simplified the decoration so that there are no frescoes or stuccowork to detract from the purity of the architecture. From my experience, almost all British and American visitors much prefer the Villa to the Rotonda.

INFORMATION

Villa Rotonda: Exterior, 15 March to 15 October, Tuesday and Thursday 10 a.m. to 12 noon and 3 p.m. to 6 p.m.
>**Interior**, 15 March to 15 October, Wednesday 10 a.m. to 12 noon and 3 p.m. to 6 p.m.
Villa Valmarana: March and April 2.30 p.m. to 5.30 p.m., May to September 3 p.m. to 6 p.m., October and November 2 p.m. to 5 p.m. daily, also on Thursday, Saturday and Sunday 10 a.m. to 12 noon
Villa Rocca Pisana, Lonigo (contact Dr Ferri, Via G. Galilei 43, 35121 Padua. Telephone: 049 38435)

Verona

Here of all places I have seene in Italy would I fix a residence
John Evelyn

DUOMO~SANT' ANASTASIA~DELLA SCALA TOMBS~ PIAZZA DELLE ERBE~PIAZZA BRA~AMPHITHEATRE~ GIARDINO GIUSTI

No visitor ever seems to have had a bad word to say about Verona. Classical scholars admired the best-preserved Roman amphitheatre in existence, Shakespearean devotees paid homage at Juliet's tomb, and, in Dickens's words, everyone enjoyed 'its fast-rushing river, picturesque old bridge, great castle, waving cypresses, and prospect so delightful'. John Evelyn, captivated by the city's beauty, would rather have lived here than anywhere else in Italy. The city's most famous site has always been the Arena, an obvious point of reference for Grand Tourists weaned on the classics. The Victorians, following Ruskin's lead, admired the unique collection of Gothic red-brick churches.

Verona was a leading opponent of the Holy Roman Emperors and reached its apogee under the Della Scala family, who ruled it from 1260 to 1387. The city fell under the control of Venice in 1405, whose rule lasted, apart from a brief interlude at the beginning of the sixteenth century, until 1797. When Venice recaptured Verona in 1517, she commissioned Sanmicheli to erect a ring of fortifications around the city, most of which still survive. These fortifications were used by the French and the Austrians in the early nineteenth century, when Verona occupied a pivotal position in north Italian politics until the Austrians were defeated by the armies of the Risorgimento in 1866.

The best place to begin a tour is by the banks of the Adige at the Ponte Pietra, a Roman bridge leading up to the medieval Castello San Pietro. The bridge was blown up in the Second World War, but has been painstakingly reconstructed with the original bricks dug up from the river bed. From here cross Piazza Broilo and pass by the campanile of the **Duomo** with its Romanesque base, surmounted by sixteenth-century Renaissance windows designed by Sanmicheli and crowned by an octagonal storey. The delightful twelfth-century carvings on the capitals of the south porch depict a monster devouring a man, supposedly Jonah in the whale's mouth, and on the opposite side a cheeky dog biting a lion's bottom.

The leading sculptor in Verona at this date was Maestro Niccolò, who sculpted the portal of the main façade in 1139, and another for the façade of San Zeno. His strength lies in his naturalistic carving of figures and animals, particularly the griffins supporting twisted columns of Verona marble, and the two hunchback figures above the door.

A beautiful semicircular choir front designed by Sanmicheli in 1534 stands at the end of the Gothic nave. In the first chapel in the left aisle hangs Titian's *Assumption* of 1535–40, not nearly as good as his earlier masterpiece in the Frari in Venice. In the second chapel in the right aisle there is a charming *Adoration of the Kings* by the late fifteenth-century painter Liberale da Verona, with a young blade of a king doffing his cap, while the foreground is littered with dogs, rabbits and children playing together, oblivious of the solemnity of the event.

Emerging from the cathedral, head south down Via Duomo and, crossing Via Emilei, where Napoleon stayed in Palazzo Forti in 1796–7 (now the Gallery of Modern Art) during his lightning campaign against the Austrians which set him on his path to glory, you arrive in front of the Dominican church of Sant' Anastasia. The brick façade, like that of so many great Gothic structures, is unfinished.

Pushing aside the heavy curtains you enter the cavernous interior, filled with a subdued twilight on even the brightest day. The church was begun in 1290 and continued over the next two centuries. Make your way past the two figures of hunchbacks supporting fonts to the Sacristy on the left of the high altar where Pisanello's famous fresco of *St George and the Princess of Trebizond*, painted in the 1430s, has been moved from the outside of the Pellegrini Chapel on the right of the high altar. The princely figure of St George prepares to mount his charger, watched by the admiring princess; in the background is a fairy-tale view of Trebizond. The horse and dogs are painted with great sympathy and realism characteristic of Pisanello's work.

Almost contemporary with Pisanello's fresco is the magnificent tomb of Cortesia Sarego on the left of the high altar. The way in which two attendants draw back the curtains to reveal general Cortesia Sarego seated proudly on his horse is typical of the Renaissance glorification of man.

Outside the church stands the Due Torri hotel where Goethe stayed in September 1786. Like so many Germans coming south through the Brenner pass, this was his first major stop on his

memorable journey to Italy. Having escaped from the claustrophobia of life in Weimar, he could hardly believe all the sensations
he was experiencing and eulogised: 'The wind that blows . . . is
charged with fragrance as if it had passed over a hill of roses.' The
hotel is now decorated with a series of period rooms, complete with
antique furniture and paintings, verging on the pretentious.

From the Due Torri head down Corso Sant' Anastasia and turn
left into the palace of the Prefettura. The courtyard leads to the
impressive, mid-fourteenth-century **Della Scala tombs**. The Della
Scala family, perhaps to increase their reputation for valour, took
the eccentric step of naming themselves after dogs. The greatest of
them called himself Cangrande (Big Dog, 1311–29), and was succeeded by Cansignorio (Lord Dog, 1329–59), and Mastino II (Mastiff,
1359–75). These tombs commemorate Cansignorio and Mastino II,
who are portrayed twice, mounted on their warhorses and lying
recumbent on their sarcophagi. The wrought-iron enclosure contains
a visual pun on the name Scala in the recurrent motif of steps (*scala*
in Italian). The tombs were particularly admired by Ruskin, who
thought that they represented the best of Veronese Gothic.

If you would like to have lunch at this point, **Arche**, at Via Arche
Scaligiere 6, next to the tombs, is in a handsome old palace, and has
been run by the same family for over 100 years. It specialises in fish,
brought fresh from the Venetian lagoon.

If you would like to continue, walk past the Scaliger tombs into
Piazza dei Signori with the statue of Dante, who was the guest of
Bartolomeo I Della Scala, in the centre. The most elegant building in
the square is the late fifteenth-century Loggia del Consiglio with four
elegant mullioned windows. The Veronese adorned the cornice with
statues of famous Romans who came from Verona, including the
poet Catullus, the architect Vitruvius and the author Pliny the
Elder, whom they poached from Lake Como.

The adjoining **Piazza delle Erbe**, built on the site of the Roman
Forum, has been the central marketplace of Verona since the Middle
Ages and is a good place to stop for a cup of coffee and enjoy the
most picturesque spot in the city. No longer just a market for vegetables (*erbe* in Italian), it is filled with all sorts of souvenir stalls. The
handsome Palazzo Maffei, on the north side, built in a mellow, yellow sandstone and dating from 1668, stands directly behind a statue
of the winged lion of St Mark, a symbol of the long period of
Venetian rule.

Taking the Via Cappello Leoni out of the south side of the square,
an alleyway on the left leads to 'Juliet's House'. Dickens took this
route in 1845 and found the house in a sad state of disrepair guarded

by 'a grim-visaged dog, viciously panting in a doorway, who would certainly have had Romeo by the leg the moment he put it over the wall'. Nowadays, the courtyard exhibits the horrors of tourism at its worst, with absurd postcards of Romeo climbing on to the balcony.

The final part of this morning's walk takes you from Piazza delle Erbe down Via Mazzini to Piazza Bra, the streets on either side full of prosperous-looking shops selling clothes and antiques and the centre of the evening *passeggiata*.

Piazza Bra, whose paving stones made of large slabs of pink Verona marble used as paving stones were much admired in the eighteenth century, is one of the pleasantest places in the city to have lunch, particularly if it is warm enough to sit outside and enjoy a view of the amphitheatre. Try the Antico Pedarena or the Tre Corone. An alternative is **Rubiani**, attached to the hotel Bologna, in Piazza Scalette Rubiani off the north side of the square, famous for its *stinco di maiale al latte* (pork in milk). If you would like to try a first-class restaurant, take Via Pelliciai off the south side of Piazza delle Erbe, turn right up Scaletta Pelliciai, and the **Dodici Apostoli** is just round the corner at Vicolo Corticella San Marco 3, housed in a medieval palace with fading frescoes on the walls. The food is excellent, particularly the *carbonara veronese* (beef in red wine stew) and the *salmone in crosta*, followed by the *pandoro con la zabaione* for dessert.

After lunch, return to Piazza Bra for a look at the **Amphitheatre**, the third largest in existence and a prime site on the Grand Tour. The Arena, initially used for gladiatorial combats, was a place of execution in the Middle Ages, the scene of tournaments in the Renaissance and of bull-baiting and plays in the seventeenth and eighteenth centuries. In 1580 the French essayist Montaigne thought it the most beautiful building he had seen in his life and neglected to look at anything else in the city. Coryate, shortly afterwards, noted that the lower arches were used as stables and for selling wine. Almost two centuries later Beckford complained bitterly at the ignorance of his guide, 'this sweet spark' who took him round and 'flourished away upon cloacas and vomitoriums with eternal fluency'.

The interior, built in the early first century AD, is still in an excellent state of preservation and is now used for an internationally famous summer opera season. The seats are, however, extremely uncomfortable, as I found to my cost during a six-hour performance of *Aida*, so bring a cushion. From December to February there is an enormous display of *presepi* (Christmas cribs) beneath the arches of the amphitheatre.

From the Piazza Bra it is a short walk across the River Adige to the **Giardino Giusti**. Via Anfiteatro leads from the north side of the amphitheatre to the Ponte Nuovo. On the far side of the river head down Via Carducci past rows of houses with pretty ironwork balconies, and turn left into Via Giusti which takes you to the entrance to Palazzo Giusti. Thomas Coryate thought it 'a second paradise' when he came here in 1608 and he was followed by a stream of admirers including the French Président de Brosses, who was lost in the maze for an hour in 1739. Goethe picked some cypress branches and sprigs of blossom from a caper bush and was surprised at the strange looks he received from passers-by as he wandered back through the town clutching them. The garden is still a place of romance; young married couples come here to have their wedding photographs taken on Saturday mornings.

The flat part of the garden behind the palace preserves its sixteenth-century character with formal beds enclosed by box hedges. The central avenue, flanked by enormous cypresses, leads your eye up above the grotto to the monstrous grinning mask. The terrace above the mask gives you the best view of the design of the box parterre. The shrubs and evergreens at the foot of the hillside were probably planted in the nineteenth century to provide an element of informality. John Evelyn, rather surprisingly for a dedicated dendrologist and the author of *Silva*, admired a cypress which he believed to be seven hundred years old, an impossibility. So famous are these gardens that the family that built them is named Giusti del Giardino in their honour.

INFORMATION

Amphitheatre: 9 a.m. to 5 p.m., closed Monday
Giardino Giusti: 8.30 a.m. to 6.30 p.m.

RESTAURANTS

Arche
Via Arche Scaligiere 6, Verona
Telephone: 045 800 7415, closed Sunday and Monday

Rubiani
Piazzetta Scaletta Rubiani 3, Verona
Telephone: 045 800 6990, closed Friday

I Dodici Apostoli
Corticella San Marco 3, Verona
Telephone: 045 596 999, closed Sunday evening and Monday

> *To this low level did art fall during the Carlovingian deca-*
> *dence and the Hungarian invasions*
>
> Hippolyte Taine

CASTELVECCHIO MUSEUM~SAN ZENO

San Zeno, the most famous of Verona's churches, lies in the eastern part of the city. You can reach it either by taking a no. 7 bus from Piazza delle Erbe or by walking from Piazza Bra. If you would prefer to walk, head down Via Roma to the **Castelvecchio Museum**, housed in the medieval castle which was used as a citadel by the Venetians and as a barracks by the French and Austrian forces after the fall of the Venetian Republic. It was transformed into a museum in 1925 and redesigned by the architect Scarpa after the Second World War. The interesting collection of Veronese works of art includes many of the best medieval sculptures removed from the various churches in the city, as well as Renaissance paintings attributed to Pisanello, Giovanni Bellini, Mantegna and Tintoretto.

From the Castelvecchio Museum walk up the river bank and turn left into Via Barbarani which leads to Piazza Carrubbio. Continue through the square to Piazza Pozza, dominated by the honey-coloured façade of **San Zeno**, one of the great Romanesque churches of northern Italy.

The church, dedicated to Verona's patron saint, was begun in 1120 but not completed until the fourteenth century. In the centre of the façade a magnificent rose window by Maestro Brioloto depicts the wheel of fortune. Beneath it the porch contains some wonderful carving. The series of panels on either side of the main door, dating from 1138, depict allegorical and religious scenes with a wealth of naturalistic detail. The most vivid scene is 'The Hunt of Theodoric', where the emperor drives a stag headlong towards the devil. The bronze doors, also dating from the twelfth century and which have long been under-going restoration, are works of great forcefulness and originality, depicting scenes from the New Testament and from the life of San Zeno. Goethe, so typical of the eighteenth century in his detestation of medieval art, thought them works of 'gloomy antiquity'. Ruskin, on the other hand, waxed lyrical over them and rated them more highly than any Renaissance work of art in Verona.

The imposing interior, with its stately arcades leading up to the high altar, was built between 1120 and 1225; the raised apse and the superb keel-haul ceiling of the nave were added in the fourteenth century. Notice the fifth capital on the left where a number of lions and dogs are racing round in a circle biting each other's tails.

The most famous painting in Verona is Mantegna's triptych of the *Madonna and Child enthroned with Saints*, painted between 1456 and 1459. The triptych's ornate frame and the brilliant colours of the figures create an extraordinarily rich effect. Mantegna's passion for the antique is very evident in the amount of classical details in the architecture. The altarpiece was removed by Napoleon to Paris after the French invasion in 1796, and the three predella panels, which have remained in France, are some of the most treasured possessions of the Louvre and the museum at Tours (they have been replaced by copies).

INFORMATION

Castelvecchio Museum: 9 a.m. to 5.30 p.m., closed Monday

Epilogue

There is certainly no place in the world where a man may travel with greater pleasure and advantage than in Italy.
Joseph Addison

What were the conclusions of all those thousands of Grand Tourists who have tasted the delights of Italy? The impact that the country made on them was almost entirely favourable, whether it was the charms of Italian women that Boswell and Byron found so irresistible, the beauty of the singing that entranced Beckford, or the splendour of the landscape. It was all very well studying the history and art from books, but there was nothing to equal the excitement of confronting it in the flesh. Byron summed it up:

> I am so convinced of the advantages of looking at mankind instead of reading about them and the bitter effects of staying at home with all the narrow prejudice of an islander, that I think there should be a law amongst us, to set our young men abroad, for a term.

The most extraordinary aspect of Italian culture is its sheer variety. Each generation admires something quite different from its predecessors. The Elizabethans studied the politics of the various states and visited their Arsenals, seventeenth-century travellers were fascinated by scientific and artistic curiosities, eighteenth-century Grand Tourists rhapsodised over the antiquities and the Victorians spent their time searching out medieval and Renaissance masterpieces.

Reactions to travellers returning home from Italy were similarly diverse. To most Elizabethans, Italy sounded a dangerous place and somewhere to be avoided. As one of them put it: 'An Englishman Italianate is a devil incarnate.' In the eighteenth century Italy was seen as the place for a young man to sow his wild oats. Dr Johnson liked the idea:

> If a young man is wild and must run after women and bad company, it is better this should be done abroad, as, on his return,

he can break off such connections, and begin at home a new man, with a character to form, and acquaintances to make.

What was so astonishing was the subtle transformation that overcame visitors to Italy. Tobias Smollett was amazed at the behaviour of Grand Tourists:

> One engages in play with an infamous gamester, and is stripped perhaps in the very first partie; another is poxed and pillaged by an antiquated cantatrice; a third is laid under contribution by a dealer in pictures. Some of them turn fiddlers, and pretend to compose, but all of them talk familiarly of the arts, and return finished connoisseurs and coxcombs, to their own country.

And the proof of their conversion is the beauty of Georgian buildings all over Britain and America, filled with paintings and works of art purchased on the Grand Tour

Italy today contains all the elements that so excited our ancestors. You can still eat 'fried Frogges' in Cremona which 'did exceedingly delight my palat', as Tom Coryate noted, stay in the hotel in Perugia where Alexandre Dumas got drunk with the two soldiers who had arrested him, and wander through the Tuscan hills which reminded Ruskin of the background of a Fra Angelico. There may be fewer *lazzaroni* sporting naked in the Bay of Naples and fewer prostitutes in Venice than the tens of thousands who attempted to entice Coryate into their boudoirs, but the Italians are still a totally unselfconscious race, and as entertaining as ever.

Perhaps the last word on the myriad delights of Italy should be left to Joseph Addison, the founder of the *Spectator*:

> There is certainly no place in the world where a man may travel with greater pleasure and advantage than in Italy. One finds something more particular in the face of the country, and more astonishing in the works of nature, than can be met with in any other part of Europe. It is the great school of music and painting, and contains in it all the noblest productions of sculpture and architecture, both ancient and modern. It abounds with cabinets and curiosities, and vast collections of all kinds of antiquities. No other country in the world has such a variety of governments that are so different in their constitutions, and so refined in their politics. There is scarce any part of the nation that is not famous in history, nor so much as a mountain or river that has not been the scene of some extraordinary action.

Bibliography

Acton, Harold and Edward Chaney, *Florence, A Travellers'
    Companion*, 1986
Acton, Harold, *Tuscan Villas*, 1984
Addison, Joseph, *Remarks on Several Parts of Italy, 1701–3*, 1705
Andersen, Hans Christian, *The Improvisatore*, 2 vols, 1845
Anderson, Patrick, *Over the Alps*, 1969
Baker, P. R., *The Fortunate Pilgrims, Americans in Italy
    1800–1860*, 1964
Bates, E.C., *Touring in 1600*, 1911
Beckford, Peter, *Italy, Spain and Portugal*, 2 vols, 1834
Berenson, Bernard, *Italian Painters of the Renaissance*, 4 vols,
    1894–1907
Blessington, Lady, *Conversations with Byron*, 1834
——— *The Idler in Italy*, 3 vols, 1839–40
Brosses, Charles de, *Lettres sur l'Italie 1739–40*, trans. Lord
    Ronald Sutherland Gower, 1897
Byron, George Gordon, Lord, *Selected Letters and Journals*,
    ed. L. A. Marchand, 1982
Casanova, Jacques, *Memoires*, trans. A. Machen, 1932
Chatfield, Judith, *A Tour of Italian Gardens*, 1988
Constant, Caroline, *The Palladio Guide*, 1985
Coryate, Thomas, *Crudities*, 1611, reprinted 2 vols 1905
Dentler, Clare Louise, *Famous Foreigners in Florence*, 1964
Dickens, Charles, *Pictures from Italy*, 1846
Doran, J., *Man and Manners at the Court of Florence 1740–86*,
    2 vols, 1876
Eustace, John Chetwode, *A Classical Tour through Italy*, 1802,
    4th edition, 1819
Evelyn, John, *The Diary*, ed. E. S. de Beer, 6 vols, 1955
Fauré, Gabriel, *Gardens of Rome*, 1960
Fenimore Cooper, James, *Gleanings in Europe*, 2 vols, 1837
Fleming, John, *Robert Adam and His Circle in Edinburgh and
    Rome*, 1963

Ford, Brinsley, 'The Grand Tour', *Apollo*, XCIX 1974

Forster, E. M., *Where Angels Fear to Tread*, 1905

—— *A Room With a View*, 1908

Forsyth, Joseph, *On Antiquities in Italy 1802–3* 1813

Fothergill, Brian, *Sir William Hamilton: Envoy Extraordinary*, 1969

Goethe, Johann Wolfgang, *Italian Journey*, trans. W. H. Auden and Elizabeth Mayer, 1962

Gunn, Peter, *Naples, A Palimpsest*, 1961

Hale, J. R., *England and the Italian Renaissance*, 1963

Hare, Augustus, *Augustus Hare in Italy*, ed. Gavin Hendersen, 1977

Hartt, Frederick, *A History of Italian Renaissance Art*, 1970

Haskell, Francis, *Rediscoveries in Art*, 1973

—— *Patrons and Painters: Italian art and society in the Age of the Baroque*, 1963

Haskell, Francis and Nicholas Penny, *Taste and the Antique, the lure of classical sculpture 1500–1900*, 1981

Hamilton, Olive, *A Paradise of Exiles*, 1974

Hawthorne, Nathaniel, *The Marble Faun*, 1884

Hibbard, Howard, *Michelangelo*, 1975

Hibbert, Christopher, *The Grand Tour*, 1987

Howard, Clare, *English Travellers of the Renaissance*, 1914

Kelly, Michael, *Reminiscences*, 2 vols, 1826

Kirby, Paul, *The Grand Tour 1700–1800*, 1952

Lassels, Richard, *The Voyage of Italy*, 1670

Lees-Milne, James, *The Earls of Creation*, 1962

Levey, Michael, 'Botticelli and Nineteenth-Century England', *Journal of the Warburg and Courtauld Institute*, vol. 23, 1960

Levey, Michael, *Tiepolo*, 1986

Lewis, Norman, *Naples '44*, 1978

Links, J. G., *Canaletto*, 1972

Massinghame, Hugh and Pauline, *The Englishman Abroad*, 1962

Masson, Georgina, *Italian Gardens*, 1961

McCarthy, Mary, *The Stones of Florence and Venice Observed*, 1972

Mead, William Edward, *The Grand Tour in the Eighteenth-Century*, 1914

Misson, François Maximilien, *A New Voyage to Italy*, 4 vols, 1739

Montaigne, Michel de, *Journal du Voyage en Italie 1580–81*, trans. L. Lautrey, 1906

Moore, John, *A View of Society and Manners in Italy*, 1792

Morgan, Lady Sydney, *Italy*, 3 vols, 1821

Morris, James, *Venice*, 1960

Morrison, H. B., *The Golden Age of Travel*, 1953

Morton, H. V., *A Traveller in Italy*, 1964
—— *A Traveller in Rome*, 1957
Moryson, Fynes, *An Itinerary Containing His Ten Years Travell*, 1617
Murray's Handbook: Italy, 1st edition ed. Sir Francis Palgrave, 1842
Murray, Peter, *The Architecture of the Italian Renaissance*, 1963
Neville Maugham, H., *The Book of Italian Travel, 1580–1900*, 1903
Nugent, Sir Thomas, *The Grand Tour*, 4 vols, 1749
Origo, Iris, *Images and Shadows*, 1970
Piozzi, Mrs Hester Lynch, *Observations and Reflections made in the Journey through France, Italy and Germany*, 1789
Pope-Hennessy, John, *Italian Gothic Sculpture*, 1955
—— *Italian Renaissance Sculpture*, 1958
—— *Italian High Renaissance and Baroque Sculpture*, 1963
Quenell, Peter, *Byron in Italy*, 1941
Ramsay, Alex and Helen Attlee, *Italian Gardens*, 1989
Rogers, Samuel, *The Italian Journal*, ed. J. R. Hale, 1956
Seed, Diane, *Eating Out in Italy*, 1989
Sharp, Samuel, *Letters from Italy*, 1767
Smith, J. T., *Nollekens and his Times*, 1828
Smollett, Tobias, *Travels through France and Italy*, 1766
Starke, Mariana, *Letters from Italy between the Years 1792 and 1798*, 2 vols, 1800
Stendhal, *Rome, Naples and Florence*, 1854
Stoye, John Walter, *English Travellers Abroad, 1604–67*, 1952
Swinburne, Henry, *The Courts of Europe at the Close of the Last Century*, 1895
Trease, Geoffrey, *The Grand Tour*, 1967
Twain, Mark, *The Innocents Abroad*, 1869
Wittkower, Rudolf, *Art and Architecture in Italy 1600–1750*, 1958
Wortley Montagu, Lady Mary, *The Complete Letters*, ed. Robert Halsband, 1965
Wright, Edward, *Some Observations made in Travelling through France, Italy etc.*, 1764
Wyck, Brooks van, *The Dream of Arcadia, American Writers 1760–1915*, 1915

Index

Abbey of Fossanova, 156
Accademia Olimpica, 276–7
Acton, Sir Harold, 39
Acton, Sir John, 151
Adam, James, 174
Adam, Robert, 36, 88, 93, 96, 100, 103, 118, 137, 153, 280
Addison, Joseph, 48, 124, 174, 208, 291; *Voyage to Italy*, 35, 59
Alban Hills, 135
Albani, Cardinal, 95–6, 111
Albany, Countess of, 37
Alberoni, 5
Alberti, Leon Battista, 12, 40, 201, 208; Sant' Andrea basilica, 13
Albornez, Cardinal, 190, 215
Aldobrandini, Cardinal Pietro, 144
Alexander VII, 104
Alfieri, Count Vittorio, 37
Allan, David, 103
Almerico, Monsignor, 280
Altichiero, 268
Amalfi, 154
Ambrosiana Library, 10
Ammannati, Bartolomeo, 102; Boboli Gardens, 56; *Fountain of Venus*, 50; Ponte Santa Trinita, 55
Ampère, Jean Jacques, 182
Ancona, 180, 182
Andersen, Hans Christian, 21, 143
Angelico, Fra, 60, 82, 196, 209; *Annunciation*, 82; *Life of the Virgin*, 82; *Madonna and Saints*, 184; *Madonna of Mercy*, 82; St Nicholas Chapel, 131; tomb of, 118
Antelami, Benedetto, 217

Antinous, 137
Apleton, Thomas, 59
Appian Way, 142
Aretino, Pietro, 77
Arezzo, 20, 77–80; Buca di San Francesco, 79; Corso Italia, 79; jousting tournament, 78; Lorenzetti, Pietro, 79; Palazzetto della Fraternità dei Laci, 78; Piazza Grande, 77; Pieve di Santa Maria, 78; restaurants, 80; San Francesco, 79
Ariccia, 143
Ariosto, Lodorico, 207
Arnold, Dr, 108
Arqua Petrarcha, 259
Arundel, Thomas Howard, 1st Earl of, 115
Asciano, 85
Ascoli Piceno, 198–9
Asolo, 270–2
Aspertini, Amico, 26
Assisi, 179, 186–9; restaurants, 188–9; San Damiano, 188; San Francesco, 180, 182, 186–7; Temple of Minerva, 188

Baciocchi, Elisa, 24, 27
Badia a Coltibuono, 65
Baglione, Cesare, 220
Bagnaia, 87–8
Bagni di Lucca, 23
Bagno Vignoni, 87
Balsimelli, Romolo, 160; *Hercules and Cacus*, 50
Balzac, Honoré de, 208
Barbaro, Daniele and Marcantonio, 272–3

Barocci, Federico: *Descent from the Cross*, 185
Barolo, 6
Barry, James, 9
Bartolomeo, Fra: *Madonna with Saints Stephen and John the Baptist*, 25
Basilica of Sant' Antonio, 268
Bassano, 273
Bassano family, 273
Bassano, Jacopo: *Nativity*, 249
Baths of Caracalla, 97
Batoni, Pompeo, 95
Baudelaire, Charles, 104
Beccafumi, Domenico: Political Virtues, frescoes of, 71; *St Catherine Receiving the Stigmata*, 76
Beckford, Peter, 3, 29, 52, 94
Beckford, William, 20, 24, 57, 59, 72, 95, 107, 150, 228–9, 244, 249, 251, 258, 261–2, 268, 277, 286, 290
Bellini, Giovanni: Accademia Gallery Madonnas, 243; *Baptism*, 277; *Coronation of the Virgin*, 182; *Madonna and Child*, 247; *Madonna and Child with Saints*, 235; *Sacra Conversazione*, 238; *St Vincent Ferrar*, 236; *Transfiguration*, 169
Belloc, Hilaire, 24
Bellotto, Bernardo, 230
Belvedere Cimbrone, 175
Belvedere Court: *Apollo Belvedere*, 132; *Laocoon and His Sons*, 131–2
Bembo, Benedetto, 220
Bembo, Cardinal Pietro, 137
Berenson, Bernard, 39, 41, 55, 62, 76, 79, 266
Bergamo, 2
Berlioz, Hector, 47, 102, 104
Bernabei, Tommaso, 82
Bernini, Gianlorenzo, 113, 210; Baldacchino, 127; Castel Gandolfo, church in, 142; Cathedra of St Peter, 128; *Fountain of the Four Rivers*, 115; Santa Maria dell' Assunzione, 143; St Peter's, 126–8

Bernini, Pietro, 100; *Apollo and Daphne*, 101; *Daniel and the Lion*, 104; *David*, 101; *Habakkuk*, 104; *Rape of Persephone*, 101
Bevagna, 193
Bevignate, Fra: Fontana Maggiore, 185
Blessington, Lady, 16, 108
Boboli Gardens, 56–7
Boccaccio, Giovanni, 40
Bologna, 207–10; Archinnasio, 212; Collegio di Spagna, 215; Palazzo Bevilacqua, 215; Palazzo di Re Enzo, 211; Piazza Maggiore, 211; Piazza Nettuno, 211; Pinacoteca Nazionale, 214; restaurants, 213, 215–16; San Giacomo Maggiore, 213; San Petronio, 211–12; San Stefano, 212; Torre d' Asinello, 213; Torre Garisenda, 213
Bomarzo, 87–8
Borghese, Camillo, 101
Borghese, Cardinal Scipione, 100
Borgia, Lucrezia, 139
Borgo Sansepolcro, 80
Borromeo, Cardinal Federico, 10
Borromini, Francesco, 99, 115, 122, 137–8; Church of Sant' Ivo alla Sapienza, 117
Boswell, James, 3, 19, 58, 69, 94, 96, 143, 181, 228, 290
Botticelli, Sandro, 10, 23, 59–60, 130; *Madonna and Child with Angels*, 168; *St Augustine*, 54
Bragadin, Marcantonio, 236
Bramante, Donato, 125, 127, 195, 200, 203; Belvedere Court, 131–2; birth place, 201; Tempietto, 273
Branacci, Cardinal Rinaldo, 166
Brandini, Federico, 204
Bregno, Andrea, 73
Brenta Canal, 261; restaurants, 263
Brera Pinacoteca, 10
Brettingham, Matthew, 157
Breughel the elder, Peter, 119; *Blind leading the Blind*, 169
Breval, John, 41
Brioloto, Maestro: San Zeno window, 288

Bromley, William, 2
Bronzino, Agnolo: Eleanor of
  Toledo, portrait of, 141
Browning, Elizabeth, 58
Browning, Pen, 240, 272
Browning, Robert, 58, 272;
  Asolando, 258, 272
Brunelleschi, 41, 43, 45–6; San
  Lorenzo, church of, 43; Santo
  Spirito, church of, 55
Brustolon, Andrea, 240
Buca di San Francesco, 79
Buckland, Reverend, 164
Buontalenti: Boboli Gardens, 56
Burano, 252–3
Burckhardt, Jacob: *Civilisation
  of the Renaissance in Italy*, 37
Burlington, Richard Boyle, 3rd
  Earl of, 275, 277–8, 280
Burne-Jones, Sir Edward, 99
Burnet, Bishop, 8
Burney, Dr Charles, 2
Byres, James, 37, 94, 104
Byron, Lord, 1, 10, 16, 21–2, 29,
  104, 120, 132, 143, 192, 208,
  211–12, 221–2, 224, 230–1,
  243, 251–2, 258–9, 262–3, 290

Caetani, Prince Gelasio, 156
Camera degli Sposi, 12
Canaletto, Il (Antonio Canal), 229
Canova, Antonio, 95, 242, 257;
  birth place, 273; Pauline
  Buonaparte, statue of, 101
Caprarola, 87, 89
Capitoline Hill, 110
Capitoline Museums, 110–11
Capodiferro, Cardinal, 122
Capodimonte Museum, 121
Capodimonte, Palazzo Reale,
  166, 168–70
Capodimonte porcelain, 150–1
Cappella Sansevero, 161
Capri, 154
Caravaggio, 95, 120; *Boy with a
  Basket of Fruit*, 102; *Calling of
  St Matthew*, 116; chiaroscuro,
  use of, 169; Contarelli Chapel
  frescoes, 116; *Conversion of
  St Paul*, 105; *Crucifixion of
  St Peter*, 105; *Entombment*,
  131; *Flagellation*, 150;

Flagellation of Christ, 169;
  Madonna of Loreto, 116;
  Martyrdom of St Matthew, 116;
  Naples, in, 150, 158; *Rest on the
  Flight into Egypt*, 119; *Seven Acts
  of Mercy*, 150, 169
Ca' Rezzonico, 240
Carpaccio, Vittorio, 235; *Legend of
  St Ursula*, 243
Carracci, Annibale, 119, 207;
  Assumption, 105; Palazzo
  Farnese, gallery in, 121
Carracci, Lodovico, 209, 215
Carriera, Rosalba, 229–30
Casanova, Jacques, 55, 138, 152,
  181, 234, 236, 244, 252, 262
Caserta, 174–5
Casimira, Maria, 190
Castel dell' Ovo, 166
Castelfranco, 270
Castel Gandolfo, 142–3
Castel Nuovo, 167
Castello di Lunghezza, 140–1
Castello Sforzesco, 10
Castelvecchio Museum, 288
Castiglione, Baldassare, 137;
  Courtier, The, 201
castrati, 180–1
Cavallini, Pietro: *Last Judgement*,
  124; *Life of the Virgin*, 124
Cavallino, Bernardo, 170
Cellini, Benvenuto, 48; *Perseus*, 51
Cenami, Bartolomeo, 28
Certosa di San Martino, 158–9
Cervantes, Miguel de, 215
Chantrey, Sir Francis, 101
Chateaubriand, Viscount François
  René de, 154, 193
Chetwode Eustace, Revd John, 32,
  96; *Classical Tour through Italy*, 9
Chigi, Agostino, 125
Chioggia, 252
Cicero, 109
Cimabue, 187
Circus Maximus, 108
Civitali, Matteo, 25
Clarke, Thomas, 55
Claude, see Lorraine, Claude
Clement XII, 111, 137
Clérisseau, Charles-Louis, 137
Cochin, Charles-Nicolas, 45
Coducci, Mauro, 233, 236

Coke, Thomas, Earl of Leicester, 14, 267
Colleoni, Bartolomeo, 2, 235
Colonna, Mengozzi, 281
Colosseum, 107
Cooper, James Fenimore, 40, 176
Cora dei Ceri, 182
Corot, Camille, 102, 140
Copley, John Singleton, 217
Cornaro, Caterina, 258, 272
Corradini, Antonio, 240
Correggio (Antonio Allegri), 208–9, 216–17; *Assumption*, 217; *Danae*, 102; *Marriage of St Jerome*, 218; *Vision of St John the Evangelist*, 217
Cortona, 20, 81–3; Museo Diocesano, 82; Piazza della Repubblica, 81–2; restaurants, 82–3; San Niccolò, 82; Santa Margherita, 82; Santa Maria del Calcinaio, 83
Coryate, Thomas, 6, 12, 227–8, 233, 235–6, 268, 270, 280, 286–7, 291
Costa, 260
Costa, Francis and Lorenzo, 213
Coutts, Thomas, 144
Cozens, John Robert, 143
Cremona, 2, 291
Crivelli, Angelo, 8
Crivelli, Carlo, 199
Crosato, Giovanni-Battista, 5, 240
Cumae, 174
Cutting, Lady Sybil, 62

da Angarona, Rinaldo, 273–4
da Caprarola, Cola, 195
da Conegliano, Cima: *Madonna and Child*, 214; *St John Baptist and Four Saints*, 247
da Cremona, Girolamo, 73
da Fabriano, Gentile: *Madonna and Child*, 196
da Faenza, Ferrau: *Last Judgement*, 194
da Firenze, Andrea, 42
da Forli, Melozzo, 200
Dali, Salvador, 88
da Maiano, Giuliano, 66–7
da Montefeltro, Federico, 179, 201–3

D' Annunzio, Gabriele: *Il Fuoco*, 264
Dante, Alighieri: *Purgatorio*, 196; *Seventh Circle of Hell*, 246
da Ponte, Antonio, 237
da Ponte, Lorenzo, 229
da Romano, Ezzelino, 258
da San Friano, Maso, 169
da Sangallo, Antonio, 121
Dashwood, Sir Francis, 97
da Vallonara, Vieri, 273–4
da Verona, Giovanni, 84
da Verona, Liberale, 73; *Adoration of the Kings*, 284
da Maiano, Benedetto, 42
David, Gerard, 17
da Vinci, Leonardo: Ambrosiana Library, collection in, 10; *Last Supper*, 9; *Portrait of a Musician*, 10
de Barbari, Jacob, 169
de Brosses, Président, 8–9, 31, 70, 94, 97, 109, 140, 145, 167, 181, 228, 233–4, 241, 249, 258, 263
Debussy, Claude, 102
de la Lande, Jean, 273
del Carretto, Ilaria, tomb of, 25
del Castagno, Andrea: Niccolo da Tolentino, portrait of, 46
della Francesca, Piero, 10; *St Nicholas of Tolentino*, 10
dell' Arca, Nicola: *Entombement*, 214
Della Scala family, 283, 285
delle Quercia, Jacopo: *Infancy of Christ*, 212
del Castagno, Andrea: *Cenacolo*, 61
del Cossa, Francesco, 209
del Grande, Antonio, 119
dell' Amatrice, Cola, 199
della Francesca, Piero, 10, 77, 201; *Annunciation*, 184; *Flagellation*, 203; *Legend of the True Cross*, 79; *Madonna del Parto*, 80; *Madonna della Misericordia*, 80; *Resurrection*, 80; *St Mary Magdalene*, 79; *St Nicholas of Tolentino*, 10
della Porta, Giacomo, 113, 127, 144
della Quercia, Jacopo: del Carretto, Ilaria, tomb of, 25
della Robbia, Luca, 41; *Cantorie*, 47

del Piombo, Sebastiano, 104;
Clement VII, portrait of, 169,
218; *Flagellation*, 125;
Metamorphoses, 126;
Polyphemus, 126
del Pollaiolo, Piero, 10
del Sarto, Andrea: *Last Supper*,
61; *Madonna and Child with
St John the Baptist*, 101
de' Medici: Anna Maria Luisa,
36; Catherine, 140–1; Cosimo II
Vecchio, 37; Cosimo III, 57;
Ferdinand, 19; Ferdinando,
102; Giuliano, 46; Lorenzo the
Magnificent, 37
de Negroponte, Antonio:
Madonna and Child, 246
Dennis, George: *Cities and
Cemeteries of Etruria*, 22
Dennistoun, James: *Memoirs of the
Dukes of Urbino*, 79, 182, 202
de' Roberti, Ercole, 210
Derry, Earl-Bishop of, 22, 37, 59,
103, 139
de Sanctis, Francesco, 100
d' Este, Cardinal Ippolito, 137, 139
d' Este, Francesco, 210
Diamante, Fra: Spoleto Duomo
frescoes, 191
Diano d' Alba, 7
di Banco, Nanni, 49
di Bartolo, Taddeo: *Last
Judgement*, 66; Trecento
frescoes, 71
di Cambio, Arnolfo, 46, 124, 196
di Cione, Nardo, 41
Dickens, Charles, 2, 14, 17, 29,
69, 140, 208–9, 233, 285
di Credi, Lorenzo: *Madonna and
Child*, 4
di Fredi, Bartolo: *Adoration of
the Magi*, 75–6
di Giorgio, Francesco, 76
di Giovanni, Matteo: *Massacre of
the Innocents*, 76; St Barbara
altarpiece, 74–5
Dilettanti Society, 96
di Paolo, Giovanni, 76
di Paolo, Jacopo: *Heaven and
Hell*, 212
di Pietro, Andrea, 275, *see also*
Palladio, Andrea

di Rienzo, Cola, 110
di Sangro, Prince Raimondo, 161
Domenichino, Il (Domenico
Zampieri), 209, 215; *Communion
of St Jerome*, 131; *Diana*, 101;
Life of St Cecilia, 116
Donatello (Donato di Bardi), 43, 46,
257; Cantorie, 47; Crucifix, 41;
David, 45; *Feast of Herod*, 73;
Gattemelata, statue of, 266, 269;
Judith, 45; *Life of St Anthony*, 268;
Prophets, 48; *St George*, 49; *St
John the Baptist*, 238; St John the
Baptist, statue of, 73; *St Mark*, 49
Dosio, Giovani Antonio, 158–9
Dossi, Dosso, 210; *Melissa*, 102
Dostoevsky, Fedor, 58
Duccio di Buoninsegna: *Madonna
dei Francescani*, 75; *Maestà*, 73
Dudley, Robert, 19
Dughet, Gaspard, 108
Dumas, Alexander, 62, 181, 291
Dundee, Bonnie (John Graham, 1st
Viscount Dundee), 265
Duomo: Castelfranco, 270; Florence,
39, 45–6; Lucca, 25; Milan, 9;
Monza, 2; Naples, 163–5; Orvieto,
196; Parma, 217; Perugia, 185;
Pisa, 30; Prato, 20; Siena, 72–3;
Spoleto, 190–1; Urbino, 204;
Verona, 283–4
Duparty, Président, 45
Dürer, Albrecht: *Four Evangelists*,
238

Eastlake, Lady, 130
Egyptian Museum, Turin, 4–5
El Greco: *Boy Blowing on a Hot
Coal*, 169
Emilia-Romagna, 207–25
Eremitani Church, 267
Evelyn, John, 15, 31, 51, 55, 100,
102, 112, 117, 127, 145, 149,
155–7, 211, 213, 228, 251, 261,
265, 280, 283

Fabris, Pietro, 173
Fagan, Robert, 95, 147
Fanzago, Cosimo, 150, 158–60
Fanzolo: Villa Emo, 272
Farnese, Alexander (Duke of
Parma), 216–17

Farnese, Pier Luigi, 216
Farnese, Cardinal Alessandro, 89, 108
Fede, Count, 138
Ferdinand IV, 174–5
Ferrara, 207–9; Palazzo Schifanoia, 210
Fiesole, 38, 62
Fiorentino, Rosso: *Marriage of the Virgin*, 43
Fischer, Johann Sigismund, 168
Flaxman, John, 22
Florence, 34–62; Baptistery, 45–6; Boboli Gardens, 56–7; Duomo, 39, 46–7; history of, 34–9; Loggia dei Lanzi, 50–1; Museo dell' Opera del Duomo, 47–8; Ognissanti, Church of, 53; Oltrarno, 52–3; Orsanmichele, Oratory of, 49; Palazzo Medici-Riccardi, 44–5; Palazzo Vecchio, 50; Piazza della Signoria, 49; Piazza Santa Maria Novella, 40; Piazza Santa Spirito, 55; Pitti Palace, 56; Ponte Santa Trinita, 55; Ponte Vecchio, 58; restaurants, 48, 51, 54, 56; River Arno, 52; San Lorenzo, 43; San Salvi, 61; Sant' Apollonia, 61; Santa Croce, 37; Santa Felicità, 58; Santa Maria del Carmine, 53; Santa Maria Novella, 40–2: Chiostro Verde, 42, Gondo Chapel, 41, Spanish Chapel, 42, Strozzi Chapel, 41, Tornabuoni Chapel, 41; Santa Trinita, 54; Santo Spirito, church of, 55; shopping, 54; St John's Day festival, 50; Uffizi, 58–60; *Venus de' Medici*, 59; Waxwork Museum, 57
Florentine Primitives, 38
Florenzi, Marchesa, 181
Foligno, 180, 193
Fontanellato, 210, 220
Forrester, James, 180
Forster, E. M., 66
Forsyth, Joseph, 29, 30, 87, 117, 234
Forum, 109
Foscarina, 262
Fox, Charles James, 152
Fragonard, Jean-Honoré, 138, 140

Francanzano, Francesco: *Life of St Gregory*, 165
Frascati, 143–5; restaurants, 145; Villa Aldobrandini, 144–5
Frazer, Sir James, 143
French Academy, 102
Fuga, Ferdinando, 123, 165
Fuseli, Henri, 59, 130

Galiffe, Jacques, 208
Galileo, 30, 35, 102, 265; trial of, 118–19
Galleria Nazionale, 218
Galleria Sabauda, 4–5
Gambara, Cardinal, 88
Garrick, David, 102, 150, 218
Gattapone, 190
Genoa, 2, 15–17; history of, 15–16; Palazzo Bianco, 17; Palazzo Rosso, 17; restaurants, 17
Gentileschi, Artemisia: *Judith and Holofernes*, 169
Genzano, 143
Gesù Nuovo, 160
Ghiberti, Lorenzo, 45–6, 49
Ghirlandaio, Domenico, 25, 55; *Last Supper*, 53–4; *Life of St Francis*, 54; *Lives of St John the Baptist and the Virgin*, 41; Santa Fina frescoes, 66; *St Jerome*, 54
Giambologna, 47–8; Cosimo I, statue of, 50; *Hercules and the Centaur*, 51; *Oceano*, 57; *Rape of the Sabine Women*, 51; *Venus Surprised by Satyrs*, 56
Gibbon, Edward, 3, 8, 24, 59, 94, 109–10, 149, 152, 230
Gibbons, Grinling, 210
Gibson, John, 113
Gigli, Benjamino, 200
Giordano, Luca, 158; *Apotheosis of the Medici*, 45
Giorgione (Giorgio Barbarelli): Castelfranco Duomo altarpiece, 259, 270–1; life of, 271; *Tempesta*, 243
Giotto di Bondone, 23, 180, 186–7, 209; Arena Chapel frescoes, 258; *Crucifixion*, 131; Palazzo della Ragione frescoes, 268; Scrovegni Chapel frescoes, 266–7

Goethe, 109, 122, 125, 130, 140, 143, 145, 149, 152, 175, 180, 229, 238, 261, 267, 277, 280, 284–5, 287–8
Goethe, Julius, 113
Gogol, Nikolai Vasilevich, 104
Goldoni, Carlo, 239–40
Gonzagas, 2, 12
Gonzago, Francesco: portrait of, 169
Gonzago, Vespasiano, 220
Gossaert, Jan, 119
Goudar, Sarah, 152
Gozzoli, Benozzo, 30; *Adoration of the Magi*, 45; *Journey of the Magi*, 45; *Life of St Augustine*, 66–7; *Life of St Francis*, 193; St Nicholas Chapel, 131; *St Sebastian*, 66;
Graham, Mrs, 267
Gray, Thomas, 36, 140
Grien, Hans Baldung, 210
Grinzane Cavour, 6–7
Grotto del Cane, 173–4
Gubbio, 182
Guercino, Il, (Giovanni Francesco Barbieri), 207; *St Sebastian Cured by Irene*, 215
Guggenheim Museum, 242

Hackert, Johann Gottlieb, 140, 143, 174
Hadfield, Charles, 36
Hadrian, 136–7
Hadrian's Villa, 136–8; Canopus, 138; Maritime Temple, 138; Piazza d' Oro, 138, *see also* Villa, Adriana
Hamilton, Emma, 77, 150, 152
Hamilton, Gavin, 135–7, 147, 157, 180
Hamilton, Sir William, 77, 137, 150–3, 173
Hancock, Sheila Butler, 31
Hare, Augustus, 156
Harvey, William, 265
Hawthorne, Nathaniel, 99, 111
Hazlitt, William, 3, 208
Heine, Heinrich, 258
Herculaneum, 149–52, 162, 171–3
Hitler, Adolf, 264
Hobbes, Thomas, 35

Hogarth, William, 257
Holbein the Younger, Hans: Erasmus, portrait of, 169, 218
Howard, Lelia and Hubert, 156
Howells, William Dean, 40, 45
Hunt, Sir William Holman, 62
Huxley, Aldous, 80

Ibsen, Hendrik, 143, 154
Ingres, Jean-Auguste-Domenique, 53, 102
Innocent X, 115, 119
Iron Crown of Lombardy, 2
Isola Bella, 7–8

James, Henry, 9, 23, 39–41, 93, 102, 187, 238
Jameson, Mrs, 60
Jenkins, Thomas, 94, 137, 143
Johnson, Dr, 290
Jones, Inigo, 115, 125, 257, 280
Jones, Thomas, 135, 180
Joyce, James, 182
Julius II, 104

Kaiserman, 145
Kauffmann, Angelica, 125, 143
Keats, John, 97, 100, 113
Keats–Shelley Memorial Museum, 103
Kelly, Michael, 152, 164, 167
Kent, William, 14, 260, 267
Killigrew, Thomas, 265

Lago di Bolsena, 87
Lake Avernus, 174
Lake Como, 7–8
Lake Maggiore, 8
Lake Nemi, 143
La Morra, 6
Landini, Taddeo, 113
Landor, Walter Savage, 38, 44
La Scala, 10
Lasinio, 22
La Spezia, 21; Gulf of, 16, 21
Lassels, Richard, 16, 24, 59, 130, 216, 266
Laurana, Luciano, 202–3
Laureti, Tomaso, 211
Lawrence, Sir Thomas, 243
Le Brun, Charles, 102
Ledoux, Claude-Nicolas, 109

Leghorn, 19
Le Langhe, 6
Leopardi, Giacomo, 200
Lewis, Norman, 164
Ligorio, Piero, 137, 139–40
Liguria, 1–17
Lindsay, Lord, 209; *Sketches of the History of Christian Art*, 79, 258
Liotard, Jean-Etienne, 5
Lippi, Filippino: *Annunciation with St Thomas Aquinas presenting Cardinal Carafa to the Virgin*, 118; *Annunciation with Saints*, 168; Branacci Chapel frescoes, 53; Carafa Chapel frescoes, 118; *Lives of St Philip and St John the Evangelist*, 41–2; *St Thomas Aquinas Confounding the Heretics*, 118; *Tobias and the three Archangels*, 4
Lippi, Filippo, 60, 102; *Annunciation*, 120; Spoleto Duomo frescoes, 191
Liszt, Franz, 104, 140
Lithgow, William, 265
Livorno, 19
Livy, 265
Loggia del Capianiato, 278
Lombardo, Pietro, 236, 246
Lombardy, 1–17
Longfellow, Henry, 40, 57–8
Longhena, Baldassare, 240, 249
Longhi, Roberto, 79
Lorenzetti, Ambrogio: Good and Bad Government, 71–2; *Madonna and Saints*, 76
Lorenzetti, Pietro, 187
Loreto, 181–2, 200–1
Lorraine, Claude, 95, 103, 108, 119, 135, 169, *see also* Claude
Lotto, Lorenzo, 101, 168, 201
Loyola, Ignatius, 208, 215
Lucca, 20, 22, 24–7; del Carretto, Ilaria, tomb of, 25; Duomo, 25; Palazzo del Mercato, 26; Palazzo Guinigi, 25; Palazzo Mansi, 26; Palazzo Pfanner, 26; restaurants, 26–7; Romanesque churches, 24–5; San Frediano, 26; San Michele, 27; Villa Reale, 27
Ludwig I of Bavaria, 181

Macaroni, Curzio, 139
Maderno, Carlo, 127, 144, 200; St Cecilia, statue of, 124
Madonna dell' Orto, 247
Madonna della Steccata, 219
Maecenas, 77
Maitani, Lorenzo, 196
Malvito, Tommaso, 165
Manetti, Rutilio di Lorenzo, 43
Mann, Sir Horace, 36, 53, 55, 57, 60
Manning, Cardinal, 99
Mantegna, Andrea, 10, 12, 257; Camera degli Sposi, frescoes, 12; *Dead Christ*, 10; Francesco Gonzago, portrait of, 169; *Madonna and Child enthroned with Saints*, 289; Martydom of St Christopher, 267; San Zeno altarpiece, 258; *St Sebastian*, 244
Mantua, 2, 12–15, 220; cafés, 13; Camera degli Sposi, 12; Palazzo del Té, 12–14; Palazzo Ducale, 12; restaurants, 13, 15; Romano's House, 13; Rotonda di San Lorenzo, 13; Sant' Andrea basilica, 13
Marche, 179–204
Marlia: Villa Reale, 27–8
Marostica, 270, 273–4
Martini, Simone: *Blessed Agostino Novello* altarpiece, 75; *Life of St Martin*, 187; *Maestà*, 71; *St Louis of Toulouse crowning Robert of Anjou King of Naples*, 168
Masaccio, 107; Branacci Chapel frescoes, 53; *Crucifixion*, 168; *Trinity with the Virgin and St John*, 41
Maser, 259; Villa Barbaro, 272
Masolino da Panicale, 107; *Madonna and Child*, 194
Massari, Giorgio, 240
Memling, Hans: *Deposition*, 120; Passion scenes, 4
Mendelssohn, Felix, 57
Menotti, Giancarlo, 190
Michelangelo, 41, 60, 73; Capitoline Square, redesign of, 110; *Crucifixion of St Peter*, 169; *David*, 50; *Deposition*, 47; *Doni Tondo*, 59–60; *Expulsion of*

Adam and Eve, 53; *Last Judgement*, 130; Palazzo Farnese, 121; *Paris and Helen*, 56; *Prisoners*, 56; *Risen Christ*, 118; St Peter's basilica, 127; San Lorenzo, 43–4; Sistine Chapel, 130

Michelozzo di Bartolomeo, 46

Milan, 1, 9–11; Ambrosiana Library, 10; Brera Pinacoteca, 10; Castello Sforzesco, 10; cuisine, 11; museums, 10; music, 10; Santa Maria delle Grazie, 9

Miller, Mrs, 1

Milton, John, 35

Mira, 262

Mirafiori, 5

Mithras, cult of, 107

Modena, 207

Montagnana, 259–60

Montagu, Lady Mary Wortley, 229

Montaigne, Michel de, 23, 28, 35, 40, 70, 80, 88, 104, 140, 147, 286

Montalcino, 85

Mont Cenis: Alpine Pass over, 1

Monte Oliveto, 84

Montefalco, 193–4

Montefiascone, 87

Montepulciano, 86

Monterchi, 80

Monterrigioni, 22

Monteverdi, 2, 12

Montrose, James Graham, 1st Marquis of, 265

Monza: Duomo, 2

Moore, Dr, 152, 229

Moore, Tom, 101

Moran, Gordon, 71

More, Jacob, 100

Morel, 27

Moreschi, Alessandro, 129

Morgan, Lady, 9, 16, 22, 77, 81, 97, 115, 117, 129, 153, 190, 218, 268

Morison, Colin, 94

Morris, William, 42

Moryson, Fynes, 14, 50, 69–70, 120, 140, 181, 236, 268

Mount Vesuvius, 152

Mozart, 10, 150

Munthe, Axel, 141

Murano, 252

Murray's *Handbook*, 97, 99, 131, 267

Museo Archeologico Nazionale, 121, 162–3

Museo Arcivescovile, 223

Museo dell' Opera del Duomo: Florence, 47–8; Siena, 73

Museo Diocesano, 82

Museo Poldi-Pezzoli, 10

Mussolini, 264

Muttoni, Francesco, 281

Naples, 149–67; antiques, 153; Bay of, 173–6; Bourbon rule, 150–1; Capodimonte Museum, 121; Cappella Sansevero, 161; Castel dell' Ovo, 166; Castel Nuovo, 167; Certosa di San Martino, 158–9; cocktail-party atmosphere, 154; Duomo, 163–5; Gerolomini, Church of, 165; Gesù Nuovo, 160; Guglia dell' Immacolata, 160; history, 149–54; Museo Archeologico Nazionale, 121, 162–3; National Gallery, 168–70; Palazzo Gravina, 159; Palazzo Reale, 166, 168–70; Piazza del Plebiscito, 166; pizzas, 161; restaurants, 161, 166–7, 170; San Domenico Maggiore, 160–1; San Gregorio Armeno, 165; San Lorenzo Maggiore, 165; Sant' Angelo a Nilo, 166; Santa Chiara, 160; Teatro San Carlo, 149–50, 167; Via Toledo, 159

Napoleon, 97, 102, 137, 246, 258, 264, 277

National Gallery of Naples, 168–70

National Gallery of Umbria, 184

Nazarines, 181

Neapolitan Baroque, 150

Nelson, Lord, 77, 150

Nemi, 143

Newman, Cardinal, 154

Niccolò, Maestro, 284

Ninfa, 156–7

Nollekens, Joseph, 94, 180

Norcia, 180, 198

Nottolini, Lorenzo, 26

Nugent, Thomas, 16, 19

Ognissanti, Church of, 53

Oratorio di San Bernadino, 76

Oratorio di San Guiseppe, 204
Orford, Lady, 62
Oriago, 262
Orsamichele, Oratory of, 49
Orsini, Vicino, 88
Orvieto, 182, 196–7; Duomo, 196;
  restaurants, 197
Ostia, 136
Ostia Antica, 146–7
Ottley, William Young, 22
Ouida (Mlle Louise de la Ramée), 38
Owen, John, 218

Pacchierotti, 24
Padua, 208, 257–8, 265–9; Basilica
  of Sant' Antonio, 268; Eremitani
  Church, 267; Palazzo della
  Ragione, 267–8; Prato della
  Valle, 269; Quattrocento art,
  265; restaurants, 269; Scrovegni
  Chapel (Arena Chapel), 266,
  267; university, 265, 267
Paestum, 149, 153, 175–6
Paganini, Niccolò, 28, 219
Palatine Hill, 108
Palazzina Mauriziana di Caccia,
  5–7
Palazzo Barbaro, 242
Palazzo Benzon, 243
Palazzo Bianco, 17
Palazzo Bevilacqua, 215
Palazzo Chiericati, 277
Palazzo Colonna, 94
Palazzo Corner-Martinengo, 243
Palazzo Dario, 242
Palazzo dei Cavalieri, 31
Palazzo dei Conservatori, 110–11
Palazzo dei Priori, 184
Palazzo dell' Accademia delle
  Scienze, 4
Palazzo della Ragione, 267–8
Palazzo del Mercato, 26
Palazzo del Museo Capitolino,
  110–12
Palazzo del Té, 12–14
Palazzo di Re Enzo, 211
Palazzo Doria-Pamphilj, 119
Palazzo Ducale: Mantua, 12;
  Sabbioneta, 220; Urbino, 202
Palazzo Farnese, 121
Palazzo Fortebraccio, 185
Palazzo Grassi, 243

Palazzo Gravina, 159
Palazzo Guiccioli, 222
Palazzo Guinigi, 25
Palazzo Guistinian, 243
Palazzo Gussoni, 245
Palazzo Labia, 237
Palazzo Mangilli-Valmarana, 244
Palazzo Mansi, 26
Palazzo Medici-Riccardi, 44–5
Palazzo Mocenigo, 243
Palazzo Nonfinito, 242
Palazzo Pfanner, 26
Palazzo Pigafetta, 279
Palazzo Porto Breganze, 279
Palazzo Pubblico, 70–1
Palazzo Reale, 166, 168–70
Palazzo Rosso, 17
Palazzo Rufolo, 175
Palazzo Schifanoia, 210
Palazzo Spada, 122
Palazzo Thiene, 277–8
Palazzo Trissino-Baston, 278
Palazzo Vecchio: Florence, 50;
  Siena, 70
Palazzo Vendramin-Calergi, 245
Palazzo Zuccari, 103
Palio, 70, 85
Palladio, Andrea, 220, 228, 246,
  248–9, 257, 275; Basilica, Piazza
  dei Signori, 278; Loggia del
  Capitaniato, 278; Palazzo Porto
  Breganze, 279; Quattro Libri,
  275, 280; Teatro Olimpico, 276–7;
  Villa Barbaro, 272–3; Villa Emo,
  272; Villa Malcontenta, 262; Villa
  Rotonda, 280–1
Panicale, 182
Pannini, Giovanni Paolo, 95;
  Charles III's Visit to Rome, 169
Pantheon, 117–18
Parco dei Mostri, 87–8
Parigi, Alfonso and Giulio: Boboli
  Gardens, 56–7
Parkinson, Dr, 101
Parma, 207–10, 216–19; Camera
  del Correggio, 218; Duomo, 217;
  Madonna della Steccata, 219;
  restaurants, 218–19; San
  Giovanni Evangelista, 217;
  Teatro Regio, 219
Parmigianino, Il (Francesa Mazzola),
  169, 208–9; St Roch, 212, 216–17

Passagno, 273
Patch, Thomas, 53, 103
Pater, Walter, 60
Pavia: Charterhouse, 2
Pellegrini, Domenico, 229
Persico, Paolo, 174
Perugia, 181, 183–6, 291; Arch of
    Augustus, 185; Collegio del
    Cambio, 183–4; Convento di
    Sant' Agnese, 185; Corso
    Vannucci, 183; Duomo, 185;
    National Gallery of Umbria,
    184; Palazzo dei Priori, 184;
    Palazzo Fortebraccio, 185;
    restaurants, 185–6; University
    of Foreigners, 185
Perugino, Pietro, 130, 179,
    183–4; *Adoration of the
    Shepherds*, 193; *Crowned
    Madonna*, 185; *Crucifixion*, 76;
    Martyrdom of St Sebastian, 182
Peruzzi, Baldassare, 125–6
Pesaro, 182
Petrarch, 77, 259
Phlegraean Fields, 173
Pianta, Francesca, 239
Piazza della Signoria, 49
Piedmont, 1–17; culinary
    tradition, 4
Pienza, 85; restaurants, 85–6
Pieve di Santa Maria, 78
Pinacoteca, 131
Pinturicchio, 73, 180, 191;
    Adoration of the Child, 104; Santa
    Maria Maggiore frescoes, 192
Piozzi, Mrs, 24
Piranesi, Giam Battista, 95, 109,
    118, 137
Pisa, 20, 29–32; Arno River, 31;
    Baptistry, 30; Botanic Garden,
    31; Campo dei Miracoli, 29;
    Campo Santo, 22, 29–30;
    Duomo, 30; festival, 31;
    Leaning Tower, 22, 29–30;
    Palazzo dei Cavalieri, 31;
    restaurants, 32; Santa Maria
    della Spina, 31–2; Santo
    Stefano dei Cavalieri, 31
Pisanello (Antonio Pisano):
    *St George and the Princess of
    Trebizond*, 284
Pisani, Alvise, 263

Pisano, Andrea: *Life of St John the
    Baptist*, 45; Museo dell' Opera del
    Duomo, panels in, 48
Pisano, Giovanni, 30, 185; Siena
    Duomo, design for, 72
Pisano, Nicola, 30, 185; Siena
    Duomo, pulpit in, 72
Pistoia, 20, 23
Pitti Palace, 56
Pius II, 85
Poldi-Pezzoli, Gian Giacomo, 10;
    museum, 10
Pompeii, 149–52, 162–3, 171–3;
    Forum, 172; restaurants, 173;
    Temple of Apollo, 172; Temple of
    Jupiter, 172; Vettii, house of, 172;
    Villa of the Mysteries, 172–3
Pomposa, Abbey of, 210
Ponte a Moriano, 28
Ponte Vecchio, 58
Pontormo, Jacopa Carrucci:
    Lamentation, 58; *Martyrdom of
    San Quintino*, 80
Pope-Henessy, Sir John, 39
Portormo, 26
Posilippo, 173; school of, 154
Poussin, Nicolas, 102
Powers, Hiram, 38
Prato: Duomo, 20
Prato della Valle, 269
Pratolino, 88
Preti, Frigimelica, 263
Preti, Mattia, 150, 170
Proust, Marcel, 234
Puccini, Giacomo, 24
Pugin, Augustus: *Contrasts*, 258

Queen Christina of Sweden, 89, 104,
    190, 193
Querini-Benzon, Countess, 243
Queriolo, Francesco: *Disillusion*, 161

Radicofani, 30, 87
Rainaldi, Girolamo, 100, 104
Ramsay, Allan, 132
Raphael, 73, 137, 208; Andrea
    Navagero and Agostino Beazzano:
    portrait of, 119; birth place, 201;
    Chigi Chapel, 104; *Entombment*,
    101; *Isaiah*, 116; *La Muta*, 203;
    Liberation of St Peter, 131;
    Madonna di Foligno, 131, 193;

St Cecilia, 214; *School of Athens*,
10; Stanze frescoes, 131; tomb
of, 118; *Transfiguration*, 125,
131; *Triumph of Galatea*, 126;
Virgin and the Unicorn, 101
Ravello, 154, 175
Ravenna, 207–8, 221–5;
Mausoleum of Galla Placidia,
222; Museo Arcivescovile, 223;
Neonian Baptistery, 223; Palazzo
Guiccioli, 222; restaurants,
224–5; San Vitale, 222; Sant'
Apollinare in Classe, 224; Sant'
Apollinare Nuovo, 223
Recanati, 200
Redentore, Il, 248
Reni, Guido, 119, 164, 207–9, 266;
Atalanta and Hippomenes, 169;
Beatrice Cenci, portrait of, 208
Revett, Nicholas, 157
Reynolds, Sir Joshua, 42, 132
Ribera, José, 150, 158, 164, 170
Ricci, Cardinal, 102
Ricci, Maddalena, 143
Ricci, Sebastiano, 229
Richardson, Jonathan, 35, 59, 111
Rimini: Tempio Malatestiano, 208
Ripon, Lord, 189
Robert, Hubert, 138, 140
Rochester, John Wilmot, 2nd Earl
of, 265
Rogers, Samuel, 104, 107, 181, 230
Romano, Giulio, 12; house, 13;
Palazzo del Té, 12–14
Rome, 93–132; antique shops, 116;
Arch of Constantine, 108; Arch
of Septimius Severus, 109; Arch
of Titus, 109; Basilica of
Maxentius, 109; Baths of
Caracalla, 97; cafés, 115–16;
Campo de' Fiori, 120; Capitoline
Hill, 110; Capitoline Museums,
110–11; Circus Maximus, 108;
Colosseum, 107; Domus
Augustana, 108; *Farnese
Hercules*, 121–2; Forum, 109;
French Academy, 102; *gelateria*,
118; history, 93–9; House of
Livia, 108; Keats–Shelley
Memorial Museum, 103; Old
University, 117; Orti Farnesiani,
108; Palatine Hill, 108; Palazzo

Colonna, 94; Palazzo dei
Conservatori, 110–11; Palazzo
del Museo Capitolino, 110–12;
Palazzo Doria-Pamphilj, 119;
Palazzo Farnese, 121; Palazzo
Spada, 122; Palazzo Zuccari,
103; Pantheon, 117–18; Piazza
Campitelli, 112; Piazza del
Popolo, 104; Piazza di Spagna,
95, 99–100; Piazza Farnese, 121;
Piazza Mattei, 112; Piazza
Minerva, 118; Piazza Navona,
99, 115; Piazza San Pietro, 126;
pizza bars, 109–10; Protestant
Cemetery, 113; restaurants,
103–5, 112–14, 118–20, 122, 126,
128, 132; Sacred Way, 109; San
Clemente, 106–7; San Luigi dei
Francesi, 116; San Pietro in
Montorio, 124; Sant' Agnese, 115;
Sant' Ivo alla Sapienza, 117;
Sant' Agostino, 116; Santa
Catherina dei Funari, 112; Santa
Cecilia, 123–4; Santa Maria del
Popolo, 104–5; Santa Maria in
Trastevere, 124; Santa Maria
sopra Minerva, 118; Santa Trinità
dei Monte, 100; Senate House,
109; shopping areas, 103; Spanish
Steps, 97, 100, 103; St Peter's,
99, 126–8; Tempietto, 125, 273;
Trastavere, 99, 123–6; Vatican,
see Vatican; Villa Borghese, 94,
100–2; Villa Medici, 102; Ville
Farnesina, 125–6
Ronciglione, 90
Rosa, Salvator, 210
Roscoe, William, 37
Rossini, Gioacchino, 167
Rotonda di San Lorenzo, 13
Rubens, Sir Peter Paul, 12, 17
Ruskin, John, 23, 25, 39, 41, 47,
60, 99, 130, 186, 209, 234–5,
243, 249, 285, 288; *Modern
Painters*, 258; *Mornings in
Florence*, 37; *Stones of Venice*,
231, 239
Russell, James, 96

Sabbioneta, 210, 220
Sacred Way, 109
St Gilles, Mme, 3

St Januarius, liquefication of blood of, 163–4
St Peter's, Rome, 96, 99; basilica, 127; forecourt, 126
Salieri, Antonio: *Europa Riconosciuta*, 10
Salimbeni, Giacomo, 204
Salimbeni, Lorenzo, 204
Saluzzo, Filippo, 161
Salviati, Francesco de, 169
Sammartino, Guiseppe: *Cristo Velato*, 161
San Clemente, 106–7
San Damiano, 188
Sandby, Paul, 143
San Domenico, 74
San Domenico Maggiore, 160–1
San Francesco: Arezzo, 79; Assisi, 180, 182, 186–7
San Francesco della Vigna, 246
San Frediano, 26
San Galgano, 84
San Giacomo Maggiore, 213
San Gimignano, 22, 65–7; Collegiata, 66; restaurants, 67; Sant' Agostino, 66
San Giorgio Maggiore, 248
San Giovanni Evangelista, 217
San Gregorio Armeno, 165
San Lorenzo, 43
San Leuccio, 174
San Lorenzo Maggiore, 165
San Luigi dei Francesi, 116
San Marino, 180
San Michele, 27
Sanmicheli, Michele, 283–4
San Niccolò, 82
San Petronio, 211–12
San Pietro, 191
San Quirico d' Orcia, 87
San Salvi, 61
San Sebastiano, 248
San Stefano dei Cavalieri, 31
Sansovino, Andrea, 200; della Rovere and Sforza tombs, 104; *Madonna and Child with St Anne*, 116
Sansovino, Jacopo, 228, 246; Biblioteca Marciana, 233; Loggetta, 233; *Madonna del Parto*, 116
Sant' Anastasia, 284

Sant' Apollinaire in Classe, 224
Sant' Apollinaire Nuovo, 223
Sant' Agnese, 115
Sant' Agostino: Rome, 116; San Gimignano, 66; Siena, 76
Sant' Andrea basilica, 13
Sant' Angelo a Nilo, 166
Sant' Antimo, 85
Sant' Apollonia, 61
Sant' Eufemia, 191
Sant' Ivo alla Sapienza, 117
Santa Catherina dei Funari, 112
Santa Cecilia, 123–4
Santa Chiara, 160
Santa Corona, 277
Santa Croce, 37
Santa Felicità, 58
Santa Margherita, 82
Santa Maria dei Miracoli, 236
Santa Maria del Calcinaio, 83
Santa Maria del Carmine, 53
Santa Maria del Popolo, 104–5
Santa Maria dell' Assunzione, 143
Santa Maria della Consolazione, 195
Santa Maria delle Grazie, 9
Santa Maria della Salute, 242
Santa Maria della Spina, 31–2
Santa Maria Gloriosa dei Frari, 238
Santa Maria in Trastevere, 124
Santa Maria sopra Minerva, 118
Santa Maria Novella, 40–2; Chiostro Verde, 42; Gondo Chapel, 41; Spanish Chapel, 42; Strozzi Chapel, 41; Tornabuoni Chapel, 41
Santa Trinita, 54
Santa Trinità dei Monte, 100
Santi Giovanni e Paolo, 236
Santo Spirito, 55
Santo Stefano, 212, 277
San Vitale, 222
San Zaccaria, 234
San Zeno, 288–9
Saraceni, Carlo, 169
Sarpi, Paolo, 245
Sassetta, Il (Stefano di Giovanni di Consolo): *Castle by a Lake*, 76; *Town by the Sea*, 76
Savoldo, Girolamo: *Tobias and the Angel*, 101
Savonarola, 46, 50
Scamozzi, Vincenzo, 220, 276–7;

Palazzo Trissino-Baston, 278; Villa Rocca Pisani, 282
Scarpa, Paolo, 288
Schippers, Thomas, 190
Schongauer, Martin: *Madonna of the Rose Garden*, 214
Scott, Geoffrey, 62
Scott, Sir Walter, 88
Scrovegni Chapel, 266
Scuola San Giorgio degli Schiavoni, 235
Sermoneta, Duchess of, 156
Severn, Joseph, 113
Sharp, Samuel, 57
Sharp, Selwyn, 230
Shaw, George Bernard, 209
Shelley, 9, 16, 21–2, 29, 40, 59, 97, 107, 113, 189, 222, 230, 259–60, 263
Siculo, Jacopo, 191
Siena, 20, 69–77; Baptistery, 73; Campo, 70; Duomo, 72–3; La Mangia tower, 70; Museo dell' Opera del Duomo, 73; Oratorio di San Bernadino, 76; paintings, 75–6; Palazzo Pubblico, 70–1; Palazzo Vecchio, 70; Palio, 70; Piccolomini Library, 73; Pinacoteca, 75; restaurants, 74–7; San Domenico, 74; Sant' Agostino, 76; St Catherine, house of, 74
Signorelli, 82, 84, 130, 200; Cappella della Madonna frescoes, 196; *Crucifixion*, 80; *Entombment*, 82; *Lamentation over the Dead Christ*, 82; *Last Judgement*, 196–7; *Madonna and Saints*, 185; *Preaching of the Antichrist*, 197; *Resurrection of the Dead*, 197
Signorelli, (school): *Madonna and Child between Saints*, 82
Sistine Chapel, 99, 129–30
Sitwell, Osbert, 56
Sitwell, Sacheverell, 88
Sixtus IV, 104
Smith, Consul, 244
Smith, Joseph, 262
Smollett, Tobias, 15, 19, 21, 96, 101, 115, 125, 153, 180, 291
Soane, Sir John, 96, 109

Sodoma, Il (Giovanni Antonio Bazzi), 84–5; Chapel of St Catherine, frescoes in, 74; *Deposition*, 76; *Epiphany*, 76; *Marriage of Alexander and Roxana*, 126; *Scorging of Christ*, 76
Solfatara di Pozzuoli, 174
Solimena, Francesco: *Expulsion of Heliodorus*, 160
Sorrento, 154
Spanish Steps, 97, 100, 103
Spello, 180, 192–3
Spence, Joseph, 36, 229
Spence, William Blundell, 62
Spencer, Lady, 102
Spoleto, 180–1, 189–92; Duomo, 190–1; Ponte delle Torri, 190; restaurants, 191–2; Rocca, 190; San Pietro, 191; Sant' Eufemia, 191
Stanzione, Massimo, 158
Stark, Freya: *A Traveller's Prelude*, 272
Starke, Mariana, 25, 59, 267
Stendhal, (Henri Beyle) 9–10, 41, 74, 167, 172
Stra: Villa Pisano, 263–4
Strange, John, 55
Stresa, 8
Stuart, James, 157
Stupinigi, 5–7
Susa, 2
Susini, Clemente, 57
Symonds, John Addington, 113, 203

Taglioni, Marie, 244
Taine, Hippolyte, 182
Talbot, Thomas Mansel, 135
Talenti, Fra Jacopo, 40
Tasso, Torquato, 207
Tavistock, Marquis of, 29
Teatro Olimpico, 276–7
Tempietto di Clitunno, 191
Tempio Malatestiano, 208
Thomas, William, 201
Tiepolo, Giam Battista, 240; *Apotheosis of the Pisani Family*, 264; Villa Vamarana, 281–2
Tiepolo, Gian Domenico: Villa Vamarana, 281–2

Tintoretto, Jacopo: *Crucifixion*, 239; *Gathering of Manna*, 249; *Jacob's Dream*, 239; *Last Judgement*, 247; *Last Supper*, 249; *Life of Christ*, 239; *Presentation of the Virgin*, 247; *Worship of the Golden Calf*, 247
Tischbein, Wilhelm, 143
Titian, 207; *Assumption*, (Duomo, Verona), 284; *Assumption*, (Frari), 238; Charles V, portrait of, 169; *Danae*, 169; *Martydom of St Lawrence*, 247; *Presentation of the Virgin*, 243; *Sacred and Profane Love*, 102; *St Peter Martyr*, 236; *Salome*, 119; *Venus of Urbino*, 59
Tivoli, 88, 136–41; Falls, 138–9; restaurants, 138; Villa Adriana, 136–8; Villa d' Este, 139–40
Todi, 194
Torcello, 251, 253
Torgiano, 195
Torrechiara, 210, 220
Torri, 84
Torrigiano, 53
Toscanini, Arturo, 219
Townley, Charles, 94, 136–7
Treaty of Tolentino, 97
Trelawny, Edward, 113
Trevi: Tempietto di Clitunno, 191
Triboli: Boboli Gardens, 56
Trissino, Gian Giorgio, 275
Tura, Cosimo, 210
Turin, 1–2; cafés, 3–4; city centre, 3; Egyptian Museum, 4–5; Galleria Sabauda, 4–5; Mirafiori, 5; Palazzo dell' Accademia delle Scienze, 4; restaurants, 4–5; Stupinigi, 5–7
Turner, Joseph Mallard William, 1, 230–1, 243
Tuscan Primitives, 22
Tuscany, 19–90
Twain, Mark, 7

Uccello, Paolo: *Battle of San Romano*, 45; Old Testament frescoes, 42; Sir John Hawkwood, portrait of, 46
Uffizi, 58–60

Umbria, 179–204
Urban VIII, 117
Urbino, 179, 182, 201–4; Duomo, 204; Oratorio di San Guiseppe, 204; Palazzo Ducale, 202; restaurants, 204

Vaccaro, Domenico Antonio, 160
Valeriano, 160
Valéry, Paul Ambroise, 181
Valsanzibio: Villa Barbarigo, 260
van Cleve, Joos: *Adoration of the Magi*, 169
van der Goes, Hugo, 17; Portinari altarpiece, 55
van der Weyden; *Visitation*, 4
Van Dyck, Sir Anthony, 17; *Children of Charles I, The*, 4
Van Eyck: *St Francis*, 4
Van Loo, Carle, 5
Vanvitelli, Gaspare, 174
Vasanzio, Giovanni, 100
Vasari, Giorgio, 78
Vatican, 129–32; Belvedere court, 131–2; Museums, 130; Pinacoteca, 131; Sistine Chapel, 129–30; Stanze, 130–1
Vecchio, Palma, 277
Velàzquez, Diego Rodriguez de Silva, 102, 210; Innocent X, portrait of, 119
Veneto, 257–89
Venice, 227–55; Accademia Gallery, 242–3; Arsenal, 246; Bridge of Sighs, 234; Burano, 252–3; Ca' d' Oro, 244; Ca' da Mosto, 244; Ca' Foscari, 243; Ca' Giustinian, 242; Ca' Pesaro, 244; Ca' Rezzonico, 240; cafés, 235; Casetta Rossa, 242; Chioggia, 252; Cini Foundation, 249; Danieli Hotel, 234; Doge's Palace, 234; Frari, 238; Gesuiti Church, 247; Ghetto, 247–8; Grand Canal, 242; Guggenheim Museum, 242; history, 227–31; Il Ridotto, 242; Lagoon, 251; Lido, 252; Madonna dell' Orto, 247; Murano, 252; music, 229–30; Palazzo Barbaro, 242; Palazzo Benzon, 243; Palazzo Corner-Martinengo, 243; Palazzo Dario, 242; Palazzo Grassi, 243;

Palazzo Guistinian, 243; Palazzo Gussoni, 245; Palazzo Labia, 237; Palazzo Mangilli-Valmarana, 244; Palazzo Mocenigo, 243; Palazzo Nonfinito, 242; Palazzo Vendramin-Calergi, 245; Piazza San Marco, 232; Piazzetta, 233; Redentore, 248; restaurants, 237, 241, 247–8, 250; Rialto Bridge, 244; Rialto, 237; San Francesco della Vigna, 246; San Giorgio Maggiore, 248; San Sebastiano, 248; San Zaccaria, 234; Santa Maria dei Miracoli, 236; Santa Maria della Salute, 242; Santi Giovanni e Paolo, 236; Scuola di San Rocco, 239; Scuola San Giorgio degli Schiavoni, 235; St Mark's, 232–3; Torcello, 251, 253

Verdi, Giuseppe, 217, 220, 242

Verona, 283–7; Amphitheatre, 286; Castelvecchio Museum, 288; Della Scala tombs, 285; Duomo, 283–4; fortifications, 283; Giardino Giusti, 287; Juliet's house, 285–6; Juliet's Tomb, 283; Piazza Bra, 286; Piazza delle Erbe, 285; Ponte Pietro, 283; restaurants, 285–6; Roman Bridge, 257; San Zeno, 288–9; Sant' Anastasia, 284

Veronese (Paolo Caliari): *Life of Esther*, 248; *Marriage of Cana*, 249; Villa Barbaro, 272–3

Verrocchio, Andrea del: *Christ and St Thomas*, 49

Via Cassia, 84

Vicenza, 259, 275–9; Accademia Olimpica, 276–7; Basilica, Piazza dei Signori, 278; Contra Porti, 278; Loggia del Capitaniato, 278; Palazzo Chiericati, 277; Palazzo Pigafetta, 279; Palazzo Porto Breganze, 279; Palazzo Thiene, 277–8; Palazzo Trissino-Baston, 278; restaurants, 279; Santa Corona, 277; Santo Stefano, 277; Teatro Olimpico, 276–7

Vignola, Il (Jacopo Barocci) 88–9, 108

Villa Adriana, 136–8; Canopus, 138; Maritime Temple, 138; Piazzo d' Oro, 138, *see* Hadrian's Villa

Villa Aldobrandini, 144–5

Villa Barbarigo, 260

Villa Barbaro, 272–3

Villa Borghese, 94, 100–2; art collection, 101; Baroque collection, 101; *Borghese Gladiator*, 101; *Dying Seneca*, 101; entrance hall, 101; gardens, 100; *Hermaphrodite*, 101; sixteenth- and seventeenth-century art, 101

Villa d' Este, 88, 137, 139–40

Villa Emo, 272

Villa Farnese, 87, 89

Villa Farnesina, 125–6

Villa Foscarini, 262

Villa Garzoni, 28

Villa Lante, 87–9

Villa Malcontenta, 261–2

Villa Mansi, 28

Villa Medici, 102

Villa of Oplontis, 172

Villa Pisano, 263–4

Villa Reale, 27–8

Villa Rocca Pisani, 282

Villa Rotonda, 280–1

Villa Torrigiani, 28

Villa Vamarana, 281–2

Virgil, 173

Viterbo, 20, 87

Vittoria, Alessandro, 273

von Stosch, Baron, 96

Wagner, Richard, 154, 234, 243

Walker, Adam, 22, 72

Waller, Edmund, 265

Walpole, Horace, 36, 53, 55, 69, 96, 172, 207, 214

Warner, Dr, 230

Warwick Vase, 136–7

Webster, John, 35

Welch, Justice, 95

West, Benjamin, 132

Whatley, Stephen, 47

Wilde, Oscar, 154

Wilson, Richard, 108, 135, 143, 191

Winckelmann, Johann Joachim, 103, 111, 153

Witmer, Theodore B., 82, 154

Wordsworth, William, 1

Wotton, Sir Henry, 245

Wright, Edward, 73, 235

York, Cardinal of, 96, 143–4

Zelotti (Giambattiste Farriati), 272

Zoffany, Johann: *Tribuna*, 36, 59

Zuccari family, 89

Zuccari, Taddeo and Federico, 139